ABOUT THIS PUBLICATION

FOR SERVICE ASSISTANCE

Customer Service
1-980.729.3505

South Carolina General Statues is published by Vision Books in Charlotte, North Carolina. Copyright 2019 by Vision Books. This book or parts thereof may not be reproduced in any form, stored in a retrieval system, or transmitted in any form by any means—electronic, mechanical, photocopy, recording or otherwise—without prior written permission of the publisher, except as provided by United States of America copyright law.

The records required by U.S. Code 2257(a) through (c) and the pertinent regulations 28 C.F.R. Cli. 1, Part 75 with respect to this publication and all materials associated with such records are maintained by The Multi-Media Group of Greater Charlotte, Publisher and available for review by Attorney General.

www.visionbooks.org

Copyright © 2019 by viion books
All rights reserved!

ISBN (13) digit: 9781790891078

123-4-56789-01234-Paperback
123-4-56789-01234-Hardback

First Edition

120620182200

Printed in the United States of America

2019 EDITION

South Carolina General Assembly General Statues - Pamphlet # 1

Printed In conjunction with the Administration of the Courts

South Carolina General Assembly General Statues
Pamphlet Reference Guide

TITLES	PAMPHLET
TITLE 1 – ADMINISTRATION OF GOVERNMENT	1
CHAPTER 1 - GENERAL PROVISIONS	1
CHAPTER 3 - GOVERNOR AND LIEUTENANT GOVERNOR	1
CHAPTER 5 - SECRETARY OF STATE	1
CHAPTER 6 - OFFICE OF THE STATE INSPECTOR GENERAL	1
CHAPTER 7 - ATTORNEY GENERAL AND SOLICITORS	1
CHAPTER 9 - EMERGENCY PROVISIONS	1
CHAPTER 10 - REMOVAL AND PLACEMENT OF CONFEDERATE FLAG	1
CHAPTER 11 - DEPARTMENT OF ADMINISTRATION	1
CHAPTER 13 - STATE HUMAN AFFAIRS COMMISSION	1
CHAPTER 15 - COMMISSION ON THE STATUS OF WOMEN	1
CHAPTER 17 - INTERSTATE COOPERATION	1
CHAPTER 18 - REVIEW OF OCCUPATIONAL REGISTRATION & LICENSING	1
CHAPTER 21 - UNIFORMITY OF LEGISLATION	1
CHAPTER 23 - STATE AGENCY RULE MAKING AND ADJUDICATION OF CONTESTED CASES	1
CHAPTER 25 - HUMAN SERVICES DEMONSTRATION PROJECT	2
CHAPTER 29 - SOUTH CAROLINA COUNCIL ON THE HOLOCAUST	2
CHAPTER 30 - DEPARTMENTS OF STATE GOVERNMENT	2
CHAPTER 31 - STATE COMMISSION FOR MINORITY AFFAIRS	2
CHAPTER 32 - SOUTH CAROLINA RELIGIOUS FREEDOM ACT	2
CHAPTER 34 - NATIONAL BUILDING CODES	2
TITLE 2 – GENERAL ASSEMBLY	
CHAPTER 1 - GENERAL PROVISIONS	2
CHAPTER 2 - LEGISLATIVE OVERSIGHT OF EXECUTIVE DEPARTMENT	3
CHAPTER 3 - ORGANIZATION, EMPLOYEES AND COMPENSATION	3
CHAPTER 5 - EMERGENCY INTERIM LEGISLATIVE SUCCESSION ACT	3
CHAPTER 7 - LEGISLATIVE ENACTMENTS	3

CHAPTER 11 - LEGISLATIVE COUNCIL	3
CHAPTER 13 - CODE COMMISSIONER AND COMMITTEE ON STATUTORY LAWS	3
CHAPTER 15 - LEGISLATIVE AUDIT COUNCIL	3
CHAPTER 17 - LOBBYISTS AND LOBBYING	3
CHAPTER 19 - ELECTION OF JUSTICES AND JUDGES	3
CHAPTER 20 - NONJUDICIAL SCREENING AND ELECTION	3
CHAPTER 35 - LOCAL GOVERNMENT STUDY COMMITTEE	3
CHAPTER 41 - JOINT COMMITTEE ON TAXATION	3
CHAPTER 47 - JOINT BOND REVIEW COMMITTEE	3
CHAPTER 48 - COMMUNITY CORRECTIONS INCENTIVE ACT	3
CHAPTER 51 - SERVICES, PROGRAMS AND FACILITIES FOR THE AGING STUDY COMMITTEE	3
CHAPTER 59 - SENATE MANAGEMENT AND OPERATIONS COMMITTEE	3
CHAPTER 65 - SOUTH CAROLINA FEDERAL AND OTHER FUNDS OVERSIGHT ACT	3
CHAPTER 66 - JEAN LANEY HARRIS FOLK HERITAGE AWARD	3
CHAPTER 67 - SOUTH CAROLINA MEDAL OF VALOR	3
CHAPTER 69 - SUBPOENAS AND SUBPOENAS DUCES TECUM	3
CHAPTER 75 - SOUTH CAROLINA RESEARCH CENTERS OF ECONOMIC EXCELLENCE	3
CHAPTER 77 - SOUTH CAROLINA HIGHER EDUCATION EXCELLENCE ENHANCEMENT PROGRAM	3
CHAPTER 79 - STATE AGENCY DEFICIT PREVENTION AND RECOGNITION	3
TITLE 3 – US GOVERNMENT, AGREEMENTS AND RELATIONS WITH	
CHAPTER 1 - CONSENT TO ACQUISITION OF LANDS BY UNITED STATES GENERALLY	3
CHAPTER 3 - SPECIFIC GRANTS OR CESSIONS OF JURISDICTION TO UNITED STATES	4
CHAPTER 5 - GRANTS OF PERPETUAL RIGHTS AND EASEMENTS TO UNITED STATES FOR DEVELOPMENT OF WATERWAYS	4
CHAPTER 7 - AGREEMENTS WITH UNITED STATES	4
CHAPTER 9 - ACQUISITION AND DISTRIBUTION OF FEDERAL SURPLUS PROPERTY	4
CHAPTER 11 - GAMBLING CRUISE ACT	4

TITLE 4 - COUNTIES
CHAPTER 1 - GENERAL PROVISIONS	4
CHAPTER 3 - BOUNDARIES OF EXISTING COUNTIES	4
CHAPTER 5 - CHANGE OF BOUNDARIES	4
CHAPTER 7 - CREATION OF NEW COUNTIES AND CONSOLIDATION OF COUNTIES	4
CHAPTER 8 - CONSOLIDATION OF POLITICAL SUBDIVISIONS	4
CHAPTER 9 - COUNTY GOVERNMENT	4
CHAPTER 10 - LOCAL SALES AND USE TAX	5
CHAPTER 11 - COUNTY OFFICERS	5
CHAPTER 12 - FEE IN LIEU OF PROPERTY TAXES	5
CHAPTER 13 - CLAIMS AGAINST COUNTIES	5
CHAPTER 15 - COUNTY BONDS	5
CHAPTER 17 - BUILDINGS AND LANDS GENERALLY	5
CHAPTER 18 - REGULATION OF WRECKERS AT SCENES OF ACCIDENTS	5
CHAPTER 19 - FIRE PROTECTION SERVICES	5
CHAPTER 20 - COMMUNITY RECREATION SPECIAL TAX DISTRICT	6
CHAPTER 21 - FIRE PROTECTION AND AMBULANCE SERVICES; MEDICAL CLINIC FACILITIES	6
CHAPTER 23 - JOINT COUNTY FIRE DISTRICTS	6
CHAPTER 25 - REGULATION OF BUILDING CONSTRUCTION	6
CHAPTER 27 - COUNTY PLANNING [REPEALED]	6
CHAPTER 29 - INDUSTRIAL DEVELOPMENT PROJECTS	6
CHAPTER 31 - JOINT COUNTY ECONOMIC OPPORTUNITY COMMISSIONS	6
CHAPTER 33 - COUNTY FAIRS	6
CHAPTER 35 - COUNTY PUBLIC WORKS IMPROVEMENT ACT	6
CHAPTER 37 - OPTIONAL METHODS FOR FINANCING TRANSPORTATION FACILITIES	6

TITLE 5 – MUNICIPLE CORPORATIONS
CHAPTER 1 - INCORPORATION	6
CHAPTER 3 - CHANGE OF CORPORATE LIMITS	6
CHAPTER 5 - SELECTION OF FORMS OF MUNICIPAL GOVERNMENT	6
CHAPTER 7 - GENERAL STRUCTURE, ORGANIZATION, POWERS, DUTIES, FUNCTIONS AND RESPONSIBILITIES OF ALL MUNICIPALITIES	6
CHAPTER 9 - MAYOR-COUNCIL FORM OF GOVERNMENT	6
CHAPTER 11 - COUNCIL FORM OF GOVERNMENT	6

CHAPTER 13 - COUNCIL-MANAGER FORM OF GOVERNMENT	7
CHAPTER 15 - NOMINATIONS AND ELECTIONS FOR MUNICIPAL OFFICES	7
CHAPTER 17 - INITIATIVE AND REFERENDUM	7
CHAPTER 19 - CIVIL SERVICE COMMISSIONS	7
CHAPTER 21 - FINANCIAL MATTERS GENERALLY	7
CHAPTER 23 - ZONING AND PLANNING [REPEALED]	7
CHAPTER 25 - BUILDING CODES AND FIRE PREVENTION	7
CHAPTER 27 - STREETS AND SIDEWALKS	7
CHAPTER 29 - OFF-STREET PARKING FACILITIES	7
CHAPTER 31 - ELECTRICITY, WATER, NATURAL GAS AND SEWERAGE SYSTEMS	7
CHAPTER 33 - ICE PLANTS	7
CHAPTER 35 - WATER FRONT IMPROVEMENTS	7
CHAPTER 37 - MUNICIPAL IMPROVEMENTS ACT OF 1999	7
CHAPTER 39 - CEMETERIES AND CEMETERY COMMISSIONS	7

TITLE 6 – LOCAL GOVERNEMENT-PROVISIONS
APPLICABLE TO SPECIAL PURPOSE DISTRICTS AND OTHER POLITICAL SUBDIVISIONS

CHAPTER 1 - GENERAL PROVISIONS	7
CHAPTER 3 - EMERGENCY SEATS OF GOVERNMENT FOR POLITICAL SUBDIVISIONS	7
CHAPTER 4 - ALLOCATION OF ACCOMMODATIONS TAX REVENUES	7
CHAPTER 5 - INVESTMENT OF FUNDS BY POLITICAL SUBDIVISIONS	8
CHAPTER 6 - SOUTH CAROLINA POOLED INVESTMENT FUND	8
CHAPTER 7 - PLANNING BY LOCAL GOVERNMENTS	8
CHAPTER 8 - BUILDING CODES ENFORCEMENT OFFICERS	8
CHAPTER 9 - BUILDING CODES	8
CHAPTER 10 - ENERGY STANDARD ACT	8
CHAPTER 11 - SPECIAL PURPOSE OR PUBLIC SERVICE DISTRICTS GENERALLY	8
CHAPTER 13 - RURAL COMMUNITY WATER DISTRICTS	8
CHAPTER 15 - SEWAGE COLLECTION, DISPOSAL AND TREATMENT BY GOVERNMENTAL ENTITIES	8
CHAPTER 16 - SOLID WASTE DISPOSAL RESOURCE RECOVERY FACILITIES ACT	8

CHAPTER 17 - REVENUE BOND REFINANCING ACT OF 1937	8
CHAPTER 19 - STATE GRANTS FOR WATER AND SEWER AUTHORITIES, DISTRICTS OR SYSTEMS	8
CHAPTER 21 - REVENUE BOND ACT FOR UTILITIES	8
CHAPTER 23 - JOINT MUNICIPAL ELECTRIC POWER AND ENERGY ACT	8
CHAPTER 24 - JOINT AGENCY ACT	9
CHAPTER 25 - JOINT AUTHORITY WATER AND SEWER SYSTEMS ACT	9
CHAPTER 27 - STATE AID TO SUBDIVISIONS ACT	9
CHAPTER 29 - SOUTH CAROLINA LOCAL GOVERNMENT COMPREHENSIVE PLANNING ENABLING ACT OF 1994	9
CHAPTER 31 - SOUTH CAROLINA LOCAL GOVERNMENT DEVELOPMENT AGREEMENT ACT	9
CHAPTER 32 - TEXTILES COMMUNITIES REVITALIZATION ACT [REPEALED]	9
CHAPTER 33 - TAX INCREMENT FINANCING FOR COUNTIES [REPEALED]	9
CHAPTER 34 - RETAIL FACILITIES REVITALIZATION ACT	9
CHAPTER 35 - RESIDENTIAL IMPROVEMENT DISTRICT ACT	9
CHAPTER 37 - BEAUFORT-JASPER WATER AND SEWER AUTHORITY	9
TITLE 7 - ELECTIONS	
CHAPTER 1 - GENERAL PROVISIONS	9
CHAPTER 3 - STATE ELECTION COMMISSION; CENTRAL REGISTRATION SYSTEM	9
CHAPTER 5 - QUALIFICATIONS AND REGISTRATION OF ELECTORS	9
CHAPTER 7 - POLLING PRECINCTS AND VOTING PLACES	10
CHAPTER 9 - PARTY ORGANIZATION	10
CHAPTER 11 - DESIGNATION AND NOMINATION OF CANDIDATES	10
CHAPTER 13 - CONDUCT OF ELECTIONS	10
CHAPTER 15 - ABSENTEE REGISTRATION AND VOTING	11
CHAPTER 17 - CANVASS OF VOTES; CERTIFICATES AND RECORDS OF RESULTS	11
CHAPTER 20 - SPECIAL PROVISIONS APPLICABLE TO FEDERAL ELECTIONS	11
CHAPTER 21 - SPECIAL PROVISIONS APPLICABLE TO ELECTION OF STATE SENATORS AND MEMBERS OF	

HOUSE OF REPRESENTATIVES	11
CHAPTER 23 - ELECTION EXPENSES	11
CHAPTER 25 - OFFENSES AGAINST THE ELECTION LAWS	11
CHAPTER 27 - COUNTY BOARDS OF REGISTRATION AND ELECTION COMMISSIONS [REPEALED]	11

Title 8 – PUBLIC OFFICES AND EMPLOYEES

CHAPTER 1 - GENERAL PROVISIONS	11
CHAPTER 3 - COMMISSIONS, OATHS AND BONDS	11
CHAPTER 5 - BUYING AND SELLING OF OFFICES PROHIBITED	11
CHAPTER 7 - ABSENCES IN MILITARY SERVICE	11
CHAPTER 9 - DELIVERY OF BOOKS, RECORDS AND MONEY TO SUCCESSOR	11
CHAPTER 11 - STATE OFFICERS AND EMPLOYEES	11
CHAPTER 12 - INTERCHANGE OF GOVERNMENT EMPLOYEES BETWEEN AND AMONG FEDERAL, STATE AND LOCAL GOVERNMENTS	11
CHAPTER 13 - ETHICS, GOVERNMENT ACCOUNTABILITY, AND CAMPAIGN REFORM	12
CHAPTER 14 - UNAUTHORIZED ALIENS AND PUBLIC EMPLOYMENT	12
CHAPTER 15 - LOCAL OR LOCAL AND STATE OFFICERS AND EMPLOYEES GENERALLY	12
CHAPTER 17 - STATE OR LOCAL EMPLOYEES GRIEVANCE PROCEDURE	12
CHAPTER 19 - MERIT SYSTEM FOR STATE-AIDED AGENCIES	12
CHAPTER 21 - FEES AND COSTS GENERALLY	12
CHAPTER 23 - DEFERRED COMPENSATION PROGRAM	12
CHAPTER 25 - GOVERNMENT VOLUNTEERS	12
CHAPTER 27 - EMPLOYMENT PROTECTION FOR REPORTS OF VIOLATIONS OF STATE OR FEDERAL LAW OR REGULATION	12
CHAPTER 29 - VERIFICATION OF LAWFUL PRESENCE IN THE UNITED STATES	12
CHAPTER 30 - RECORDING AND REPORTING IMMIGRATION LAW VIOLATIONS	12

TITLE 9 – RETIREMENT SYSTEMS

CHAPTER 1 - SOUTH CAROLINA RETIREMENT SYSTEM	13
CHAPTER 2 - RETIREMENT AND PRERETIREMENT ADVISORY PANEL	13

CHAPTER 3 - COVERAGE OF PUBLIC OFFICERS AND EMPLOYEES UNDER FEDERAL SOCIAL SECURITY ACT	13
CHAPTER 4 - SOUTH CAROLINA PUBLIC EMPLOYEE BENEFIT AUTHORITY	13
CHAPTER 5 - STATE RETIREMENT AND SOCIAL SECURITY ACT OF 1955	13
CHAPTER 8 - RETIREMENT SYSTEM FOR JUDGES AND SOLICITORS	13
CHAPTER 9 - RETIREMENT SYSTEM FOR MEMBERS OF GENERAL ASSEMBLY	13
CHAPTER 10 - NATIONAL GUARD RETIREMENT SYSTEM	13
CHAPTER 11 - POLICE OFFICERS RETIREMENT SYSTEM	14
CHAPTER 12 - QUALIFIED EXCESS BENEFITS ARRANGEMENTS	14
CHAPTER 13 - FIREMEN'S PENSION FUNDS IN CITIES	14
CHAPTER 15 - ANNUITY CONTRACTS FOR EMPLOYEES OF SCHOOLS AND EDUCATIONAL INSTITUTIONS	14
CHAPTER 16 - RETIREMENT SYSTEM FUNDS	14
CHAPTER 17 - OPTIONAL RETIREMENT PROGRAM FOR PUBLICLY-SUPPORTED FOUR-YEAR AND POSTGRADUATE INSTITUTIONS OF HIGHER EDUCATION [REPEALED]	14
CHAPTER 18 - QUALIFIED DOMESTIC RELATIONS ORDERS	14
CHAPTER 20 - STATE OPTIONAL RETIREMENT PROGRAM	14
CHAPTER 21 - THE SOUTH CAROLINA RETIREMENT SYSTEMS CLAIMS PROCEDURES ACT	14
TITLE 10 – PUBLIC BUILDINGS AND PROPERTY	
CHAPTER 1 - GENERAL PROVISIONS	14
CHAPTER 3 - GOVERNOR'S MANSION AND LACE HOUSE COMMISSION	14
CHAPTER 5 - CONSTRUCTION AND RENOVATION OF PUBLIC BUILDINGS AND OTHER PROJECTS	14
CHAPTER 7 - INSURANCE ON PUBLIC BUILDINGS AND PROPERTY	14
CHAPTER 9 - MINERALS AND MINERAL INTERESTS IN PUBLIC LANDS	14
CHAPTER 11 - TRESPASSES AND OFFENSES	15
TITLE 11 – PUBLIC FINANCE	
CHAPTER 1 - GENERAL PROVISIONS	15
CHAPTER 3 - COMPTROLLER GENERAL	15

CHAPTER 5 - STATE TREASURER	15
CHAPTER 7 - STATE AUDITOR	15
CHAPTER 9 - STATE FINANCES GENERALLY	15
CHAPTER 11 - STATE BUDGET SYSTEM	15
CHAPTER 13 - DEPOSIT OF STATE FUNDS	15
CHAPTER 14 - DEFEASANCE OF OUTSTANDING PUBLIC BONDS, NOTES, AND OTHER OBLIGATIONS	15
CHAPTER 15 - BONDS OF POLITICAL SUBDIVISIONS	15
CHAPTER 17 - BORROWING BY STATE, STATE AGENCIES, AND POLITICAL UNITS IN ANTICIPATION OF ISSUANCE OF BONDS	15
CHAPTER 18 - SOUTH CAROLINA VOLUME CAP ALLOCATION ACT	15
CHAPTER 19 - BORROWING IN ANTICIPATION OF FEDERAL GRANTS	15
CHAPTER 21 - ADVANCED REFUNDING OF BONDS OF PUBLIC AGENCIES	15
CHAPTER 23 - PLEDGE OF REVENUES TO SECURE PAYMENT OF BONDS	15
CHAPTER 25 - PUBLIC PRINTING AND STATE PUBLICATIONS	15
CHAPTER 27 - EFFECT OF NEW ARTICLE X OF CONSTITUTION ON BONDED AND OTHER TYPES OF INDEBTEDNESS	15
CHAPTER 29 - PAYMENT OF STATE GENERAL OBLIGATION BONDS PURSUANT TO ARTICLE 10 OF CONSTITUTION	16
CHAPTER 31 - EXCHANGE OF COUPON BONDS FOR FULLY REGISTERED BONDS	16
CHAPTER 35 - SOUTH CAROLINA CONSOLIDATED PROCUREMENT CODE	16
CHAPTER 37 - SOUTH CAROLINA RESOURCES AUTHORITY ACT	16
CHAPTER 38 - ISSUANCE OF CAPITAL IMPROVEMENT BONDS IN DENOMINATIONS OF LESS THAN ONE THOUSAND DOLLARS	16
CHAPTER 39 - JOINT LEGISLATIVE COMMITTEE ON ENERGY	16
CHAPTER 40 - SOUTH CAROLINA INFRASTRUCTURE FACILITIES AUTHORITY ACT	16
CHAPTER 41 - STATE GENERAL OBLIGATION ECONOMIC DEVELOPMENT BOND ACT	16

CHAPTER 42 - SOUTH CAROLINA COMPREHENSIVE INFRASTRUCTURE DEVELOPMENT ACT	16
CHAPTER 43 - SOUTH CAROLINA TRANSPORTATION INFRASTRUCTURE BANK ACT	16
CHAPTER 44 - HIGH GROWTH SMALL BUSINESS JOB CREATION ACT	16
CHAPTER 45 - VENTURE CAPITAL INVESTMENT ACT OF SOUTH CAROLINA	16
CHAPTER 46 - SOUTH CAROLINA HYDROGEN INFRASTRUCTURE DEVELOPMENT ACT	17
CHAPTER 47 - TOBACCO ESCROW FUND ACT	17
CHAPTER 48 - TOBACCO QUALIFIED ESCROW FUND ENFORCEMENT	17
CHAPTER 49 - TOBACCO SETTLEMENT REVENUE MANAGEMENT AUTHORITY ACT	17
CHAPTER 50 - SOUTH CAROLINA RURAL INFRASTRUCTURE ACT	17
CHAPTER 51 - SOUTH CAROLINA RESEARCH UNIVERSITY INFRASTRUCTURE ACT	17
CHAPTER 53 - SOUTH CAROLINA ENTERPRISE INFORMATION SYSTEM	17
CHAPTER 55 - STATE FISCAL ACCOUNTABILITY AUTHORITY	17
CHAPTER 56 - MICROENTERPRISE DEVELOPMENT	17
CHAPTER 57 - IRAN DIVESTMENT ACT	17

TITLE 12 – TAXATION

CHAPTER 2 - GENERAL PROVISIONS	17
CHAPTER 3 - SOUTH CAROLINA TAX REALIGNMENT COMMISSION	17
CHAPTER 4 - THE SOUTH CAROLINA DEPARTMENT OF REVENUE	17
CHAPTER 6 - SOUTH CAROLINA INCOME TAX ACT	17
CHAPTER 8 - INCOME TAX WITHHOLDING	18
CHAPTER 10 - ENTERPRISE ZONE ACT OF 1995	18
CHAPTER 11 - INCOME TAX ON BANKS	18
CHAPTER 13 - INCOME TAX ON BUILDING AND LOAN ASSOCIATIONS	18
CHAPTER 14 - ECONOMIC IMPACT ZONE COMMUNITY DEVELOPMENT ACT OF 1995	18
CHAPTER 15 - SOUTH CAROLINA LIFE SCIENCES ACT	18
CHAPTER 16 - ESTATE TAX	18
CHAPTER 20 - CORPORATION LICENSE FEES	18

CHAPTER 21 - STAMP AND BUSINESS LICENSE TAX	18
CHAPTER 22 - COIN-OPERATED MACHINES AND OTHER DEVICES	18
CHAPTER 23 - LICENSE TAXES ON OTHER BUSINESSES	18
CHAPTER 24 - DEED RECORDING FEE	18
CHAPTER 28 - MOTOR FUELS SUBJECT TO USER FEES	19
CHAPTER 33 - ALCOHOLIC BEVERAGES TAXES	19
CHAPTER 35 - THE SIMPLIFIED SALES AND USE TAX ADMINISTRATION ACT	19
CHAPTER 36 - SOUTH CAROLINA SALES AND USE TAX ACT	19
CHAPTER 37 - ASSESSMENT OF PROPERTY TAXES	20
CHAPTER 39 - COUNTY AUDITORS	20
CHAPTER 43 - COUNTY EQUALIZATION AND REASSESSMENT	20
CHAPTER 44 - FEE IN LIEU OF TAX SIMPLIFICATION ACT	20
CHAPTER 45 - COUNTY TREASURERS AND COLLECTION OF TAXES	20
CHAPTER 49 - ENFORCED COLLECTION OF TAXES GENERALLY	20
CHAPTER 51 - ALTERNATE PROCEDURE FOR COLLECTION OF PROPERTY TAXES	21
CHAPTER 53 - TAX COLLECTION BY DEPARTMENT OF REVENUE	21
CHAPTER 54 - UNIFORM METHOD OF COLLECTION AND ENFORCEMENT OF TAXES LEVIED AND ASSESSED BY SOUTH CAROLINA DEPARTMENT OF REVENUE	21
CHAPTER 55 - OVERDUE TAX DEBT COLLECTION ACT	21
CHAPTER 56 - SETOFF DEBT COLLECTION ACT	21
CHAPTER 57 - UNIFORM FEDERAL TAX LIEN REGISTRATION ACT	21
CHAPTER 58 - SOUTH CAROLINA TAXPAYERS' BILL OF RIGHTS	21
CHAPTER 59 - FORFEITED LANDS	21
CHAPTER 60 - SOUTH CAROLINA REVENUE PROCEDURES ACT	21
CHAPTER 61 - SUITS TO CLEAR TAX TITLES	21
CHAPTER 62 - SOUTH CAROLINA MOTION PICTURE INCENTIVE ACT	21
CHAPTER 63 - ENERGY FREEDOM AND RURAL DEVELOPMENT ACT	21
CHAPTER 65 - SOUTH CAROLINA TEXTILES	

COMMUNITIES REVITALIZATION ACT	21
CHAPTER 67 - SOUTH CAROLINA ABANDONED BUILDINGS REVITALIZATION ACT	21

TITLE 13 – PLANNING RESEARCH AND DEVELOPMENT

CHAPTER 1 - GENERAL PROVISIONS	22
CHAPTER 2 - AUTHORITY TO AGREE--GOVERNING BOARD MEMBERSHIP	22
CHAPTER 7 - NUCLEAR ENERGY	22
CHAPTER 11 - NEW HORIZONS DEVELOPMENT AUTHORITY	22
CHAPTER 12 - TRIDENT ECONOMIC DEVELOPMENT FINANCE AUTHORITY	22
CHAPTER 13 - SOUTHERN GROWTH POLICIES AGREEMENT	22
CHAPTER 15 - TRI-COUNTY COLISEUM COMMISSION	22
CHAPTER 17 - SOUTH CAROLINA RESEARCH AUTHORITY	22
CHAPTER 19 - MIDLANDS AUTHORITY	22
CHAPTER 21 - EDISTO DEVELOPMENT AUTHORITY	22

TITLE 14 - COURTS

CHAPTER 1 - GENERAL PROVISIONS	22
CHAPTER 2 - ABOLITION OF CERTAIN COURTS AND OFFICES	22
CHAPTER 3 - SUPREME COURT	22
CHAPTER 5 - CIRCUIT COURTS	23
CHAPTER 7 - JURIES AND JURORS IN CIRCUIT COURTS	23
CHAPTER 8 - COURT OF APPEALS	23
CHAPTER 9 - COUNTY COURTS	23
CHAPTER 11 - MASTERS AND REFEREES	23
CHAPTER 13 - COURT REPORTING	23
CHAPTER 15 - COURT STENOGRAPHERS AND BAILIFFS	23
CHAPTER 17 - CLERKS OF COURTS	23
CHAPTER 23 - PROBATE COURTS	23
CHAPTER 25 - MUNICIPAL COURTS	23
CHAPTER 27 - JUDICIAL COUNCIL	23
CHAPTER 29 - VETERANS TREATMENT COURT PROGRAM	23
CHAPTER 31 - MENTAL HEALTH COURT PROGRAM	23

TITLE 15 – CIVIL REMEDIES AND PROCEDURE

CHAPTER 1 - GENERAL PROVISIONS	24
CHAPTER 3 - LIMITATION OF CIVIL ACTIONS	24
CHAPTER 5 - PARTIES	24
CHAPTER 7 - VENUE	24
CHAPTER 9 - SUMMONSES, ORDERS OF PUBLICATION AND SERVICE OF PAPERS GENERALLY	24

CHAPTER 11 - NOTICE OF LIS PENDENS	24
CHAPTER 17 - ARREST AND BAIL IN CIVIL ACTIONS	24
CHAPTER 19 - ATTACHMENT	24
CHAPTER 27 - TRIAL AND CERTAIN INCIDENTS THEREOF	24
CHAPTER 28 - VIDEOTAPED DEPOSITIONS	24
CHAPTER 29 - LEGAL NOTICES, GENERALLY	24
CHAPTER 31 - REFEREES AND MASTERS	24
CHAPTER 32 - NONECONOMIC DAMAGE AWARDS	24
CHAPTER 33 - VERDICTS	24
CHAPTER 35 - JUDGMENTS AND DECREES GENERALLY	24
CHAPTER 36 - SOUTH CAROLINA FRIVOLOUS CIVIL PROCEEDINGS SANCTIONS ACT	24
CHAPTER 37 - COSTS	24
CHAPTER 38 - SOUTH CAROLINA CONTRIBUTION AMONG TORTFEASORS ACT	24
CHAPTER 39 - EXECUTIONS AND JUDICIAL SALES GENERALLY	24
CHAPTER 41 - HOMESTEAD AND OTHER EXEMPTIONS	24
CHAPTER 43 - ABATEMENT OF NUISANCES	24
CHAPTER 47 - UNIFORM INTERSTATE DEPOSITIONS AND DISCOVERY ACT	25
CHAPTER 48 - UNIFORM ARBITRATION ACT	25
CHAPTER 49 - CHANGE OF NAME	25
CHAPTER 50 - STRUCTURED SETTLEMENT PROTECTION ACT	25
CHAPTER 51 - DEATH BY WRONGFUL ACT AND LYNCHING	25
CHAPTER 53 - DECLARATORY JUDGMENTS	25
CHAPTER 61 - PARTITION	25
CHAPTER 63 - QUO WARRANTO AND SCIRE FACIAS	25
CHAPTER 65 - RECEIVERSHIP AND OTHER PROVISIONAL REMEDIES	25
CHAPTER 67 - RECOVERY OF REAL PROPERTY	25
CHAPTER 69 - RECOVERY OF PERSONAL PROPERTY	25
CHAPTER 72 - JURISDICTION OF CIRCUIT COURT	25
CHAPTER 73 - SELLERS OF DEFECTIVE PRODUCTS	25
CHAPTER 74 - LIABILITY EXEMPTION FOR DONORS OF FOOD	25
CHAPTER 75 - SUITS INVOLVING MISCELLANEOUS ACTS OF WRONGFUL CONDUCT	25
CHAPTER 77 - SUITS INVOLVING STATE, STATE AGENCIES AND OFFICIALS AND UNITED STATES	25

CHAPTER 78 - SOUTH CAROLINA TORT CLAIMS ACT	25
CHAPTER 79 - MEDICAL MALPRACTICE ACTIONS	25
CHAPTER 81 - SUCCESSOR ASBESTOS-RELATED LIABILITY FAIRNESS ACT	25
CHAPTER 82 - LIMITATION ON LIABILITY OF LAND POSSESSORS TO TRESPASSERS – TRESPASSER RESPONSIBILITY ACT	25

TITLE 16 – CRIMES AND OFFENSES

CHAPTER 1 - FELONIES AND MISDEMEANORS; ACCESSORIES	26
CHAPTER 3 - OFFENSES AGAINST THE PERSON	26
CHAPTER 5 - OFFENSES AGAINST CIVIL RIGHTS	26
CHAPTER 7 - OFFENSES AGAINST THE PEACE	26
CHAPTER 8 - OFFENSES PROMOTING CIVIL DISORDER	26
CHAPTER 9 - OFFENSES AGAINST PUBLIC JUSTICE	26
CHAPTER 11 - OFFENSES AGAINST PROPERTY	27
CHAPTER 13 - FORGERY, LARCENY, EMBEZZLEMENT, FALSE PRETENSES AND CHEATS	27
CHAPTER 14 - FINANCIAL TRANSACTION CARD CRIME ACT	27
CHAPTER 15 - OFFENSES AGAINST MORALITY AND DECENCY	27
CHAPTER 16 - COMPUTER CRIME ACT	27
CHAPTER 17 - OFFENSES AGAINST PUBLIC POLICY	27
CHAPTER 19 - GAMBLING AND LOTTERIES	27
CHAPTER 21 - OFFENSES INVOLVING MOTOR VEHICLE TITLES	27
CHAPTER 23 - OFFENSES INVOLVING WEAPONS	27
CHAPTER 25 - CRIMINAL DOMESTIC VIOLENCE	27
CHAPTER 27 - ANIMAL FIGHTING AND BAITING ACT	27

TITLE 17 – CRIMINAL PROCEDURE

CHAPTER 1 - GENERAL PROVISIONS	28
CHAPTER 3 - DEFENSE OF INDIGENTS	28
CHAPTER 5 - CORONERS AND MEDICAL EXAMINERS	28
CHAPTER 7 - AUTOPSIES AND INQUEST ON THE DEAD	28
CHAPTER 9 - EXTRADITION	28
CHAPTER 11 - INTERSTATE AGREEMENT ON DETAINERS	28
CHAPTER 13 - ARREST, PROCESS, SEARCHES AND SEIZURES	28
CHAPTER 15 - BAIL AND RECOGNIZANCES	28
CHAPTER 17 - HABEAS CORPUS	28
CHAPTER 19 - INDICTMENTS	28

CHAPTER 21 - VENUE	28
CHAPTER 22 - INTERVENTION PROGRAMS	28
CHAPTER 23 - PLEADING AND TRIAL	28
CHAPTER 24 - MENTALLY ILL OR INSANE DEFENDANTS	28
CHAPTER 25 - JUDGMENT AND EXECUTION	28
CHAPTER 27 - UNIFORM POST-CONVICTION PROCEDURE ACT	28
CHAPTER 28 - POST-CONVICTION DNA TESTING AND PRESERVATION OF EVIDENCE	28
CHAPTER 29 - PEN REGISTERS AND TRAP AND TRACE DEVICES	28
CHAPTER 30 - INTERCEPTION OF WIRE, ELECTRONIC, OR ORAL COMMUNICATIONS	28
TITLE 18 - APPEALS	
CHAPTER 1 - GENERAL PROVISIONS	29
CHAPTER 3 - APPEALS FROM MAGISTRATES IN CRIMINAL CASES	29
CHAPTER 7 - APPEALS TO CIRCUIT AND COUNTY COURTS IN OTHER CASES	29
CHAPTER 9 - APPEALS TO SUPREME COURT AND COURT OF APPEALS	29
TITLE 19 - EVIDENCE	
CHAPTER 1 - GENERAL PROVISIONS	29
CHAPTER 3 - PROOF OF ORDINANCES AND LAWS	29
CHAPTER 5 - PUBLIC DOCUMENTS, RECORDS AND BOOKS	29
CHAPTER 7 - COMPELLING ATTENDANCE OF WITNESSES	29
CHAPTER 9 - UNIFORM ACT TO SECURE THE ATTENDANCE OF WITNESSES FROM WITHOUT A STATE IN CRIMINAL PROCEEDINGS	29
CHAPTER 11 - COMPETENCY OF WITNESSES	29
CHAPTER 21 - PERPETUATION OF EVIDENCE	29
TITLE 20 – DOMESTIC RELATIONS	
CHAPTER 1 - MARRIAGE	29
CHAPTER 3 - DIVORCE	29
CHAPTER 4 - PROTECTION FROM DOMESTIC ABUSE	29
CHAPTER 5 - PROPERTY RIGHTS OF MARRIED WOMEN	29
CHAPTER 7 - CHILDREN'S CODE [REPEALED]	29
TITLE 21 – ESTATES, TRUSTS, GUARDIANS AND FIDUCIARIES	
CHAPTER 21 - NATURAL AND PARENTALLY APPOINTED GUARDIANS	30

CHAPTER 29 - TRUST COMPANIES	30

TITLE 22 – MAGISTRATES AND CONSTABLES

CHAPTER 1 - MAGISTRATES GENERALLY	30
CHAPTER 2 - SELECTION OF MAGISTRATES AND MAGISTRATES' JURY	30
CHAPTER 3 - JURISDICTION AND PROCEDURE IN MAGISTRATES' COURTS	30
CHAPTER 5 - MAGISTRATES' POWERS AND DUTIES I IN CRIMINAL MATTERS	30
CHAPTER 7 - FEES AND COSTS OF MAGISTRATES	30
CHAPTER 8 - MAGISTRATES' COMPENSATION	30
CHAPTER 9 - CONSTABLES	

TITLE 23 – LAW ENFORCEMENT AND PUBLIC SAFETY

CHAPTER 1 - GENERAL PROVISIONS	30
CHAPTER 3 - SOUTH CAROLINA LAW ENFORCEMENT DIVISION	30
CHAPTER 4 - CRIMINAL JUSTICE COMMITTEE AND PROGRAMS	30
CHAPTER 6 - DEPARTMENT OF PUBLIC SAFETY	30
CHAPTER 7 - STATE CONSTABLES	30
CHAPTER 9 - STATE FIRE MARSHAL	30
CHAPTER 10 - SOUTH CAROLINA FIRE ACADEMY	31
CHAPTER 11 - SHERIFFS--ELECTION, QUALIFICATIONS AND VACANCIES IN OFFICE	31
CHAPTER 13 - DEPUTY SHERIFFS GENERALLY	31
CHAPTER 15 - GENERAL POWERS AND DUTIES OF SHERIFFS AND DEPUTY SHERIFFS	31
CHAPTER 17 - LIABILITIES OF SHERIFFS AND DEPUTY SHERIFFS	31
CHAPTER 19 - SHERIFFS' FEES AND ACCOUNTING WITH SUCCESSOR	31
CHAPTER 20 - LAW ENFORCEMENT ASSISTANCE AND SUPPORT ACT	31
CHAPTER 21 - POLICE COMMISSIONERS IN CITIES OF 20,000 TO 50,000	31
CHAPTER 23 - LAW ENFORCEMENT TRAINING COUNCIL AND CRIMINAL JUSTICE ACADEMY	31
CHAPTER 24 - OFF-DUTY PRIVATE JOBS OF LAW ENFORCEMENT OFFICERS	31
CHAPTER 25 - LAW ENFORCEMENT OFFICERS HALL OF FAME	31

CHAPTER 27 - POLICE DISTRICTS IN UNINCORPORATED COMMUNITIES	31
CHAPTER 28 - RESERVE POLICE OFFICERS	31
CHAPTER 29 - SUBVERSIVE ACTIVITIES REGISTRATION ACT [REPEALED]	31
CHAPTER 31 - FIREARMS	31
CHAPTER 33 - MISSILES	31
CHAPTER 35 - FIREWORKS AND EXPLOSIVES	31
CHAPTER 36 - EXPLOSIVES CONTROL ACT	31
CHAPTER 37 - SAFETY GLAZING MATERIALS	31
CHAPTER 39 - HAZARDOUS SUBSTANCES ACT	31
CHAPTER 41 - ARSON REPORTING-IMMUNITY ACT	32
CHAPTER 43 - MODULAR BUILDINGS CONSTRUCTION ACT	32
CHAPTER 47 - PUBLIC SAFETY COMMUNICATIONS CENTER	32
CHAPTER 49 - FIREFIGHTER MOBILIZATION	32
CHAPTER 50 - SOUTH CAROLINA CRIMESTOPPERS ACT	32
CHAPTER 51 - REDUCED CIGARETTE IGNITION PROPENSITY STANDARDS AND FIREFIGHTER PROTECTION ACT	32
TITLE 24 – CORRECTIONS, JAILS, PROBATIONS, PAROLES AND PARDONS	
CHAPTER 1 - DEPARTMENT OF CORRECTIONS	32
CHAPTER 3 - STATE PRISON SYSTEM	32
CHAPTER 5 - JAILS AND JAILERS	32
CHAPTER 7 - COUNTY AND MUNICIPAL CHAIN GANGS	32
CHAPTER 9 - JAIL AND PRISON INSPECTION PROGRAM	32
CHAPTER 11 - INTERSTATE CORRECTIONS COMPACT	32
CHAPTER 13 - PRISONERS GENERALLY	32
CHAPTER 19 - CORRECTION AND TREATMENT OF YOUTHFUL OFFENDERS	32
CHAPTER 21 - PROBATION, PAROLE AND PARDON	32
CHAPTER 22 - CLASSIFICATION SYSTEM AND ADULT CRIMINAL OFFENDER MANAGEMENT SYSTEM	33
CHAPTER 23 - CASE CLASSIFICATION SYSTEM AND COMMUNITY CORRECTIONS PLAN	33
CHAPTER 25 - PALMETTO UNIFIED SCHOOL DISTRICT NO. 1	33
CHAPTER 26 - SOUTH CAROLINA SENTENCING GUIDELINES COMMISSION	33
CHAPTER 27 - INMATE LITIGATION	33
CHAPTER 28 - SENTENCING REFORM OVERSIGHT COMMITTEE	33
TITLE 25 – MILITARY, CIVIL DEFENSE AND VETERAN	

AFFAIRS
CHAPTER 1 - MILITARY CODE 33
CHAPTER 3 - SOUTH CAROLINA STATE GUARD 33
CHAPTER 7 - TREASON; SABOTAGE 33
CHAPTER 9 - EMERGENCY MEASURES 33
CHAPTER 11 - DIVISION OF VETERANS' AFFAIRS 33
CHAPTER 12 - VETERAN'S UNCLAIMED CREMATED REMAINS 33
CHAPTER 13 - CONFEDERATE PENSIONS 33
CHAPTER 15 - OTHER PROVISIONS FOR BENEFIT OF VETERANS 33
CHAPTER 17 - SOUTH CAROLINA MILITARY MUSEUM 33
CHAPTER 19 - PRISONERS OF WAR COMMISSION 33
CHAPTER 21 - VETERANS' TRUST FUND 33
TITLE 26 – NOTARIES PUBLIC AND ACKNOWLEDGEMENTS
CHAPTER 1 - NOTARIES PUBLIC 34
CHAPTER 3 - UNIFORM RECOGNITION OF ACKNOWLEDGMENTS ACT 34
CHAPTER 6 - UNIFORM ELECTRONIC TRANSACTIONS ACT 34
TITLE 27 – PROPERTY AND CONVEYANCES
CHAPTER 1 - GENERAL PROVISIONS 34
CHAPTER 2 - COORDINATE SYSTEM FOR DEFINING LOCATION OF POINTS WITHIN STATE 34
CHAPTER 3 - LIMITATION ON LIABILITY OF LANDOWNERS 34
CHAPTER 5 - ESTATES AND CONSTRUCTION OF DOCUMENTS CREATING ESTATES 34
CHAPTER 6 - UNIFORM STATUTORY RULE AGAINST PERPETUITIES 34
CHAPTER 7 - FORM AND EXECUTION OF CONVEYANCES 34
CHAPTER 8 - CONSERVATION EASEMENT ACT 34
CHAPTER 11 - CONFIRMATION OF TITLES 34
CHAPTER 13 - PROPERTY OWNERSHIP BY ALIENS 34
CHAPTER 15 - CATAWBA INDIAN LANDS 34
CHAPTER 16 - CATAWBA INDIAN CLAIMS SETTLEMENT ACT 34
CHAPTER 18 - UNIFORM UNCLAIMED PROPERTY ACT 34
CHAPTER 19 - ESCHEAT OF LAND AND PERSONAL PROPERTY 34
CHAPTER 21 - DISPOSITION OF CONFISCATED AND STOLEN PROPERTY 34
CHAPTER 23 - PAROL, FRAUDULENT, AND OTHER VOID GIFTS OR CONVEYANCES 35

CHAPTER 25 - ASSIGNMENTS FOR THE BENEFIT OF
    CREDITORS   35
CHAPTER 27 - BETTERMENTS   35
CHAPTER 29 - UNIFORM LAND SALES PRACTICE ACT   35
CHAPTER 31 - HORIZONTAL PROPERTY ACT   35
CHAPTER 32 - VACATION TIME SHARING PLANS   35
CHAPTER 33 - LANDLORD AND TENANT GENERALLY   35
CHAPTER 35 - CREATION, CONSTRUCTION, AND
    TERMINATION OF LEASEHOLD ESTATES   35
CHAPTER 37 - EJECTMENT OF TENANTS   35
CHAPTER 39 - RENT   35
CHAPTER 40 - RESIDENTIAL LANDLORD AND TENANT ACT   35
CHAPTER 41 - UNDERTENANTS OF LIFE TENANTS   35
CHAPTER 43 - CEMETERIES   35
CHAPTER 45 - ABANDONED AND LOANED CULTURAL
    PROPERTY   35
CHAPTER 47 - MANUFACTURED HOME PARK TENANCY ACT   35
CHAPTER 50 - THE RESIDENTIAL PROPERTY CONDITION
    DISCLOSURE ACT   35

TITLE 28 - EMINENT DOMAIN
CHAPTER 2 - THE EMINENT DOMAIN PROCEDURE ACT   36
CHAPTER 3 - STATE AUTHORITIES EMINENT DOMAIN ACT   36
CHAPTER 11 - RELOCATION ASSISTANCE   36

TITLE 29 – MORTGAGES AND OTHER LIENS
CHAPTER 1 - GENERAL PROVISIONS   36
CHAPTER 3 - MORTGAGES AND DEEDS OF TRUST
    GENERALLY   36
CHAPTER 4 - REVERSE MORTGAGES   36
CHAPTER 5 - MECHANICS' LIENS   36
CHAPTER 6 - PAYMENTS TO CONTRACTORS,
    SUBCONTRACTORS, AND SUPPLIERS   36
CHAPTER 7 - LIENS OF LABORERS AND OTHERS ON
CONTRACT PRICE   36
CHAPTER 9 - LIENS ON SHIPS AND VESSELS   36
CHAPTER 11 - LIEN OF MINING AND MANUFACTURING
    EMPLOYEES   36
CHAPTER 13 - AGRICULTURAL LIENS   36
CHAPTER 15 - MISCELLANEOUS LIENS FOR SERVICES,
    DAMAGES, STORAGE OR MATERIALS   36

TITLE 30 – PUBLIC RECORDS
CHAPTER 1 - PUBLIC RECORDS, REPORTS AND OFFICIAL

DOCUMENTS	36
CHAPTER 2 - FAMILY AND PERSONAL IDENTIFYING INFORMATION PRIVACY PROTECTION	36
CHAPTER 4 - FREEDOM OF INFORMATION ACT	37
CHAPTER 5 - RECORDING GENERALLY	37
CHAPTER 6 - UNIFORM REAL PROPERTY ELECTRONIC RECORDING ACT	37
CHAPTER 7 - RECORDATION ESSENTIAL TO VALIDITY	37
CHAPTER 9 - INDEXING AND FILING	37
CHAPTER 11 - RECORDATION OF DEEDS AND DOCUMENTS OF RAILROADS	37
CHAPTER 13 - RECORDATION OF MARKETING CONTRACTS	37
CHAPTER 15 - RECORDATION OF VETERANS' DISCHARGE	37

TITLE 31 – HOUSING AND REDEVELOPMENT

CHAPTER 1 - STATE HOUSING LAW	37
CHAPTER 3 - HOUSING AUTHORITIES LAW	37
CHAPTER 5 - HOUSING CO-OPERATION LAW	37
CHAPTER 6 - TAX INCREMENT FINANCING FOR REDEVELOPMENT PROJECTS	37
CHAPTER 7 - TAX INCREMENT FINANCING FOR COUNTIES	37
CHAPTER 9 - IMPROVEMENT TO LAND BY MUNICIPALITIES	37
CHAPTER 10 - COMMUNITY DEVELOPMENT LAW	37
CHAPTER 11 - HOUSING FOR NATIONAL DEFENSE ACTIVITIES	38
CHAPTER 12 - REDEVELOPMENT OF FEDERAL MILITARY INSTALLATIONS AND OTHER DEFENSE SITES	38
CHAPTER 13 - MODERATE TO LOW INCOME HOUSING	38
CHAPTER 15 - DWELLINGS UNFIT FOR HUMAN HABITATION	38
CHAPTER 17 - MOBILE HOMES AND HOUSE TRAILERS	38
CHAPTER 18 - SHOOTING RANGE PROTECTION ACT	38
CHAPTER 19 - INVESTMENTS IN HOUSING OBLIGATIONS	38
CHAPTER 21 - FAIR HOUSING LAW	38
CHAPTER 22 - WILLIAM C. MESCHER LOCAL HOUSING TRUST FUND ENABLING ACT	38
CHAPTER 23 - SOUTH CAROLINA COMMUNITY LAND TRUST	38

TITLE 32 – CONTRACTS AND AGENTS

CHAPTER 1 - GAMBLING AND FUTURE CONTRACTS	38
CHAPTER 2 - CONTRACTS AGAINST PUBLIC POLICY	38
CHAPTER 3 - STATUTE OF FRAUDS	38
CHAPTER 7 - PRENEED FUNERAL CONTRACTS	38
CHAPTER 8 - CREMATION AUTHORIZATIONS AND	

PROCEDURES	38
CHAPTER 9 - SEPARATE COMPOSITION OF ONE OF JOINT DEBTORS	38
CHAPTER 11 - AGENTS ACTING AFTER DEATH OF PRINCIPAL	38
CHAPTER 13 - CONTRACT FOR REIMBURSEMENT OF FEDERAL MANUFACTURER'S EXCISE TAX	38
TITLE 33 – CORPORATIONS, PARTNERSHIPS AND ASSOCIATIONS	
CHAPTER 1 - GENERAL PROVISIONS	39
CHAPTER 2 - INCORPORATION	39
CHAPTER 3 - PURPOSES AND POWERS	39
CHAPTER 4 - NAME	39
CHAPTER 5 - OFFICE AND AGENT	39
CHAPTER 6 - SHARES AND DISTRIBUTIONS	39
CHAPTER 7 - SHAREHOLDERS	39
CHAPTER 8 - DIRECTORS AND OFFICERS	39
CHAPTER 9 - DOMESTICATION OF A FOREIGN CORPORATION	39
CHAPTER 10 - AMENDMENT OF ARTICLES OF INCORPORATION AND BYLAWS	39
CHAPTER 11 - MERGER AND SHARE EXCHANGE	39
CHAPTER 12 - SALE OF ASSETS	39
CHAPTER 13 - DISSENTERS' RIGHTS	39
CHAPTER 14 - DISSOLUTION	39
CHAPTER 15 - FOREIGN CORPORATIONS	39
CHAPTER 16 - RECORDS AND REPORTS	39
CHAPTER 18 - STATUTORY CLOSE CORPORATION SUPPLEMENT	39
CHAPTER 19 - PROFESSIONAL CORPORATION SUPPLEMENT	39
CHAPTER 20 - TRANSITION PROVISIONS	39
CHAPTER 27 - TRANSFER OF STOCK IN CUSTODY OF CLEARING CORPORATIONS	39
CHAPTER 31 - SOUTH CAROLINA NONPROFIT CORPORATION ACT	39
CHAPTER 36 - CORPORATIONS NOT-FOR-PROFIT FINANCED BY FEDERAL OR STATE LOANS	40
CHAPTER 37 - BUSINESS DEVELOPMENT CORPORATIONS	40
CHAPTER 38 - SOUTH CAROLINA BENEFIT CORPORATION ACT	40

CHAPTER 39 - COUNTY BUSINESS DEVELOPMENT CORPORATIONS	40
CHAPTER 41 - UNIFORM PARTNERSHIP ACT	40
CHAPTER 42 - UNIFORM LIMITED PARTNERSHIP ACT	40
CHAPTER 44 - UNIFORM LIMITED LIABILITY COMPANY ACT OF 1996	40
CHAPTER 45 - COOPERATIVE ASSOCIATIONS GENERALLY	40
CHAPTER 46 - TELEPHONE COOPERATIVE ACT	41
CHAPTER 47 - MARKETING COOPERATIVE ASSOCIATIONS	41
CHAPTER 49 - ELECTRIC COOPERATIVES	41
CHAPTER 53 - BUSINESS TRUSTS	41
CHAPTER 56 - SOLICITATION OF CHARITABLE FUNDS	41
CHAPTER 57 - NONPROFIT RAFFLES FOR CHARITABLE PURPOSES	41
TITLE 34 – BANKING, FINANCIAL INSTITUTIONS AND MONEY	
CHAPTER 1 - STATE BOARD OF FINANCIAL INSTITUTIONS	41
CHAPTER 3 - BANKS AND BANKING GENERALLY	41
CHAPTER 5 - MANAGEMENT OF BANK BY CONSERVATORS	41
CHAPTER 6 - SOUTH CAROLINA UNIFORM PRUDENT MANAGEMENT OF INSTITUTIONAL FUNDS ACT	41
CHAPTER 7 - REORGANIZATION OF INSOLVENT BANKS	41
CHAPTER 9 - BANK CAPITAL AND CAPITAL STOCK	41
CHAPTER 11 - BANK DEPOSITS	41
CHAPTER 12 - COUNTY AND MULTI-COUNTY CHECK CLEARING HOUSES	41
CHAPTER 13 - BANK LOANS AND INVESTMENTS	41
CHAPTER 15 - BANK ACTING AS FIDUCIARY	41
CHAPTER 19 - SAFE-DEPOSIT BOXES	41
CHAPTER 21 - BANKS AND CORPORATIONS DOING TRUST BUSINESS	41
CHAPTER 24 - SOUTH CAROLINA BANK HOLDING COMPANY ACT [REPEALED]	41
CHAPTER 25 - SOUTH CAROLINA BANKING AND BRANCHING EFFICIENCY ACT OF 1996	42
CHAPTER 26 - SOUTH CAROLINA CREDIT UNION ACT	42
CHAPTER 27 - COOPERATIVE CREDIT UNIONS	42
CHAPTER 28 - SAVINGS ASSOCIATIONS	42
CHAPTER 29 - CONSUMER FINANCE LAW	42
CHAPTER 30 - A STATE SAVINGS BANK CHARTER IN SOUTH CAROLINA	42

CHAPTER 31 - MONEY AND INTEREST	43
CHAPTER 33 - BANKER'S BANKS	43
CHAPTER 36 - LOAN BROKERS	43
CHAPTER 39 - DEFERRED PRESENTMENT SERVICES	43
CHAPTER 41 - CHECK-CASHING SERVICES	43
CHAPTER 43 - SOUTH CAROLINA COMMUNITY ECONOMIC DEVELOPMENT ACT	43
CHAPTER 45 - SAVINGS PROMOTION CONTESTS	43

TITLES 35 - SECURITIES

CHAPTER 1 - SOUTH CAROLINA UNIFORM SECURITIES ACT OF 2005	43
CHAPTER 2 - CONTROL SHARE ACQUISITIONS; BUSINESS COMBINATIONS	43
CHAPTER 5 - NOMINEE REGISTRATION OF SECURITIES HELD BY CORPORATE FIDUCIARIES	43
CHAPTER 6 - UNIFORM TRANSFER ON DEATH SECURITY REGISTRATION ACT	43
CHAPTER 7 - UNIFORM ACT FOR SIMPLIFICATION OF FIDUCIARY SECURITY TRANSFERS [REPEALED]	43
CHAPTER 9 - INSIDER TRADING IN SECURITIES OF DOMESTIC STOCK INSURANCE COMPANIES [REPEALED]	43
CHAPTER 11 - SOUTH CAROLINA ANTI-MONEY LAUNDERING ACT	43

TITLE 36 – COMMERCIAL CODE

CHAPTER 1 - COMMERCIAL CODE - GENERAL PROVISIONS	44
CHAPTER 2 - COMMERCIAL CODE - SALES	44
CHAPTER 2A - COMMERCIAL CODE - LEASES	44
CHAPTER 3 - COMMERCIAL CODE - NEGOTIABLE INSTRUMENTS	44
CHAPTER 4 - COMMERCIAL CODE - BANK DEPOSITS AND COLLECTIONS	45
CHAPTER 4A - COMMERCIAL CODE - FUNDS TRANSFERS	45
CHAPTER 5 - COMMERCIAL CODE - LETTERS OF CREDIT	45
CHAPTER 6 - COMMERCIAL CODE - BULK TRANSFERS WAREHOUSE RECEIPTS [REPEALED]	45
CHAPTER 7 - COMMERCIAL CODE - WAREHOUSE RECEIPTS, BILLS OF LADING AND OTHER DOCUMENTS OF TITLE	45
CHAPTER 8 - COMMERCIAL CODE - INVESTMENT SECURITIES	45
CHAPTER 9 - COMMERCIAL CODE - SECURED	

TRANSACTIONS	46
CHAPTER 10 - COMMERCIAL CODE - EFFECTIVE DATE AND REPEALER	46
CHAPTER 11 - EFFECTIVE DATE AND TRANSITION PROVISIONS FOR THE 1981 UNIFORM COMMERCIAL CODE AMENDMENTS	46

TITLE 37 – CONSUMER PROTECTION CODE

CHAPTER 1 - GENERAL PROVISIONS AND DEFINITIONS	46
CHAPTER 2 - CREDIT SALES	46
CHAPTER 3 - LOANS	47
CHAPTER 4 - INSURANCE	47
CHAPTER 5 - REMEDIES AND PENALTIES	47
CHAPTER 6 - ADMINISTRATION	47
CHAPTER 7 - CONSUMER CREDIT COUNSELING	47
CHAPTER 8 - WAGE EARNER RECEIVERSHIP	47
CHAPTER 9 - EFFECTIVE DATE AND REPEALER	47
CHAPTER 10 - MISCELLANEOUS LOAN PROVISIONS	47
CHAPTER 11 - LICENSING AND REGULATION OF CONTINUING CARE RETIREMENT COMMUNITIES	47
CHAPTER 13 - REGULATION OF THE SUBLEASING AND LOAN ASSUMPTION OF MOTOR VEHICLES	47
CHAPTER 15 - PRIZES AND GIFTS	47
CHAPTER 16 - PREPAID LEGAL SERVICES	47
CHAPTER 17 - DISCOUNT MEDICAL PLAN ORGANIZATIONS	47
CHAPTER 20 - CONSUMER IDENTITY THEFT PROTECTION	47
CHAPTER 22 - MORTGAGE LENDING	47
CHAPTER 23 - HIGH-COST AND CONSUMER HOME LOANS	47
CHAPTER 25 - LIMITATIONS ON DISPENSING OF AN OPHTHALMIC CONTACT LENS OR LENSES	48
CHAPTER 29 - PALMETTOPRIDE	48
CHAPTER 30 - GUARANTEED ASSET PROTECTION	48

TITLE 38 - INSURANCE

CHAPTER 1 - TITLE AND DEFINITIONS	48
CHAPTER 2 - PENALTIES	
CHAPTER 3 - THE DEPARTMENT OF INSURANCE	48
CHAPTER 5 - AUTHORITY AND REQUIREMENTS TO TRANSACT BUSINESS	48
CHAPTER 7 - FEES AND TAXES	48
CHAPTER 9 - CAPITAL, SURPLUS, RESERVES, AND OTHER FINANCIAL MATTERS	48
CHAPTER 10 - PROTECTED CELL INSURANCE COMPANIES	48

CHAPTER 12 - SOUTH CAROLINA INVESTMENTS LAWS	48
CHAPTER 13 - EXAMINATIONS, INVESTIGATIONS, RECORDS, AND REPORTS	49
CHAPTER 14 - SPECIAL PURPOSE REINSURANCE VEHICLE MODEL ACT	49
CHAPTER 15 - SURETY INSURERS	49
CHAPTER 17 - RECIPROCAL INSURANCE	49
CHAPTER 19 - DOMESTIC MUTUAL INSURERS	49
CHAPTER 21 - INSURANCE HOLDING COMPANY REGULATORY ACT	49
CHAPTER 23 - INSIDER TRADING IN SECURITIES OF DOMESTIC STOCK INSURERS	49
CHAPTER 25 - UNAUTHORIZED TRANSACTION OF INSURANCE BUSINESS	49
CHAPTER 26 - ADMINISTRATIVE SUPERVISION OF INSURERS ACT	49
CHAPTER 27 - INSURERS' REHABILITATION AND LIQUIDATION ACT	49
CHAPTER 29 - SOUTH CAROLINA LIFE AND ACCIDENT AND HEALTH INSURANCE GUARANTY ASSOCIATION	49
CHAPTER 31 - SOUTH CAROLINA PROPERTY AND CASUALTY INSURANCE GUARANTY ASSOCIATION	50
CHAPTER 33 - HEALTH MAINTENANCE ORGANIZATIONS	50
CHAPTER 35 - MUTUAL BENEVOLENT AID ASSOCIATIONS	50
CHAPTER 38 - FRATERNAL BENEFIT SOCIETIES	50
CHAPTER 39 - INSURANCE PREMIUM SERVICE COMPANIES	50
CHAPTER 41 - MULTIPLE EMPLOYER SELF-INSURED HEALTH PLAN	50
CHAPTER 43 - INSURANCE PRODUCERS AND AGENCIES	50
CHAPTER 44 - MANAGING GENERAL AGENTS ACT	50
CHAPTER 45 - INSURANCE BROKERS AND SURPLUS LINES INSURANCE	50
CHAPTER 46 - REINSURANCE INTERMEDIARY ACT	50
CHAPTER 47 - INSURANCE ADJUSTERS	50
CHAPTER 48 - PUBLIC INSURANCE ADJUSTERS	50
CHAPTER 49 - MOTOR VEHICLE PHYSICAL DAMAGE APPRAISERS	50
CHAPTER 51 - ADMINISTRATORS OF INSURANCE BENEFIT PLANS	50
CHAPTER 53 - BAIL BONDSMEN AND RUNNERS	50
CHAPTER 55 - CONDUCT OF INSURANCE BUSINESS	50

CHAPTER 57 - TRADE PRACTICES	51
CHAPTER 59 - CLAIMS PRACTICES	51
CHAPTER 61 - INSURANCE CONTRACTS GENERALLY	51
CHAPTER 63 - INDIVIDUAL LIFE INSURANCE	51
CHAPTER 65 - GROUP LIFE INSURANCE	51
CHAPTER 67 - VARIABLE CONTRACTS	51
CHAPTER 69 - INDIVIDUAL ANNUITIES	51
CHAPTER 70 - UTILIZATION REVIEWS AND PRIVATE REVIEW AGENTS	51
CHAPTER 71 - ACCIDENT AND HEALTH INSURANCE	51
CHAPTER 72 - LONG TERM CARE INSURANCE ACT	52
CHAPTER 73 - PROPERTY, CASUALTY, INLAND MARINE, AND SURETY RATES AND RATE-MAKING ORGANIZATIONS	52
CHAPTER 74 - HEALTH INSURANCE POOL	52
CHAPTER 75 - PROPERTY, CASUALTY, AND TITLE INSURANCE GENERALLY	52
CHAPTER 77 - AUTOMOBILE INSURANCE	52
CHAPTER 78 - SERVICE CONTRACTS	52
CHAPTER 79 - MEDICAL MALPRACTICE INSURANCE	52
CHAPTER 81 - LEGAL MALPRACTICE INSURANCE	52
CHAPTER 83 - JOINT UNDERWRITING ASSOCIATION FOR WRITING OF PROFESSIONAL LIABILITY INSURANCE	53
CHAPTER 85 - CONSOLIDATIONS AND MORTGAGE INSURANCE	53
CHAPTER 87 - REGULATION AND TAXATION OF RISK RETENTION GROUPS AND PURCHASING GROUPS	53
CHAPTER 89 - DAY CARE JOINT UNDERWRITING ASSOCIATION	53
CHAPTER 90 - CAPTIVE INSURANCE COMPANIES	53
CHAPTER 91 - JOINT UNDERWRITING ASSOCIATION FOR PRIVATE PASSENGER AND COMMERCE AUTOMOBILE INSURANCE [INOPERATIVE]	53
CHAPTER 93 - PRIVACY OF GENETIC INFORMATION	53
CHAPTER 95 - INTERSTATE INSURANCE PRODUCT REGULATION COMPACT [EXPIRED]	53
CHAPTER 97 - PORTABLE ELECTRONICS INSURANCE	53
TITLE 39 – TRADE AND COMMENCE	
CHAPTER 1 - GENERAL PROVISIONS	53
CHAPTER 3 - TRUSTS, MONOPOLIES AND RESTRAINTS OF TRADE	53

CHAPTER 4 - ABUSIVE ASSERTIONS RELATING TO INTELLECTUAL PROPERTY	53
CHAPTER 5 - UNFAIR TRADE PRACTICES	53
CHAPTER 6 - FAIR PRACTICES OF FARM, CONSTRUCTION, INDUSTRIAL, AND OUTDOOR POWER EQUIPMENT MANUFACTURERS, DISTRIBUTORS, WHOLESALERS, AND DEALERS	53
CHAPTER 7 - FAIR TRADE ACT	53
CHAPTER 8 - TRADE SECRETS	54
CHAPTER 9 - WEIGHTS AND MEASURES	54
CHAPTER 11 - PUBLIC WEIGHMASTERS	54
CHAPTER 13 - NAMES OF BUSINESS ESTABLISHMENTS [REPEALED]	54
CHAPTER 14 - SOUTH CAROLINA LANDOWNER AND ADVERTISING PROTECTION AND PROPERTY VALUATION ACT	54
CHAPTER 15 - LABELS AND TRADEMARKS	54
CHAPTER 16 - SALE OF FINE PRINTS; DISCLOSURE REQUIREMENTS	54
CHAPTER 17 - CONTAINERS AND GRADES	54
CHAPTER 19 - WAREHOUSES AND WAREHOUSEMEN GENERALLY	54
CHAPTER 20 - SELF-SERVICE STORAGE FACILITIES	54
CHAPTER 21 - STATE WAREHOUSE SYSTEM [REPEALED]	54
CHAPTER 22 - STATE WAREHOUSE SYSTEM	54
CHAPTER 23 - ADULTERATED, MISBRANDED OR NEW DRUGS AND DEVICES	54
CHAPTER 24 - DRUG PRODUCT SELECTION ACT	54
CHAPTER 25 - ADULTERATED OR MISBRANDED FOOD AND COSMETICS	54
CHAPTER 27 - FLOUR AND BREAD	54
CHAPTER 29 - CORN MEAL AND GRITS	54
CHAPTER 31 - RICE	54
CHAPTER 33 - MILK AND MILK PRODUCTS MARKETING	54
CHAPTER 35 - BUTTER AND CHEESE IMITATIONS	54
CHAPTER 37 - ICE CREAM, ICE MILK AND OTHER FROZEN DESSERTS	55
CHAPTER 39 - EGGS AND BABY CHICKS	55
CHAPTER 41 - GASOLINE, LUBRICATING OILS AND OTHER PETROLEUM PRODUCTS	55
CHAPTER 43 - LIQUEFIED PETROLEUM GASES [REPEALED]	55

CHAPTER 45 - PAINT, PAINT OIL AND TURPENTINE [REPEALED]	55
CHAPTER 47 - ANHYDROUS AMMONIA [REPEALED]	55
CHAPTER 49 - ELECTRIC STORAGE BATTERIES	55
CHAPTER 51 - ANTI-FREEZE	55
CHAPTER 53 - PRODUCTS MADE BY BLIND PERSONS	55
CHAPTER 54 - ASSISTIVE TECHNOLOGY WARRANTY ACT	55
CHAPTER 55 - CEMETERIES [REPEALED]	55
CHAPTER 57 - BUSINESS OPPORTUNITY SALES ACT	55
CHAPTER 59 - FRANCHISE AGREEMENTS RELATING TO RETAIL AND REPURCHASE OF FARM IMPLEMENTS, ETC.	55
CHAPTER 61 - MOTOR CLUB SERVICES ACT	55
CHAPTER 63 - TEXTILE FIBER PRODUCTS	55
CHAPTER 65 - PAYMENT OF POST-TERMINATION CLAIMS TO SALES REPRESENTATIVES	55
CHAPTER 69 - MOLD LIEN AND RETENTION	55
CHAPTER 73 - STATE COMMODITY CODE	55
CHAPTER 75 - REGROOVED AND REGROOVABLE TIRES	55

TITLE 40 – PROFESSIONS AND OCCUPATIONS

CHAPTER 1 - PROFESSIONS AND OCCUPATIONS	56
CHAPTER 2 - ACCOUNTANTS	56
CHAPTER 3 - ARCHITECTS	56
CHAPTER 5 - ATTORNEYS-AT-LAW	56
CHAPTER 6 - AUCTIONEERS	56
CHAPTER 7 - BARBERS AND BARBERING	56
CHAPTER 8 - SOUTH CAROLINA PERPETUAL CARE CEMETERY ACT	56
CHAPTER 9 - CHIROPRACTORS AND CHIROPRACTIC	56
CHAPTER 10 - FIRE PROTECTION SPRINKLER SYSTEMS ACT	56
CHAPTER 11 - CONTRACTORS	56
CHAPTER 13 - COSMETOLOGY AND COSMETOLOGISTS	56
CHAPTER 15 - DENTISTS, DENTAL HYGIENISTS, AND DENTAL TECHNICIANS	57
CHAPTER 18 - PRIVATE SECURITY AND INVESTIGATION AGENCIES	57
CHAPTER 19 - EMBALMERS AND FUNERAL DIRECTORS	57
CHAPTER 20 - SOUTH CAROLINA DIETETICS LICENSURE ACT	57
CHAPTER 21 - [RESERVED]	57

CHAPTER 22 - ENGINEERS AND SURVEYORS	57
CHAPTER 23 - ENVIRONMENTAL CERTIFICATION BOARD	57
CHAPTER 24 - EYE CARE CONSUMER PROTECTION	57
CHAPTER 25 - PRACTICE OF SPECIALIZING IN HEARING AIDS ACT	57
CHAPTER 26 - COMMERCIAL INSPECTORS	57
CHAPTER 27 - JUNK DEALERS	57
CHAPTER 28 - LANDSCAPE ARCHITECTS	57
CHAPTER 29 - UNIFORM STANDARDS CODE FOR MANUFACTURED HOUSING	57
CHAPTER 30 - MASSAGE/BODYWORK PRACTICE ACT	58
CHAPTER 31 - NATUROPATHY	58
CHAPTER 33 - NURSES	58
CHAPTER 35 - LONG TERM HEALTH CARE ADMINISTRATORS	58
CHAPTER 36 - OCCUPATIONAL THERAPISTS	58
CHAPTER 37 - OPTOMETRISTS	58
CHAPTER 38 - OPTICIANS	58
CHAPTER 39 - PAWNBROKERS	58
CHAPTER 41 - PEDDLERS AND HAWKERS, HORSE TRADERS, AND FORTUNETELLERS	58
CHAPTER 43 - SOUTH CAROLINA PHARMACY PRACTICE ACT	58
CHAPTER 45 - PHYSICAL THERAPISTS	59
CHAPTER 47 - PHYSICIANS AND MISCELLANEOUS HEALTH CARE PROFESSIONALS	59
CHAPTER 49 - PLUMBERS AND PLUMBING	59
CHAPTER 51 - PODIATRISTS AND PODIATRY	59
CHAPTER 53 - POLYGRAPH EXAMINERS ACT	59
CHAPTER 54 - DEALERS IN PRECIOUS METALS	59
CHAPTER 55 - PSYCHOLOGISTS	59
CHAPTER 56 - STATE BOARD OF PYROTECHNIC SAFETY	59
CHAPTER 57 - REAL ESTATE BROKERS, SALESMEN, AND PROPERTY MANAGERS	59
CHAPTER 58 - LICENSING OF MORTGAGE BROKERS ACT	60
CHAPTER 59 - RESIDENTIAL HOME BUILDERS	60
CHAPTER 60 - SOUTH CAROLINA REAL ESTATE APPRAISER LICENSE AND CERTIFICATION ACT	60
CHAPTER 61 - SANITARIANS	60
CHAPTER 63 - SOCIAL WORKERS	60
CHAPTER 65 - SOIL CLASSIFIERS	60

CHAPTER 67 - SPEECH PATHOLOGISTS AND AUDIOLOGISTS	60
CHAPTER 68 - REGULATION OF PROFESSIONAL EMPLOYER ORGANIZATIONS	60
CHAPTER 69 - VETERINARIANS	60
CHAPTER 71 - LIABILITY OF MEMBERS OF PROFESSIONAL COMMITTEES	60
CHAPTER 73 - [RESERVED]	61
CHAPTER 75 - PROFESSIONAL COUNSELORS, MARRIAGE AND FAMILY THERAPISTS, AND LICENSED PSYCHO-EDUCATIONAL SPECIALISTS	61
CHAPTER 77 - GEOLOGIST	61
CHAPTER 79 - SOUTH CAROLINA ALARM SYSTEM BUSINESS ACT	61
CHAPTER 80 - SOUTH CAROLINA FIREFIGHTERS EMPLOYMENT AND REGISTRATION ACT	61
CHAPTER 81 - STATE ATHLETIC COMMISSION	61
CHAPTER 82 - LIQUID PETROLEUM GAS	61
CHAPTER 83 - REGISTRATION OF IMMIGRATION ASSISTANCE SERVICES ACT	61
TITLE 41 – LABOR AND EMPLOYMENT	
CHAPTER 1 - GENERAL PROVISIONS	61
CHAPTER 3 - DEPARTMENT AND DIRECTOR OF LABOR, LICENSING, AND REGULATION	61
CHAPTER 7 - RIGHT TO WORK	61
CHAPTER 8 - ILLEGAL ALIENS AND PRIVATE EMPLOYMENT	61
CHAPTER 10 - PAYMENT OF WAGES	61
CHAPTER 11 - PAYMENT OF WAGES [REPEALED]	61
CHAPTER 13 - CHILD LABOR	61
CHAPTER 14 - BOILER SAFETY ACT	62
CHAPTER 15 - OCCUPATIONAL HEALTH AND SAFETY	62
CHAPTER 16 - SOUTH CAROLINA ELEVATOR CODE	62
CHAPTER 17 - CONCILIATION OF INDUSTRIAL DISPUTES	62
CHAPTER 18 - SOUTH CAROLINA AMUSEMENT RIDES SAFETY CODE	62
CHAPTER 19 - PERSONAL SERVICE CONTRACTS [REPEALED]	62
CHAPTER 21 - FUTURE VOLUNTEER FIREFIGHTERS ACT OF SOUTH CAROLINA	62
CHAPTER 23 - AGRICULTURAL LABOR CONTRACTS [REPEALED]	62

CHAPTER 25 - PRIVATE PERSONNEL PLACEMENT SERVICES	62
CHAPTER 27 - EMPLOYMENT AND WORKFORCE – GENERAL PROVISIONS	62
CHAPTER 29 - EMPLOYMENT AND WORKFORCE – DEPARTMENT OF EMPLOYMENT AND WORKFORCE	62
CHAPTER 31 - CONTRIBUTIONS AND PAYMENTS TO THE UNEMPLOYMENT TRUST FUND	62
CHAPTER 33 - EMPLOYMENT AND WORKFORCE - FUNDS	62
CHAPTER 35 - EMPLOYMENT AND WORKFORCE – BENEFITS AND CLAIMS THEREFOR	63
CHAPTER 37 - EMPLOYMENT AND WORKFORCE – EMPLOYER'S COVERAGE	63
CHAPTER 39 - EMPLOYMENT AND WORKFORCE – PROTECTION OF RIGHTS AND BENEFITS	63
CHAPTER 41 - EMPLOYMENT AND WORKFORCE – OFFENSES, PENALTIES AND LIABILITIES	63
CHAPTER 42 - STATE EMPLOYMENT SERVICE	63
CHAPTER 43 - SOUTH CAROLINA JOBS - ECONOMIC DEVELOPMENT FUND ACT	63
CHAPTER 44 - PALMETTO SEED CAPITAL FUND LIMITED PARTNERSHIP	63
CHAPTER 45 - COORDINATING COUNCIL FOR ECONOMIC DEVELOPMENT [REPEALED]	63
TITLE 42 – WORKER'S COMPENSATION	
CHAPTER 1 - GENERAL PROVISIONS	63
CHAPTER 3 - WORKERS' COMPENSATION COMMISSION	63
CHAPTER 5 - INSURANCE AND SELF-INSURANCE	63
CHAPTER 7 - FUNDS	63
CHAPTER 9 - COMPENSATION AND PAYMENT	63
CHAPTER 11 - OCCUPATIONAL DISEASES	63
CHAPTER 13 - IONIZING RADIATION INJURY	64
CHAPTER 15 - NOTICE OF ACCIDENT; FILING OF CLAIMS; MEDICAL ATTENTION AND EXAMINATION	64
CHAPTER 17 - AWARDS PROCEDURE	64
CHAPTER 19 - RECORDS AND REPORTS	64
TITLE 43 – SOCIAL SERVICES	
CHAPTER 1 - STATE DEPARTMENT AND BOARD OF SOCIAL SERVICES	64
CHAPTER 3 - COUNTY DEPARTMENTS AND BOARDS OF SOCIAL SERVICES	64

CHAPTER 5 - PUBLIC AID, ASSISTANCE AND RELIEF GENERALLY	64
CHAPTER 7 - MEDICAL AND HOSPITAL CARE	64
CHAPTER 21 - DIVISION AND ADVISORY COUNCIL ON AGING	64
CHAPTER 25 - COMMISSION FOR THE BLIND	64
CHAPTER 26 - OPERATION OF VENDING FACILITIES BY BLIND PERSONS	64
CHAPTER 31 - VOCATIONAL REHABILITATION	64
CHAPTER 33 - RIGHTS OF PHYSICALLY DISABLED PERSONS	64
CHAPTER 35 - ADULT PROTECTION	64
CHAPTER 38 - INVESTIGATION OF HEALTH FACILITIES BY OMBUDSMAN	64
CHAPTER 39 - MIDLANDS HUMAN RESOURCES DEVELOPMENT COMMISSION	64
CHAPTER 41 - GLEAMNS HUMAN RESOURCES COMMISSION	64
CHAPTER 43 - DILLON-MARION HUMAN RESOURCES COMMISSION	65
CHAPTER 45 - COMMUNITY ECONOMIC OPPORTUNITY ACT OF 1983	65
CHAPTER 47 - COUNTY HUMAN RESOURCES COMMISSION	65
TITLE 44 - HEALTH	
CHAPTER 1 - DEPARTMENT OF HEALTH AND ENVIRONMENTAL CONTROL	65
CHAPTER 2 - STATE UNDERGROUND PETROLEUM ENVIRONMENTAL RESPONSE BANK ACT	65
CHAPTER 3 - LOCAL HEALTH BOARDS AND DISTRICTS	65
CHAPTER 4 - EMERGENCY HEALTH POWERS	65
CHAPTER 5 - STATE HEALTH PLANNING AND DEVELOPMENT ACT	65
CHAPTER 6 - DEPARTMENT OF HEALTH AND HUMAN SERVICES	65
CHAPTER 7 - HOSPITALS, TUBERCULOSIS CAMPS AND HEALTH SERVICES DISTRICTS	65
CHAPTER 8 - COMMUNITY ORAL HEALTH COORDINATOR	66
CHAPTER 9 - STATE DEPARTMENT OF MENTAL HEALTH	66
CHAPTER 10 - INTERSTATE HEALTHCARE COMPACT	66
CHAPTER 11 - ORGANIZATION AND CONTROL OF STATE MENTAL HEALTH FACILITIES	66

CHAPTER 13 - ADMISSION, DETENTION AND REMOVAL OF PATIENTS AT STATE MENTAL HEALTH FACILITIES 66
CHAPTER 15 - LOCAL MENTAL HEALTH PROGRAMS, BOARDS AND CENTERS 66
CHAPTER 17 - CARE AND COMMITMENT OF MENTALLY ILL PERSONS 66
CHAPTER 20 - SOUTH CAROLINA INTELLECTUAL DISABILITY, RELATED DISABILITIES, HEAD INJURIES, AND SPINAL CORD INJURIES ACT 66
CHAPTER 21 - DEPARTMENT OF DISABILITIES AND SPECIAL NEEDS FAMILY SUPPORT SERVICES 66
CHAPTER 22 - RIGHTS OF MENTAL HEALTH PATIENTS 66
CHAPTER 23 - PROVISIONS APPLICABLE TO BOTH MENTALLY ILL PERSONS AND PERSONS OF INTELLECTUAL DISABILITIES 66
CHAPTER 24 - COMMITMENT OF CHILDREN IN NEED OF MENTAL HEALTH TREATMENT 66
CHAPTER 25 - INTERSTATE COMPACT ON MENTAL HEALTH 66
CHAPTER 26 - RIGHTS OF CLIENTS WITH INTELLECTUAL DISABILITY 66
CHAPTER 27 - PATIENTS AT FEDERAL INSTITUTIONS 66
CHAPTER 28 - SELF-SUFFICIENCY TRUST FUND; DISABILITY TRUST FUND; AID FOR DEVELOPMENTALLY DISABLED, MENTALLY ILL, AND PHYSICALLY HANDICAPPED PERSONS 67
CHAPTER 29 - CONTAGIOUS AND INFECTIOUS DISEASES 67
CHAPTER 30 - HEALTH CARE PROFESSIONAL COMPLIANCE ACT 67
CHAPTER 31 - TUBERCULOSIS 67
CHAPTER 32 - BODY PIERCING 67
CHAPTER 33 - SICKLE CELL ANEMIA 67
CHAPTER 34 - TATTOOING 67
CHAPTER 35 - CANCER 67
CHAPTER 36 - ALZHEIMER'S DISEASE AND RELATED DISORDERS 67
CHAPTER 37 - CARE OF THE NEWLY BORN 67
CHAPTER 38 - HEAD AND SPINAL CORD INJURIES 67
CHAPTER 39 - DIABETES INITIATIVE OF SOUTH CAROLINA 67
CHAPTER 40 - AGENT ORANGE INFORMATION AND ASSISTANCE PROGRAM 67
CHAPTER 41 - ABORTIONS 67

CHAPTER 43 - DISPOSITIONS OF HUMAN BODIES AND PARTS; POST-MORTEM EXAMINATIONS	67
CHAPTER 44 - BIRTH DEFECTS	67
CHAPTER 48 - SEXUALLY VIOLENT PREDATOR ACT	67
CHAPTER 49 - DEPARTMENT OF ALCOHOL AND OTHER DRUG ABUSE SERVICES	67
CHAPTER 52 - ALCOHOL AND DRUG ABUSE COMMITMENT	68
CHAPTER 53 - POISONS, DRUGS AND OTHER CONTROLLED SUBSTANCES	68
CHAPTER 54 - DRUG DEALER LIABILITY ACT	68
CHAPTER 55 - WATER, SEWAGE, WASTE DISPOSAL AND THE LIKE	68
CHAPTER 56 - SOUTH CAROLINA HAZARDOUS WASTE MANAGEMENT ACT	68
CHAPTER 59 - THE RIVER BASINS ADVISORY COMMISSIONS	68
CHAPTER 61 - EMERGENCY MEDICAL SERVICES	68
CHAPTER 63 - VITAL STATISTICS	68
CHAPTER 66 - ADULT HEALTH CARE CONSENT ACT	68
CHAPTER 67 - LITTER CONTROL [REPEALED]	68
CHAPTER 69 - LICENSURE OF HOME HEALTH AGENCIES	68
CHAPTER 70 - LICENSURE OF IN-HOME CARE PROVIDERS ACT	68
CHAPTER 71 - LICENSURE OF HOSPICE PROGRAMS	68
CHAPTER 74 - RADIOLOGIC TECHNOLOGISTS	69
CHAPTER 75 - ATHLETIC TRAINERS' ACT OF SOUTH CAROLINA	69
CHAPTER 76 - AUTOMATED EXTERNAL DEFIBRILLATORS	69
CHAPTER 77 - DEATH WITH DIGNITY ACT	69
CHAPTER 78 - EMERGENCY SERVICES NON-RESUSCITATION ORDER	69
CHAPTER 79 - PHYSICAL FITNESS SERVICES ACT	69
CHAPTER 81 - BILL OF RIGHTS FOR RESIDENTS OF LONG-TERM CARE FACILITIES	69
CHAPTER 87 - ASBESTOS ABATEMENT LICENSE	69
CHAPTER 89 - LICENSING OF BIRTHING CENTERS	69
CHAPTER 93 - INFECTIOUS WASTE MANAGEMENT	69
CHAPTER 95 - CLEAN INDOOR AIR ACT	69
CHAPTER 96 - SOUTH CAROLINA SOLID WASTE POLICY AND MANAGEMENT ACT	69
CHAPTER 99 - INSECT STING EMERGENCY TREATMENT	

ACT	69
CHAPTER 107 - THE DRUG-FREE WORKPLACE ACT	69
CHAPTER 113 - PROVIDER SELF-REFERRAL	69
CHAPTER 115 - PHYSICIANS' PATIENT RECORDS ACT	69
CHAPTER 117 - PRESCRIPTION INFORMATION PRIVACY ACT	69
CHAPTER 122 - COUNTY GRANTS FUND FOR ADOLESCENT PREGNANCY PREVENTION INITIATIVES	69
CHAPTER 125 - OSTEOPOROSIS PREVENTION AND TREATMENT EDUCATION	69
CHAPTER 128 - SOUTH CAROLINA YOUTH SMOKING PREVENTION ACT	70
CHAPTER 130 - SOUTH CAROLINA OVERDOSE PREVENTION ACT	70
CHAPTER 132 - DIRECT SUBMISSION OF CLAIMS FOR ANATOMIC PATHOLOGY SERVICES	70
CHAPTER 135 - THE ASBESTOS AND SILICA CLAIMS PROCEDURE ACT OF 2006	70
CHAPTER 137 - THE RIGHT TO TRY ACT	70

Title 45 – HOTELS, MOTELS, RESTAURANTS AND BOARDINGHOUSES

CHAPTER 1 - GENERAL PROVISIONS	70
CHAPTER 2 - THE LODGING ESTABLISHMENT ACT	70
CHAPTER 3 - REGULATION BY MUNICIPALITIES	70
CHAPTER 4 - SOUTH CAROLINA BED AND BREAKFAST ACT	70
CHAPTER 5 - SAFETY REGULATIONS	71
CHAPTER 7 - TOURIST CAMPS AND ROADHOUSES	71
CHAPTER 9 - EQUAL ENJOYMENT AND PRIVILEGES TO PUBLIC ACCOMMODATIONS	71

TITLE 46 - AGRICULTURE

CHAPTER 1 - GENERAL PROVISIONS; OFFENSES	71
CHAPTER 3 - DEPARTMENT AND COMMISSIONER OF AGRICULTURE	71
CHAPTER 5 - AGRICULTURE COMMISSION	71
CHAPTER 7 - CLEMSON UNIVERSITY	71
CHAPTER 9 - STATE CROP PEST COMMISSION	71
CHAPTER 10 - BOLL WEEVIL ERADICATION	71
CHAPTER 11 - PEST CONTROL COMPACT	71
CHAPTER 13 - PESTICIDE CONTROL ACT	71
CHAPTER 15 - AGRICULTURAL MARKETING GENERALLY	71
CHAPTER 17 - AGRICULTURAL COMMODITIES MARKETING	71

CHAPTER 19 - LOCAL MARKETING AUTHORITIES AND FARM MARKETING CENTERS	71
CHAPTER 21 - SEEDS; PLANTS; SEED AND PLANT CERTIFICATION	71
CHAPTER 23 - NOXIOUS WEEDS	71
CHAPTER 25 - FERTILIZERS	71
CHAPTER 26 - AGRICULTURAL LIMING MATERIALS AND LANDPLASTER	71
CHAPTER 27 - SOUTH CAROLINA COMMERCIAL FEED ACT	71
CHAPTER 29 - COTTON	71
CHAPTER 30 - TOBACCO ECONOMY	71
CHAPTER 31 - FLUE-CURED TOBACCO	71
CHAPTER 33 - SHIPMENT AND SALE OF TREES, PLANTS AND SHRUBS	71
CHAPTER 35 - NEGLECTED OR ABANDONED ORCHARDS	71
CHAPTER 37 - INTRODUCTION OF HONEY BEES INTO STATE	71
CHAPTER 39 - FARMERS' ASSOCIATIONS	71
CHAPTER 40 - GRAIN DEALERS GUARANTY FUND	71
CHAPTER 41 - DEALERS AND HANDLERS OF AGRICULTURAL PRODUCTS	72
CHAPTER 42 - SAMPLING, GRADING AND INSPECTION OF GRAINS AND OILSEEDS	72
CHAPTER 45 - NUISANCE SUITS RELATED TO AGRICULTURAL OPERATIONS	72
CHAPTER 49 - SUPERVISION AND REGULATION OF MILK AND MILK PRODUCTS	72
CHAPTER 50 - SOUTHERN INTERSTATE DAIRY COMPACT	72
CHAPTER 51 - AQUACULTURE PERMIT ASSISTANCE OFFICE	72
CHAPTER 53 - AGRITOURISM ACTIVITY LIABILITY	72
CHAPTER 55 - INDUSTRIAL HEMP CULTIVATION	72
TITLE 47 – ANIMALS, LIVESTOCK AND POULTRY	
CHAPTER 1 - CRUELTY TO ANIMALS	72
CHAPTER 3 - DOGS AND OTHER DOMESTIC PETS	72
CHAPTER 4 - STATE LIVESTOCK-POULTRY HEALTH COMMISSION	72
CHAPTER 5 - RABIES CONTROL	72
CHAPTER 6 - PSEUDORABIES CONTROL AND ERADICATION ACT	72
CHAPTER 7 - ESTRAYS; LIVESTOCK TRESPASSING OR	

RUNNING AT LARGE	72
CHAPTER 9 - LIVESTOCK GENERALLY	72
CHAPTER 11 - SALE, GRADING AND INSPECTION OF LIVESTOCK	72
CHAPTER 13 - DISEASES AND INFECTIONS	72
CHAPTER 15 - FEEDING OF GARBAGE TO SWINE	73
CHAPTER 17 - MEAT AND MEAT FOOD	73
CHAPTER 19 - POULTRY PRODUCTS INSPECTION LAW	73
CHAPTER 20 - CONFINED SWINE FEEDING OPERATIONS	73
CHAPTER 21 - FARM ANIMAL, CROP OPERATION, AND RESEARCH FACILITIES PROTECTION ACT	73
CHAPTER 22 - RENDERING OF LIVESTOCK AND POULTRY RAW MATERIAL	73

TITLE 48 – ENVIRONMENT PROTECTION AND CONSERVATION

CHAPTER 1 - POLLUTION CONTROL ACT	73
CHAPTER 2 - ENVIRONMENTAL PROTECTION FUNDS	73
CHAPTER 3 - POLLUTION CONTROL FACILITIES	73
CHAPTER 4 - DEPARTMENT OF NATURAL RESOURCES	73
CHAPTER 5 - SOUTH CAROLINA WATER QUALITY REVOLVING FUND AUTHORITY ACT	73
CHAPTER 7 - FEDERAL CONSERVATION ACT	73
CHAPTER 9 - SOIL AND WATER CONSERVATION DISTRICTS LAW	73
CHAPTER 11 - WATERSHED CONSERVATION DISTRICTS	73
CHAPTER 14 - THE STORMWATER MANAGEMENT AND SEDIMENT REDUCTION ACT	73
CHAPTER 15 - LOW COUNTRY RESOURCES, CONSERVATION AND DEVELOPMENT AUTHORITY	73
CHAPTER 17 - CROSSROADS OF HISTORY RESOURCE, CONSERVATION AND DEVELOPMENT AUTHORITY	74
CHAPTER 18 - EROSION AND SEDIMENT REDUCTION ACT OF 1983	74
CHAPTER 20 - SOUTH CAROLINA MINING ACT	74
CHAPTER 21 - INTERSTATE MINING COMPACT	74
CHAPTER 22 - THE SOUTH CAROLINA GEOLOGICAL SURVEY UNIT OF THE DEPARTMENT OF NATURAL RESOURCES	74
CHAPTER 23 - FORESTRY GENERALLY	74
CHAPTER 25 - FORESTRY DISTRICTS	74
CHAPTER 27 - REGISTRATION OF FORESTERS	74

CHAPTER 28 - FOREST RENEWAL PRACTICES	74
CHAPTER 29 - FOREST PEST OUTBREAKS	74
CHAPTER 30 - PRIMARY FOREST PRODUCT ASSESSMENT	74
CHAPTER 31 - EMERGENCY POWERS OF GOVERNOR TO PROTECT FORESTS	74
CHAPTER 33 - SOUTH CAROLINA FOREST FIRE PROTECTION ACT	74
CHAPTER 34 - SOUTH CAROLINA PRESCRIBED FIRE ACT	74
CHAPTER 35 - REGULATION OF FIRES ON CERTAIN LANDS	74
CHAPTER 36 - SOUTH CAROLINA FOREST BEST MANAGEMENT PRACTICES ACT	74
CHAPTER 37 - SOUTHEASTERN INTERSTATE FOREST FIRE PROTECTION COMPACT	74
CHAPTER 39 - COASTAL TIDELANDS AND WETLANDS	74
CHAPTER 40 - BEACH RESTORATION AND IMPROVEMENT TRUST ACT	74
CHAPTER 41 - INTERSTATE COMPACT TO CONSERVE OIL AND GAS	75
CHAPTER 43 - OIL AND GAS EXPLORATION, DRILLING, TRANSPORTATION, AND PRODUCTION	75
CHAPTER 44 - SOUTH CAROLINA OIL SPILL RESPONDERS LIABILITY ACT	75
CHAPTER 45 - SOUTH CAROLINA SEA GRANT CONSORTIUM	75
CHAPTER 46 - ATLANTIC INTERSTATE LOW-LEVEL RADIOACTIVE WASTE COMPACT IMPLEMENTATION ACT	75
CHAPTER 49 - SOUTH CAROLINA MOUNTAIN RIDGE PROTECTION ACT OF 1984	75
CHAPTER 52 - ENERGY EFFICIENCY	75
CHAPTER 53 - TRANSPORTATION OF LITTER	75
CHAPTER 54 - TAKE PALMETTO PRIDE IN WHERE YOU LIVE	75
CHAPTER 55 - SOUTH CAROLINA ENVIRONMENTAL AWARENESS AWARD	75
CHAPTER 56 - INNOVATION IN ENVIRONMENTAL APPROACHES	75
CHAPTER 57 - ENVIRONMENTAL AUDIT PRIVILEGE AND VOLUNTARY DISCLOSURE	75
CHAPTER 59 - THE SOUTH CAROLINA CONSERVATION BANK ACT	75
CHAPTER 60 - SOUTH CAROLINA MANUFACTURER	

RESPONSIBILITY AND CONSUMER CONVENIENCE INFORMATION TECHNOLOGY EQUIPMENT COLLECTION AND RECOVERY ACT	75
TITLE 49 – WATERS, WATER RESOURCES AND DRAINAGE	
CHAPTER 1 - GENERAL PROVISIONS	75
CHAPTER 3 - WATER RESOURCES PLANNING AND COORDINATION ACT	76
CHAPTER 4 - SOUTH CAROLINA SURFACE WATER WITHDRAWAL, PERMITTING USE, AND REPORTING ACT	76
CHAPTER 5 - GROUNDWATER USE AND REPORTING ACT	76
CHAPTER 6 - AQUATIC PLANT MANAGEMENT	76
CHAPTER 7 - BUSHY PARK AUTHORITY	76
CHAPTER 9 - FLOODING OF CEMETERIES OR BURIAL GROUNDS BY POWER OR WATER COMPANIES	76
CHAPTER 11 - DAMS	76
CHAPTER 17 - DRAINAGE OR LEVEE DISTRICTS UNDER 1911 ACT	76
CHAPTER 19 - DRAINAGE DISTRICTS UNDER 1920 ACT	76
CHAPTER 21 - INTERBASIN TRANSFER OF WATER [REPEALED]	76
CHAPTER 23 - SOUTH CAROLINA DROUGHT RESPONSE ACT	76
CHAPTER 25 - OFFICE OF STATE CLIMATOLOGY	76
CHAPTER 27 - LAKE WYLIE MARINE COMMISSION	76
CHAPTER 28 - LAKE WATEREE MARINE ADVISORY COMMISSION	76
CHAPTER 29 - SOUTH CAROLINA SCENIC RIVERS ACT	76
CHAPTER 30 - PUBLIC WATERS NUISANCE ABATEMENT ACT	76
CHAPTER 33 - LAKE PAUL A. WALLACE AUTHORITY	76
TITLE 50 – FISH, GAME AND WATERCRAFT	
CHAPTER 1 - GENERAL PROVISIONS	76
CHAPTER 2 - FOREST MANAGEMENT PROTECTION ACT	77
CHAPTER 3 - DEPARTMENT OF NATURAL RESOURCES	77
CHAPTER 5 - MARINE RESOURCES ACT	77
CHAPTER 9 - HUNTING AND FISHING LICENSES	77
CHAPTER 11 - PROTECTION OF GAME	78
CHAPTER 12 - INTERSTATE WILDLIFE VIOLATOR COMPACT	78
CHAPTER 13 - PROTECTION OF FISH	78
CHAPTER 15 - NONGAME AND ENDANGERED SPECIES	78

CHAPTER 16 - IMPORTATION OF WILDLIFE	78
CHAPTER 18 - AQUACULTURE	78
CHAPTER 19 - SPECIAL HUNTING AND FISHING PROVISIONS FOR CERTAIN COUNTIES AND AREAS	79
CHAPTER 20 - INTERSTATE BOATING VIOLATION COMPACT	79
CHAPTER 21 - EQUIPMENT AND OPERATION OF WATERCRAFT	79
CHAPTER 23 - WATERCRAFT AND OUTBOARD MOTORS	79
CHAPTER 25 - BOATING AND SURFING AT PARTICULAR LOCALITIES	79
CHAPTER 26 - ALL-TERRAIN VEHICLE SAFETY ACT	79
TITLE 51 – PARKS, RECREATION AND TOURISM	
CHAPTER 1 - DEPARTMENT OF PARKS, RECREATION AND TOURISM	79
CHAPTER 3 - STATE PARKS	79
CHAPTER 5 - SCENIC RIVERS [REPEALED]	79
CHAPTER 7 - HUNTING ISLAND, BEAUFORT COUNTY	79
CHAPTER 9 - FORT WATSON MEMORIAL	79
CHAPTER 11 - RECREATION LAND TRUST FUND	79
CHAPTER 13 - REGIONAL DISTRICTS, COMMISSIONS AND AUTHORITIES	79
CHAPTER 15 - MUNICIPAL PARKS, RECREATIONAL FACILITIES AND THE LIKE	79
CHAPTER 17 - HERITAGE TRUST PROGRAM	79
CHAPTER 18 - WAR BETWEEN THE STATES HERITAGE TRUST PROGRAM	80
CHAPTER 19 - OLD EXCHANGE BUILDING COMMISSION	80
CHAPTER 21 - COMMITTEE ON TOURISM [REPEALED]	80
CHAPTER 22 - LEGACY TRUST FUND	80
CHAPTER 23 - GRANTS FOR PARKS AND RECREATION	80
TITLE 52 – AMUSEMENTS AND ATHLETIC CONTESTS	
CHAPTER 1 - CIRCUSES, CARNIVALS AND OTHER TRAVELING SHOWS	80
CHAPTER 3 - MOTION PICTURES, SPORTING EVENTS AND CONCERTS	80
CHAPTER 5 - HORSE RACING	80
CHAPTER 7 - STATE AND COUNTY ATHLETIC COMMISSIONS [REPEALED]	80
CHAPTER 9 - ENDURANCE CONTESTS [REPEALED]	80
CHAPTER 11 - POOL AND BILLIARDS [REPEALED]	80
CHAPTER 13 - DANCE HALLS	80

CHAPTER 15 - COIN-OPERATED MACHINES AND DEVICES AND OTHER AMUSEMENTS [REPEALED]	80
CHAPTER 17 - BINGO GAMES [REPEALED]	80
CHAPTER 19 - BUNGEE JUMPING	80
CHAPTER 21 - ICE OR ROLLER SKATING LIABILITY IMMUNITY	80
TITLE 53 – SUNDAYS, HOLIDAYS AND OTHER SPECIAL DAYS	
CHAPTER 1 - SUNDAYS	80
CHAPTER 3 - SPECIAL DAYS	81
CHAPTER 5 - LEGAL HOLIDAYS	81
TITLE 54 – PORTS AND MARITIME MATTERS	
CHAPTER 1 - GENERAL PROVISIONS	81
CHAPTER 3 - SOUTH CAROLINA STATE PORTS AUTHORITY	81
CHAPTER 5 - PORT AND TERMINAL UTILITIES AND COMMISSIONS IN CITIES	81
CHAPTER 6 - SAVANNAH RIVER MARITIME COMMISSION	81
CHAPTER 7 - SHIPWRECKS AND SALVAGE OPERATIONS	81
CHAPTER 9 - OFFENSES RELATING TO SEAMEN	81
CHAPTER 11 - INTERFERENCE WITH NAVIGATION	81
CHAPTER 13 - TRESPASS ON PRIVATE DOCKS	81
CHAPTER 15 - PILOTS AND PILOTAGE	81
CHAPTER 17 - SOUTH CAROLINA MARITIME SECURITY ACT	81
TITLE 55 - AERONAUTICS	
CHAPTER 1 - GENERAL PROVISIONS	81
CHAPTER 3 - STATE LAW FOR AERONAUTICS	81
CHAPTER 5 - STATE AERONAUTICAL REGULATORY ACT	81
CHAPTER 7 - REGISTRATION OF AIRCRAFT [REPEALED]	81
CHAPTER 8 - UNIFORM AIRCRAFT FINANCIAL RESPONSIBILITY ACT [REPEALED]}	81
CHAPTER 9 - SOUTH CAROLINA AIRPORTS ACT	82
CHAPTER 11 - PARTICULAR AIRPORTS	82
CHAPTER 13 - PROTECTION OF AIRPORTS AND AIRPORT PROPERTY	82
CHAPTER 15 - RELOCATION ASSISTANCE	82
CHAPTER 17 - REGIONAL AIRPORT DISTRICTS	82
TITLE 56 – MOTOR VEHICLES	
CHAPTER 1 - DRIVER'S LICENSE	82
CHAPTER 2 - SPECIALIZED VEHICLES	83
CHAPTER 3 - MOTOR VEHICLE REGISTRATION AND LICENSING	83

CHAPTER 5 - UNIFORM ACT REGULATING TRAFFIC ON HIGHWAYS	84
CHAPTER 7 - TRAFFIC TICKETS	85
CHAPTER 9 - MOTOR VEHICLE FINANCIAL RESPONSIBILITY ACT	85
CHAPTER 10 - MOTOR VEHICLE REGISTRATION AND FINANCIAL SECURITY	85
CHAPTER 11 - ROAD TAX ON MOTOR CARRIERS	85
CHAPTER 15 - REGULATION OF MANUFACTURERS, DISTRIBUTORS AND DEALERS	85
CHAPTER 16 - REGULATION OF MOTORCYCLE MANUFACTURERS, DISTRIBUTORS, DEALERS, AND WHOLESALERS	85
CHAPTER 17 - CRIMINAL PENALTIES	85
CHAPTER 19 - PROTECTION OF TITLES TO AND INTERESTS IN MOTOR VEHICLES	85
CHAPTER 21 - REGULATION OF TRAFFIC AT STATE INSTITUTIONS	85
CHAPTER 23 - DRIVER TRAINING SCHOOLS	85
CHAPTER 25 - NONRESIDENT TRAFFIC VIOLATOR COMPACTS	85
CHAPTER 27 - PROFESSIONAL HOUSEMOVING	85
CHAPTER 28 - ENFORCEMENT OF MOTOR VEHICLE EXPRESS WARRANTIES	85
CHAPTER 29 - MOTOR VEHICLE CHOP SHOP, STOLEN, AND ALTERED PROPERTY ACT	85
CHAPTER 31 - RENTAL OF PRIVATE PASSENGER AUTOMOBILES	86
CHAPTER 32 - MOTOR VEHICLE DAMAGE DISCLOSURE ACT	86
CHAPTER 35 - IDLING RESTRICTIONS FOR COMMERCIAL DIESEL VEHICLES	86
TITLE 57 – HIGHWAYS, BRIDGES AND FERRIES	
CHAPTER 1 - GENERAL PROVISIONS	86
CHAPTER 3 - DEPARTMENT OF TRANSPORTATION	86
CHAPTER 5 - STATE HIGHWAY SYSTEM	86
CHAPTER 7 - OBSTRUCTION OR DAMAGE TO ROADS OR DRAINAGE	86
CHAPTER 9 - ABANDONMENT OR CLOSING OF STREETS, ROADS OR HIGHWAYS	86
CHAPTER 11 - FINANCIAL MATTERS	86

CHAPTER 13 - PROVISIONS AFFECTING BRIDGES ONLY	86
CHAPTER 15 - PROVISIONS AFFECTING FERRIES ONLY	86
CHAPTER 17 - COUNTY ROADS, BRIDGES AND FERRIES GENERALLY	86
CHAPTER 19 - COUNTY ROAD TAXES AND ASSESSMENTS	86
CHAPTER 21 - PAVING DISTRICTS IN COUNTIES WITH CITY OF OVER 70,000	86
CHAPTER 23 - HIGHWAY BEAUTIFICATION AND SCENIC ROUTES	86
CHAPTER 25 - OUTDOOR ADVERTISING	86
CHAPTER 27 - JUNKYARD CONTROL	86

TITLE 58 – PUBLIC UTILITIES, SERVICES AND CARRIERS

CHAPTER 1 - GENERAL PROVISIONS	87
CHAPTER 2 - UTILITY SERVICE WHERE STATE BOUNDARIES CLARIFIED	87
CHAPTER 3 - PUBLIC SERVICE COMMISSION	87
CHAPTER 4 - OFFICE OF REGULATORY STAFF	87
CHAPTER 5 - GAS, HEAT, WATER, SEWERAGE COLLECTION AND DISPOSAL, AND STREET RAILWAY COMPANIES	87
CHAPTER 7 - SPECIAL PROVISIONS AFFECTING GAS, WATER OR PIPELINE COMPANIES	87
CHAPTER 9 - TELEPHONE, TELEGRAPH AND EXPRESS COMPANIES	87
CHAPTER 11 - RADIO COMMON CARRIERS	87
CHAPTER 12 - CABLE TELEVISION	87
CHAPTER 13 - CARRIERS GENERALLY	88
CHAPTER 15 - RAILROAD, STREET RAILWAY, STEAMBOAT AND CANAL COMPANIES	88
CHAPTER 17 - THE GENERAL RAILROAD LAW	88
CHAPTER 21 - ELECTRIC, INTERURBAN AND STREET RAILWAYS	88
CHAPTER 23 - MOTOR VEHICLE CARRIERS	88
CHAPTER 25 - REGIONAL TRANSPORTATION AUTHORITY LAW	88
CHAPTER 27 - ELECTRIC UTILITIES AND ELECTRIC COOPERATIVES	88
CHAPTER 31 - PUBLIC SERVICE AUTHORITY	89
CHAPTER 33 - UTILITY FACILITY SITING AND ENVIRONMENTAL PROTECTION	89
CHAPTER 36 - UNDERGROUND FACILITY DAMAGE PREVENTION ACT	89

CHAPTER 37 - ENERGY SUPPLY AND EFFICIENCY	89
CHAPTER 39 - SOUTH CAROLINA DISTRIBUTED ENERGY RESOURCE PROGRAM	89
CHAPTER 40 - NET ENERGY METERING	89
TITLE 59 - EDUCATION	
CHAPTER 1 - GENERAL PROVISIONS	89
CHAPTER 2 - SOUTH CAROLINA COLLEGE INVESTMENT PROGRAM	89
CHAPTER 3 - STATE SUPERINTENDENT OF EDUCATION	89
CHAPTER 4 - SOUTH CAROLINA TUITION PREPAYMENT PROGRAM	89
CHAPTER 5 - STATE BOARD OF EDUCATION	89
CHAPTER 6 - MONITORING IMPLEMENTATION OF EDUCATION IMPROVEMENT PROGRAM	89
CHAPTER 7 - EDUCATIONAL TELEVISION COMMISSION	89
CHAPTER 10 - PHYSICAL EDUCATION, SCHOOL HEALTH SERVICES, AND NUTRITIONAL STANDARDS	89
CHAPTER 11 - COMPACT FOR EDUCATION	89
CHAPTER 13 - COUNTY SUPERINTENDENTS OF EDUCATION	89
CHAPTER 15 - COUNTY BOARDS OF EDUCATION	90
CHAPTER 16 - SOUTH CAROLINA VIRTUAL SCHOOL PROGRAM	90
CHAPTER 17 - SCHOOL DISTRICTS	90
CHAPTER 18 - EDUCATION ACCOUNTABILITY ACT	90
CHAPTER 19 - SCHOOL TRUSTEES	90
CHAPTER 20 - EDUCATION FINANCE ACT OF 1977	90
CHAPTER 21 - STATE AID FOR SCHOOLS	90
CHAPTER 23 - SCHOOL BUILDINGS AND OTHER SCHOOL PROPERTY	90
CHAPTER 24 - SCHOOL ADMINISTRATORS	90
CHAPTER 25 - TEACHERS	90
CHAPTER 26 - TRAINING, CERTIFICATION AND EVALUATION OF PUBLIC EDUCATORS	90
CHAPTER 27 - INTERSTATE AGREEMENT ON QUALIFICATION	90
CHAPTER 28 - PARENTAL INVOLVEMENT IN THEIR CHILDREN'S EDUCATION	90
CHAPTER 29 - SUBJECTS OF INSTRUCTION	90
CHAPTER 30 - BASIC SKILLS ASSESSMENT PROGRAM [REPEALED]	91

CHAPTER 31 - TEXTBOOKS	91
CHAPTER 32 - COMPREHENSIVE HEALTH EDUCATION PROGRAM	91
CHAPTER 33 - SPECIAL EDUCATION FOR HANDICAPPED CHILDREN	91
CHAPTER 34 - BLIND PERSONS' LITERACY RIGHTS AND EDUCATION	91
CHAPTER 35 - KINDERGARTENS	91
CHAPTER 36 - PRESCHOOL PROGRAMS FOR CHILDREN WITH DISABILITIES	91
CHAPTER 37 - SCHOOLS FOR ELEEMOSYNARY INSTITUTIONS	91
CHAPTER 38 - SOUTH CAROLINA EDUCATION BILL OF RIGHTS FOR CHILDREN IN FOSTER CARE	91
CHAPTER 39 - HIGH SCHOOLS	91
CHAPTER 40 - CHARTER SCHOOLS	91
CHAPTER 41 - GRANTS TO STUDENTS ATTENDING PRIVATE SCHOOLS	91
CHAPTER 43 - ADULT EDUCATION GENERALLY	91
CHAPTER 44 - COMMUNITY EDUCATION	91
CHAPTER 45 - HOME-STUDY SCHOOLS	91
CHAPTER 46 - INTERSTATE COMPACT ON EDUCATIONAL OPPORTUNITY FOR MILITARY CHILDREN	91
CHAPTER 47 - SCHOOL FOR THE DEAF AND THE BLIND	91
CHAPTER 48 - SPECIAL SCHOOL OF SCIENCE AND MATHEMATICS	91
CHAPTER 49 - JOHN DE LA HOWE SCHOOL	91
CHAPTER 50 - SOUTH CAROLINA GOVERNOR'S SCHOOL FOR THE ARTS AND HUMANITIES	91
CHAPTER 51 - THE WIL LOU GRAY OPPORTUNITY SCHOOL	91
CHAPTER 52 - SOUTH CAROLINA SCHOOL-TO-WORK TRANSITION ACT OF 1994 [REPEALED]	92
CHAPTER 53 - TECHNICAL AND VOCATIONAL EDUCATION AND TRAINING	92
CHAPTER 54 - SOUTH CAROLINA EMPLOYMENT REVITALIZATION ACT	92
CHAPTER 55 - JUNIOR COLLEGE COURSES	92
CHAPTER 56 - BEAUFORT-JASPER HIGHER EDUCATION COMMISSION	92
CHAPTER 57 - WESTERN CAROLINA HIGHER EDUCATION COMMISSION	92

CHAPTER 58 - NONPUBLIC POST-SECONDARY INSTITUTION LICENSING	92
CHAPTER 59 - SOUTH CAROLINA EDUCATION AND ECONOMIC DEVELOPMENT ACT	92
CHAPTER 63 - PUPILS GENERALLY	92
CHAPTER 65 - ATTENDANCE OF PUPILS	92
CHAPTER 66 - SCHOOL SAFETY COORDINATORS	92
CHAPTER 67 - TRANSPORTATION OF PUPILS; SCHOOL BUSES	92
CHAPTER 69 - SCHOOL FUNDS GENERALLY	93
CHAPTER 71 - SCHOOL BONDS	93
CHAPTER 73 - SCHOOL TAXES	93
CHAPTER 101 - COLLEGES AND INSTITUTIONS OF HIGHER LEARNING GENERALLY	93
CHAPTER 102 - ATHLETE AGENTS AND STUDENT ATHLETES	93
CHAPTER 103 - STATE COMMISSION ON HIGHER EDUCATION	93
CHAPTER 104 - INITIATIVES FOR RESEARCH AND ACADEMIC EXCELLENCE	93
CHAPTER 105 - SOUTH CAROLINA CAMPUS SEXUAL ASSAULT INFORMATION ACT	93
CHAPTER 106 - SOUTH CAROLINA CAMPUS SEX CRIMES PREVENTION ACT	93
CHAPTER 107 - STATE INSTITUTION BONDS	93
CHAPTER 108 - MID-CAROLINA COMMISSION FOR HIGHER EDUCATION	93
CHAPTER 109 - EDUCATIONAL FACILITIES AUTHORITY ACT FOR PRIVATE NONPROFIT INSTITUTIONS OF HIGHER LEARNING	93
CHAPTER 110 - SOUTH CAROLINA CRITICAL NEEDS NURSING INITIATIVE ACT	93
CHAPTER 111 - SCHOLARSHIPS	93
CHAPTER 112 - DETERMINATION OF RATES OF TUITION AND FEES	93
CHAPTER 113 - TUITION GRANTS	93
CHAPTER 114 - SOUTH CAROLINA NATIONAL GUARD COLLEGE ASSISTANCE PROGRAM ACT	93
CHAPTER 115 - STATE EDUCATION ASSISTANCE ACT	93
CHAPTER 116 - CAMPUS SECURITY DEPARTMENT	93
CHAPTER 117 - UNIVERSITY OF SOUTH CAROLINA	94

CHAPTER 118 - SOUTH CAROLINA ACADEMIC ENDOWMENT INCENTIVE ACT OF 1997	94
CHAPTER 119 - CLEMSON UNIVERSITY	94
CHAPTER 121 - THE CITADEL, THE MILITARY UNIVERSITY OF SOUTH CAROLINA	94
CHAPTER 122 - THE CITADEL HOUSING REVENUE BONDS	94
CHAPTER 123 - THE MEDICAL UNIVERSITY OF SOUTH CAROLINA	94
CHAPTER 125 - WINTHROP UNIVERSITY	94
CHAPTER 127 - SOUTH CAROLINA STATE UNIVERSITY	94
CHAPTER 129 - PALMER COLLEGE	94
CHAPTER 130 - THE COLLEGE OF CHARLESTON	94
CHAPTER 131 - PARKING FACILITIES AT THE COLLEGE OF CHARLESTON	94
CHAPTER 133 - FRANCIS MARION UNIVERSITY	94
CHAPTER 135 - LANDER COLLEGE	94
CHAPTER 136 - COASTAL CAROLINA UNIVERSITY	94
CHAPTER 139 - EARLY CHILD DEVELOPMENT AND ACADEMIC ASSISTANCE	94
CHAPTER 141 - NATIONAL EDUCATION GOALS	94
CHAPTER 142 - STUDENTS FIRST FINANCIAL RESOURCES FOR SCHOLARSHIPS AND TUITION	94
CHAPTER 143 - CHILDREN'S EDUCATION ENDOWMENT	94
CHAPTER 144 - PUBLIC SCHOOL FACILITIES ASSISTANCE	94
CHAPTER 145 - SINGLE-GENDER COLLEGE	94
CHAPTER 146 - STATE SCHOOL FACILITIES BONDS ACT	94
CHAPTER 147 - HIGHER EDUCATION REVENUE BOND ACT	94
CHAPTER 149 - LEGISLATIVE INCENTIVES FOR FUTURE EXCELLENCE (LIFE) SCHOLARSHIPS	95
CHAPTER 150 - SOUTH CAROLINA EDUCATION LOTTERY ACT	95
CHAPTER 151 - SOUTH CAROLINA LIGHTRAIL CONSORTIUM	95
CHAPTER 152 - SOUTH CAROLINA FIRST STEPS TO SCHOOL READINESS	95
CHAPTER 153 - ENDOWMENT FUNDS	95
CHAPTER 154 - JESSICA HORTON ACT	95
CHAPTER 155 - SOUTH CAROLINA READ TO SUCCEED ACT	95
CHAPTER 156 - CHILD EARLY READING DEVELOPMENT AND EDUCATION PROGRAM	95

TITLE 60 – LIBRARIES, ARCHIVES, MUSEUMS AND ARTS

CHAPTER 1 - SOUTH CAROLINA STATE LIBRARY	95
CHAPTER 2 - STATE DOCUMENTS DEPOSITORY	95
CHAPTER 3 - LIBRARY OF SUPREME COURT	95
CHAPTER 4 - CONFIDENTIAL LIBRARY RECORDS	95
CHAPTER 9 - STATE AND COUNTY AID FOR SCHOOL LIBRARIES	95
CHAPTER 11 - ARCHIVES ACT AND CIVIL WAR SESQUICENTENNIAL ADVISORY BOARD	95
CHAPTER 12 - PROTECTION OF STATE-OWNED OR LEASED HISTORIC PROPERTIES	95
CHAPTER 13 - SOUTH CAROLINA MUSEUM COMMISSION AND INSTITUTE OF ARCHEOLOGY AND ANTHROPOLOGY	95
CHAPTER 15 - SOUTH CAROLINA ARTS COMMISSION	96
CHAPTER 17 - SOUTH CAROLINA CONFEDRATE RELIC ROOM AND MILITARY MUSEUM COMMISSION	96

TITLE 61 – ALCOHOL AND ALCOHOLIC BEVERAGES

CHAPTER 1 - GENERAL PROVISIONS [REPEALED]	96
CHAPTER 2 - GENERAL PROVISIONS	96
CHAPTER 3 - ALCOHOLIC BEVERAGE CONTROL ACT [REPEALED]	96
CHAPTER 4 - BEER, ALE, PORTER, AND WINE	96
CHAPTER 5 - REGULATION OF TRANSPORTATION, POSSESSION, CONSUMPTION AND SALE OF ALCOHOLIC BEVERAGES [REPEALED]	96
CHAPTER 6 - ALCOHOLIC BEVERAGE CONTROL ACT	96
CHAPTER 7 - IMPORTATION OF ALCOHOLIC BEVERAGES [REPEALED]	96
CHAPTER 8 - NUISANCES	96
CHAPTER 9 - BEER, ALE, PORTER AND WINE [REPEALED]	96
CHAPTER 10 - ALCOHOL	96
CHAPTER 11 - ALCOHOL [REPEALED]	96
CHAPTER 12 - DISBURSEMENT OF REVENUE FOR PROGRAMS FOR ALCOHOLICS, DRUG ABUSERS, AND DRUG ADDICTS	96
CHAPTER 13 - NUISANCES, OFFENSES AND ENFORCEMENT [REPEALED]	96

TITLE 62 – SOUTH CAROLINA PROBATE CODE

ARTICLE 1. GENERAL PROVISIONS, DEFINITIONS, AND PROBATE JURISDICTION OF COURT	97
ARTICLE 2. INTESTATE SUCCESSION AND WILLS	97

ARTICLE 3. PROBATE OF WILLS AND ADMINISTRATION	97
ARTICLE 4. LOCAL AND FOREIGN PERSONAL REPRESENTATIVES; ANCILLARY ADMINISTRATION	97
ARTICLE 5. PROTECTION OF PERSONS UNDER DISABILITY AND THEIR PROPERTY	98
ARTICLE 6. NONPROBATE TRANSFERS	98
ARTICLE 7. SOUTH CAROLINA TRUST CODE	99
ARTICLE 8. SOUTH CAROLINA UNIFORM POWER OF ATTORNEY ACT	99
TITLE 63 – SOUTH CAROLINA CHILDREN'S CODE	
CHAPTER 1 - STATE POLICY AND GENERAL PROVISIONS	99
CHAPTER 3 - FAMILY COURT	99
CHAPTER 5 - LEGAL STATUS OF CHILDREN	99
CHAPTER 7 - CHILD PROTECTION AND PERMANENCY	100
CHAPTER 9 - ADOPTIONS	100
CHAPTER 11 - CHILDREN'S SERVICES AGENCIES	100
CHAPTER 13 - CHILDCARE FACILITIES	101
CHAPTER 15 - CHILD CUSTODY AND VISITATION	101
CHAPTER 17 - PATERNITY AND CHILD SUPPORT	101
CHAPTER 19 - JUVENILE JUSTICE CODE	102
CHAPTER 21 - PERSONS WITH DISABILITIES RIGHT TO PARENT ACT	102

Title 1 - Administration of the Government

CHAPTER 1

General Provisions

ARTICLE 1

Jurisdiction and Boundaries of State

SECTION 1-1-10. Jurisdiction and boundaries of the State.

The sovereignty and jurisdiction of this State extends to all places within its bounds, which are declared to be as follows:

The northern line beginning at a point at the low-water mark of the Atlantic Ocean on the eastern shore of Bird Island, runs in a northwest direction through monuments established at latitude 33° 51' 07.8792" N. , longitude 78° 32' 32.6210" W., at latitude 33° 51' 36.4626" N., longitude 78° 33' 06.1937" W., and at latitude 33° 51' 50.7214" N., longitude 78° 33' 22.9448" W., (coordinates based on North American Datum 1927), following existing monuments to a stake in a meadow; thence, in a direction due west, a distance of sixty-two miles, to a point where it intersects the Charleston Road (at sixty-one miles) near the Waxhaw Creek; thence N. 2° 12 1/2' E. eight miles to a gum tree on the southeastern corner of the Catawba Indian Reservation as laid out in 1764; thence following the eastern and northern boundary lines of said Catawba Indian Reservation to where such northern boundary line crosses the thread of the Catawba River; thence up the thread of said river to the confluence of the north and south forks thereof; thence west to a point at latitude 35° 11' 46.41502" N. and longitude 082° 12' 57.37020" W. , North American Datum 1983-86 (NAD 83-86) marked by a brass screw in a stone inscribed "S.C. 1815" on one side and "N.C., Sept 15" on the other; thence westward as recorded by a set of 34 plats signed by Gary W. Thompson and Sidney C. Miller, co-chairmen of the North Carolina-South Carolina Joint Boundary Commission, dated 12/20/2005 (sets available at the South Carolina Department of Archives and History, the South Carolina Geodetic Survey, the Greenville County Register of Deeds and the Pickens County Register of Deeds) to a point at latitude 35° 12' 00.31689" N. and longitude 082° 17' 27.89089" W., North American Datum 1983-86 (NAD 83-86), marked by a brass disk stamped with "POINT 1, 2004, NORTH CAROLINA, SOUTH CAROLINA, STATE BOUNDARY LINE" and set in a concrete monument; thence southwestward (according to the previously referenced plats) to a point at latitude 35° 11' 43.48762" N. and longitude 082° 17' 38.97840" W., North American Datum 1983-86 (NAD 83-86), marked by an aluminum disk on an iron pin, stamped with "2, 2001, NC, SC, STATE LINE" on the ridge line dividing the waters of the north fork of the Pacolet River from the north fork of the Saluda River; thence westward along the various courses of said ridge (according to the previously referenced plats) to a point at latitude 35° 05' 07.96924" N. and longitude 082° 47' 01.49862" W., North American Datum 1983-86 (NAD 83-86), where the Cherokee boundary of 1897 intersected the ridge, now marked by a brass disk stamped with "BLACKBURN, 1996, NORTH CAROLINA, SOUTH CAROLINA, STATE BOUNDARY LINE" and set in a concrete monument; thence from said point (as recorded on a plat, North Carolina/South Carolina State Boundary from Indian Camp Mountain to the Chattooga River, dated May 2005, copies available at the South Carolina Department of Archives and History and the South Carolina Geodetic Survey) following a geodetic line to latitude 35° 00' 04.88130" N. and longitude 083° 06' 30.84455" W., NAD 83-86, marked by the "+" in the inscription "LAT 35, AD 1813, NC + SC" chiseled on Commissioners' Rock on the east bank of the Chattooga River; thence following a geodetic line with a geodetic azimuth of 270 degrees to the centerline of the Chattooga River.

The lateral seaward boundary between North Carolina and South Carolina from the low-water mark of the Atlantic Ocean shall be and is hereby designated as a continuation of the North Carolina-South Carolina boundary line as described by monuments located at latitude 33° 51' 50.7214" N., longitude 78° 33' 22.9448" W., at latitude 33° 51' 36.4626" N., longitude 78° 33' 06.1937" W., and at latitude 33° 51' 07.8792" N., longitude 78° 32' 32.6210" W., (coordinates based on North American Datum 1927), in a straight line projection of said line to the seaward limits of the states' territorial jurisdiction, such line to be extended on the same bearing insofar as a need for further delimitation may arise.

From the state of Georgia, this State is divided by the Savannah River, at the point where the northern edge of the navigable channel of the Savannah River intersects the seaward limit of the state's territorial jurisdiction; thence generally along the northern edge of the navigable channel up the Savannah River; thence along the northern edge of the sediment basin to the Tidegate; thence to the confluence of the Tugaloo and Seneca Rivers; thence up the Tugaloo River to the confluence of the Tallulah and the Chattooga Rivers; thence up the Chattooga River to the 35th parallel of north latitude, which is the boundary of North Carolina, the line being midway between the banks of said respective rivers when the water is at ordinary stage, except in the lower reaches of the Savannah River, as hereinafter described. And when the rivers are broken by islands of natural formation which, under the Treaty of Beaufort, are reserved to the state of Georgia, the line is midway between the island banks and the South Carolina banks when the water is at ordinary stage, except in the lower reaches of the Savannah River, as hereinafter described.

The boundary between Georgia and South Carolina along the lower reaches of the Savannah River, and the lateral seaward boundary, is more particularly described as follows and depicted in "Georgia - South Carolina Boundary Project, Lower Savannah River Segment, Portfolio of Maps" prepared by the United States Department of Commerce, National Oceanic and Atmospheric Administration, National Ocean Service, National Geodetic Survey, Remote Sensing Division - 2001 (copies available at the South Carolina Department of Archives and History and the South Carolina Geodetic Survey):

Beginning at a point where the thread of the northernmost branch of the Savannah River equidistant between its banks intersects latitude 32° 07' 00" N., (North American Datum 1983-86), located in the Savannah River, and proceeding in a southeasterly direction down the thread of the Savannah River equidistant between the banks of the Savannah River on Hutchinson Island and on the mainland of South Carolina including the small downstream island southeast of the aforesaid point, at ordinary stage, until reaching the vicinity of Pennyworth Island;

Proceeding thence easterly down the thread of the northernmost channel of the Savannah River known as the Back River as it flows north of Pennyworth Island, making the transition to the said northernmost channel using the equidistant method between Pennyworth Island, the Georgia bank on Hutchinson Island, and the South Carolina mainland bank, thence to the thread of the said northernmost channel equidistant from the South Carolina mainland bank and Pennyworth Island at ordinary stage, around Pennyworth Island;

Proceeding thence southeasterly to the thread of the northern channel of the Savannah River equidistant from the Georgia bank on Hutchinson Island and the South Carolina mainland bank, making the transition utilizing the equidistant method between Pennyworth Island, the Georgia bank on Hutchinson Island, and the South Carolina mainland bank;

Proceeding thence southeasterly down the thread of the Savannah River equidistant from the Hutchinson Island and South Carolina mainland banks of the river at ordinary stage, through the tide gates, until reaching the northwestern (farthest upstream) boundary of the "Back River Sediment Basin", as defined in the "Annual Survey-1992, Savannah Harbor, Georgia, U. S. Coastal Highway, No. 17 to the Sea", U. S. Army Corps of Engineers, Savannah District as amended by the Examination Survey-1992 charts for the Savannah Harbor Deepening Project, Drawings No. DSH 1 12/107, (hereinafter the "Channel Chart");

Proceeding thence along the said northwestern boundary to its intersection with the northern boundary of the Back River Sediment Basin; thence southeasterly until said northern boundary intersects the northern boundary of the main navigational channel as depicted on the Channel Chart at the point designated as SR-34 (latitude 32° 05' 01.440" N., longitude 081° 02' 17.252" W., North American Datum (NAD 1983-86);

Proceeding thence toward the mouth of the Savannah River along the northern boundary of the main navigational channel at the new channel limit as depicted on the Channel Chart, via Oglethorpe Range through point SR-33 (latitude 32° 05' 17.168" N., longitude 081° 01' 34.665" W., NAD 1983-86), Fort Jackson Range through point SR-32 (latitude 32° 05' 30.133" N., longitude 081° 01' 17.750" W., NAD 1983-86), the Bight Channel through points SR-31 (latitude 32° 05' 55.631" N., longitude 081° 01' 02.480" W., NAD 1983-86), SR-30 (latitude 32° 06' 06.272" N., longitude 081° 00' 44.802" W., NAD 1983-86), SR-29 (latitude 32° 06' 09.053" N., longitude 081° 00' 31.887" W., NAD 1983-86), SR-28 (latitude 32° 06' 08.521" N., longitude 081° 00' 15.498" W., NAD 1983-86), and SR-27 (latitude 32° 06' 01.565" N., longitude 080° 59' 58.406" W., NAD 1983-86), Upper Flats Range through points SR-26 (latitude 32° 05' 41.698" N., longitude 080° 59' 31.968" W., NAD 1983-86) and SR-25 (latitude 32° 05' 02.819" N., longitude 080° 59' 12.644" W., NAD 1983-86), Lower Flats Range through points SR-24 (latitude 32° 04' 46.375" N., longitude 080° 59' 00.631" W., NAD 1983-86), SR-23 (latitude 32° 04' 40.209" N., longitude 080° 58' 49.947" W., NAD 1983-86), SR-22 (latitude 32° 04' 28.679" N., longitude 080° 58' 18.895" W., NAD 1983-86), and SR-21 (latitude 32° 04' 22.274" N., longitude 080° 57' 34.449" W. , NAD 1983-86), Long Island Crossing Range through points SR-20 (latitude 32° 04' 13.042" N., longitude 080° 57' 14.511" W., NAD 1983-86), and SR-19 (latitude 32° 02' 30.984" N., longitude 080° 55' 30.308' W., NAD 1983-86) and New Channel Range following the northern boundary of the Rehandling Basin and the northern boundary of the Oyster Bed Island Turning Basin back to the northern edge of the main navigational channel, thence through points SR-17 (latitude 32° 02' 07.661" N., longitude 080° 53' 39.379" W., NAD 1983-86) and SR-16 (latitude 32° 02' 07.533" N., longitude 080° 53' 31.663" W., NAD 1983-86), to a point at latitude 32° 02' 08"

N., longitude 080° 53' 25" W., NAD 1983-86 (now marked by Navigational Buoy "24") near the eastern end of Oyster Bed Island;

Proceeding thence from a point at latitude 32° 02' 08" N., longitude 080° 53' 25" W., NAD 1983-86 (now marked by Navigational Buoy R "24") on a true azimuth of 0° 0' 0" (true north) to the mean low low-water line of Oyster Bed Island; thence easterly along the said mean low low-water line of Oyster Bed Island to the point at which the said mean low low-water line of Oyster Bed Island intersects the Oyster Bed Island Training Wall;

Proceeding thence easterly along the mean low low-water line of the southern edge of the Oyster Bed Island Training Wall to its eastern end; thence continuing the same straight line to its intersection with the Jones Island Range line;

Proceeding thence southeasterly along the Jones Island Range line until reaching the northern boundary of the main navigational channel as depicted on the Channel Chart;

Proceeding thence southeasterly along the northern boundary of the main navigational channel as depicted on the Channel Chart, via Jones Island Range and Bloody Point Range, to a point at latitude 31° 59' 16.700" N. , longitude 080° 46' 02.500" W., NAD 1983-86 (now marked by Navigational Buoy "6"); and finally,

Proceeding from a point at latitude 31° 59' 16.700" N., longitude 080° 46' 02.500" W., NAD 1983-86 (now marked by Navigational Buoy "6") extending southeasterly to the federal-state boundary on a true azimuth of 104 degrees (bearing of S76°E), which describes the line being at right angles to the baseline from the southernmost point of Hilton Head Island and the northernmost point of Tybee Island, drawn by the Baseline Committee in 1970.

Should the need for further delimitation arise, the boundary shall further extend southeasterly on above-described true azimuth of 104 degrees (bearing of S76°E).

Provided, further, that nothing in this section shall in any way be considered to govern or affect in any way the division between the states of the remaining assimilative capacity that is, the capacity to receive wastewater and other discharges without violating water quality standards, of the portion of the Savannah River described in this section.

HISTORY: 1962 Code Section 39-1; 1952 Code Section 39-1; 1942 Code Section 2038; 1932 Code Section 2038; Civ. C. '22 Section 1; Civ. C. '12 Section 1; Civ. C. '02 Section 1; G. S. 1; R. S. 1; 1923 (33) 114; 1970 (56) 2051; 1978 Act No. 413, Section 1; 1978 Act No. 414, Section 1; 1978 Act No. 416, Section 1; 1996 Act No. 375, Section 1; 1998 Act No. 341, Section 1; 2008 Act No. 264, Section 1, eff June 4, 2008.

Effect of Amendment

The 2008 amendment substantially rewrote the second undesignated paragraph; in the fifth undesignated paragraph, added the clause at the end starting with "and depicted in"; and made changes in the fifteenth and sixteenth undesignated paragraphs.

SECTION 1-1-20. Effect of change of State boundary on bordering lands.

Whenever the location of the State line has been or may be re-established and corrected by competent authority, the lines of bordering lands which were established and fixed according to the previous location of the State line shall not be changed by reason of such re-establishment and correction of the State line.

HISTORY: 1962 Code Section 39-2; 1952 Code Section 39-2; 1942 Code Section 2039; 1932 Code Section 2039; Civ. C. '22 Section 2; Civ. C. '12 Section 2; 1906 (25) 63.

ARTICLE 3

Executive Department

SECTION 1-1-110. What officers constitute executive department.

The executive department of this State is hereby declared to consist of the following officers, that is to say: The Governor and Lieutenant Governor, the Secretary of State, the State Treasurer, the Attorney General and the solicitors, the Adjutant General, the Comptroller General, the State Superintendent of Education, the Commissioner of Agriculture and the Director of the Department of Insurance.

HISTORY: 1962 Code Section 1-1; 1952 Code Section 1-1; 1942 Code Section 3082; 1932 Code Section 3082; Civ. C. '22 Section 766; Civ. C. '12 Section 682; Civ. C. '02 Section 613; G. S. 464; R. S. 530; 1865 (13) 350; 1941 (42) 119; 1960 (51) 1646; 1993 Act No. 181, Section 2.

SECTION 1-1-120. Vacancies in executive department.

In case any vacancy shall occur in the office of Secretary of State, State Treasurer, Comptroller General, Attorney General or Adjutant General, such vacancy shall be filled by election by the General Assembly, a majority of the votes cast being necessary to a choice. If such vacancy occur during the recess of the General Assembly, the Governor shall fill the vacancy by appointment until an election by the General Assembly at the session next ensuing such vacancy.

HISTORY: 1962 Code Section 1-2; 1952 Code Section 1-2; 1942 Code Section 3083; 1932 Code Section 3083; Civ. C. '22 Section 767; Civ. C. '12 Section 683; Civ. C. '02 Section 614; G. S. 465; R. S. 531; 1875 (15) 935; 1942 (42) 1446.

ARTICLE 7

Public Employment

SECTION 1-1-540. Written employment applications required.

State, county and municipal officers, departments, boards and commissions, and all school districts in this State, shall require applications in writing for employment by them, upon such application forms as they may severally prescribe, which shall include information as to active or honorary membership in or affiliation with all membership associations and organizations. The provisions of this section shall not apply to any office or position which by law is filled by the vote of the qualified electors in any general or special election.

HISTORY: 1962 Code Section 1-36; 1956 (49) 1747; (50) 234.

SECTION 1-1-550. Honorably discharged veterans shall have preference for public employment.

Honorably discharged members of the United States Armed Forces who are given employment preference by the United States Government, now and hereafter, shall be given preference for appointment and employment in every public department and upon all public works in this State insofar as such preference may be practicable; age, loss of limb or other physical impairment which does not in fact incapacitate shall not be deemed to disqualify them, provided they possess the capacity of skill and knowledge necessary to discharge the duties of the position involved. Provided, that any public department operating on a merit system shall give preferences similar to those given by the United States Government to eligible members discharged from the Armed Forces insofar as such preferences may be practicable.

HISTORY: 1962 Code Section 1-37; 1968 (55) 2541.

ARTICLE 9

State Emblems, Pledge to State Flag, Official Observances

SECTION 1-1-610. Official State gem stone.

The amethyst is the official gem stone of the State.

HISTORY: 1962 Code Section 1-363.2; 1969 (56) 441.

SECTION 1-1-615. American History Month designated.

The month of February in every year is designated American History Month. South Carolinians are encouraged to sponsor and participate in appropriate observances of American History Month.

HISTORY: 1988 Act No. 418, Section 1.

SECTION 1-1-616. African American History Month designated.

The month of February of every year is also designated African American History Month in South Carolina to be observed concurrently with American History Month as provided in Section 1-1-615, but with emphasis on the contributions of African Americans to the growth, development, culture, and institutions of our country. South Carolinians are encouraged to sponsor and participate in appropriate observances of African American History Month.

HISTORY: 2012 Act No. 131, Section 2, eff March 13, 2012.

Editor's Note

2012 Act No. 131, Section 1, provides as follows:

"The General Assembly finds that:

"(1) Black History Month, now to be designated as African American History Month in South Carolina, began as 'Negro History Week', which was created in 1926 by Carter G. Woodson, a noted African American historian, scholar, educator, and publisher. It became a month-long celebration in 1976. The month of February was chosen to coincide with the birthdays of Frederick Douglass and Abraham Lincoln;

"(2) African Americans of all generations have contributed greatly to the growth, development, culture, and institutions of the United States; and

"(3) to declare the month of February of each year as African American History Month in our State to honor the significant contributions to our country of these outstanding individuals."

SECTION 1-1-617. Endometriosis Awareness Month.

The month of March in every year is designated as "Endometriosis Awareness Month". South Carolinians are encouraged to sponsor and participate in relevant educational activities and events in the observance of "Endometriosis Awareness Month".

HISTORY: 2014 Act No. 166 (S.983), Section 1, eff May 16, 2014.

SECTION 1-1-618. Airborne Heritage Day designated.

August sixteenth of each year is designated as South Carolina Airborne Heritage Day.

HISTORY: 2007 Act No. 11, Section 1, eff April 18, 2007.

SECTION 1-1-620. Official State stone.

Blue granite is the official stone of the State.

HISTORY: 1962 Code Section 1-363.3; 1969 (56) 441.

SECTION 1-1-625. Official State reptile.

The loggerhead turtle (Caretta caretta) is the official reptile of the State.

HISTORY: 1988 Act No. 588, Section 1.

SECTION 1-1-630. Official State bird.

The Carolina Wren is the official bird of the State.

HISTORY: 1962 Code Section 28-2; 1952 Code Section 28-2; 1942 Code Section 1777; 1939 (41) 483; 1948 (45) 1758; 1952 (47) 2179.

SECTION 1-1-635. Official State wild game bird.

The South Carolina Wild Turkey (Meleagris Gallopavo) is the official wild game bird of the State.

HISTORY: 1976 Act No. 508, Section 1.

SECTION 1-1-640. Official State fish.

The striped bass or rockfish is the official fish of the State.

HISTORY: 1962 Code Section 28-2.1; 1972 (57) 2508.

SECTION 1-1-645. Official State insect.

(A) The Carolina mantid, Stagmomantis carolina (Johannson) , or praying mantis, is the official insect of the State.

(B) A statement in substantially the following form must be printed in the next edition and all subsequent editions of the South Carolina Legislative Manual in the appropriate section:

The State Insect

The Carolina mantid, Stagmomantis carolina (Johannson), or praying mantis, was designated the state insect by the General Assembly by Act 591 of 1988, for the following reasons: it is a native, beneficial insect that is easily recognizable throughout the State; it symbolizes the importance of the natural science of entomology and its special role in all forms of agriculture in helping to control harmful insects; and it provides a perfect specimen of living science for the school children of this State.

HISTORY: 1988 Act No. 591, Section 1.

SECTION 1-1-647. Official State butterfly.

The tiger swallowtail is designated as the official state butterfly.

HISTORY: 1994 Act No. 319, Section 1.

SECTION 1-1-650. Official State animal.

The white-tailed deer (odocoileus virginianus) is the official animal of the State.

HISTORY: 1962 Code Section 28-2.2; 1972 (57) 2508.

SECTION 1-1-655. Official State dog.

The Boykin Spaniel is the official dog of the State.

HISTORY: 1985 Act No. 31, Section 1.

SECTION 1-1-660. Official State tree.

The palmetto tree is hereby designated and adopted as the official tree of the State.

HISTORY: 1962 Code Section 29-11; 1952 Code Section 29-11; 1942 Code Section 3284-11; 1939 (41) 99.

SECTION 1-1-665. Official State dance.

The shag is the official dance of the State.

HISTORY: 1984 Act No. 329, Section 1.

SECTION 1-1-667. Official State waltz.

"The Richardson Waltz" is designated as the official state waltz.

HISTORY: 2000 Act No. 389, Part I, Section 3.

Editor's Note

2000 Act No. 389, Part I, Section 1, provides as follows:

Sections 1 through 4 of this act are known and may be cited as the "Richardson Waltz Act".

SECTION 1-1-670. Official pledge to State flag.

The pledge to the flag of South Carolina shall be as follows:

"I salute the flag of South Carolina and pledge to the Palmetto State love, loyalty and faith."

HISTORY: 1962 Code Section 1-95; 1966 (54) 2271.

SECTION 1-1-674. State Pecan Festival.

The South Carolina Pecan Festival in Florence County is designated as the official State Pecan Festival.

HISTORY: 2011 Act No. 9, Section 1, eff April 12, 2011.

SECTION 1-1-675. State Botanical Garden.

The Botanical Garden of Clemson University is designated the State Botanical Garden.

HISTORY: 1992 Act No. 288, Section 1.

SECTION 1-1-676. Official State lowcountry handcraft.

The sweet grass basket is the official state lowcountry handcraft.

HISTORY: 2006 Act No. 234, Section 1, eff February 21, 2006.

SECTION 1-1-677. Official State grass.

Indian Grass, Sorghastrum nutans, is designated as the official grass of the State. In making this designation, the General Assembly makes no warranty or endorsement of Indian Grass as a commercial product, but recognizes Indian Grass as a native, nonnoxious plant, with a historical, continuing, widespread, and beneficial existence in South Carolina.

HISTORY: 2001 Act No. 94, Section 2.

SECTION 1-1-680. Official State fruit.

The peach is the official fruit of the State.

HISTORY: 1984 Act No. 360, Section 2.

SECTION 1-1-681. Official state vegetable.

Collard greens are the official vegetable of the State.

HISTORY: 2011 Act No. 38, Section 1, eff June 2, 2011.

SECTION 1-1-682. Official state snack food.

Boiled peanuts are the official state snack food. Nothing in this section requires or encourages any school district in this State to serve peanuts to students, especially students with food allergies.

HISTORY: 2006 Act No. 270, Section 2, eff May 1, 2006.

SECTION 1-1-683. Official state picnic cuisine.

Barbecue is designated as the official State Picnic Cuisine of South Carolina.

HISTORY: 2014 Act No. 231 (S.1136), Section 1, eff June 2, 2014.

SECTION 1-1-685. Official State song.

"South Carolina On My Mind" is designated as an official state song to help inspire pride in our State and improve the quality of life among all South Carolinians, and to promote the image of South Carolina beyond our borders by further developing tourism and industry through the attraction of vacationers, prospective investors, and new residents.

HISTORY: 1984 Act No. 302, Section 1.

SECTION 1-1-688. Official State music.

The spiritual is the official music of the State.

HISTORY: 1999 Act No. 64, Section 1.

SECTION 1-1-689. Official State popular music.

Beach music is designated as the official state popular music of South Carolina.

HISTORY: 2001 Act No. 15, Section 2.

SECTION 1-1-690. Official State beverage.

Milk is the official state beverage.

HISTORY: 1984 Act No. 360, Section 4.

SECTION 1-1-691. Official state fossil.

The Columbian Mammoth is designated as the official State Fossil of South Carolina.

HISTORY: 2014 Act No. 177 (H.4482), Section 1, eff May 16, 2014.

SECTION 1-1-692. Official State hospitality beverage.

South Carolina grown tea is designated as the official hospitality beverage of the State.

HISTORY: 1995 Act No. 31, Section 1.

SECTION 1-1-693. Official State opera.

Porgy and Bess is designated as the official opera of this State. The State and any of its agencies, departments, or political subdivisions may not use any copyrighted or proprietary material from Porgy and Bess without the express written permission from the estates of Dubose Heyward, George Gershwin, and

Ira Gershwin or the management company responsible for licensing productions of this opera in part or in its entirety.

HISTORY: 2001 Act No. 94, Section 1.

SECTION 1-1-694. Official State Tobacco Museum.

(A) The South Carolina Tobacco Museum is the official tobacco museum of the State of South Carolina. The designation of the South Carolina Tobacco Museum as the official tobacco museum of the State is an honorary designation and does not bind the State in any way.

(B) The official designation does not create a new state agency or educational institution or qualify the South Carolina Tobacco Museum for state funds.

(C) The official designation does not confer any liability upon the State.

(D) The official designation does not sanction by the State any activity, philosophy, or course of action conducted, published, or undertaken by the South Carolina Tobacco Museum.

HISTORY: 2004 Act No. 222, Section 1, eff April 29, 2004.

SECTION 1-1-695. Official State shell.

The Lettered Olive, Oliva sayana, is the official shell of the State.

HISTORY: 1984 Act No. 360, Section 6.

SECTION 1-1-696. Official State language.

The English language is the official language of the State of South Carolina.

HISTORY: 1987 Act No. 25, Section 1.

SECTION 1-1-697. Use of language other than English prohibited.

Neither this State nor any political subdivision thereof shall require, by law, ordinance, regulation, order, decree, program, or policy, the use of any language other than English; provided, however, that nothing in Sections 1-1-696 through 1-1-698 shall prohibit a state agency or a political subdivision of the

State from requiring an applicant to have certain degrees of knowledge of a foreign language as a condition of employment where appropriate.

HISTORY: 1987 Act No. 25, Section 2.

SECTION 1-1-698. Exceptions to prohibition against use of language other than English.

Sections 1-1-696 through 1-1-698 do not prohibit any law, ordinance, regulation, order, decree, program, or policy requiring educational instruction in a language other than English for the purpose of making students who use a language other than English proficient in English or making students proficient in a language in addition to English.

HISTORY: 1987 Act No. 25, Section 3.

SECTION 1-1-699. Official State amphibian.

The Spotted Salamander, Ambystoma maculatum, is designated as the official state amphibian.

HISTORY: 1999 Act No. 79, Section 1.

SECTION 1-1-700. Official State American Folk Dance.

The square dance is the official American Folk Dance of the State.

HISTORY: 1994 Act No. 329, Section 1.

SECTION 1-1-701. Official State spider.

The "Carolina Wolf Spider", Hogna carolinensis, is designated as the official state spider.

HISTORY: 2000 Act No. 389, Part II, Section 7.

SECTION 1-1-702. Official State tapestry.

The tapestry, "From the Mountains to the Sea", is designated as the official state tapestry.

HISTORY: 2000 Act No. 354, Section 1.

SECTION 1-1-703. Official State tartan.

The Carolina Tartan is designated as the official tartan of the State of South Carolina.

HISTORY: 2002 Act No. 303, Section 1.

SECTION 1-1-704. Official State wildflower.

Goldenrod (solidago altissima) is the official state wildflower.

HISTORY: 2003 Act No. 31, Section 1.

SECTION 1-1-705. Official State railroad museum.

The South Carolina Railroad Museum in Fairfield County is the official railroad museum of the State of South Carolina, upon the payment of a fee of five dollars to the Secretary of State.

HISTORY: 1997 Act No. 155, Part II, Section 60A.

SECTION 1-1-706. Official State military academy.

(A) Camden Military Academy is designated as the official military academy of the State. The designation of Camden Military Academy as the official military academy of the State is an honorary designation and does not bind the State in any way.

(B) The official designation does not create a new state agency or educational institution or qualify Camden Military Academy for state funds.

(C) The official designation does not confer any liability of the State.

HISTORY: 2001 Act No. 56, Section 1.

SECTION 1-1-707. Official State Hall of Fame.

(A) The South Carolina Hall of Fame located in the Myrtle Beach Convention Center, operated by South Carolina Hall of Fame, Inc. , an eleemosynary corporation certified by the Secretary of State on June 1, 1963, is the official state Hall of Fame. The official designation is an honorary designation and does not bind the State in any way.

(B) The official designation does not create a new state agency or educational institution or qualify the South Carolina Hall of Fame for state funds.

(C) The official designation does not confer any liability upon the State.

(D) The official designation does not sanction by the State any activity, philosophy, or course of action conducted, published, or undertaken by the Hall of Fame.

HISTORY: 2001 Act No. 107, Section 1.

SECTION 1-1-708. Official State folk art and crafts center.

The South Carolina Artisans Center, a nonprofit organization, located in Walterboro is designated as the official folk art and crafts center of the State of South Carolina.

HISTORY: 2000 Act No. 256, Section 1.

SECTION 1-1-709. Official State rural drama theater.

(A) The Abbeville Opera House is designated as the official state rural drama theater of the State. The designation of the Abbeville Opera House as the official state rural drama theater of the State is an honorary designation and does not bind the State in any way.

(B) The official designation does not create a new state agency or educational institution or qualify the Abbeville Opera House for state funds.

(C) The official designation does not confer any liability of the State.

(D) The official designation does not sanction by the State any activity, philosophy, or course of action conducted, published, or undertaken by the Abbeville Opera House.

HISTORY: 2001 Act No. 48, Section 1.

SECTION 1-1-710. Official State color.

The color indigo blue worn on the uniform of Colonel William Moultrie's soldiers and adopted as the background of the South Carolina State flag, is designated as the official color of the State of South Carolina.

HISTORY: 2008 Act No. 200, Section 1, eff April 16, 2008.

SECTION 1-1-711. Official state duck.

The "wood duck" (Aix sponsa) also known as the summer duck and the Carolina duck is designated as the official state duck.

HISTORY: 2009 Act No. 58, Section 1, eff upon approval (became law without the Governor's signature on June 3, 2009).

SECTION 1-1-712. Official state marine mammal.

The "bottlenose dolphin" (Tursiops truncatus) is designated as the official state marine mammal.

HISTORY: 2009 Act No. 58, Section 2, eff upon approval (became law without the Governor's signature on June 3, 2009).

SECTION 1-1-713. Official state migratory marine mammal.

The "northern right whale" (Eubalaena glacialis) is designated as the official state migratory marine mammal.

HISTORY: 2009 Act No. 58, Section 3, eff upon approval (became law without the Governor's signature on June 3, 2009).

SECTION 1-1-713A. Official state emblem of United States Armed Forces who have given their lives in the line of duty.

The Honor and Remember Flag is designated as the official State Emblem of Service and Sacrifice by those in United States Armed Forces who have given their lives in the line of duty.

HISTORY: 2012 Act No. 237, Section 1, eff June 18, 2012.

SECTION 1-1-714. Official state heritage horse.

The Marsh Tacky is designated as the official State Heritage Horse of South Carolina.

HISTORY: 2010 Act No. 240, Section 2, eff June 11, 2010.

SECTION 1-1-714A. Official state heritage work animal.

The mule is hereby designated as the official State Heritage Work Animal of South Carolina.

HISTORY: 2010 Act No. 240, Section 3, eff June 11, 2010.

ARTICLE 11

Census

SECTION 1-1-715. United States Census of 2010 adopted.

The United States Census of 2010 is adopted as the true and correct enumeration of the inhabitants of this State, and of the several counties, municipalities, and other political subdivisions of this State.

HISTORY: 2003 Act No. 55, Section 2; 2011 Act No. 71, Pt I, Section 1, eff June 28, 2011; 2011 Act No. 75, Pt I, Section 1, eff August 1, 2011.

Code Commissioner's Note

This section was codified at the direction of the Code Commissioner.

Effect of Amendment

The 2011 amendments substituted "2010" for "2000".

ARTICLE 13

Reports to Governor or General Assembly

SECTION 1-1-810. Annual accountability reports by agencies and departments of state government.

Each agency and department of state government shall submit an annual accountability report to the Governor and the General Assembly covering a period from July first to June thirtieth, unless otherwise directed by the specific statute governing the department or institution.

HISTORY: 1962 Code Section 1-44; 1952 Code Section 1-44; 1942 Code Section 2096; 1932 Code Section 2096; 1929 (36) 225; 1931 (37) 278; 1933 (38) 490; 1960 (51) 1746; 1995 Act No. 145, Part II, Section 43A.

SECTION 1-1-820. Contents of annual accountability reports.

The annual accountability report required by Section 1-1-810 must contain the agency's or department's mission, objectives to accomplish the mission, and performance measures that show the degree to which objectives are being met.

HISTORY: 1962 Code Section 1-45; 1952 Code Section 1-45; 1942 Code Section 2097; 1932 Code Section 2097; Civ. C. '22 Section 58; Civ. C. '12 Section 48; Civ. C. '02 Section 45; 1896 (22) 202; 1960 (51) 1779; 1995 Act No. 145, Part II, Section 43B.

SECTION 1-1-830. One report shall not be embraced in another.

No State officer shall embrace in his report the report of another State officer which is required to be published by law, but he may make such reference thereto as may be necessary, including a brief recapitulation thereof, when necessary to the proper understanding of such report.

HISTORY: 1962 Code Section 1-46; 1952 Code Section 1-46; 1942 Code Section 2102; 1932 Code Section 2102; Civ. C. '22 Section 63; Civ. C. '12 Section 53; Civ. C. '02 Section 50; R. S. 50; 1886 (19) 310.

SECTION 1-1-840. Special reports.

The Governor or the General Assembly, or either branch thereof by resolution, may call upon any department or institution at any time for such special reports as may be deemed in the interest of the public welfare.

HISTORY: 1962 Code Section 1-47; 1952 Code Section 1-47; 1942 Code Section 2096; 1932 Code Section 2096; 1929 (36) 225; 1931 (37) 278; 1933 (38) 490.

ARTICLE 15

Reporting of Expenditures of State Appropriated Funds, Personal Data and the Like

SECTION 1-1-970. Personnel data required to be furnished quarterly.

All agencies, departments and institutions of state government shall furnish to the State Personnel Division not later than fifteen days following the close of the second quarter of each even-numbered year a current personnel organization chart in a form prescribed by the division showing all authorized positions, the personnel grade and compensation of each and indications as to whether such positions are filled or vacant.

All agencies, departments and institutions of state government shall furnish to the State Personnel Division not later than fifteen days following the close of each quarter except the second quarter of each even-numbered year any and all changes or alterations to the personnel organization chart in a form prescribed by the division.

The State Personnel Division shall ensure that all reports submitted to the division by agencies, departments and institutions of state government are accurate and up-to-date and, based on that information, shall furnish to the Legislative Audit Council organizational charts and alterations to existing charts for each such agency, department and institution in such form as the division and Audit Council shall determine.

The charts prepared by the division shall be furnished to the Audit Council not later than thirty days following the end of each quarter.

HISTORY: 1976 Act No. 561, Section 7; 1977 Act No. 101, Section 3.

SECTION 1-1-980. Penalties for failure to cooperate with implementation of reporting procedures.

All service agencies of the State shall cooperate with individual agencies, departments and institutions of State government in the implementation of this article. Any person who falsifies any report, statement or document required under this article shall be subject to punishment pursuant to Section 16-9-30 of the Code. Wilful failure to comply with the reporting requirements of this article shall be deemed misfeasance in office and subject the chief executive authority of the offending agency, department or institution to the penalties therefor.

HISTORY: 1976 Act No. 561, Section 8.

SECTION 1-1-990. Reports and information deemed public records; dissemination of copies.

All reports and information assembled pursuant to the provisions of this article are considered "public records" as defined in the Freedom of Information Act of 1972. Commencing on July 1, 1985, and thereafter, the Comptroller General shall furnish copies of the information when requested by authorized parties. The provisions of subsection (2) of Section 11-35-1230 of the 1976 Code of Laws govern fiscal reporting.

HISTORY: 1976 Act No. 561, Section 9; 1985 Act No. 201, Part II, Section 2A.

SECTION 1-1-1000. Partial exemption granted law enforcement agencies.

The provisions of this article shall not be construed to require any law enforcement agency to report in detail expenditures which would jeopardize the necessary confidentiality of its operations, but all such agencies shall report the total amount of funds expended for payments to informants and for purchases of illegal substances in connection with criminal investigations.

HISTORY: 1976 Act No. 561, Section 10.

SECTION 1-1-1020. Purchase of equipment by Office of State Treasurer for lease or resale to entities of state government; funding.

(A) The Office of State Treasurer is authorized to provide financing arrangements under the master lease program on behalf of boards, commissions, institutions, and agencies of state government for the purpose of renting, leasing, or purchasing office equipment, telecommunications equipment, energy conservation equipment, medical equipment, data processing equipment, and related software in accordance with procurement statutes and regulations.

(B) The Office of State Treasurer shall negotiate the terms of any financing arrangement and prescribe the procedures necessary to administer this program.

(C) When providing financing as described in subsection (A) of this section, the Office of State Treasurer shall ensure that repayment schedules provide sufficient funds to defray the cost of administering this program. The Office of State Treasurer shall retain such funds as are necessary to defray administrative costs. Any excess funds at year-end must be deposited to the credit of the general fund of the State.

HISTORY: 1981 Act No. 178 Part II, Section 19; 1982 Act No. 466 Part II, Section 27; 1990 Act No. 612, Part II, Section 12; 1994 Act No. 497, Section 10B; 2002 Act No. 286, Section 1.

SECTION 1-1-1025. Insurance on state data processing and telecommunications facilities.

The State Fiscal Accountability Authority, through its Insurance Reserve Fund, shall provide insurance against the accidental or deliberate destruction of data processing and telecommunications facilities operated by the State. The insurance shall specifically include replacement cost of hardware and software systems and specialized environmental systems and shall also provide for an alternate processing location should replacement or repair of the original processing location exceed ten calendar days.

HISTORY: 1982 Act No. 466, Part II, Section 25.

Code Commissioner's Note

At the direction of the Code Commissioner, references in this section to the offices of the former State Budget and Control Board, Office of the Governor, or other agencies, were changed to reflect the transfer of them to the Department of Administration or other entities, pursuant to the directive of the South Carolina Restructuring Act, 2014 Act No. 121, Section 5(D)(1), effective July 1, 2015.

SECTION 1-1-1030. Governmental or quasi-governmental entity not to pay contingency fee or bonus to private counsel without prior written agreement.

Notwithstanding any other provision of law, effective July 1, 1993, no governmental agency or quasi-governmental entity or agency shall pay a contingency fee or bonus to private counsel retained by such agency or entity for legal representation, unless such contingency fee or bonus arrangement has been reduced to writing setting forth the parameters of the employment and the terms of payment prior to the initiation of such representation.

HISTORY: 1993 Act No. 164, Part II, Section 107.

SECTION 1-1-1035. Expenditure of state or Medicaid funds to perform abortions.

No state funds or Medicaid funds shall be expended to perform abortions, except for those abortions authorized by federal law under the Medicaid program.

HISTORY: 2000 Act No. 387, Part II, Section 35.

SECTION 1-1-1040. Links to websites posting department's monthly state procurement card statements or information; redaction.

All agencies, departments, and institutions of state government must be responsible for providing on their Internet websites a link to the Internet website of any agency, other than the individual agency, department, or institution, that posts on its Internet website that agency's, department's, or institution's monthly state procurement card statements or monthly reports containing all or substantially all the same information contained in the monthly state procurement card statements. The link must be to the specific webpage or section on the website of the agency where the state procurement card information for the state agency, department, or institution can be found. The information posted may not contain the state procurement card number. Any information that is expressly prohibited from public disclosure by federal or state law or regulation must be redacted from any posting required by this section.

HISTORY: 2011 Act No. 74, Pt II, Section 2.B, eff August 1, 2011.

Editor's Note

2011 Act No. 74, Pt. II, Section 2.C, provides as follows:

"This SECTION takes effect upon approval by the Governor, and public institutions of higher learning to which this SECTION applies shall have one year from the effective date of this act to comply with its requirements."

ARTICLE 19

Salaries of State Officers

SECTION 1-1-1210. Annual salaries of certain state officers.

The annual salaries of the state officers listed below are:

Governor $98,000

Lieutenant Governor 43,000 Secretary of State 85,000 State Treasurer 85,000 Attorney General 85,000 Comptroller General 85,000 Superintendent of Education 85,000 Adjutant General 85,000 Commissioner of Agriculture 85,000

These salaries must be increased by two percent on July 1, 1991, and on July first of each succeeding year through July 1, 1994.

A state officer whose salary is provided in this section may not receive compensation for ex officio service on any state board, committee, or commission.

HISTORY: 1985 Act No. 201, Part II, Section 11; 1989 Act No. 189, Part II, Section 9.

ARTICLE 20

Reporting and Records of State Boards and Commissions Membership

SECTION 1-1-1310. State boards and commissions; notification of membership changes; contents.

Each state board and commission must send written notification to the Secretary of State's Office of any appointment, election, resignation, or vacancy in the membership of its board or commission. The notification must be sent within two weeks of the appointment, election, resignation, or vacancy and must include:

(1) the governing statute or Executive Order authorizing the appointment or election;

(2) the board or commission's address, phone number, fax number, and e-mail address, if any;

(3) the member's name;

(4) the member's district, circuit, seat, or position, if applicable;

(5) when the member's term begins and ends;

(6) the qualifications for membership on the board or commission and any specific requirements for the member's position;

(7) whether the member is eligible to receive compensation for his service;

(8) the name of the former member; and

(9) in the case of an appointment or election, whether it is a reappointment or reelection of an incumbent.

HISTORY: 2002 Act No. 182, Section 1.

ARTICLE 21

Workplace Domestic Violence Policy

SECTION 1-1-1410. Development and implementation of workplace domestic violence policy; zero tolerance policy statement.

Every state agency, based upon guidelines developed by the Office of Human Resources, Department of Administration, shall develop and implement an agency workplace domestic violence policy which must include, but is not limited to, a zero tolerance policy statement regarding acts or threats of domestic violence in the workplace and safety and security procedures.

HISTORY: 2003 Act No. 92, Section 7.

Code Commissioner's Note

At the direction of the Code Commissioner, references in this section to the offices of the former State Budget and Control Board, Office of the Governor, or other agencies, were changed to reflect the transfer of them to the Department of Administration or other entities, pursuant to the directive of the South Carolina Restructuring Act, 2014 Act No. 121, Section 5(D)(1), effective July 1, 2015.

ARTICLE 23

Repeal of Joint Resolution Calling for Balanced Federal Budget; Disavowal of Calls for Constitutional Convention

SECTION 1-1-1510. In general.

(A) Joint Resolution 775 of 1976 is repealed.

(B) The General Assembly of the State of South Carolina disavows any other calls or applications for a constitutional convention made to Congress prior to the effective date of this act, by any means expressed, including, but not limited to, S. 1024 of 1978.

(C) The Secretary of State is directed to forward copies of this act bearing the Great Seal of the State to the following persons: The President and Vice President of the United States, the Speaker of the House of Representatives, and each member of the South Carolina Congressional Delegation in Washington, D.C.

HISTORY: 2004 Act No. 314, Sections 1, 2, 3, eff July 16, 2004.

Code Commissioner's Note

This article was added and 2004 Act No. 314, Sections 1 to 3 codified at the direction of the Code Commissioner.

Editor's Note

The introduction to 2004 Act No. 314 provides as follows:

"Whereas, the General Assembly of the State of South Carolina, acting with the best of intentions, at various times and during various sessions, has previously made applications to Congress to call one or more conventions to propose either a single amendment concerning a specific subject or to call a general convention to propose an unspecified and unlimited number of amendments to the United States Constitution, pursuant to the provisions of Article V thereof; and

"Whereas, former Chief Justice of the Supreme Court of the United States of America Warren E. Burger, former Associate Justice of the United States Supreme Court Arthur J. Goldberg, and other leading constitutional scholars agree that such a convention may propose sweeping changes to the Constitution, any limitations or restrictions purportedly imposed by the states in applying for such a convention or conventions to the contrary notwithstanding, thereby creating an imminent peril to the well-established rights of the citizens and the duties of various levels of government; and

"Whereas, the Constitution of the United States of America has been amended many times in the history of this nation and may be amended many more times, without the need to resort to a constitutional convention, and has been interpreted for more than two hundred years and has been found to be a sound document which protects the lives and liberties of the citizens; and

"Whereas, there is no need for, rather, there is great danger in, a new constitution or in opening the Constitution to sweeping changes, the adoption of which would only create legal chaos in this nation and only begin the process of another two centuries of litigation over its meaning and interpretation. Now, therefore,"

ARTICLE 25

Video Conferencing

SECTION 1-1-1610. Use for performing administrative hearings; evidence of cost savings requirement; annual reports.

An administrative state agency performing administrative hearings within this State may make use of existing video conferencing capabilities. There must be evidence that a cost savings will be recognized by using video conferencing, as opposed to holding an administrative hearing where all parties must be in attendance at one particular location. A report of video conferencing activities and any related cost savings must be submitted annually, before January fifteenth, to the House Ways and Means Committee and the Senate Finance Committee.

HISTORY: 2008 Act No. 353, Section 2, Pt 20F, eff July 1, 2009.

CHAPTER 3

Governor and Lieutenant Governor

ARTICLE 1

General Provisions Affecting Governor

SECTION 1-3-10. Departments, agencies and the like shall furnish information requested by Governor.

The departments, bureaus, divisions, officers, boards, commissions, institutions and other agencies or undertakings of the State, upon request, shall immediately furnish to the Governor, in such form as he may require, any information desired by him in relation to their respective affairs or activities.

HISTORY: 1962 Code Section 1-101; 1952 Code Section 1-101; 1942 Code Section 3216; 1932 Code Section 3216; Civ. C. '22 Section 912; 1919 (31) 187.

SECTION 1-3-20. Salary of Governor.

The Governor shall receive such annual salary as may be provided by the General Assembly.

HISTORY: 1962 Code Section 1-102; 1952 Code Section 1-102; 1942 Code Section 3090; 1932 Code Section 3090; Civ. C. '22 Section 775; Civ. C. '12 Section 691; Civ. C. '02 Section 621; G. S. 473; R. S. 537; 1865 (13) 350; 1893 (21) 416; 1919 (31) 4; 1924 (33) 1182; 1948 (45) 1716; 1954 (48) 1566; 1960 (51) 1779; 1963 (53) 358 [478]; 1966 (54) 2424; 1969 (56) 444; 1973 (58) 623.

SECTION 1-3-30. Executive chamber, official papers and records.

The Governor shall be furnished with a suitable office, to be called the executive chamber, in which all petitions, memorials, letters and other official papers and documents addressed to or received by him shall be methodically arranged and kept, with proper indexes therefor. He shall keep a record in proper books of:

(1) All his messages to the General Assembly;

(2) All bills presented to him in obedience to the provisions of the Constitution and all objections he may make to any of them;

(3) All official communications, proclamations and orders issuing from his office; and

(4) All other matters which he may think it important to preserve.

HISTORY: 1962 Code Section 1-103; 1952 Code Section 1-103; 1942 Code Section 3090; 1932 Code Section 3090; Civ. C. '22 Section 775; Civ. C. '12 Section 691; Civ. C. '02 Section 621; G. S. 473; R. S. 537; 1865 (13) 350; 1893 (21) 416; 1919 (31) 4; 1924 (33) 1182.

SECTION 1-3-40. Private secretary of Governor.

The Governor shall be allowed a private secretary, to be appointed by him, who shall under the direction of the Governor keep an accurate record under proper dates of all transactions, opinions and other official matters and acts occurring during his period of office. Said record shall, under certain restrictions, be open to the inspection of the members of the General Assembly. He shall also perform such clerical and other duties as may be required of him by the Governor, in connection with the duties of the office of Governor.

HISTORY: 1962 Code Section 1-104; 1952 Code Section 1-104; 1942 Code Section 3091; 1932 Code Section 3901; Civ. C. '22 Section 776; Civ. C. '12 Section 692; Civ. C. '02 Section 622; G. S. 474; R. S. 538; 1865 (13) 350; 1868 (14) 11; 1869 (14) 246; 1893 (21) 416.

SECTION 1-3-50. Personal staff of Governor for ceremonial occasions; military secretary.

Whenever the Governor shall desire the attendance of a personal staff upon any ceremonial occasion he shall detail therefor such officers as he may choose from the active list of the National Guard of South Carolina, resident in or nearest to the place where such ceremonies are to be held, and the officers detailed shall attend in uniform at the time and place designated and shall constitute the personal staff of the Governor for that occasion, reverting upon completion of such duty to their regular assignments. The Governor may appoint as his military secretary any officer of the United States Army detailed for duty with the militia of this State, and such officer shall have the rank of colonel and the title "Military Secretary to the Governor".

HISTORY: 1962 Code Section 1-105; 1952 Code Section 1-105; 1950 (46) 1881.

ARTICLE 3

Installation of Governor; Vacancy in Office

SECTION 1-3-110. Date of installation of Governor.

The Governor shall be installed on the first Wednesday following the second Tuesday in January following his election; but in case the Governor is unable to be installed on the day herein provided, he shall be installed as soon thereafter as is practicable.

HISTORY: 1962 Code Section 1-111; 1952 Code Section 1-111; 1942 Code Section 3085; 1932 Code Section 3085; Civ. C. '22 Section 770; Civ. C. '12 Section 686; 1911 (27) 142; 1979 Act No. 29, Section 1.

SECTION 1-3-120. Vacancy in office of both Governor and Lieutenant Governor.

In case of the removal, death, resignation or disability of both the Governor, and the Lieutenant Governor, the President of the Senate pro tempore shall perform the duties and exercise the powers of Governor until such disability shall have been removed or until the next general election, at which a Governor shall be elected by the electors duly qualified, as is prescribed by Section 3 of Article IV of the Constitution.

HISTORY: 1962 Code Section 1-112; 1952 Code Section 1-112; 1942 Code Section 3086; 1932 Code Section 3086; Civ. C. '22 Section 771; Civ. C. '12 Section 687; Civ. C. '02 Section 617; G. S. 469; R. S. 533; 1868 (14) 101.

SECTION 1-3-130. Disability of Governor, Lieutenant Governor and President of Senate pro tempore.

In case of the disability, from whatever cause, of the Governor, the Lieutenant Governor, and the President of the Senate pro tempore, the Speaker of the House of Representatives shall perform the duties and exercise the powers of Governor, in like manner and upon like conditions as are prescribed by Section 1-3-120.

HISTORY: 1962 Code Section 1-113; 1952 Code Section 1-113; 1942 Code Section 3087; 1932 Code Section 3087; Civ. C. '22 Section 772; Civ. C. '12 Section 688; Civ. C. '02 Section 618; G. S. 470; R. S. 534; 1868 (14) 102.

SECTION 1-3-140. Disability of all of officers enumerated in Sections 1-3-120 and 1-3-130.

In case of the disability, from whatever cause, of all of the officers enumerated in Sections 1-3-120 and 1-3-130, the General Assembly, if it shall be in session, by a joint vote shall elect a person duly qualified to fill the office of Governor in like manner, and upon the like conditions, as are prescribed by Section 1-3-120.

HISTORY: 1962 Code Section 1-114; 1952 Code Section 1-114; 1942 Code Section 3088; 1932 Code Section 3088; Civ. C. '22 Section 773; Civ. C. '12 Section 689; Civ. C. '02 Section 619; G. S. 471; R. S. 535; 1868 (14) 102.

SECTION 1-3-150. Term of Governor elected pursuant to Section 1-3-140.

Whenever a Governor shall be elected as provided in Section 1-3-140, he shall immediately enter upon the discharge of the duties of his office and shall continue to discharge them during the residue of the term.

HISTORY: 1962 Code Section 1-115; 1952 Code Section 1-115; 1942 Code Section 3089; 1932 Code Section 3089; Civ. C. '22 Section 774; Civ. C. '12 Section 690; Civ. C. '02 Section 620; G. S. 472; R. S. 536; 1868 (14) 102.

ARTICLE 5

Appointment and Removal of Officers

SECTION 1-3-210. Filling vacancies when Senate not in session.

During the recess of the Senate, vacancy which occurs in an office filled by an appointment of the Governor with the advice and consent of the Senate may be filled by an interim appointment of the Governor. The Governor must report the interim appointment to the Senate and must forward a formal appointment at its next ensuing regular session.

If the Senate does not advise and consent thereto prior to sine die adjournment of the next ensuing regular session, the office shall be vacant and the interim appointment shall not serve in hold over status notwithstanding any other provision of law to the contrary. A subsequent interim appointment of a different person to a vacancy created by a failure of the Senate to grant confirmation to the original interim appointment shall expire on the second Tuesday in January following the date of such subsequent interim appointment and the office shall be vacant.

HISTORY: 1962 Code Section 1-121; 1952 Code Section 1-121; 1942 Code Section 3093; 1932 Code Section 3093; Civ. C. '22 Section 778; Civ. C. '12 Section 694; Civ. C. '02 Section 624; G. S. 476, 477; R. S. 540; 1868 (14) 66; 1870 (14) 376; 1871 (15) 690; 1876 (16); 1877 (16) 249; 1878 (16) 571, 609, 766; 1882 (18) 1111; 1890 (20) 697; 1896 (22) 154; 1901 (23) 701; 1920 (31) 704, 908; 1922 (32) 938; 1945 (44) 156; 1954 (48) 1745; Const. 1895, Art. 12, Section 2; 1963 (53) 512; 1993 Act No. 181, Section 3.

SECTION 1-3-215. Appointments by the Governor requiring advice and consent of Senate.

(A) Appointments by the Governor requiring the advice and consent of the Senate must be transmitted to the Senate and must contain at a minimum the following information:

(1) the title of the office to which the individual is being appointed;

(2) the designation of any special seat, discipline, interest group or other designated entity that the individual is representing or is chosen from;

(3) the full legal name of the individual being appointed;

(4) the current street or mailing address and telephone number;

(5) the county, counties, district or other geographic area or political subdivision being represented;

(6) the name of the individual being replaced if the appointment is not an initial appointment; and

(7) the commencement and ending date of the term of office.

(B) When an appointment has been confirmed by the Senate, evidence of such confirmation shall be transmitted to the Secretary of State by the Clerk of the Senate and the Secretary of State must thereafter obtain the necessary oath and evidence of bond if required. The taking of the oath of office and filing of any requisite bond shall fully vest the person appointed with the full rights, privileges and powers of the office. The notice of confirmation transmitted by the Senate shall be conclusive as to the validity of an appointment and the issuance of a commission by the Secretary of State after obtaining the requisite documentation is a ministerial act.

HISTORY: 1993 Act No. 183, Section 4; 1993 Act No. 181, Section 4.

SECTION 1-3-220. Appointment of certain officers by Governor.

The following appointments shall be made by the Governor and are in addition to those appointments by the Governor authorized in other provisions in the Code:

(1) An appointment to fill any vacancy in an office of the executive department as defined in Section 1-1-110 occurring during a recess of the General Assembly. The term of such appointment shall be until the vacancy be filled by a general election or by the General Assembly in the manner provided by law.

(2) An appointment to fill any vacancy in a county office. The person so appointed shall hold office, in all cases in which the office is elective, until the next general election and until his successor shall qualify; and in the case of offices originally filled by appointment and not by election, until the adjournment of the session of the General Assembly next after such vacancy has occurred. The Governor may remove for cause any person so appointed by him under the provisions of this paragraph to fill any such vacancy.

(3) Proxies to represent the share of the State in the Cheraw and Coalfields Railroad Company and in the Cheraw and Salisbury Railroad Company.

(4) The chief constable of the State, whensoever in his judgment any public emergency shall require it or when necessary to the due execution of legal process.

HISTORY: 1962 Code Section 1-122; 1952 Code Section 1-122; 1942 Code Section 3094; 1932 Code Section 3094; Civ. C. '22 Section 779; Civ. C. '02 Section 625; G. S. 477; R. S. 541; 1818 (16) 723; 1840 (11) 147; 1875 (15) 935; 1877 (16) 263; 1878 (16) 656, 716; 1884 (18) 691; 1903 (24) 19; 1960 (51) 1917; 1993 Act No. 181, Section 5.

SECTION 1-3-230. Appointment of poet laureate.

The Governor may name and appoint some outstanding and distinguished man of letters as poet laureate for the State of South Carolina.

HISTORY: 1962 Code Section 1-123; 1952 Code Section 1-123; 1942 Code Section 3094; 1932 Code Section 3094; Civ. C. '22 Section 779; Civ. C. '12 Section 695; Civ. C. '02 Section 625; G. S. 477; R. S. 541; 1875 (15) 935; 1909 (26) 127; 1911 (27) 5; 1924 (33) 1016; 1933 (38) 296; 1934 (38) 1299.

SECTION 1-3-240. Removal of officers by Governor.

(A) Any officer of the county or State, except:

(1) an officer whose removal is provided for in Section 3 of Article XV of the State Constitution;

(2) an officer guilty of the offense named in Section 8 of Article VI of the State Constitution; or

(3) pursuant to subsection (B) of this section, an officer of the State appointed by the Governor, either with or without the advice and consent of the Senate; who is guilty of malfeasance, misfeasance, incompetency, absenteeism, conflicts of interest, misconduct, persistent neglect of duty in office, or incapacity must be subject to removal by the Governor upon any of the foregoing causes being made to appear to the satisfaction of the Governor. Before removing any such officer, the Governor shall inform him in writing of the specific charges brought against him and give him an opportunity on reasonable notice to be heard.

(B) A person appointed to a state office by the Governor, either with or without the advice and consent of the Senate, other than those officers enumerated in subsection (C), may be removed from office by the Governor at his discretion by an Executive Order removing the officer.

(C)(1) Persons appointed to the following offices of the State may be removed by the Governor for malfeasance, misfeasance, incompetency, absenteeism, conflicts of interest, misconduct, persistent neglect of duty in office, or incapacity:

(a) Workers' Compensation Commission;

(b) Department of Transportation Commission;

(c) Ethics Commission;

(d) Election Commission;

(e) Professional and Occupational Licensing Boards;

(f) Juvenile Parole Board;

(g) Probation, Parole and Pardon Board;

(h) Director of the Department of Public Safety;

(i) Board of the Department of Health and Environmental Control, excepting the chairman;

(j) Chief of State Law Enforcement Division;

(k) South Carolina Lottery Commission;

(l) Executive Director of the Office of Regulatory Staff;

(m) Directors of the South Carolina Public Service Authority appointed pursuant to Section 58-31-20. A director of the South Carolina Public Service Authority also may be removed for his breach of any duty arising under Section 58-31-55 or 58-31-56. The Governor must not request a director of the South Carolina Public Service Authority to resign unless cause for removal, as established by this subsection, exists. Removal of a director of the South Carolina Public Service Authority, except as is provided by this section or by Section 58-31-20(A), must be considered to be an irreparable injury for which no adequate remedy at law exists;

(n) State Ports Authority;

(o) State Inspector General; and

(p) State Adjutant General.

(2) Upon the expiration of an officeholder's term, the individual may continue to serve until a successor is appointed and qualifies.

HISTORY: 1962 Code Section 1-124; 1952 Code Section 1-124; 1942 Code Section 3098; 1932 Code Section 3098; 1924 (33) 997; 1993 Act No. 181, Section 6; 2001 Act No. 59, Section 3; 2004 Act No. 175, Section 1, eff March 4, 2004; 2005 Act No. 137, Section 1, eff May 25, 2005; 2007 Act No. 114, Section 3, eff June 27, 2007; 2009 Act No. 73, Section 16, eff June 16, 2009; 2012 Act No. 105, Section 1, eff January 1, 2012; 2014 Act No. 224 (H.3540), Section 1, eff March 5, 2015.

Editor's Note

2014 Act No. 224, Section 4, provides as follows:

"SECTION 4. This act takes effect upon the ratification of amendments to Section 7, Article VI, and Section 4, Article XIII of the Constitution of this State deleting the requirement that the Adjutant General be elected by the qualified electors of this State and providing that he be appointed by the Governor."

2015 Act No. 1 (S.8) Sections 1.A, 1.B, eff March 5, 2015, ratified amendments to Section 7, Article VI, and Section 4, Article XIII of the Constitution.

Effect of Amendment

The 2004 amendment added subsection (C)(12).

The 2005 amendment, in subsection (C), designated paragraph (1) and under it redesignated items (1) to (12) as subparagraphs (a) to (l), in subparagraph (b), substituted "Reserved" for "Commission of the Department of Revenue", and added subparagraph (m) relating to the officers who may be removed by the governor; and designated paragraph (2) making nonsubstantive changes.

The 2007 amendment, in subsection (C)(1)(b), substituted "Department of Transportation Commission" for "Reserved".

The 2009 amendment added subsection (C)(1)(n) relating to State Ports Authority.

The 2012 amendment inserted subsection (C)(1)(o) and made other nonsubstantive changes.

2014 Act No. 224, Section 1, effective March 5, 2015, added subsection (C)(1)(p), relating to the Adjutant General.

SECTION 1-3-245. Removal from office of member of state board for three consecutive unexcused absences; vacancy created; requirement of chairman to notify appointing authority; exclusion for ex officio member or designee.

(A) A member of a state board, council, commission, or committee who has three consecutive unexcused absences from regularly scheduled meetings held by the particular board, council, commission, or committee is considered removed from the board, council, commission, or committee and a vacancy is created. The chairman of the board, council, commission, or committee immediately shall notify the Governor or appropriate appointing authority of the member's three consecutive unexcused absences and of the resulting vacancy. An unexcused absence must be defined by each respective board, council, commission, or committee in rules governing its operation.

(B) This section does not apply to an ex officio member of a state board, council, commission, or committee or to a designee of an ex officio member.

HISTORY: 1995 Act No. 79, Section 1.

SECTION 1-3-250. Appeal by officer removed by Governor.

An officer, other than a state officer appointed by the Governor pursuant to subsection (B) of Section 1-3-240, shall have the right of appeal from any order of removal by the Governor under Section 1-3-240 to the resident or presiding judge of the circuit in which the officer resides. The judge shall hear and determine the appeal both as to law and fact upon the record as made before the Governor and upon additional evidence as he shall see fit to allow. The notice of appeal shall be served upon the Governor, or his secretary, within five days after the service upon the officer of the order of the Governor removing him and shall state the grounds for the appeal and name the circuit judge to whom the appeal is taken. The Governor shall transmit to the judge the record in the case, including a copy of the order of removal, grounds of removal, evidence in support of removal and return of service, and any other matter which in his judgment may be considered by the court. The circuit judge within twenty days after the taking of the appeal, or in such shorter time as may be practical, shall hear and determine the appeal, after giving to the parties reasonable notice of the time and place of hearing. The hearing may be had and judgment may be rendered in open court, or at chambers within or without the circuit. Any appeal from the order of the circuit court must be taken in the manner provided by the South Carolina Appellate Court Rules.

HISTORY: 1962 Code Section 125; 1952 Code Section 1-125; 1942 Code Section 3098; 1932 Code Section 3098; 1924 (33) 997; 1960 (51) 1736; 1993 Act No. 181, Section 7; 1999 Act No. 55, Section 1.

SECTION 1-3-260. Removal procedure as additional to other removal procedures.

The power and procedure of removal conferred and provided for in Sections 1-3-240 and 1-3-250 are additional to any other removal powers or procedure authorized by statute.

HISTORY: 1962 Code Section 1-126; 1952 Code Section 1-126; 1942 Code Section 3098; 1932 Code Section 3098; 1924 (33) 997.

SECTION 1-3-270. Filling of vacancies created by removal pursuant to Section 1-3-240.

Any vacancy created under the authority vested by Section 1-3-240 shall be filled as provided by the Constitution and statute laws of the State relating to the filling of a vacancy in the office in which such vacancy is so created.

HISTORY: 1962 Code Section 1-127; 1952 Code Section 1-127; 1942 Code Section 3098; 1932 Code Section 3098; 1924 (33) 997.

ARTICLE 7

Maintenance of Peace and Order

SECTION 1-3-410. Governor may act to prevent violence.

The Governor may take such measures and do all and every act and thing which he may deem necessary in order to prevent violence or threats of violence to the person or property of citizens of the State and to maintain peace, tranquility and good order in the State, and in any political subdivision thereof, and in any particular area of the State designated by him.

HISTORY: 1962 Code Section 1-128; 1957 (50) 521.

SECTION 1-3-420. Proclamation of emergency by Governor.

The Governor, when in his opinion the facts warrant, shall, by proclamation, declare that, because of unlawful assemblage, violence or threats of violence, or a public health emergency, as defined in Section 44-4-130, a danger exists to the person or property of any citizen and that the peace and tranquility of the State, or any political subdivision thereof, or any particular area of the State designated by him, is threatened, and because thereof an emergency, with reference to such threats and danger, exists.

The Governor, upon the issuance of a proclamation as provided for in this section, must immediately file the proclamation in the Office of the Secretary of State, which proclamation is effective upon issuance and remain in full force and effect until revoked by the Governor.

HISTORY: 1962 Code Section 1-129; 1957 (50) 521; 2002 Act No. 339, Section 3.

SECTION 1-3-430. Orders to prevent danger.

In all such cases when the Governor shall issue his proclamation as provided in Section 1-3-420 he may further, cope with such threats and danger, order and direct any person or group of persons to do any act which would in his opinion prevent or minimize danger to life, limb or property, or prevent a breach of the peace; and he may order any person or group of persons to refrain from doing any act or thing which would, in his opinion, endanger life, limb or property, or cause, or tend to cause, a breach of the peace, or endanger the peace and good order of the State or any section or community thereof, and he shall have full power by use of all appropriate available means to enforce such order or proclamation.

HISTORY: 1962 Code Section 1-130; 1957 (50) 521.

SECTION 1-3-440. Further powers of Governor.

For the purposes already stated the Governor may take and exercise any or all of the following actions:

(1) Call out the military forces of the State (State militia) or any unit or units thereof and order and direct them to take such action as in his judgment may be

necessary to avert any threatened danger and to maintain peace and good order;

(2) Order any and all law enforcement officers of the State or any of its subdivisions to do whatever may be deemed necessary to maintain peace and good order;

(3) Order the discontinuance of any transportation or other public facilities, or, in the alternative, direct that such facilities be operated by a State agency; or

(4) Authorize, order or direct any State, county or city official to enforce the provisions of such proclamation in the courts of the State by injunction, mandamus, or other appropriate legal action.

HISTORY: 1962 Code Section 1-130.1; 1957 (50) 521.

SECTION 1-3-450. Intervention by Governor in situations of violence or public disorder.

The Governor may intervene in any situation where there exists violence or threats of violence to persons or property and take complete control thereof to prevent violence, riotous conduct, public disorder or breaches of the peace.

HISTORY: 1962 Code Section 1-30.2; 1957 (50) 521.

SECTION 1-3-460. Governor's powers under article shall be supplemental to powers granted by other laws of State.

The powers granted in this article are supplemental to and in aid of powers now vested in the Governor under the Constitution, statutory laws and police powers of the State.

HISTORY: 1962 Code Section 1-30.3; 1957 (50) 521.

SECTION 1-3-470. Lowering flags upon death in line of duty of firefighter or law enforcement officer.

The Governor on the day of burial or other service for any firefighter or law enforcement officer in this State who died in the line of duty shall order all flags on state buildings to be flown at half-mast in tribute to the deceased firefighter or law enforcement officer. The Governor shall also request that flags over the buildings of the political subdivisions of this State similarly be flown at half-mast for this purpose.

HISTORY: 1987 Act No. 104, Section 1.

SECTION 1-3-480. Authority of Governor to authorize national guard to support federal, state and local law enforcement agencies in drug enforcement matters; delegation of authority.

(A) The Governor, as Commander-in-Chief of the organized militia of this State and in accordance with Title 32, United States Code, Section 112, may authorize or direct the South Carolina National Guard to assist and support federal, state, and local law enforcement agencies in drug interdiction, counterdrug activities, and demand reduction activities. The Governor may delegate his authority under this section to the Adjutant General who is specifically authorized to enter into mutual assistance and support agreements with law enforcement agencies operating within this State for activities within this State.

(B) The Governor, with the consent of Congress, is authorized to enter into compacts and agreements for the deployment of the National Guard with governors of other states concerning drug interdiction, counterdrug activities, and demand reduction activities. To facilitate these agreements, the General Assembly ratifies the National Guard Mutual Assistance Counterdrug Activities Compact, codified at Section 1-3-490. Article I, Section 10 of the Constitution of the United States permits a state to enter into a compact or agreement with another state, subject to the consent of Congress. Congress, through enactment of 4 U.S.C. Section 112, has given its consent for states to enter such compacts for cooperative effort and mutual assistance in the prevention of crime.

HISTORY: 1992 Act No. 379, Section 1; 1995 Act No. 113, Section 1.

SECTION 1-3-490. National Guard Mutual Assistance Counterdrug Activities Compact.

The National Guard Mutual Assistance Counterdrug Activities Compact is hereby enacted into law and entered into by the State of South Carolina with all other states legally joining, in the form substantially as follows:

THE NATIONAL GUARD MUTUAL ASSISTANCE COUNTERDRUG ACTIVITIES COMPACT

ARTICLE I

Purpose

The purposes of this compact are to:

(A) provide for mutual assistance and support among the party states in the utilization of the National Guard in drug interdiction, counterdrug activities, and demand reduction activities;

(B) permit the National Guard of this State to enter into mutual assistance and support agreements, on the basis of need, with one or more law enforcement agencies operating within this State, for activities within this State, or with a National Guard of one or more other states, whether the activities are within or outside this State in order to facilitate and coordinate efficient, cooperative enforcement efforts directed toward drug interdiction, counterdrug activities, and demand reduction activities;

(C) permit the National Guard of this State to act as a receiving and a responding state as defined within this compact and to ensure the prompt and effective delivery of National Guard personnel, assets, and services to agencies or areas that are in need of increased support and presence;

(D) permit and encourage a high degree of flexibility in the deployment of National Guard forces in the interest of efficiency;

(E) maximize the effectiveness of the National Guard in situations which permit its utilization under this compact;

(F) provide protection for the rights of National Guard personnel when performing duty in other states in counterdrug activities; and

(G) ensure uniformity of state laws in the area of National Guard involvement in interstate counterdrug activities by incorporating the uniform laws within the compact.

ARTICLE II

Entry into Force and Withdrawal

(A) This compact becomes effective when enacted by any two states. Thereafter, this compact becomes effective as to another state upon its enactment.

(B) A party state may withdraw from this compact by enacting a statute repealing the compact, but no withdrawal shall take effect until one year after the governor of the withdrawing state has given notice in writing of the withdrawal to the governors of all other party states.

ARTICLE III

Mutual Assistance and Support

(A) As used in this article:

(1) "Drug interdiction and counterdrug activities" means the use of National Guard personnel, while not in federal service, in law enforcement support activities that are intended to reduce the supply or use of illegal drugs in the United States. These activities include, but are not limited to:

(a) providing information obtained during either the normal course of military training or operations or during counterdrug activities to federal, state, or local law enforcement officials that may be relevant to a violation of a federal or state law within the jurisdiction of these officials;

(b) making available equipment, including associated supplies or spare parts, base facilities, or research facilities of the National Guard to a federal, state, or local civilian law enforcement official for law enforcement purposes, in accordance with other applicable law;

(c) providing available National Guard personnel to train federal, state, or local civilian law enforcement in the operation and maintenance of equipment, including equipment made available pursuant to this provision, in accordance with other applicable law;

(d) providing available National Guard personnel to operate and maintain equipment provided to federal, state, or local law enforcement officials pursuant to activities defined and referred to in this compact;

(e) operation and maintenance of equipment and facilities of the National Guard or law enforcement agencies used for the purposes of drug interdiction and counterdrug activities;

(f) providing available National Guard personnel to operate equipment for the detection, monitoring, and communication of the movement of air, land, and sea traffic, to facilitate communications in connection with law enforcement programs, to provide transportation for civilian law enforcement personnel;

(g) providing available National Guard personnel, equipment, and support for administrative, interpretive, analytic, or other purposes;

(h) providing available National Guard personnel and other equipment to aid federal, state, and local officials and agencies otherwise involved in the prosecution or incarceration of individuals processed within the criminal justice system who have been arrested for criminal acts involving the use, distribution, or transportation of controlled substances as defined in 21 U.S.C. 801 et seq. or in accordance with other applicable law.

(2) "Demand reduction" means providing available National Guard personnel, equipment, support, and coordination to federal, state, local, and civic organizations and agencies for the purposes of the prevention of drug abuse and the reduction in the demand for illegal drugs.

(3) "Requesting state" means the state whose governor requested assistance in the area of counterdrug activities.

(4) "Responding state" means the state furnishing assistance, or requested to furnish assistance, in the area of counterdrug activities.

(5) "Law enforcement agency" means a lawfully established federal, state, or local public agency that is responsible for the prevention and detection of crime and the enforcement of penal, traffic, regulatory, game, immigration, postal, customs, or controlled substances laws.

(6) "Official" means the appointed, elected, or designated representative of an agency, institution, or organization authorized to conduct those activities for which support is requested.

(7) "Mutual assistance and support agreement" means an agreement between the National Guard of this State and one or more law enforcement agencies or

between the National Guard of this State and the National Guard of one or more other states, consistent with the purposes of this compact.

(8) "Party state" means a state that has lawfully enacted this compact.

(9) "State" means each of the several states of the United States, the District of Columbia, the Commonwealth of Puerto Rico, or a territory or possession of the United States.

(B) Upon the request of the governor of a party state for assistance in drug interdiction, counterdrug activities, and demand reduction activities, the governor of a responding state shall have authority under this compact to send to a requesting state and place under the temporary operational control of the appropriate National Guard or military authorities of that state, for the purposes of providing the requested assistance, all or a part of the National Guard forces of his state. The exercise of his discretion in this regard must be conclusive.

(C) The governor of a party state may withhold the National Guard forces of his state from deployment in a requesting state and recall the forces deployed in a requesting state.

(D) The National Guard of this State is authorized to engage in counterdrug activities and demand reduction activities.

(E) The Adjutant General of this State, in order to further the purposes of this compact, may enter into a mutual assistance and support agreement with one or more law enforcement agencies of this State, and with the National Guard of other party states to provide personnel, assets, and services in the area of counterdrug activities and demand reduction activities provided that all parties to the agreement are not specifically prohibited by law to perform these activities.

(F) The agreement must set forth the powers, rights, and obligations of the parties to the agreement, where applicable, as follows:

(1) the duration of the agreement;

(2) the organization, composition, and nature of a separate legal entity created by the agreement;

(3) the purpose of the agreement;

(4) the manner of financing the agreement and establishing and maintaining the budget of the agreement;

(5) the method to be employed in accomplishing the partial or complete termination of the agreement and for disposing of property upon a partial or complete termination;

(6) provision for administering the agreement, which may include creation of a joint board responsible for its administration;

(7) the manner of acquiring, holding, and disposing of real and personal property used in the agreement;

(8) the minimum standards for National Guard personnel implementing the provisions of this agreement;

(9) the minimum insurance required of each party to the agreement;

(10) the chain of command or delegation of authority to be followed by National Guard personnel acting under the provisions of the agreement;

(11) the duties and authority that the National Guard personnel of each party state may exercise; and

(12) other necessary and proper matters.

(G) As a condition precedent to an agreement becoming effective, the agreement must be submitted to and receive the approval of the Office of the Attorney General of South Carolina. The Attorney General may delegate his approval authority to the appropriate attorney for the South Carolina National Guard subject to those conditions which he decides are appropriate. The delegation must be in writing and:

(1) the Attorney General, or his agent in the South Carolina National Guard, shall approve an agreement submitted to him under this provision unless he finds that it is not in proper form, does not meet the requirements set forth in this provision, or does not conform to the laws of South Carolina. If the Attorney General disapproves an agreement, he shall provide a written explanation to the Adjutant General of the National Guard;

(2) if the Attorney General, or his authorized agent, approves an agreement within thirty days after its submission to him, it is considered approved by him;

(3) whenever National Guard forces of a party state are engaged in drug interdiction, counterdrug activities, and demand reduction activities, they personally must not be held liable for an act or omission which occurs during the performance of their duty.

ARTICLE IV

Responsibilities

(A) Nothing in this compact may be construed as a waiver of benefits, privileges, immunities, or rights provided for National Guard personnel performing duty pursuant to Title 32 of the United States Code, nor shall anything in this compact be construed as a waiver of coverage provided for under the Federal Tort Claims Act. If National Guard personnel performing counterdrug activities do not receive rights, benefits, privileges, and immunities provided for National Guard personnel provided in this section, then the following provisions apply:

(1) Whenever National Guard forces of a responding state are engaged in another state in carrying out the purposes of this compact, the members engaged shall have the same powers, duties, rights, privileges, and immunities as members of the National Guard forces of the requesting state. The requesting state shall save and hold members of the National Guard forces of the responding state harmless from civil liability for acts or omissions which occur in the performance of their duty while engaged in carrying out the purposes of this compact, whether responding forces are serving the requesting state within the borders of the responding state or are attached to the requesting state for purposes of operational control.

(2) Subject to the provisions of items (3), (4), and (5) of this subsection, liability that may arise under the laws of the requesting state or the responding states, on account of or in connection with a request for assistance or support, must be assumed and borne by the requesting state.

(3) A requesting state rendering aid or assistance pursuant to this compact must be reimbursed by the requesting state for loss or damage to, or expense incurred in the operation of, equipment answering a request for aid, and for the cost of the materials, transportation, and maintenance of National Guard personnel and equipment incurred in connection with the request, provided that

nothing contained in this provision prevents a responding state from assuming the loss, damage, expense, or other cost.

(4) Unless there is a written agreement to the contrary, each party shall provide, in the same amounts and manner as if they were on duty within their state, for pay and allowances of the personnel of its National Guard units while engaged in another state pursuant to this compact and while going to and returning from duty pursuant to this compact.

(5) Each party state providing the payment of compensation and death benefits to injured members and the representatives of deceased members of its National Guard forces in case the members sustain injuries or are killed within their own state shall provide for the payment of compensation and death benefits in the same manner and on the same terms in the event the members sustain injury or are killed while rendering assistance or support pursuant to this compact. These benefits and compensation are expense items reimbursable pursuant to item (3) of this subsection.

(B) Officers and enlisted personnel of the National Guard performing duties pursuant to this compact must be subject to and governed by the provisions of their home state's Code of Military Justice whether they are performing duties within or outside their home state. If a National Guard member commits, or is suspected of committing, a criminal offense while performing duties pursuant to this compact outside his home state, he may be returned immediately to his home state and that state must be responsible for disciplinary action. However, nothing in this section abrogates the general criminal jurisdiction of the state in which the offense occurred.

ARTICLE V

Delegation

Nothing in this compact must be construed to prevent the governor of a party state from delegating his responsibilities or authority respecting the National Guard, provided that this delegation is in accordance with law. For purposes of this compact, however, the Governor shall not delegate the power to request assistance from another state.

ARTICLE VI

Limitations

Nothing in this compact shall:

(1) authorize or permit National Guard units or personnel to be placed under the operational control of a person not having the National Guard rank or status required by law for the command in question; or

(2) deprive a properly convened court of jurisdiction over an offense or a defendant because the National Guard, while performing duties pursuant to this compact, was utilized in achieving an arrest or indictment.

ARTICLE VII

Construction and Severability

This compact must be liberally construed to effectuate its purpose. The provisions of this compact are severable and if a phrase, clause, sentence, or provision of this compact is declared to be contrary to the Constitution of the United States or of a state or its applicability to any government, agency, person, or circumstance is held invalid, the validity of the remainder of this compact and its applicability to any government, agency, person, or circumstance must not be affected. If this compact is held contrary to the Constitution of a participating state, the compact shall remain in full force and effect upon the remaining party state and in full force and effect upon the state affected as to all severable matters.

HISTORY: 1995 Act No. 113, Section 2.

ARTICLE 9

Lieutenant Governor

SECTION 1-3-610. Compensation.

The Lieutenant Governor shall receive such annual salary as may be provided by the General Assembly.

HISTORY: 1962 Code Section 1-131; 1952 Code Section 1-131; 1942 Code Section 3100; 1932 Code Section 3100; Civ. C. '22 Section 782; Civ. C. '12 Section 698; Civ. C. '02 Section 627; G. S. 481; R. S. 544; 1865 (13) 350; 1868 (14) 135; 1871 (15) 531; 1878 (16) 246; 1893 (21) 416; 1919 (31) 4; 1924 (33)

1182; 1966 (54) 2424; Const. 1895, Art. 3 Sections 2, 5-9, 13, 20; 1969 (56) 444; 1973 (58) 623.

SECTION 1-3-620. Office of Lieutenant Governor to be part-time.

Beginning with the term of the Lieutenant Governor elected in 1982, the duties of such office shall be part-time.

HISTORY: 1981 Act No. 178, Part II, Section 22.

CHAPTER 5

Secretary of State

SECTION 1-5-10. Compensation.

The Secretary of State shall receive such annual salary as may be provided by the General Assembly, and the fees or perquisites of the office shall be paid into the Treasury of the State.

HISTORY: 1962 Code Section 1-201; 1952 Code Section 1-201; 1942 Code Section 3101; 1932 Code Section 3101; Civ. C. '22 Section 783; Civ. C. '12 Section 699; G. S. 483, 484; R. S. 546, 547; 1786 (4) 751; 1865 (13) 350; 1924 (33) 1182; 1948 (45) 1716; 1954 (48) 1566; 1957 (50) 404; 1969 (56) 444; 1973 (58) 623.

SECTION 1-5-20. Bond.

The Secretary of State, before entering upon the duties of his office, shall execute a bond with two or more good sureties in the penal sum of ten thousand dollars for the faithful discharge of the duties of his office.

HISTORY: 1962 Code Section 1-202; 1952 Code Section 1-202; 1942 Code Section 3101; 1932 Code Section 3101; Civ. C. '22 Section 783; Civ. C. '12 Section 699; G. S. 483, 484; R. S. 546, 547; 1786 (4) 751; 1865 (13) 350; 1924 (33) 1182.

SECTION 1-5-30. Responsibility for executive records and papers.

The Secretary of State shall, during the absence of the Governor from Columbia, be placed in charge of the records and papers in the executive chamber. He shall keep in Columbia all the books, records and papers belonging thereto.

HISTORY: 1962 Code Section 1-204; 1952 Code Section 1-204; 1942 Code Section 3101; 1932 Code Section 3101; Civ. C. '22 Section 783; Civ. C. '12 Section 699; G. S. 483, 484; R. S. 546, 547; 1786 (4) 751; 1865 (13) 350; 1924 (33) 1182.

SECTION 1-5-40. Duty to monitor state boards and commissions; certification of dates of terms of office.

(A) The office of Secretary of State is designated as the state office whose responsibility it is to monitor positions on the state boards and commissions specified in this subsection and any elected or appointed state boards and commissions established after the effective date of this section. The dates of the terms of office for appointments to boards and commissions made with the advice and consent of the Senate are the dates as certified to the Secretary of State by the Senate. The dates of the terms of office for all other elected or appointed boards and commissions are the dates certified to the Secretary of State by the Governor for his direct appointments and the dates for the terms of office for members of boards and commissions elected by the General Assembly shall be the dates as certified to the Secretary of State by the clerks of the two houses. The specified boards and commissions referred to in this subsection are:

(1) Accountancy, Board of

(2) Aging, Division on Advisory Council

(3) Agriculture Commission

(4) Architectural Examiners, State Board of

(5) Arts Commission

(6) Athletic Commission

(7) Auctioneer's Commission

(8) Accessibility Committee for the Building Codes Council

(9) Blind, Commission for the

(10) Builders Commission, Residential

(11) Building Code Council

(12) College of Charleston Board of Trustees

(13) Children's Trust Fund Board of Trustees

(14) Children, Foster Care Review Board

(15) Chiropractic Examiners, State Board of

(16) The Citadel Board of Visitors

(17) Clemson University Board of Trustees

(18) Coastal Carolina University Board of Trustees

(19) Consumer Affairs, Commission on

(20) Contractors' Licensing Board

(21) Cosmetology, State Board of

(22) Professional Counselors, Associate Counselors and Marital and Family Therapists, State Board of Examiners

(23) Deaf and Blind, School for the

(24) Dentistry Board

(25) Disabilities and Special Needs Commission

(26) Education, State Board of

(27) Education Board, Southern Regional

(28) Education Council

(29) Educational Television Commission

(30) Election Commission

(31) Department of Employment and Workforce

(32) Registration for Professional Engineers and Land Surveyors

(33) Environmental Certification Board

(34) Ethics Commission

(35) Financial Institutions, Board of

(36) Fisheries Commission, Atlantic States Marine

(37) Office of General Services, State Fleet Management

(38) Forestry Commission

(39) Francis Marion University Board of Trustees

(40) Funeral Service Board

(41) Geologists, Board of Registration for

(42) Governor's Mansion and Lace House Commission

(43) DHEC

(a) Board of Health and Environmental Control

(b) Office of Ocean and Coastal Resource Management Board

(44) Higher Education Commission

(45) Holocaust, Council on the

(46) Housing, Finance and Development Authority

(47) Human Affairs Commission

(48) Indigent Defense, Commission on

(49) Intergovernmental Relations, Advisory Commission on

(50) Jobs and Economic Development Authority

(51) John de la Howe School

(52) Judicial Merit Selection Commission

(53) Juvenile Justice, Dept. of, Board of Juvenile Parole

(54) Lander University Board of Trustees

(55) Law Examiners Board

(56) Legislative Audit Council

(57) Library Board

(58) Liquefied Petroleum Gas Board

(59) Long Term Health Care Administrators, Board of

(60) Manufactured Housing Board

(61) Maternal, Infant and Child Health, Council on

(62) Medical Examiners, Board of

(63) Medical University of South Carolina Board of Trustees

(64) Mental Health, State Department of, Commission

(65) Migrant Farm Workers Commission

(66) Mining Council

(67) Minority Affairs, Commission for

(68) Museum Commission

(69) Natural Resources, Department of

(a) Natural Resources Board

(b) Heritage Trust Advisory Board

(70) Nuclear Advisory Council

(71) Nursing, Board of

(72) Occupational Health and Safety Review Board

(73) Occupational Therapy, Board of

(74) Old Exchange Building Commission

(75) Opportunity School, Wil Lou Gray Board of Trustees

(76) Opticianry, Board of Examiners in

(77) Optometry, Board of Examiners in

(78) Patriots Point Development Authority

(79) Pharmacy, Board of

(80) Physical Therapy Examiners, State Board of

(81) Podiatry Examiners, Board of

(82) Ports Authority Board

(83) Prisoner of War Commission

(84) Probation, Parole and Pardon Services, Board of

(85) Prosecution Coordination, Commission on

(86) Psychology, Board of Examiners in

(87) Public Service Authority, Board of Directors

(88) Public Service Commission

(89) Pyrotechnic Safety, Board of

(90) Radiation Control Technical Advisory Council

(91) Real Estate Commission

(92) Real Estate Appraisers Board

(93) Reorganization Commission

(94) Salary, Executive and Performance Evaluation Commission

(95) Social Work Examiners, Board of

(96) South Carolina State University Board of Trustees

(97) Speech-Language Pathology and Audiology, Board of Examiners

(98) Tax Board of Review

(99) Technical and Comprehensive Education, Board for

(100) Transportation Department Commission

(101) University of South Carolina Board of Trustees

(102) Veterinary Medical Examiners, Board of

(103) Vocational Rehabilitation, Board of

(104) Winthrop University Board of Trustees

(105) Women, Governor's Office, Commission on

(106) Workers' Compensation Commission

(107) South Carolina First Steps to School Readiness Board of Trustees.

(B) The Secretary must keep in a public record available for inspection an up-to-date compilation of the membership of the boards and commissions listed in subsection (A) and information about the memberships received from state boards and commissions pursuant to Section 1-1-1310 so that members of the General Assembly and interested citizens may be informed of the current composition of these boards and commissions. This compilation must include:

(1) length of term for each office;

(2) the month and year in which terms have expired or will expire;

(3) terms which have expired;

(4) vacancies;

(5) the body or authority which elects or appoints, as appropriate;

(6) any qualifications including, but not limited to, residency requirements or limitations required for a particular vacancy; and

(7) any additional information received from state boards or commissions as required by Section 1-1-1310.

(C) The Secretary must publicize vacancies, expired terms, and those terms expiring within one year on a semiannual basis statewide.

HISTORY: 1998 Act No. 368, Section 1; 2002 Act No. 182, Section 2; 2014 Act No. 287 (H.3428), Section 22, eff June 18, 2014.

Code Commissioner's Note

Pursuant to the directive to the Code Commissioner in 2010 Act No. 146, Section 122, "Department of Employment and Workforce" was substituted for all references to "Employment Security Commission", and "Executive Director of the Department of Employment and Workforce" or "executive director" was substituted for all references to the "Chairman of the Employment Security Commission" or "chairman" that refer to the Chairman of the Employment Security Commission, as appropriate.

Effect of Amendment

2014 Act No. 287, Section 22, added subsection (A)(107), related to the South Carolina First Steps to School Readiness Board of Trustees.

SECTION 1-5-50. Fees for searching or copying records.

The Secretary of State may establish and collect fees, not to exceed the actual cost of searching for or making copies of records. These records must be furnished at the lowest possible cost to the person requesting the records. The agency also may charge a reasonable hourly rate for making records available to the public and require a reasonable deposit of such costs before searching for or making copies of the records. Fees collected pursuant to this section may be retained by the agency and used to defray the expenses associated with purchasing and maintaining computer and telephone facsimile equipment and rent.

HISTORY: 2002 Act No. 356, Section 1, Pt VII.A.

SECTION 1-5-60. Fees associated with collection of dishonored checks.

The Secretary of State may establish, collect, and retain fees to recover the costs associated with the collection of dishonored checks returned to the agency due to insufficient funds. These fees must be retained and expended by the agency to defray collection expenses and any unused amount must be carried forward to the succeeding fiscal year and used for the same purposes.

HISTORY: 2002 Act No. 356, Section 1, Pt VII.B.

Title 1 - Administration of the Government

CHAPTER 6

Office of the State Inspector General

SECTION 1-6-10. Definitions.

As used in this title:

(1) "Agency" means an authority, board, branch, commission, committee, department, division, or other instrumentality of the executive department of

state government, including administrative bodies. "Agency" includes a body corporate and politic established as an instrumentality of the State. "Agency" does not include:

(a) the judicial department of state government;

(b) quasijudicial bodies of state government;

(c) the legislative department of state government; or

(d) political subdivisions.

(2) "Business relationship" means dealings of a person with an agency seeking, obtaining, establishing, maintaining, or implementing:

(a) a pecuniary interest in a contract or purchase with the agency; or

(b) a license or permit requiring the exercise of judgment or discretion by the agency.

(3) "Employee" means an individual who is employed by an agency on a full-time, part-time, temporary, intermittent, or hourly basis. "Employee" includes an individual who contracts with an agency for personal services.

(4) 'Person' means:

(a) an individual, labor union and organization, joint apprenticeship committee, partnership, association, corporation, legal representative, mutual company, joint-stock company, trust, unincorporated organization, trustee, trustee in bankruptcy, receiver, or other legal or commercial entity located in part or in whole in the State or doing business in the State;

(b) the State and any agency or local subdivision of an agency; or

(c) a political subdivision.

(5) "Political subdivision" includes a county, city, municipality, town, village, township, district, authority, special purpose district, school district, other local government entity, or other public corporation or entity whether organized and existing under charter or general law.

(6) "Special state appointee" means a person who is:

(a) not a state officer or employee; and

(b) elected or appointed to an authority, a board, a commission, a committee, a council, a task force, or other body designated by name that:

(i) is authorized by statute or Executive Order; and

(ii) functions in a policy or an advisory role in the executive, including the administrative, department of state government, including a separate body corporate and politic.

(7) "State officer" means any of the following:

(a) the Governor;

(b) the Lieutenant Governor;

(c) the Secretary of State;

(d) the State Comptroller General;

(e) the State Treasurer;

(f) the Attorney General;

(g) the Superintendent of Education;

(h) the Commissioner of Agriculture; or

(i) the Adjutant General.

(8) "Wrongdoing" means action by an agency which results in substantial abuse, misuse, destruction, or loss of substantial public funds or public resources. "Wrongdoing" also includes an allegation that a public employee has intentionally violated federal or state statutory law or regulations or other political subdivision ordinances or regulations or a code of ethics, which violation is not merely technical or of a minimum nature.

HISTORY: 2012 Act No. 105, Section 2, eff January 1, 2012.

SECTION 1-6-20. Office of State Inspector General established; duties; appointment and removal; information and documents.

(A) There is hereby established the Office of the State Inspector General that consists of the State Inspector General, who is the director of the office, and a staff of deputy inspectors general, investigators, auditors, and clerical employees employed by the State Inspector General as necessary to carry out the duties of the State Inspector General and as are authorized by law. The State Inspector General shall fix the salaries of all staff subject to the funds authorized in the annual general appropriation act.

(B) The State Inspector General is responsible for investigating and addressing allegations of fraud, waste, abuse, mismanagement, misconduct, violations of state or federal law, and wrongdoing in agencies.

(C) The Governor shall appoint the State Inspector General with the advice and consent of the Senate for a term of four years. A Governor may reappoint the State Inspector General for additional terms. The State Inspector General's compensation must not be reduced during the State Inspector General's uninterrupted continued tenure in office.

(D) The State Inspector General:

(1) may be removed from office only by the Governor as provided in Section 1-3-240(C);

(2) must be selected without regard to political affiliation and on the basis of integrity, capability for strong leadership, and demonstrated ability in accounting, auditing, financial analysis, law, management analysis, public administration, investigation, or criminal justice administration or other closely related fields;

(3) is entitled to receive compensation set by the Governor and approved by the State Fiscal Accountability Authority.

(E) Upon request of the State Inspector General for information or assistance, all agencies are directed to fully cooperate with and furnish the State Inspector General with all documents, reports, answers, records, accounts, papers, and other necessary data and documentary information to perform the mission of the State Inspector General.

(F) Except for information declared confidential under this chapter, records of the Office of the State Inspector General are subject to public inspection under Chapter 4, Title 30.

HISTORY: 2012 Act No. 105, Section 2, eff January 1, 2012.

Code Commissioner's Note

At the direction of the Code Commissioner, the reference in subsection (F) to "Chapter 4 of this title" was changed to "Chapter 4, Title 30".

At the direction of the Code Commissioner, references in this section to the offices of the former State Budget and Control Board, Office of the Governor, or other agencies, were changed to reflect the transfer of them to the Department of Administration or other entities, pursuant to the directive of the South Carolina Restructuring Act, 2014 Act No. 121, Section 5(D)(1), effective July 1, 2015.

SECTION 1-6-30. Powers of the State Inspector General.

The State Inspector General may:

(1) initiate, supervise, and coordinate investigations authorized by this chapter;

(2) recommend policies and carry out other activities designed to deter, detect, and eradicate fraud, waste, abuse, mismanagement, misconduct, violations of state or federal law, and wrongdoing in state government;

(3) receive complaints alleging a violation of a statute or rule relating to the purchase of goods or services by a current or former employee, state officer, special state appointee, or person who has a business relationship with an agency;

(4) receive complaints from any individual, including those employed by any agency, alleging fraud, waste, abuse, mismanagement, misconduct, violations of state or federal law, and wrongdoing in an agency;

(5) adopt rules and regulations for administering the Office of the State Inspector General;

(6) offer every employee, state officer, special state appointee, and person who has a business relationship with an agency training in the Rules of Conduct pursuant to Article 7, Chapter 13, Title 8 of the South Carolina Code of Laws;

(7) provide advice to an agency on developing, implementing, and enforcing policies and procedures to prevent or reduce the risk of fraudulent or wrongful acts within the agency;

(8) recommend legislation to the Governor and General Assembly to strengthen public integrity laws; and

(9) annually submit a report to the Governor, President Pro Tempore of the Senate, and Speaker of the House of Representatives detailing the State Inspector General's activities.

HISTORY: 2012 Act No. 105, Section 2, eff January 1, 2012.

SECTION 1-6-40. Mandatory reports of misconduct to Governor, agency head, and law enforcement; agency report of disciplinary and preventative action.

(A) If the State Inspector General has reasonable cause to believe that fraud, waste, abuse, mismanagement, misconduct, or wrongdoing has occurred or is occurring, he must report the suspected conduct to:

(1) the Governor; and

(2) the head of the agency affected by the conduct or employing the person allegedly engaged in the suspected conduct.

(B) In addition to the reporting requirements in subsection (A), if the State Inspector General has reasonable cause to believe that a crime has occurred or is occurring, he must report the conduct to the appropriate state or federal law enforcement agencies and prosecuting authorities that have jurisdiction over the matter.

(C) In addition to fully cooperating with the State Inspector General's investigation, the head of the agency employing a person allegedly engaged in the suspected conduct is responsible for submitting a report to the State Inspector General describing any and all actions taken with the employee and within the agency to prevent the alleged conduct from occurring again.

HISTORY: 2012 Act No. 105, Section 2, eff January 1, 2012.

SECTION 1-6-50. Investigatory powers; subpoena; report and advice; civil actions.

The State Inspector General has the following powers:

(A) As part of an investigation, the State Inspector General may:

(1) administer oaths;

(2) examine witnesses under oath;

(3) issue subpoenas and subpoenas duces tecum; and

(4) examine the records, reports, audits, reviews, papers, books, recommendations, contracts, correspondence, or any other documents maintained by an agency.

(B) The State Inspector General may apply to a circuit court for an order holding an individual in contempt of court if the individual refuses to give sworn testimony under a subpoena issued by the State Inspector General or otherwise disobeys a subpoena or subpoena duces tecum issued by the State Inspector General.

(C) For an investigation that results in a report, the State Inspector General must prepare a written report that remains confidential until it is issued as a final report. The State Inspector General is the authority who determines if an investigation requires a report. The State Inspector General, in his discretion, may give an agency advice or recommendations that remain confidential and are not issued as a report.

(D) If the Attorney General has elected not to file a civil action for the recovery of funds misappropriated, diverted, missing, or unlawfully gained, the State Inspector General may file a civil action for the recovery of the funds pursuant to Section 1-6-70 of this chapter.

HISTORY: 2012 Act No. 105, Section 2, eff January 1, 2012.

SECTION 1-6-60. Evidence of ethics violation; complaint.

If the State Inspector General investigates and determines that there is specific and credible evidence that a current or former employee, a current or former state officer, a current or former special state appointee, or a person who has or had a business relationship with an agency has violated the code of ethics, the State Inspector General may file a complaint with the Ethics Commission and represent the State in any proceeding before the Ethics Commission.

HISTORY: 2012 Act No. 105, Section 2, eff January 1, 2012.

SECTION 1-6-70. Evidence of misconduct resulting in financial loss; report to Attorney General; civil actions.

(A) This section applies if the State Inspector General finds evidence of misfeasance, malfeasance, nonfeasance, misappropriation, fraud, or other misconduct that has resulted in a financial loss to the State or in an unlawful benefit to an individual in the conduct of state business.

(B) If the State Inspector General finds evidence described in subsection (A), the State Inspector General shall certify a report of the matter to the Attorney General and provide the Attorney General with any relevant documents, transcripts, written statements, or other evidence. Not later than one hundred eighty days after receipt of the report from the State Inspector General, the Attorney General must do one of the following:

(1) file a civil action, including an action upon a state officer's official bond, to secure for the State the recovery of funds misappropriated, diverted, missing, or unlawfully gained. Upon request of the Attorney General, the State Inspector General shall assist the Attorney General in the investigation, preparation, and prosecution of the civil action;

(2) inform the State Inspector General that the Attorney General does not intend to file a civil action for the recovery of funds misappropriated, diverted, missing, or unlawfully gained. If the Attorney General elects not to file a civil action, the Attorney General must return to the State Inspector General all documents, transcripts, written statements, or other evidence initially provided by the State Inspector General; or

(3) inform the State Inspector General that the Attorney General is diligently reviewing the matter and after further review may file a civil action for the recovery of funds misappropriated, diverted, missing, or unlawfully gained. However, if more than three hundred sixty-five days have passed since the

State Inspector General certified the report to the Attorney General, and the Attorney General has neither filed a civil action nor informed the State Inspector General that he does not intend to file a civil action, the Attorney General loses the authority to file a civil action for the recovery of funds misappropriated, diverted, missing, or unlawfully gained and must return to the State Inspector General all documents, transcripts, written statements, or other evidence provided by the State Inspector General.

(C) The State Inspector General may file a civil action for the recovery of funds misappropriated, diverted, missing, or unlawfully gained if the State Inspector General has found evidence described in subsection (A) and reported to the Attorney General pursuant to subsection (B) and:

(1) the Attorney General has elected pursuant to subsection (B)(2) not to file a civil action for the recovery of funds misappropriated, diverted, missing, or unlawfully gained; or

(2) pursuant to subsection (B)(3), more than three hundred sixty-five days have passed since the State Inspector General certified the report to the Attorney General pursuant to subsection (B), and the Attorney General has not filed a civil action.

(D) If the State Inspector General has found evidence pursuant to subsection (A), the State Inspector General may institute forfeiture proceedings as allowed by law in a court having jurisdiction in a county where property derived from or realized through the misappropriation, diversion, disappearance, or unlawful gain of state funds is located, unless a prosecuting attorney has already instituted forfeiture proceedings against that property.

HISTORY: 2012 Act No. 105, Section 2, eff January 1, 2012.

SECTION 1-6-80. Evidence of criminal activity; certification and information to be provided to prosecuting attorney.

(A) If the State Inspector General discovers evidence of criminal activity, the State Inspector General shall certify to the appropriate prosecuting attorney the following information:

(1) the identity of a person who may be involved in the criminal activity; and

(2) the criminal statute that the State Inspector General believes has been violated.

(B) In addition, the State Inspector General must provide the prosecuting attorney with any relevant documents, transcripts, written statements, or other evidence. If the prosecuting attorney decides to prosecute the crime described in the information certified to the prosecuting attorney, or any other related crimes, the State Inspector General must cooperate with the prosecuting attorney in the investigation and prosecution of the case. Upon request of the prosecuting attorney, the State Inspector General may participate on behalf of the State in a resulting criminal trial.

HISTORY: 2012 Act No. 105, Section 2, eff January 1, 2012.

SECTION 1-6-90. Toll-free public telephone number for receiving information.

The State Inspector General must establish a toll-free public telephone number for the purpose of receiving information concerning fraud, waste, abuse, mismanagement, misconduct, violations of state or federal law, and wrongdoing in an agency. The phone number must be prominently posted by all agencies, in clear view of all employees and the public, and in a conspicuous location on the agency's Internet website.

HISTORY: 2012 Act No. 105, Section 2, eff January 1, 2012.

SECTION 1-6-100. Confidentiality of identity of person reporting information in good faith; public inspection; exception.

(A) If an individual discloses information alleging fraud, waste, abuse, mismanagement, misconduct, violations of state or federal law, and wrongdoing in an agency in good faith to the State Inspector General, the individual's identity is confidential and must not be disclosed to anyone other than the Governor, the staff of the Office of the State Inspector General, or an authority to whom the investigation is subsequently referred or certified, unless:

(1) the State Inspector General makes a written determination that it is in the public interest to disclose the individual's identity; or

(2) the individual consents in writing to disclosure of the individual's identity.

(B) After an investigation is completed and a report is issued pursuant to Section 1-6-50(C), the investigative records of the State Inspector General are subject to public inspection pursuant to Chapter 4 of this title. However, if an individual's identity is confidential pursuant to subsection (A), the individual's identity or any information that reasonably might lead to the discovery of the individual's identity must not be disclosed, except as pursuant to subsection (A) or subsection (E).

(C) This subsection does not apply to a person who is a party to an action brought by the State Inspector General. Information received by the State Inspector General is not required to be produced in the course of discovery, unless ordered by a court after a showing of particularized need and proof that the information requested cannot be obtained from another source.

(D) Except as provided in subsection (E), a person commits the misdemeanor of unlawful disclosure of confidential information if he knowingly or intentionally discloses:

(1) confidential information or records; or

(2) the identity of a person whose identity is confidential under subsection (A).

A person convicted pursuant to this subsection must be fined not more than one thousand dollars or imprisoned not more than one year. If the person convicted is an officer or employee of the State, he must be dismissed from office or employment and is ineligible to hold any public office in this State for a period of five years after the conviction.

(E) A person may disclose confidential information, records, or an individual's identity that is confidential pursuant to subsection (A) if the Governor authorizes the disclosure of this information in the public interest.

HISTORY: 2012 Act No. 105, Section 2, eff January 1, 2012.

CHAPTER 7

Attorney General and Solicitors

ARTICLE 1

Attorney General and Assistants

SECTION 1-7-10. Compensation of Attorney General.

The Attorney General shall receive such annual salary as may be provided by the General Assembly.

HISTORY: 1962 Code Section 1-231; 1952 Code Section 1-231; 1942 Code Section 3112; 1932 Code Section 3112; Civ. C. '22 Section 795; Civ. C. '12 Section 710; Civ. C. '02 Section 638; G. S. 495; R. S. 555; 1877 (16) 247; 1880 (17) 372; 1919 (31) 4; 1924 (33) 1182; 1946 (44) 2596; 1948 (45) 1716; 1954 (48) 1566; 1957 (50) 404; 1969 (56) 444; 1973 (58) 623.

SECTION 1-7-20. Bond of Attorney General.

Before entering upon the duties of his office, the Attorney General shall execute a bond, with two good sureties, to this State in the sum of ten thousand dollars for the faithful discharge of his office.

HISTORY: 1962 Code Section 1-232; 1952 Code Section 1-232; 1942 Code Section 3113; 1932 Code Section 3113; Civ. C. '22 Section 796; Civ. C. '12 Section 711; Civ. C. '02 Section 639; G. S. 496; R. S. 556; 1812 (5) 675.

SECTION 1-7-30. Appointment of Assistant Attorneys General.

The Attorney General shall appoint the Assistant Attorneys General.

HISTORY: 1962 Code Section 1-232.1; 1952 Code Section 1-232.1; 1942 Code Section 3112; 1932 Code Section 3112; Civ. C. '22 Section 795; Civ. C. '12 Section 710; Civ. C. '02 Section 638; G. S. 495; R. S. 555; 1877 (16) 247; 1880 (17) 372; 1919 (31) 4; 1924 (33) 1182.

SECTION 1-7-40. Appearance for State in Supreme Court and other courts and tribunals.

He shall appear for the State in the Supreme Court and the court of appeals in the trial and argument of all causes, criminal and civil, in which the State is a party or interested, and in these causes in any other court or tribunal when required by the Governor or either branch of the General Assembly.

HISTORY: 1962 Code Section 1-233; 1952 Code Section 1-233; 1942 Code Section 3114; 1932 Code Section 3114; Civ. C. '22 Section 797; Civ. C. '12

Section 712; Civ. C. '02 Section 640; G. S. 497; R. S. 557; 1868 (14) 88; 1999 Act No. 55, Section 2.

SECTION 1-7-50. Defense of actions against public officers and employees.

In the event that any officer or employee of the State, or of any political subdivision thereof, be prosecuted in any action, civil or criminal, or special proceeding in the courts of this State, or of the United States, by reason of any act done or omitted in good faith in the course of his employment, it is made the duty of the Attorney General, when requested in writing by any such officer or employee, to appear and defend the action or proceeding in his behalf. Such appearance may be by any member of his staff or by any solicitor or assistant solicitor when directed to do so by the Attorney General.

HISTORY: 1962 Code Section 1-234; 1960 (51) 1627.

SECTION 1-7-55. Counter-claims, cross-actions, or other actions on behalf of public officers and employees.

When the Attorney General undertakes to defend any civil action or proceeding on behalf of any officer or employee of the State, or of any political subdivision of the State, he may, in his discretion, upon the request of the officer or employee, enter and prosecute a counter-claim, cross-action, or any other appropriate action in the suit on behalf of the officer or employee.

HISTORY: 1984 Act No. 305, Section 1.

SECTION 1-7-60. Investigation required prior to defense of actions against public officers and employees; effect of insurance.

Before any such defense, however, is undertaken, an investigation shall be made of the facts on which the action or special proceedings are based and unless, in the opinion of the Attorney General, it appears that the officer or employee was acting in good faith, without malice, and in the course of his employment, the investigation shall proceed no further, nor shall any defense be provided for him by virtue of this section and Section 1-7-50. The investigation herein required to be made may be made by the Attorney General, any member of his staff, or by any solicitor or assistant solicitor when directed to do so by the Attorney General. In the event that it should appear that any such officer or employee is covered by any policy of insurance, under the terms of which the carrier is required to provide counsel, the Attorney General may, in his discretion, make no further investigation and provide no representation for any such party.

HISTORY: 1962 Code Section 1-234.1; 1960 (51) 1627.

SECTION 1-7-70. Information obtained pursuant to Sections 1-7-50 and 1-7-60 shall be confidential and inadmissible as evidence.

Any and all information obtained by virtue of the provisions of Sections 1-7-50 and 1-7-60 shall be considered confidential and shall not be admissible as evidence in any such action or special proceeding, and no reference thereto shall be made in any such trial or hearing.

HISTORY: 1962 Code Section 1-234.2; 1960 (51) 1627.

SECTION 1-7-80. Conditions attached to appropriation for Attorney General for expenses of litigation.

The annual appropriation for the Attorney General for the expenses of litigation is subject to the following conditions:

(1) the Attorney General shall conduct all litigation which may be necessary for any department of the state government or any of the boards connected therewith, and all these boards or departments are forbidden to employ any counsel for any purpose except through the Attorney General and upon his advice;

(2) out of this appropriation the Attorney General shall pay for dockets for the several circuit solicitors and those other expenses as he may deem advisable.

HISTORY: 1962 Code Section 1-235; 1952 Code Section 1-235; 1942 Code Section 3194; 1932 Code Section 3194; Civ. C. '22 Section 890; Civ. C. '12 Section 810; 1909 (26) 281; 1992 Act No. 347, Section 1.

SECTION 1-7-85. Reimbursement of costs in representing State in criminal proceedings and State and its officers and agencies in civil and administrative proceedings.

Notwithstanding any other provision of law, the Office of the Attorney General may obtain reimbursement for its costs in representing the State in criminal proceedings and in representing the State and its officers and agencies in civil and administrative proceedings. These costs may include, but are not limited to, attorney fees or investigative costs or costs of litigation awarded by court order or settlement, travel expenditures, depositions, printing, transcripts, and personnel costs. Reimbursement of these costs may be obtained by the Office of the Attorney General from the budget of an agency or officer that it is representing or from funds generally appropriated for legal expenses, with the approval of the State Budget and Control Board.

HISTORY: 2008 Act No. 353, Section 2, Pt 10C, eff July 1, 2009.

Code Commissioner's Note

At the direction of the Code Commissioner, reference in this section to the former Budget and Control Board has not been changed pursuant to the directive of the South Carolina Restructuring Act, 2014 Act No. 121, Section 5(D)(1), until further action by the General Assembly.

SECTION 1-7-90. Advice to General Assembly and Governor.

The Attorney General shall, when required by either branch of the General Assembly, attend during their sessions and give his aid and advice in the arrangement and preparation of legislative documents and business; and he shall give his opinion upon questions of law submitted to him by either branch thereof, or by the Governor.

HISTORY: 1962 Code Section 1-236; 1952 Code Section 1-236; 1942 Code Section 3119; 1932 Code Section 3116; Civ. C. '22 Section 799; Civ. C. '12 Section 714; Civ. C. '02 Section 642; G. S. 499; R. S. 559; 1868 (14) 88.

SECTION 1-7-100. Advice to solicitors; attendance at grand jury and trials.

The Attorney General shall consult with and advise the solicitors in matters relating to the duties of their offices. When, in his judgment, the interest of the State requires it he shall:

(1) Assist the solicitors by attending the grand jury in the examination of any case in which the party accused is charged with a capital offense; and

(2) Be present at the trial of any cause in which the State is a party or interested and, when so present, shall have the direction and management of such prosecution or suit.

HISTORY: 1962 Code Section 1-237; 1952 Code Section 1-237; 1942 Code Section 3116; 1932 Code Section 3116; Civ. C. '22 Section 799; Civ. C. '12 Section 714; Civ. C. '02 Section 642; G. S. 499; R. S. 559; 1868 (14) 88.

SECTION 1-7-110. Advice to State officers and Public Service Commission.

He shall, when required by the Secretary of State, State Treasurer, Adjutant General, Comptroller General, or any other State officer or the Public Service Commission, consult and advise with them, respectively, on questions of law relating to their official business.

HISTORY: 1962 Section 1-238; 1952 Code Section 1-238; 1942 Code Section 3120; 1932 Code Sections 2127, 3120; Civ. C. '22 Sections 88, 802; Civ. C. '12 Sections 78, 717; Civ. C. '02 Sections 75, 645; G. S. 51, 502; R. S. 72, 562; 1868 (14) 88, 89; 1890 (20) 705.

SECTION 1-7-115. Duties of Division of Securities devolved upon Attorney General.

(A) The duties, functions, and responsibilities of the Division of Securities of the office of the Secretary of State are hereby devolved upon the Attorney General's office on July 1, 1996. All personnel, appropriations, and full-time equivalent positions of the Division of Securities also shall be transferred to the Attorney General's office on July 1, 1996.

(B) The Attorney General shall administer the South Carolina Uniform Securities Act as contained in Chapter 1 of Title 35 of the 1976 Code and shall serve ex officio as the Securities Commissioner.

HISTORY: 1996 Act No. 458, Part II, Section 27A, B.

SECTION 1-7-117. Duties of Division of Public Charities devolved upon Attorney General.

(A) The duties, functions, and responsibilities of the Division of Public Charities of the office of the Secretary of State are devolved upon the Attorney General's office on July 1, 1996. All personnel, appropriations, and full-time equivalent positions of the Division of Public Charities also are transferred to the Attorney General's office on July 1, 1996.

(B) The Attorney General shall administer the "South Carolina Solicitation of Charitable Funds Act" as contained in Chapter 56 of Title 33 of the 1976 Code.

HISTORY: 1996 Act No. 458, Part II, Section 28A, B.

SECTION 1-7-120. Action against intruders on property of State.

The Attorney General when, in his judgment, the interest of the State requires it shall file and prosecute information or other process against persons who intrude upon the lands, rights or property of the State or commit or erect any nuisance thereon.

HISTORY: 1962 Code Section 1-239; 1952 Code Section 1-239; 1942 Code Section 3115; 1932 Code Section 3115; Civ. C. '22 Section 798; Civ. C. '12 Section 713; Civ. C. '02 Section 641; G. S. 498; R. S. 558; 1868 (14) 88.

SECTION 1-7-130. Protection of public charities and prosecution of corporations.

The Attorney General shall enforce the due application of funds given or appropriated to public charities within the State, prevent breaches of trust in the administration thereof and, when necessary, prosecute corporations which fail to make to the General Assembly any report or return required by law.

HISTORY: 1962 Code Section 1-240; 1952 Code Section 1-240; 1942 Code Section 3117; 1932 Code Section 3117; Civ. C. '22 Section 800; Civ. C. '12 Section 715; Civ. C. '02 Section 643; G. S. 500; R. S. 560; 1868 (14) 88; 1950 (46) 2214.

SECTION 1-7-140. Annual report to General Assembly.

The Attorney General shall annually make a report to the General Assembly of:

(1) the cases argued, tried, or conducted by him in the Supreme Court, the court of appeals, and circuit courts during the preceding year; and

(2) other information in relation to the criminal laws and observations and statements as, in his opinion, the proper and efficient administration of the criminal law requires.

HISTORY: 1962 Code Section 1-241; 1952 Code Section 1-241; 1942 Code Section 3121; 1932 Code Section 3121; Civ. C. '22 Section 803; Civ. C. '12 Section 718; Civ. C. '02 Section 646; G. S. 503; R. S. 563; 1868 (14) 89; 1980 Act No. 462, Section 2; 1985 Act No. 97; 1999 Act No. 55, Section 3.

SECTION 1-7-150. Accounting to Treasurer; deposit of funds.

(A) The Attorney General shall account to the State Treasurer for all fees, bills of costs, and monies received by him by virtue of his office.

(B) All monies, except investigative costs or costs of litigation awarded by court order or settlement, awarded the State of South Carolina by judgment or settlement in actions or claims brought by the Attorney General on behalf of the State or one of its agencies or departments must be deposited in the general fund of the State, except for monies recovered for losses or damages to natural resources, which must be deposited in the Mitigation Trust Fund, or where some other disposition is required by law.

HISTORY: 1962 Code Section 1-242; 1952 Code Section 1-242; 1942 Code Section 3124; 1932 Code Section 3124; Civ. C. '22 Section 806; Civ. C. '12 Section 721; Civ. C. '02 Section 649; G. S. 506; R. S. 566; 1868 (14) 89; 1998 Act No. 419, Section PT. 2, Section 18.

SECTION 1-7-160. Hiring of attorneys.

A department or agency of state government may not hire a classified or temporary attorney as an employee except upon the written approval of the Attorney General and at compensation approved by him. All of these attorneys at all times are under the supervision and control of the Attorney General except as otherwise provided by law unless prior approval by the State Budget and Control Board is obtained. This section does not apply to an attorney hired by the General Assembly or the Judicial department.

HISTORY: 2008 Act No. 353, Section 2, Pt 10A, eff July 1, 2009.

Code Commissioner's Note

At the direction of the Code Commissioner, reference in this section to the former Budget and Control Board has not been changed pursuant to the directive of the South Carolina Restructuring Act, 2014 Act No. 121, Section 5(D)(1), until further action by the General Assembly.

SECTION 1-7-170. Engaging attorney on fee basis.

(A) A department or agency of state government may not engage on a fee basis an attorney at law except upon the written approval of the Attorney General and upon a fee as must be approved by him. This section does not apply to the employment of attorneys in special cases in inferior courts when the fee to be paid does not exceed two hundred fifty dollars or exceptions approved by the State Budget and Control Board. This section does not apply to an attorney hired by the General Assembly or the judicial department.

(B) A public institution of higher learning shall engage and compensate outside counsel in accordance with policies and procedures adopted by the State Fiscal Accountability Authority for matters of bonded indebtedness, public finance, borrowing, and related financial matters.

HISTORY: 2008 Act No. 353, Section 2, Pt 10B, eff July 1, 2009; 2011 Act No. 74, Pt VI, Section 9, eff August 1, 2011.

Code Commissioner's Note

At the direction of the Code Commissioner, reference in (A) to the former Budget and Control Board has not been changed pursuant to the directive of the South Carolina Restructuring Act, 2014 Act No. 121, Section 5(D)(1), until further action by the General Assembly. Reference in (B) to the former Budget and Control Board was changed to the State Fiscal Accountability Authority pursuant to the directive of the South Carolina Restructuring Act, 2014 Act No. 121, Section 5(D)(1).

Effect of Amendment

The 2011 amendment inserted subsection identifier (A) in the first paragraph and added subsection (B) relating to outside counsel.

ARTICLE 3

Solicitors, Assistants, and Investigators

SECTION 1-7-310. Number, election and terms of solicitors.

There is one solicitor for each judicial circuit, to be elected by the qualified electors of the circuit, who holds his office for the term of four years. The term of office of a solicitor begins at noon on the first Wednesday following the second Tuesday in January following his election and ends at noon on the first Wednesday following the second Tuesday in January four years later. A solicitor must be licensed to practice law by the South Carolina Bar at the time of his election and throughout his term.

HISTORY: 1962 Code Section 1-250; 1973 (58) 47; 1998 Act No. 359, Section 6; 2005 Act No. 20, Section 1, eff March 22, 2005.

Effect of Amendment

The 2005 amendment added the second sentence setting forth the beginning and ending of the solicitor's term.

SECTION 1-7-320. Solicitors shall perform duties of Attorney General and assist in prosecutions.

Solicitors shall perform the duty of the Attorney General and give their counsel and advice to the Governor and other State officers, in matters of public concern, whenever they shall be, by them, required to do so; and they shall assist the Attorney General, or each other, in all suits of prosecution in behalf of this State when directed so to do by the Governor or called upon by the Attorney General.

HISTORY: 1962 Code Section 1-251; 1952 Code Section 1-251; 1942 Code Section 3126; 1932 Code Section 3126; Civ. C. '22 Section 808; Civ. C. '12 Section 723; 1877 (16) 246; 1893 (21) 417; 1906 (25) 120; 1919 (31) 101.

SECTION 1-7-325. Solicitors to be full-time state employees; compensation; secretary.

The solicitors of this state shall be full-time employees of the State of South Carolina, provided, however, that any solicitor serving in office on July 1, 1976, whose term of office expires in the year 1979 shall not be required to be full time as provided by this section until the expiration of his term in 1979. Each solicitor shall receive an annual salary and a monthly expense allowance as is provided by the General Assembly.

When a solicitor is required to serve out of his circuit, he shall also receive such subsistence and mileage as is authorized by law for circuit judges while holding court without the county in which they reside. Each solicitor shall have one full-time secretary who shall receive such annual salary as may be provided by the General Assembly.

HISTORY: 1976 Act No. 690 Art. IX, Section 1; 1977 Act No. 119.

SECTION 1-7-330. Attendance at circuit courts; preparation and publication of docket.

The solicitors shall attend the courts of general sessions for their respective circuits. Preparation of the dockets for general sessions courts shall be exclusively vested in the circuit solicitor and the solicitor shall determine the order in which cases on the docket are called for trial. Provided, however, that no later than seven days prior to the beginning of each term of general sessions court, the solicitor in each circuit shall prepare and publish a docket setting forth the cases to be called for trial during the term.

HISTORY: 1962 Code Section 1-252; 1952 Code Section 1-252; 1942 Code Section 3132; 1932 Code Section 3132; Civ. C. '22 Section 814; Civ. C. '12 Section 729; Civ. C. '02 Section 655; G. S. 510; R. S. 572; 1842 (11) 222; Const. 1895, Art. 5, Section 29; 1972 (57) 2477; 1980 Act No. 462, Section 3.

For validity of this section, see State v. Langford, 400 S.C. 421, 735 S.E.2d 471 (S.C. 2012).

SECTION 1-7-340. Attendance at inquests and preliminary hearings in capital cases.

The several solicitors of the State shall attend all inquests and preliminary hearings in capital cases when requested by the coroner or the sheriff.

HISTORY: 1962 Code Section 1-252.1; 1954 (48) 1566.

SECTION 1-7-350. Representation of State institutions, departments and agencies; assignment to criminal matters outside circuit.

The several solicitors of the State shall, within their respective circuits, in cooperation with, and as assigned by the Attorney General, represent in all matters, both civil and criminal, all institutions, departments, and agencies of the

State. Likewise in criminal matters outside their circuits, and in extradition proceedings in other states, they shall be subject to the call of the Attorney General, who shall have the exclusive right, in his discretion, to so assign them in case of the incapacity of the local solicitor or otherwise.

HISTORY: 1962 Code Section 1-252.2; 1954 (48) 1566.

SECTION 1-7-360. Compensation of solicitors; disposition of defendants' costs; expenses for services performed outside circuit.

The circuit solicitors of the various judicial circuits of this State shall each receive such annual salary, payable monthly, as may be provided by the General Assembly. Such salaries shall be in lieu of all charges against the State and the counties. All costs from defendants shall be paid over by each solicitor to the county treasurer for the use of the State.

It shall be the duty of the solicitors to perform the services required in Sections 1-7-340 and 1-7-350, and in no instance, civil or criminal, shall they receive for such services any additional compensation, except that they shall be entitled to expense allowance, as provided for State employees and officers, when performing such services outside of their respective circuits.

HISTORY: 1962 Code Section 1-254; 1952 Code Section 1-254; 1942 Code Section 3127; 1932 Code Section 3127; Civ. C. '22 Section 809; Civ. C. '12 Section 724; 1877 (16) 246; 1893 (21) 417; 1906 (25) 120; 1919 (31) 101; 1954 (48) 1566.

SECTION 1-7-370. When solicitors may defend accused persons.

The solicitors may defend any persons brought to trial before any criminal courts of this State when their duty shall not require them to prosecute such persons and their assistance shall not be required against such persons by the Governor or Attorney General.

HISTORY: 1962 Code Section 1-255; 1952 Code Section 1-255; 1942 Code Section 3126; 1932 Code Section 3126; Civ. C. '22 Section 808; Civ. C. '12 Section 723; 1877 (16) 246; 1893 (21) 417; 1906 (25) 120; 1919 (31) 101.

SECTION 1-7-380. Litigation against the State prohibited.

The several solicitors of the State shall not engage in litigation against the State or any of its departments.

HISTORY: 1962 Code Section 1-255.1; 1954 (48) 1566.

SECTION 1-7-390. Vacancies.

In case any circuit solicitor shall cease to reside in his circuit, his office shall become vacant. In case any vacancy shall occur in such office by death, resignation or otherwise, the vacancy thereby created shall be filled by the Governor, by and with the advice and consent of the Senate. The judge residing in the circuit of the solicitor, whose office shall thus become vacant, shall certify such vacancy to the Governor.

HISTORY: 1962 Code Section 1-256; 1952 Code Section 1-256; 1942 Code Section 3125; 1932 Code Section 3125; Civ. C. '22 Section 807; Civ. C. '12 Section 722; Civ. C. '02 Section 650; G. S. 515; R. S. 567; 1812 (5) 675; 1876 (16) 152; 1936 (39) 1456.

SECTION 1-7-396. Full-time solicitor's investigator to have police power.

Any investigator employed by a solicitor who is required to devote full time to his duties and receives compensation on a full-time basis shall be granted the police powers that are granted to a deputy sheriff. The investigator shall exercise his authority within the jurisdictional territory of the solicitor. Investigators who qualify to be granted police power shall be required to post bond and take the oath as required of constables.

HISTORY: 1979 Act No. 170, Section 1.

SECTION 1-7-400. Circuit solicitors disabled by intoxication.

Any circuit solicitor who shall, while in the public discharge of the duties of his office, be drunk or intoxicated or in any extent disabled by reason of the use of intoxicating liquors from the proper discharge of his duties shall be guilty of a misdemeanor and upon conviction thereof shall be punished by a fine of not less than one hundred nor more than one thousand dollars and imprisoned not less than one month nor more than one year, in the discretion of the court, and shall be dismissed from his office. And whenever it shall be brought to the attention of the Attorney General that any circuit solicitor has been charged with an offense mentioned in this section, he shall prepare a bill of indictment against such officer and prosecute it in the county where the offense was committed. And if such officer is duly convicted, the Attorney General shall cause to be forwarded to the Governor of the State a record of such conviction, upon the receipt of which the Governor shall forthwith declare the office to be vacant and order an election to fill it.

HISTORY: 1962 Code Section 1-257; 1952 Code Section 1-257; 1942 Code Section 1529; 1932 Code Section 1529; Cr. C. '22 Section 476; Cr. C. '12 Section 550; Cr. C. '02 Section 393; G. S. 2560; R. S. 310; 1873 (15) 486.

SECTION 1-7-405. Appointment of assistant solicitors, investigators and secretaries.

Each solicitor may appoint as many assistant solicitors, investigators and secretaries as he deems necessary and whose salaries are provided by the counties of the circuit in which they serve. They shall serve at the pleasure of the solicitor and shall have such responsibilities as he directs.

HISTORY: 1976 Act No. 690, Art. IX, Section 2; 1977 Act No. 119, Section 1.

SECTION 1-7-406. Full-time assistant solicitor and investigator for each judicial circuit.

Notwithstanding any other provision of law, each judicial circuit of this State, in addition to its other assistant solicitors, shall have one assistant solicitor and one investigator who shall be full-time employees. Such assistant solicitor and investigator for each circuit shall be appointed by the solicitor of that circuit, shall serve at his pleasure and shall have such responsibilities as the solicitor directs. The compensation of each such assistant solicitor and investigator or such other staff as may be designated by each solicitor for his circuit and related employment expenses shall be as provided by the General Assembly in the annual general appropriations act. Nothing contained herein shall prohibit the funds so provided for such staff to be designated by the solicitor as being utilized with local and federal funds.

HISTORY: 1979 Act No. 191, Section 1.

SECTION 1-7-407. Receipt and disbursement of funds for employment of assistant solicitor and investigator.

Each solicitor shall enter into an agreement with a county within his circuit to administer the funds so provided and the funds shall be directed to the administering county. The administering county shall account for the receipt and disbursement of the funds separately from any other funds administered by the county.

The solicitors may expend the funds for the employment of additional assistant solicitors, investigators and payment of expenses related to employment of such additional personnel, including fringe benefits and travel.

Personnel employed under the provisions of Sections 1-7-406 through 1-7-407. shall be employees of the administering county but all personnel costs, including fringe benefits, shall be paid by the administering county from funds provided under provisions of Sections 1-7-406 through 1-7-407.

HISTORY: 1979 Act No. 191, Section 2.

SECTION 1-7-408. Repealed by 2005 Act No. 164, Section 37, eff June 10, 2005.

Editor's Note

Former Section 1-7-408 was entitled "Report of expenditures" and was derived from 1979 Act No. 191, Section 3.

SECTION 1-7-410. Additional duties of solicitor for fourteenth judicial circuit.

The circuit solicitor of the fourteenth judicial circuit shall advise with and aid the grand jury of Colleton County in its duties and the coroner or magistrate of Colleton County in inquisitions.

HISTORY: 1962 Code Section 1-257.1; 1959 (51) 81.

SECTION 1-7-420. Assistant solicitor for first judicial circuit.

The solicitor of the first judicial circuit may, upon the approval of a majority of the Dorchester County legislative delegation, appoint an attorney who is a resident of Dorchester County as his assistant who shall perform any of the duties and functions imposed by law upon the circuit solicitor relating to Dorchester County. The term of the assistant solicitor shall be coterminous with that of the solicitor and he shall receive such compensation as may be provided by law. The compensation of the assistant solicitor and any other expenses incurred pursuant to the provisions of this section shall be borne by Dorchester County.

In Dorchester County, appointments made pursuant to this section are governed by the provisions of Act 512 of 1996.

HISTORY: 1962 Code Section 1-257.1:1; 1970 (56) 2073.

SECTION 1-7-430. Additional assistant solicitor for first judicial circuit.

The solicitor of the first judicial circuit may appoint an assistant solicitor, who shall be a licensed attorney-at-law residing in the circuit, to serve at the pleasure of the solicitor and have such responsibility as the solicitor shall direct. The salary to be paid such assistant solicitor shall be paid from funds provided by Public Law 90-351, The Omnibus Crime Control and Safe Streets Act of 1968, as amended.

HISTORY: 1962 Code Section 1-257.1:2; 1974 (58) 2989.

SECTION 1-7-440. Assistant solicitor for third judicial circuit.

The solicitor of the third judicial circuit may appoint an assistant solicitor, who shall be a licensed attorney at law residing in the circuit, to serve at the pleasure of the solicitor and have such responsibility as the solicitor shall direct. The solicitor shall also determine the salary to be paid such assistant solicitor and such salary shall be paid from funds provided by Public Law 90-351, The Omnibus Crime Control and Safe Streets Act of 1968, as amended.

HISTORY: 1962 Code Section 1-257.1:3; 1971 (57) 24.

SECTION 1-7-450. Assistant solicitor for fourth judicial circuit.

The solicitor of the fourth judicial circuit may appoint an attorney, who is a resident of the circuit, as an assistant solicitor, who shall perform such duties and functions as may be assigned him by the solicitor. His term shall be coterminous with that of the solicitor and he shall receive as compensation for his services such salary as may provided by the General Assembly, one fourth of which shall be paid by each county of the circuit.

HISTORY: 1962 Code Section 1-257.2; 1966 (54) 2014.

SECTION 1-7-460. Assistant solicitors for fifth judicial circuit.

The circuit solicitor of the fifth judicial circuit may appoint competent attorneys, who are residents of the circuit, as assistant solicitors who shall perform any and all of the duties and functions imposed by law upon the circuit solicitor as the solicitor shall authorize, designate and direct. The solicitor shall designate in which county of the circuit such assistant solicitors shall perform their duties. The assistant solicitors shall be appointed by the solicitor to serve for the same term as the solicitor. The assistant solicitors performing services in Kershaw County shall receive as compensation for their services such annual salary as may be provided by the Kershaw County Council and the assistant solicitors performing services in Richland County shall receive as compensation for their services such annual salary as may be provided by the Richland County Council.

HISTORY: 1962 Code Section 1-258; 1959 (48) 139; 1975 (59) 819.

SECTION 1-7-470. Assistant solicitor for seventh judicial circuit.

The circuit solicitor of the seventh judicial circuit may appoint a competent attorney, who is a resident of Spartanburg County, as assistant solicitor. He shall perform any and all of the duties and functions now or hereafter imposed by law upon the circuit solicitor in Spartanburg County, as the solicitor of the circuit shall authorize, designate and direct. The assistant solicitor shall be appointed by the solicitor of the seventh judicial circuit and shall after appointment be commissioned by the Governor; provided, however, the solicitor of the seventh judicial circuit shall have the right to remove the assistant solicitor from office at his pleasure, and in no event can the assistant solicitor be appointed for a period beyond the term of office of the circuit solicitor. The assistant solicitor shall receive from Spartanburg County as compensation for his services such sum per year as may be provided by the General Assembly, payable the first and fifteenth of each month, and eight hundred dollars per year for travel.

The assistant solicitor shall appear and represent the State in magistrates' courts when requested by the sheriff's department or the highway patrol located in Spartanburg County. He shall further prosecute appeals from magistrates' courts in that county.

HISTORY: 1962 Code Section 1-260; 1953 (48) 401.

SECTION 1-7-480. Assistant solicitor for eighth judicial circuit.

There is hereby created the office of assistant solicitor for the eighth judicial circuit, the qualifications for which shall be the same as those of a solicitor. The assistant solicitor shall be appointed by and serve at the pleasure of the circuit solicitor and shall perform such duties as may be assigned to him by the solicitor.

The assistant solicitor shall receive an annual salary equal to one half of that received by the solicitor. He shall also receive the same amount for expenses as received by the solicitor. Each county in the circuit shall pay its pro rata share of such salary and expense allowance based upon population according to the latest official United States census. Such amounts shall be paid monthly in equal payments by the treasurer of each county in the circuit from the general fund of the county.

HISTORY: 1962 Code Section 1-260.01; 1970 (56) 2276.

SECTION 1-7-490. Assistant solicitors for ninth judicial circuit.

The Circuit Solicitor for the Ninth Judicial Circuit may appoint seven competent attorneys, each of whom are residents of the circuit, as his assistants who shall perform any and all of the duties and functions now or hereafter imposed by law upon the circuit solicitor as the solicitor of the circuit shall authorize, designate and direct. The assistant circuit solicitors shall be designated in their appointment as first, second, third, fourth, fifth and sixth assistants for Charleston County and assistant circuit solicitor for Berkeley County. The first and second assistants shall enter upon their duties upon the approval of the majority of the Charleston County Legislative Delegation. The first assistant shall receive such compensation for his services as may be provided by law and the second assistant such compensation as may be provided by law to be paid by the County of Charleston. The third assistant shall receive such compensation for his services as may be provided by law, such compensation to be paid from federal funds or from funds appropriated by the Governing Body of Charleston County. The fourth assistant shall devote full time to his duties as assistant solicitor and shall receive such compensation for his services as may be provided by law to be paid from funds appropriated by the Governing Body of Charleston County. The fifth assistant shall receive such compensation for his services as may be provided by law to be paid from funds appropriated by the Governing Body of Charleston County. The sixth assistant shall devote full time to his duties as assistant solicitor and shall receive such compensation for his services as may be provided by law to be paid from funds appropriated by the Governing Body of Charleston County or from federal funds made available to the Governing Body of Charleston County for such purpose. The assistant circuit solicitor for Berkeley County shall enter upon his duties upon the approval of the majority of the Berkeley County Legislative Delegation and shall receive such compensation for his services as may be provided by law to be paid by the County of Berkeley.

HISTORY: 1962 Code Section 1-260.1; 1952 (47) 2076; 1966 (54) 2154; 1969 (56) 2; 1975 (59) 74; 1975 (59) 574; 1976 Act No. 480, Section 1; 1976 Act No. 660, Section 1.

SECTION 1-7-500. Assistant solicitor for tenth judicial circuit.

The solicitor of the tenth judicial circuit may employ a lawyer residing in his circuit to assist in performing the duties of his office. The term of office shall be at the pleasure of the solicitor; however, such term shall not extend beyond the term of office of the employing solicitor; provided, that the person named by the solicitor shall be confirmed by a majority of the members of the Anderson and Oconee delegations.

The salary for the person provided by this section shall be such sum annually as may be provided by the General Assembly, to be paid as follows: Seventy per cent shall be paid by Anderson County and thirty per cent shall be paid by Oconee County and such sum shall be paid by the two counties in the same manner that county officers are paid by such counties. The assistant solicitor may receive from time to time such further compensation as the General Assembly may provide.

HISTORY: 1962 Code Section 1-260.2; 1957 (50) 325.

SECTION 1-7-510. Assistant solicitor for thirteenth judicial circuit.

The solicitor of the thirteenth judicial circuit may appoint an attorney who is a resident of Greenville County as his full-time assistant who shall perform any of the duties and functions imposed by law upon the circuit solicitor relating to Greenville County. The term of the assistant solicitor shall be coterminous with that of the solicitor and he shall receive such compensation as may be provided by the county council for Greenville County. The compensation of the assistant solicitor and any other expenses incurred pursuant to the provisions of this section shall be borne by Greenville County.

HISTORY: 1962 Code Section 1-260.6; 1973 (58) 219.

SECTION 1-7-520. Assistant solicitor for fourteenth judicial circuit.

There is hereby created the office of assistant solicitor for the fourteenth circuit, the qualifications for which shall be the same as those of a solicitor. The assistant solicitor shall be appointed by and serve at the pleasure of the circuit solicitor and shall perform such duties as may be assigned to him by the solicitor.

The assistant solicitor shall receive an annual salary equal to one half of that received by the solicitor. He shall also receive the same amount for expenses as received by the solicitor. Each county in the circuit shall pay its pro rata share of such salary and expense allowance based upon population according to the latest official United States census. Such amounts shall be paid monthly in equal payments by the treasurer of each county in the circuit from the general fund of the county.

HISTORY: 1962 Code Section 1-260.7; 1969 (56) 716.

SECTION 1-7-530. Assistant solicitor for sixteenth judicial circuit.

The solicitor of the sixteenth judicial circuit may appoint an attorney who is a resident of the circuit as an assistant solicitor who shall perform such duties and functions as may be assigned to him by the solicitor. The term of office shall be for a period of one year and the assistant solicitor shall receive for his services such compensation as is provided for in the appropriations acts of Union and York Counties.

HISTORY: 1962 Code Section 1-260.9; 1971 (57) 26.

SECTION 1-7-533. Special investigator for third judicial circuit.

The solicitor of the third judicial circuit may appoint a special investigator to serve at the pleasure of the solicitor and have such responsibility as the solicitor shall direct. The solicitor shall determine the salary to be paid the investigator which shall be paid from such funds as may be provided by law. The investigator, while engaged in official duties of his office, is authorized to carry a pistol or other handgun. He shall give a bond in the sum of two thousand dollars which shall be in the same form and under the same conditions as required for police officers. He shall be commissioned by the Governor and shall have all the powers and duties provided for constables in Section 23-1-60, Code of Laws of South Carolina, 1976, and shall be a "police officer" as defined in Section 9-11-10.

HISTORY: 1976 Act No. 491, Section 1.

SECTION 1-7-540. Special investigator and assistant special investigator for ninth judicial circuit.

The circuit solicitor for the ninth judicial circuit may appoint two competent residents of the circuit who shall be designated as special investigator and assistant special investigator for his office. The special investigator and assistant special investigator shall work under the direction of the solicitor as full-time employees. Their appointment shall be for a period not exceeding the term for which the solicitor was elected. The special investigator and assistant special investigator shall each give a bond in the sum of two thousand dollars, which shall be in the same form and provide the same conditions as required by law of peace officers. The special investigator and assistant special investigator shall be commissioned by the Governor and shall have all the powers, rights and duties, within the ninth judicial circuit, as any State constable, as provided in Section 23-1-60. The special investigator and assistant special investigator shall be "police officers," as defined in Section 9-11-10. The special investigator shall receive such salary as may be provided by law, and an expense allowance of not less than fifteen hundred dollars, such sums to be paid by the Governing Body of Charleston County. The assistant special investigator shall receive such compensation for his services as may be provided by law, such compensation to be paid from federal funds or from funds appropriated by the Governing Body of Charleston County.

HISTORY: 1962 Code Section 1-260.3; 1966 (54) 2155; 1969 (56) 656; 1975 (59) 74.

ARTICLE 5

Provisions Affecting Attorney General and Solicitors

SECTION 1-7-710. Defense of persons claiming under State.

In all cases wherein the right of the State may be involved, the persons claiming under the State shall call on the Attorney General, or on the solicitors in their respective districts, to defend the right of the State; on failure whereof, the record of such case shall not be adduced as evidence to substantiate any claim against the State.

HISTORY: 1962 Code Section 1-261; 1952 Code Section 1-261; 1942 Code Section 3129; 1932 Code Section 3129; Civ. C. '22 Section 811; Civ. C. '12 Section 726; Civ. C. '02 Section 652; G. S. 507; R. S. 569; 1808 (5) 571.

SECTION 1-7-720. Suits for penalties.

The Attorney General and solicitors shall sue for the penalties incurred by any public officer or board of public officers.

HISTORY: 1962 Code Section 1-262; 1952 Code Section 1-262; 1942 Code Section 3130; 1932 Code Section 3130; Civ. C. '22 Section 812; Civ. C. '12 Section 727; Civ. C. '02 Section 653; G. S. 508; R. S. 570; 1813 (5) 709; 1814 (5) 733; 1815 (6) 9; 1844 (11) 295.

SECTION 1-7-730. Examination of offices of county officers.

The Attorney General and solicitors shall annually, at such times as they may deem expedient, examine into the condition of the offices of the clerk of the court of common pleas and general sessions, of the sheriff and of the register of deeds in the counties of the respective solicitors and ascertain if such officers have discharged the duties which now are, or shall be, required of them; and they shall make a report of the condition of said offices and of the manner in which said officers have discharged their duties to the circuit court in each county, respectively, at the fall term in each year, and also to the General Assembly at its annual session.

HISTORY: 1962 Code Section 1-263; 1952 Code Section 1-263; 1942 Code Section 3131; 1932 Code Section 3131; Civ. C. '22 Section 813; Civ. C. '12 Section 728; Civ. C. '02 Section 654; G. S. 509; R. S. 571; 1837 (6) 577; 1997 Act No. 34, Section 1.

SECTION 1-7-740. Legal assistance to Dairy Board.

Whenever legal assistance is needed by the State Dairy Board it must be furnished by the Attorney General's Office.

HISTORY: 1984 Act No. 370, Section 2.

SECTION 1-7-750. Circuit solicitors authorized to employ outside counsel.

A circuit solicitor may employ outside counsel, in his discretion, without approval of the Attorney General, for civil forfeiture proceedings arising from criminal activity or from estreatment of bail bonds. In any other matter, the circuit solicitor must obtain written approval of the Attorney General prior to retaining counsel to or filing a civil cause of action.

HISTORY: 2011 Act No. 52, Section 3, eff January 1, 2012.

Editor's Note

2011 Act No. 52, Section 7, provides as follows:

"SECTION 7. This act takes effect January 1, 2012, and applies to all actions that accrue on or after the effective date except the provisions of SECTION 3 do not apply to any matter pending on the effective date of this act."

ARTICLE 7

Commission on Prosecution Coordination

SECTION 1-7-910. Commission on Prosecution Coordination created.

There is created a commission to coordinate all activities involving the prosecution of criminal cases in this State. The commission is known as the South Carolina Commission on Prosecution Coordination.

HISTORY: 1990 Act No. 485, Section 1.

SECTION 1-7-920. Commission membership.

The commission is composed of the following persons for terms as indicated:

(1) the Chairmen of the Senate and House Judiciary Committees for the terms for which they are elected or their legislative designees;

(2) the Chief of the South Carolina Law Enforcement Division for the term for which he is appointed;

(3) the Director of the Department of Public Safety shall serve during the term for which he is appointed;

(4) a director of a Judicial Circuit Pretrial Intervention Program appointed by the Governor for a term of two years;

(5) a Judicial Circuit Victim-Witness Assistance Advocate appointed by the Governor for a term of two years;

(6) five judicial circuit solicitors appointed by the Governor for a term of four years. However, upon initial appointment, the Governor shall select one for a two-year term, two for a three-year term, and two for a four-year term. If a solicitor appointed to the commission is not re-elected, a vacancy occurs and it must be filled pursuant to the provisions of Section 1-7-930.

HISTORY: 1990 Act No. 485, Section 1; 1996 Act No. 337, Section 1.

SECTION 1-7-930. Vacancies.

If a vacancy occurs, it must be filled for the remainder of the term in the same manner as the initial appointment.

HISTORY: 1990 Act No. 485, Section 1.

SECTION 1-7-940. Duties.

(A) The commission has the following duties:

(1) coordinate all administrative functions of the offices of the solicitors and any affiliate services operating in conjunction with the solicitors' offices;

(2) submit the budgets of the solicitors and their affiliate services to the General Assembly;

(3) encourage and develop legal education programs and training programs for solicitors and their affiliate services, organize and provide seminars to help increase the effectiveness and efficiency of the prosecution of criminal cases in this State, and act as a clearinghouse and distribution source for publications involving solicitors and their affiliate services and provide legal updates on matters of law affecting the prosecution of cases in this State;

(4) provide blank indictments for the circuit solicitors.

(B) Nothing in this section may be construed to displace or otherwise affect the functions and responsibilities of the State Victim/Witness Assistance Program as established in Section 16-3-1410.

HISTORY: 1990 Act No. 485, Section 1; 1992 Act No. 347, Section 2.

SECTION 1-7-950. Election of chairman and officers.

The chairman of the commission must be elected by a majority vote of the membership of the commission for a two-year term. A majority of the entire membership constitutes a quorum. Other officers as needed by the commission must be elected in the same manner.

HISTORY: 1990 Act No. 485, Section 1.

SECTION 1-7-960. Executive director; staff.

The commission has the authority to appoint an executive director who shall serve at the pleasure of the commission. He is responsible for the day-to-day operation of the commission and the coordination of the work with other state agencies. The commission has the authority to hire additional staff as provided for in the annual appropriations act in order to perform the duties of the commission.

HISTORY: 1990 Act No. 485, Section 1.

SECTION 1-7-970. Compensation; expenses.

Members of the commission shall serve without pay but are allowed the usual mileage, per diem, and subsistence as provided by law for members of state boards, committees, and commissions. The executive director of the commission shall approve all vouchers for necessary expenses which must be paid from an appropriation as provided for by the General Assembly for the operation of the commission.

HISTORY: 1990 Act No. 485, Section 1.

SECTION 1-7-980. Funding.

Funding for the commission must be derived from the per capita funding for state services for solicitors based upon a formula to be determined by the commission.

HISTORY: 1990 Act No. 485, Section 1.

SECTION 1-7-990. Promulgation of regulations.

The Commission on Prosecution Coordination may promulgate those regulations necessary to assist it in performing its required duties as provided by this chapter.

HISTORY: 1993 Act No. 48, Section 1.

SECTION 1-7-1000. Salaries of circuit solicitors.

Circuit solicitors shall receive a salary as provided by the General Assembly in the annual general appropriations act.

HISTORY: 1996 Act No. 458, Part II, Section 25C.

CHAPTER 9

Emergency Provisions

ARTICLE 1

Emergency Interim Executive and Judicial Succession

SECTION 1-9-10. Short title.

This article shall be known and may be cited as the "Emergency Interim Executive and Judicial Succession Act."

HISTORY: 1962 Code Section 1-1001; 1962 (52) 2198.

SECTION 1-9-20. Definitions.

Unless otherwise clearly required by the context, as used in this article:

(a) "Unavailable" means either that a vacancy in office exists and there is no deputy authorized to exercise all of the powers and discharge the duties of the office, or that the lawful incumbent of the office (including any deputy exercising the powers and discharging the duties of an office because of a vacancy) and his duly authorized deputy are absent or unable to exercise the powers and discharge the duties of the office.

(b) "Emergency interim successor" means a person designated pursuant to this article, in the event the officer is unavailable, to exercise the powers and discharge the duties of an office until a successor is appointed or elected and qualified as may be provided by the Constitution, statutes, charters and ordinances or until the lawful incumbent is able to resume the exercise of the powers and discharge the duties of the office.

(c) "Office" includes all State and local offices, the powers and duties of which are defined by the Constitution, statutes, charters, and ordinances, except the office of Governor, and except those in the General Assembly and the judiciary.

(d) "Attack" means any attack or series of attacks by an enemy of the United States causing, or which may cause, substantial damage or injury to civilian property or persons in the United States in any manner by sabotage or by the use of bombs, missiles, shellfire, or atomic, radiological, chemical, bacteriological, or biological means or other weapons or processes.

(e) "Political subdivision" includes counties, cities, towns, villages, townships, districts, authorities, and other public corporations and entities whether organized and existing under charter or general law.

HISTORY: 1962 Code Section 1-1002; 1962 (52) 2198.

SECTION 1-9-30. Emergency interim successors to office of Governor.

In the event that the Governor, for any of the reasons specified in the Constitution, is not able to exercise the powers and discharge the duties of his office, or is unavailable, and in the event the Lieutenant Governor, President pro tempore of the Senate, and the Speaker of the House of Representatives be for any of the reasons specified in the Constitution not able to exercise the powers and discharge the duties of the office of Governor, or be unavailable, the Secretary of State, State Treasurer or Attorney General shall, in the order named, if the preceding named officers be unavailable, exercise the powers and discharge the duties of the office of Governor until a new Governor is elected and qualifies, or until a preceding named officer becomes available; provided, however, that no emergency interim successor to the aforementioned offices may serve as Governor.

HISTORY: 1962 Code Section 1-1003; 1962 (52) 2198.

SECTION 1-9-40. Designation of successors by State officers; powers; duties; vacancies.

All State officers, subject to such regulations as the Governor (or other official authorized under the Constitution and this article to exercise the powers and discharge the duties of the office of Governor) may issue, shall, upon approval of this article, in addition to any deputy authorized pursuant to law to exercise all of the powers and discharge the duties of the office, designate by title emergency interim successors and specify their order of succession. The officer shall review and revise, as necessary, designations made pursuant to this article to insure their current status. The officer will designate a sufficient number of such emergency interim successors so that there will be not less than three nor more than seven such deputies or emergency interim successors or any combination thereof, at any time. In the event that any State officer is unavailable following an attack, and in the event his deputy, if any, is also unavailable, the powers of his office shall be exercised and the duties of his office shall be discharged by his designated emergency interim successors in the order specified. Such emergency interim successors shall exercise the powers and discharge the duties only until such time as the Governor under the Constitution or authority other than this article (or other official authorized under the Constitution or this article to exercise the powers and discharge the duties of the office of Governor) may, where a vacancy exists, appoint a successor to fill the vacancy or until a successor is otherwise appointed, or elected and qualified as provided by law; or an officer (or his deputy or a preceding named emergency interim successor) becomes available to exercise or resume the exercise of the powers and discharge the duties of his office.

HISTORY: 1962 Code Section 1-1004; 1962 (52) 2198.

SECTION 1-9-50. Authorization of qualified local governments to enact ordinances providing for emergency interim successors to local offices.

With respect to local offices for which the governing bodies of cities, towns, villages, townships, and counties may enact resolutions or ordinances relative to the manner in which vacancies will be filled or temporary appointments to office made, such bodies are hereby authorized to enact resolutions or ordinances providing for emergency interim successors to offices of such governmental units. Such resolutions and ordinances shall not be inconsistent with the provisions of the article.

HISTORY: 1962 Code Section 1-1005; 1962 (52) 2198.

SECTION 1-9-60. Applicability of emergency interim successor provisions to officers of political subdivisions not included in Section 1-9-50.

The provisions of this section shall be applicable to officers of political subdivisions (including, but not limited to, cities, towns, villages, townships and counties, as well as school, fire, power, water, sewer, watershed conservation, soil conservation, public service and drainage districts) not included in Section 1-9-50. Such officers, subject to such regulations as the executive head of the political subdivision may issue, shall upon approval of this article, designated by title (if feasible) or by named person, emergency interim successors and specify their order of succession. The officer shall review and revise, as necessary, designations made pursuant to this article to insure their current status. The officer will designate a sufficient number of persons so that there will be not less than three, nor more than seven, deputies or emergency interim successors or any combination thereof, at any time. In the event that any officer of any political subdivision (or his deputy provided for pursuant to law) is unavailable, the powers of the office shall be exercised and duties shall be discharged by his designated emergency interim successors in the order specified. The emergency interim successor shall exercise the powers and discharge the duties of the office to which designated until such time as a vacancy which may exist shall be filled in accordance with the Constitution or statutes; or until the officer (or his deputy or a preceding emergency interim successor) again becomes available to exercise the powers and discharge the duties of his office.

HISTORY: 1962 Code Section 1-1006; 1962 (52) 2198.

SECTION 1-9-70. Emergency interim successors for judges.

In the event that any judge of any court is unavailable to exercise the powers and discharge the duties of his office, and in the event no other judge authorized to act in the event of absence, disability or vacancy or no special judge appointed in accordance with the provisions of the Constitution or statutes is available to exercise the powers and discharge the duties of such office, the duties of the office shall be discharged and the powers exercised by the special emergency judges hereinafter provided for:

(a) The Governor, upon approval of this article, shall designate for each member of the Supreme Court special emergency judges in the number of not less than three nor more than seven for each member of the court, and shall specify the order of their succession.

(b) The Chief Justice of the Supreme Court in consultation with the other members of the court, upon approval of this article, shall designate for each court of record except the Supreme Court, special emergency judges in the number of not less than three nor more than seven for each judge of the courts, and shall specify the order of their succession.

(c) The judge of the circuit court, upon approval of this article, shall designate not less than three special emergency judges for courts not of record within that circuit and shall specify their order of succession.

The special emergency judges shall, in the order specified, exercise the powers and discharge the duties of such office in case of the unavailability of the regular judge or persons immediately preceding them in the designation. The designating authority shall review and revise, as necessary, designations made pursuant to this article to insure their current status.

The special emergency judges shall discharge the duties and exercise the powers of such office until such time as a vacancy which may exist shall be filled in accordance with the Constitution and statutes or until the regular judge or one preceding the designee in the order of succession becomes available to exercise the powers and discharge the duties of the office.

HISTORY: 1962 Code Section 1-1007; 1962 (52) 2198.

SECTION 1-9-80. Oath of successors.

At the time of their designation, emergency interim successors and special emergency judges shall take such oath as may be required for them to exercise the powers and discharge the duties of the office to which they may succeed. Notwithstanding any other provision of law, no person, as a prerequisite to the exercise of the powers or discharge of the duties of an office to which he succeeds, shall be required to comply with any other provision of law relative to taking office.

HISTORY: 1962 Code Section 1-1008; 1962 (52) 2198.

SECTION 1-9-90. Duration of successors' authority to exercise powers and duties.

Officials authorized to act as Governor pursuant to this article, emergency interim successors and special emergency judges are empowered to exercise the powers and discharge the duties of an office as herein authorized only after an attack upon the United States, as defined herein, has occurred. The General Assembly by concurrent resolution, may at any time terminate the authority of the emergency interim successors and special emergency judges to exercise the powers and discharge the duties of office, as herein provided.

HISTORY: 1962 Code Section 1-1009; 1962 (52) 2198.

SECTION 1-9-100. Designated successors shall serve at pleasure of designating authority prior to assuming new duties of an office.

Until such time as the persons designated as emergency interim successors or special emergency judges are authorized to exercise the powers and discharge the duties of an office in accordance with this article, including Section 1-9-90 hereof, the persons shall serve in their designated capacities at the pleasure of the designating authority and may be removed or replaced by the designating authority at any time, with or without cause.

HISTORY: 1962 Code Section 1-1010; 1962 (52) 2198.

SECTION 1-9-110. Governor shall adjudicate disputes.

Any dispute concerning a question of fact arising under this article with respect to an office in the executive branch of the State government (except a dispute of fact relative to the office of Governor) shall be adjudicated by the Governor (or other official authorized under the Constitution and this article to exercise the powers and discharge the duties of the office of Governor) and his decision shall be final.

HISTORY: 1962 Code Section 1-1011; 1962 (52) 2198.

ARTICLE 3

Emergency Seats of State Government

SECTION 1-9-210. Declaration of emergency seats of government by Governor.

Whenever, due to an emergency resulting from the effects of enemy attack, or the anticipated effects of a threatened enemy attack, it becomes imprudent, inexpedient or impossible to conduct the affairs of State government at the normal location of the seat thereof in the city of Columbia in Richland County, the Governor shall, as often as the exigencies of the situation require, by proclamation, declare an emergency temporary location, or locations, for the seat of government at such place, or places, within or without this State as he may deem advisable under the circumstances, and shall take such action and issue such orders as may be necessary for an orderly transition of the affairs of State government to such emergency temporary location, or locations. Such emergency temporary location, or locations, shall remain as the seat of government until the General Assembly shall by law establish a new location, or locations, or until the emergency is declared to be ended by the Governor and the seat of government is returned to its normal location.

HISTORY: 1962 Code Section 1-1021; 1962 (52) 2196.

SECTION 1-9-220. Official acts at emergency location shall be valid.

During such time as the seat of government remains at such emergency temporary location, or locations, all official acts now or hereafter required by law to be performed at the seat of government by any officer, agency, department or authority of this State, including the convening and meeting of the General Assembly in regular, extraordinary, or emergency session, shall be as valid and binding when performed at such emergency temporary location, or locations, as if performed at the normal location of the seat of government.

HISTORY: 1962 Code Section 1-1022; 1962 (52) 2196.

SECTION 1-9-230. Provisions of this article shall control.

The provisions of this article shall control and be supreme in the event it shall be employed notwithstanding the provisions or any other law to the contrary or in conflict herewith.

HISTORY: 1962 Code Section 1-1023; 1962 (52) 2196.

CHAPTER 10

Removal and Placement of Confederate Flag

Code Commissioner's Note

Chapter 10 was added at the direction of the Code Commissioner.

SECTION 1-10-10. Flags authorized to be flown atop State House dome, in chambers of Senate and House of Representatives and on grounds of Capitol Complex; members' offices as "chambers"; private individual wearing, carrying or displaying flag on capitol grounds.

(A) As of 12:00 noon on the effective date of this act, and permanently thereafter, the only flags authorized to be flown atop the dome of the State House, in the chambers of the Senate and House of Representatives, and on the grounds of the Capitol Complex shall be as authorized in this section.

The flags authorized to be flown atop the dome of the State House and in the chambers of the Senate and House of Representatives are the United States Flag and the South Carolina State Flag.

From any funds appropriated to the Department of Administration, the Division of General Services of the Department of Administration, or its successor in interest, shall ensure that the flags authorized above shall be placed at all times as directed in this section and shall replace the flags at appropriate intervals as may be necessary due to wear.

(B) The provisions of this section may only be amended or repealed upon passage of an act which has received a two-thirds vote on the third reading of the bill in each branch of the General Assembly.

(C) The term "chambers" of the House or Senate for the purposes of this section does not include individual members' offices. The provisions of this section do not prohibit a private individual on the capitol complex grounds from wearing as a part of his clothing or carrying or displaying any type of flag including a Confederate Flag.

HISTORY: 2000 Act No. 292, Section 1; 2015 Act No. 90 (S.897), Section 1, eff July 9, 2015.

Code Commissioner's Note

At the direction of the Code Commissioner, references in this section to the offices of the former State Budget and Control Board, Office of the Governor, or other agencies, were changed to reflect the transfer of them to the Department of Administration or other entities, pursuant to the directive of the South Carolina Restructuring Act, 2014 Act No. 121, Section 5(D)(1), effective July 1, 2015.

Editor's Note

2015 Act No. 90, Section 2, provides as follows:

"SECTION 2. The South Carolina Infantry Battle Flag of the Confederate States of America [the Battle Flag of the Army of Northern Virginia (General Robert E. Lee's Army) the South Carolina, Georgia, Florida Department version] shall be permanently removed from its location on the south side of the Confederate Soldier Monument. The South Carolina Infantry Battle Flag of the Confederate States of America shall be permanently removed from its location on the Capitol Complex Grounds within twenty-four hours of the effective date of this act. Upon its removal, the flag shall be transported to the Confederate Relic Room for appropriate display. The flagpole on which the flag is flown and the area adjacent to the monument and flagpole must be returned to its previous condition by the Division of General Services."

Effect of Amendment

2015 Act No. 90, Section 1, amended the section, providing for removal of the South Carolina Infantry Battle Flag of the Confederate States of America from the grounds of the Capitol Complex.

SECTION 1-10-20. Confederate Flags from above rostrums of Senate and House of Representatives chambers to be placed and displayed in State Museum.

The actual Confederate Flags (Naval Jack) removed from above the rostrum in the chambers of the House of Representatives and the Senate must be placed and permanently displayed in a suitable location in the State Museum.

HISTORY: 2000 Act No. 292, Section 1.

SECTION 1-10-30. Confederate Flag from dome to be placed and displayed in State Museum.

The actual Confederate Flag (Naval Jack) which is flying on the effective date of this act and which is removed from the dome of the State House must be placed and permanently displayed in a suitable location in the State Museum.

HISTORY: 2000 Act No. 292, Section 6.

Title 1 - Administration of the Government

CHAPTER 11

Department of Administration

ARTICLE 1

General Provisions

Editor's Note

1988 Act No. 658, Part II, Section 18A directed that Sections 1-11-10 through 1-11-420 be designated as Article 1 of Chapter 11, Title 1, and be entitled "General Provisions".

SECTION 1-11-10. Department of Administration established; transfer of offices, divisions, other agencies.

(A) There is hereby created, within the executive branch of the state government, the Department of Administration, headed by a director appointed by the Governor upon the advice and consent of the Senate who only may be removed pursuant to Section 1-3-240(B). Effective July 1, 2015, the following offices, divisions, or components of the former State Budget and Control Board, Office of the Governor, or other agencies are transferred to, and incorporated into, the Department of Administration:

(1) the Division of General Services, including Business Operations, Facilities Management, State Building and Property Services, and Agency Services, including surplus property, intrastate mail, parking, state fleet management, except that the Division of General Services shall not be transferred to the Department of Administration until the Director of the Department of

Administration enters into a memorandum of understanding with appropriate officials of applicable legislative and judicial agencies or departments meeting the requirements of this subsection. There shall be a single memorandum of understanding involving the Department of Administration and the legislative and judicial branches with appropriate officials of each to be signatories to the memorandum of understanding.

(a) The memorandum of understanding shall provide for:

(i) continued use of existing office space;

(ii) a method for the allocation of new, additional, or different office space;

(iii) adequate parking;

(iv) a method for the allocation of new, additional, or different parking;

(v) the provision of appropriate levels of electrical, mechanical, maintenance, energy management, fire protection, custodial, project management, safety and building renovation, and other services currently provided by the General Services Division of the State Budget and Control Board;

(vi) the provision of water, electricity, steam, and chilled water to the offices, areas, and facilities occupied by the applicable agencies;

(vii) the ability for each agency or department to maintain building access control for its allocated office space; and

(viii) access control for the Senate and House chambers and courtrooms as appropriate.

(b) The parties may modify the memorandum of understanding by mutual consent at any time.

(c) The General Services Division must provide the services described in subsection (a) and any other maintenance and support, at a level that is greater than or equal to what is provided prior to the effective date of this act, to each building on the Capitol Complex, including the Supreme Court, without charge. The General Services Division must coordinate with the appropriate officials of applicable legislative and judicial agencies or departments when providing these services to the buildings and areas controlled by those agencies;

(2) the State Office of Human Resources;

(3) the Guardian Ad Litem Program as established in Article 5, Chapter 11, Title 63;

(4) the Office of Economic Opportunity, the office designated by the Governor to be the state administering agency that is responsible for the receipt and distribution of the federal funds as allocated to South Carolina for the implementation of Title VI, Public Law 97-35;

(5) the Developmental Disabilities Council as established by Executive Order in 1971 and reauthorized in 2010;

(6) the Continuum of Care for Emotionally Disturbed Children as established in Article 13, Chapter 11, Title 63;

(7) the Division for Review of the Foster Care of Children as established by Article 7, Chapter 11, Title 63;

(8) the Children's Case Resolution System as established by Article 11, Chapter 11, Title 63;

(9) the Client Assistance Program;

(10) the Division of Veterans' Affairs as established by Chapter 11, Title 25;

(11) the Commission on Women as established by Chapter 15, Title 1;

(12) the Office of Victims Assistance, including the South Carolina Victims Advisory Board and the Victims Compensation Fund, both as established by Article 13, Chapter 3, Title 16;

(13) the Crime Victims' Ombudsman as established by Article 16, Chapter 3, Title 16;

(14) the Governor's Office of Ombudsman;

(15) the Division of Small and Minority Business Contracting and Certification, as established pursuant to Article 21, Chapter 35, Title 11, formerly known as the Small and Minority Business Assistance Office;

(16) the Division of State Information Technology, including the Data Center, Telecommunications and Information Technology Services, the South Carolina Enterprise Information System, and the Division of Information Security; and

(17) the Nuclear Advisory Council as established in Article 9, Chapter 7, Title 13.

(B)(1) The Division of State Information Technology must submit the Statewide Strategic Information Technology Plan to the Director of the Department of Administration by September 1, 2015, and biennially thereafter. The director shall review the Statewide Strategic Information Technology Plan and recommend to the Governor priorities for state government enterprise information technology projects and resource requirements. The director also shall review information technology spending by state agencies and evaluate whether greater efficiencies, more effective services, and cost savings can be achieved through streamlining, standardizing, and consolidating agency information technology.

(2) All oversight concerning the South Carolina Enterprise Information System must remain as provided in Chapter 53, Title 11.

(C) The Department of Administration shall use the existing resources of each division, insofar as it promotes efficiency and effectiveness, transferred to the department including, but not limited to, funding, personnel, equipment, and supplies from the board's administrative support units, including, but not limited to, the Office of the Executive Director, Office of General Counsel, and the Office of Internal Operations. "Funding" means state, federal, and other funds. Vacant FTEs at the State Budget and Control Board also may be used to fill needed positions at the department. No new FTEs may be assigned to the department without authorization from the General Assembly.

(D) No later than December 31, 2015, the department's director shall submit a report to the President Pro Tempore of the Senate and the Speaker of the House of Representatives that contains an analysis of and recommendations regarding the most appropriate organizational placement for each component of the Office of Executive Policy and Programs as of the effective date of this act. The department shall solicit input from and consider the recommendation of affected constituencies while developing its report.

(E) The Department of Administration shall, during the absence of the Governor from Columbia, be placed in charge of the records and papers in the executive chamber kept pursuant to Section 1-3-30.

HISTORY: 1962 Code Section 1-351; 1952 Code Section 1-351; 1950 (46) 3605; 2014 Act No. 121 (S.22), Pt III, Section 4.A, eff July 1, 2015.

Effect of Amendment

2014 Act No. 121, Section 4A, rewrote the section.

SECTION 1-11-20. Transfer of offices, divisions, other agencies from State Budget and Control Board to appropriate entities.

Effective July 1, 2015:

(A) The South Carolina Confederate Relic Room and Military Museum is transferred from the State Budget and Control Board and is governed by the South Carolina Confederate Relic Room and Military Museum Commission, as established in Section 60-17-10.

(B) The State Energy Office is transferred from the State Budget and Control Board to the Office of Regulatory Staff.

(C) The offices, divisions, or components of the State Budget and Control Board named in this subsection are transferred to, and incorporated into, the Rural Infrastructure Authority as established in Section 11-50-30. All functions, powers, duties, responsibilities, and authority vested in the agencies and authorities, including their governing boards, if any, named in this subsection are devolved upon the Rural Infrastructure Authority and the authority shall constitute the agencies and authorities, including their governing boards, if any, named in this subsection:

(1) Local Government Division in support of the local government loan program as established in Section 1-11-25;

(2) Water Resources Coordinating Council as established in Section 11-37-200(A); and

(3) Division of Regional Development as established in Section 11-42-40.

(D) The regulation of minerals and mineral interests on public land, and the regulation of Geothermal Resources as provided in Chapter 9, Title 10 is transferred to, and incorporated into, the Department of Health and Environmental Control.

(E) The Procurement Services Division of the State Budget and Control Board is transferred to, and incorporated into, the State Fiscal Accountability Authority.

(F) The State Auditor is transferred to, and incorporated into, the State Fiscal Accountability Authority.

(G) South Carolina Infrastructure Facilities Authority as established in Chapter 40, Title 11 and the South Carolina Water Quality Revolving Fund Authority in support of water quality projects and federal loan programs as established in Chapter 5, Title 48 are transferred to, and incorporated into, the State Fiscal Accountability Authority.

HISTORY: 1962 Code Section 1-352; 1952 Code Section 1-352; 1950 (46) 3605, 3608; 2005 Act No. 164, Section 2, eff June 10, 2005; 2014 Act No. 121 (S.22), Pt III, Section 4.B, eff July 1, 2015.

Effect of Amendment

The 2005 amendment made nonsubstantive changes in the first sentence and rewrote the second sentence which formerly read "The State Auditor shall be the director of the Finance Division, ex officio, and the directors of the other divisions shall be employed by the State Budget and Control Board for such time and compensation, not greater than the term and compensation for the State Auditor, as shall be fixed by the Board in its judgment".

2014 Act No. 121, Section 4.B, rewrote the section.

SECTION 1-11-22. Organization of staff.

Notwithstanding any other provision of law, the Department of Administration may organize its staff as it deems most appropriate to carry out the various duties, responsibilities and authorities assigned to it and to its various divisions.

HISTORY: 1983 Act No. 151, Part II, Section 27.

Code Commissioner's Note

At the direction of the Code Commissioner, references in this section to the offices of the former State Budget and Control Board, Office of the Governor, or other agencies, were changed to reflect the transfer of them to the Department of Administration or other entities, pursuant to the directive of the South Carolina Restructuring Act, 2014 Act No. 121, Section 5(D)(1), effective July 1, 2015.

SECTION 1-11-23. Filling vacancy in position of Director of Budget Division.

Vacancies in the position of Director of the Budget Division of the State Budget and Control Board must be filled by appointment of the Budget and Control Board.

HISTORY: 1992 Act No. 501, Part II Section 13E.

Code Commissioner's Note

At the direction of the Code Commissioner, reference in this section to the former Budget and Control Board has not been changed pursuant to the directive of the South Carolina Restructuring Act, 2014 Act No. 121, Section 5(D)(1), until further action by the General Assembly.

SECTION 1-11-25. Local Government Division.

There is hereby established a Local Government Division within the Rural Infrastructure Authority to act as a liaison for financial grants from the funds available to the authority. The division shall be under the supervision of a director who shall be appointed by and who shall serve at the pleasure of the Director of the Rural Infrastructure Authority. He may employ such staff as may be approved by the Director of the Rural Infrastructure Authority. The division shall be responsible for certifying grants to local governments from both federal and state funds. The term "local government" shall mean any political entity below the state level. Notwithstanding the fact that the Local Government Division is now a part of the Rural Infrastructure Authority, where certain grants of the division depending upon their funding source require additional approvals other than the division and the authority before they may be made, those additional approvals also must be secured.

The division shall establish guidelines and procedures which public entities shall follow in applying for grants. The director shall make known to these entities the availability of all grants available through the authority and shall make periodic reports to the General Assembly and the Office of the Governor. The reports shall contain information concerning the amount of funds available from both federal and state sources, requests for grants and the status of such requests and such other information as the director may deem appropriate. The director shall maintain such records as may be necessary for the efficient operation of the office.

HISTORY: 1978 Act No. 632, Part II, Section 6; 2014 Act No. 121 (S.22), Pt VI, Section 16.A, eff July 1, 2015.

Effect of Amendment

2014 Act No. 121, Section 16.A, rewrote the section.

SECTION 1-11-26. Use of funds from Rural Infrastructure Authority; penalties for misuse.

(A) Grant funds received by a public entity from the Rural Infrastructure Authority must be deposited in a separate fund and may not be commingled with other funds, including other grant funds. Disbursements may be made from this fund only on the written authorization of the individual who signed the grant application filed with the division, or his successor, and only for the purposes specified in the grant application. A person violating the provisions of this section is guilty of a misdemeanor and, upon conviction, must be fined five thousand dollars or imprisoned for six months, or both.

(B) It is not a defense to an indictment alleging a violation of this section that grant funds received were used by a grantee or subgrantee for governmental purposes other than those specified in the grant application or that the purpose for which the grant was made was accomplished by funds other than grant funds.

(C) The Division of Local Government of the Rural Infrastructure Authority shall furnish a copy of this section to a grantee when the grant is awarded.

HISTORY: 1990 Act No. 612, Part II, Section 14A; 2014 Act No. 121 (S.22), Pt VI, Section 16.B, eff July 1, 2015.

Effect of Amendment

2014 Act No. 121, Section 16.B, in subsection (A), substituted "public entity from the Rural Infrastructure Authority" for "county, municipality, political subdivision, or other entity from the Division of Local Government of the State Budget and Control Board"; in subsection (B), deleted "from the Division of Local Government" before "grant funds received", and deleted "by the Division of Local Government" before "grant was made"; and in subsection (C), substituted "Rural Infrastructure Authority" for "State Budget and Control Board".

SECTION 1-11-50. Certain funds of Revenue and Fiscal Affairs Office and the Executive Budget Office carried forward.

If funds accumulated by the Revenue and Fiscal Affairs Office and the Executive Budget Office, under contract for the provision of goods and services not covered by the offices' appropriated funds, are not expended during the preceding fiscal years, these funds may be carried forward and expended for the costs associated with the provision of these goods and services.

HISTORY: 1995 Act No. 145, Part II, Section 26A.

Code Commissioner's Note

At the direction of the Code Commissioner, references in this section to the offices of the former State Budget and Control Board, Office of the Governor, or other agencies, were changed to reflect the transfer of them to the Department of Administration or other entities, pursuant to the directive of the South Carolina Restructuring Act, 2014 Act No. 121, Section 5(D)(1).

SECTION 1-11-55. Leasing of real property for governmental bodies.

(1) "Governmental body" means a state government department, commission, council, board, bureau, committee, institution, college, university, technical school, agency, government corporation, or other establishment or official of the executive branch of this State. Governmental body excludes the General Assembly, Legislative Council, the Legislative Services Agency, the judicial department and all local political subdivisions such as counties, municipalities, school districts, or public service or special purpose districts.

(2) The Division of General Services of the Department of Administration is hereby designated as the single central broker for the leasing of real property for governmental bodies. No governmental body shall enter into any lease agreement or renew any existing lease except in accordance with the provisions

of this section. However, a technical college, with the approval by the State Board for Technical and Comprehensive Education, and a public institution of higher learning, may enter into any lease agreement or renew any lease agreement up to one hundred thousand dollars annually for each property or facility.

(3) When any governmental body needs to acquire real property for its operations or any part thereof and state-owned property is not available, it shall notify the Division of General Services of its requirement on rental request forms prepared by the division. Such forms shall indicate the amount and location of space desired, the purpose for which it shall be used, the proposed date of occupancy and such other information as General Services may require. Upon receipt of any such request, General Services shall conduct an investigation of available rental space which would adequately meet the governmental body's requirements, including specific locations which may be suggested and preferred by the governmental body concerned. When suitable space has been located which the governmental body and the division agree meets necessary requirements and standards for state leasing as prescribed in procedures of the department as provided for in subsection (5) of this section, General Services shall give its written approval to the governmental body to enter into a lease agreement. All proposed lease renewals shall be submitted to General Services by the time specified by General Services.

(4) The department shall adopt procedures to be used for governmental bodies to apply for rental space, for acquiring leased space, and for leasing state-owned space to nonstate lessees.

(5) Any participant in a property transaction proposed to be entered who maintains that a procedure provided for in this section has not been properly followed, may request review of the transaction by the Director of the Division of General Services of the Department of Administration or his designee.

HISTORY: 1997 Act No. 153, Section 2; 2002 Act No. 333, Section 1; 2002 Act No. 356, Section 1, Pt VI.P(1); 2011 Act No. 74, Pt VI, Section 13, eff August 1, 2011; 2013 Act No. 31, Section 1, eff May 21, 2013; 2014 Act No. 121 (S.22), Pt V, Section 7.A, eff July 1, 2015.

Code Commissioner's Note

The last sentence in subsection (2), which was added by 2011 Act No. 74, was inadvertently omitted from 2014 Act No. 121 due to a scrivener's error. At the direction of the Code Commissioner, this sentence has been retained in subsection (2).

Effect of Amendment

The 2011 amendment, in subsection (2), added the third sentence relating to technical colleges.

The 2013 amendment, in subsection (1), substituted "Legislative Services Agency" for "Office of Legislative Printing, Information and Technology Systems".

2014 Act No. 121, Section 7.A, in subsection (1), substituted "agency, government corporation, or other establishment or official of the executive branch" for "legislative body, agency, government corporation, or other establishment or official of the executive, judicial, or legislative branches"; in subsection (2), substituted "Division of General Services of the Department of Administration" for "Budget and Control Board"; in subsection (3) substituted "division" for "office" in three instances, and substituted "department" for "board"; in subsection (4), substituted "department" for "board"; and in subsection (5), substituted "Division of General Services of the Department of Administration" for "Office of General Services".

SECTION 1-11-56. Program to manage leasing; procedures.

(A) The Division of General Services of the Department of Administration, in an effort to ensure that funds authorized and appropriated for rent are used in the most efficient manner, is directed to develop a program to manage the leasing of all public and private space of a governmental body. The department must submit regulations for the implementation of this section to the General Assembly as provided in the Administrative Procedures Act, Chapter 23, Title 1. The department's regulations, upon General Assembly approval, shall include procedures for:

(1) assessing and evaluating agency needs, including the authority to require agency justification for any request to lease public or private space;

(2) establishing standards for the quality and quantity of space to be leased by a requesting agency;

(3) devising and requiring the use of a standard lease form (approved by the Attorney General) with provisions which assert and protect the state's prerogatives including, but not limited to, a right of cancellation in the event of:

(a) a nonappropriation for the renting agency;

(b) a dissolution of the agency; and

(c) the availability of public space in substitution for private space being leased by the agency;

(4) rejecting an agency's request for additional space or space at a specific location, or both;

(5) directing agencies to be located in public space, when available, before private space can be leased;

(6) requiring the agency to submit a multiyear financial plan for review by the department with copies sent to Ways and Means Committee and Senate Finance Committee, before any new lease for space is entered into; and

(7) requiring prior review by the Joint Bond Review Committee and the requirement of State Fiscal Accountability Authority approval before the adoption of any new or renewal lease that commits more than two hundred thousand dollars annually in rental or lease payments or more than one million dollars in such payments in a five-year period.

(B) Leases or rental agreements involving amounts below the thresholds provided in subsection (A)(7) may be executed by the Department of Administration without this prior review by the Joint Bond Review Committee and approval by the State Fiscal Accountability Authority.

(C) The threshold requirements requiring review by the Joint Bond Review Committee and approval by the State Fiscal Accountability Authority as contained in subsection (A)(7) also apply to leases or rental agreements with nonstate entities whether or not the state or its agencies or departments is the lessee or lessor.

HISTORY: 1997 Act No. 153, Section 2; 2014 Act No. 121 (S.22), Pt V, Section 7.B, eff July 1, 2015.

Effect of Amendment

2014 Act No. 121, Section 7.B, added subsection designator (A); in subsection (A), substituted "Division of General Services of the Department of Administration" for "State Budget and Control Board", substituted "a governmental body" for "state agencies", and added the second sentence relating to regulations; in subsection (A)(6), substituted "department" for "board's budget office", and deleted text relating to prior review by the Joint Bond Review Committee; rewrote subsection (A)(7); and added subsections (B) and (C) .

SECTION 1-11-58. Annual inventory and report; review; sale of surplus property.

(A)(1) Every state agency, as defined by law, shall annually perform an inventory and prepare a report of all residential and surplus real property owned by it. The report shall be submitted to the Department of Administration, Division of General Services, on or before June thirtieth and shall indicate current use, current value, and projected use of the property. Property not currently being utilized for necessary agency operations shall be made available for sale and funds received from the sale of the property shall revert to the general fund.

(2) The Division of General Services shall review the annual reports addressing real property submitted to it and determine the real property which is surplus to the State. A central listing of such property will be maintained for reference in reviewing subsequent property acquisition needs of agencies.

(3) Upon receipt of a request by an agency to acquire additional property, the Division of General Services shall review the surplus property list to determine if the agency's needs may be met from existing state-owned property. If such property is identified, the division shall act as broker in transferring the property to the requesting agency under terms and conditions that are mutually agreeable to the agencies involved.

(4) The department may authorize the Division of General Services to sell any unassigned surplus real property. The division shall have the discretion to determine the method of disposal to be used, which possible methods include: auction, sealed bids, listing the property with a private broker or any other method determined by the division to be commercially reasonable considering the type and location of property involved.

(B) The procedures involving surplus real property sales under this section also are subject to the approvals required in Section 1-11-65 for surplus real property sales above five hundred thousand dollars.

HISTORY: 1997 Act No. 153, Section 2; 2014 Act No. 121 (S.22), Pt V, Section 7.B, eff July 1, 2015.

Code Commissioner's Note

In 2012 the Code Commissioner substituted "as defined by law" for "as defined by Section 1-19-40 in Subsection (1).

Editor's Note

2004 Act No. 248, Part IB, Section 73.18, subsection (A), provides as follows:

"(A) It is the intent of the General Assembly to establish a comprehensive central property and office facility management process to plan for the needs of state government agencies and to achieve maximum efficiency and economy in the use of state owned or state leased real properties. The Budget and Control Board is directed to identify all state owned properties whether titled in the name of the state or an agency or department, and all agencies and departments of state government are upon request to provide the Board all documents related to the title and acquisition of the real properties that are occupied or used by the agency or titled in the name of the agency. Except for any properties where the Board determines title should not transfer because the properties are subject to reverter clauses or other restraints upon transfer of title to the State, or where the Board determines the state would be best served by not receiving title, and with the exception of properties, highways and roadways owned by the Department of Transportation, title of any property held in a state agency or department name is effectively transferred to the state under the control of the Budget and Control Board upon the effective date of this Act. Further, the Budget and Control Board is directed to approve a long-term plan no later than November 1, 2004, for the real property and space needs of all state agencies. Based on the plan, state owned buildings and properties that the Board determines are not needed shall be sold with the approval of the Board. Upon determination by the Board that a property should be sold, the agency is required to sell the property and remit the proceeds as directed herein. In addition existing debt on facilities and buildings may be refinanced with Board approval.

"The proceeds, net of selling expenses, from the sale of surplus properties shall be used to reduce the Fiscal Year 2001-02 accumulated budgetary general fund operating deficit as provided in this section. A schedule of future proceeds from surplus by fiscal year shall be provided as a part of the plan.

"The property that the Board should consider for sale includes but is not limited to:

"This provision applies to all state agencies and departments except: institutions of higher learning; the Public Service Authority; the Ports Authority; the MUSC Hospital Authority; the Myrtle Beach Air Force Redevelopment Authority; the Department of Transportation; and the Charleston Naval Complex Redevelopment Authority.

"This provision is comprehensive and supersedes any conflicting provisions concerning title and acquisition and disposition of state owned real property whether in permanent law, temporary law or by provision elsewhere in this Act.

"Funds derived from sales and refinancing pursuant to this provision are to be used as provided in this section, except in those instances where the Board determines that the funds should be applied to debt payments related to the property."

Effect of Amendment

2014 Act No. 121, Section 7.B, added subsection designator (A); in subsection (A)(1), substituted "Department of Administration, Division of" for "State Budget and Control Board, Office of"; in subsection (A)(2), substituted "Division" for "Office" and "shall review" for "will review"; in subsection (A)(3), substituted "Division" for "Office", substituted "may be met" for "can be met", and substituted "division" for "Office of General Services"; in subsection (A)(4), substituted "department may authorize the Division" for "Budget and Control Board may authorize the Office", and twice substituted "division" for "Office of General Services"; and added subsection (B).

SECTION 1-11-65. Approval and recordation of real property transactions involving governmental bodies.

(A) All transactions involving real property, made for or by any governmental bodies, excluding political subdivisions of the State, must be approved by and recorded with the Department of Administration for transactions of one million dollars or less. For transactions of more than one million dollars, approval of the State Fiscal Accountability Authority is required in lieu of the department, although the recording will be with the department. Upon approval of the transaction, there must be recorded simultaneously with the deed, a certificate of acceptance, which acknowledges the department's and authority's approval of the transaction as required. The county recording authority cannot accept for recording any deed not accompanied by a certificate of acceptance. The department and authority may exempt a governmental body from the provisions of this subsection.

(B) All state agencies, departments, and institutions authorized by law to accept gifts of tangible personal property shall have executed by its governing body an acknowledgment of acceptance prior to transfer of the tangible personal property to the agency, department, or institution.

HISTORY: 1985 Act No. 201, Part II, Section 5; 1989 Act No. 26, Section 1; 1997 Act No. 153, Section 2; 2014 Act No. 121 (S.22), Pt V, Section 7.C, eff July 1, 2015.

Editor's Note

Except for designation of the paragraphs, this section and former Section 1-11-57 were identical. For consistency, Section 1-11-57 is treated as an amendment to this section.

Effect of Amendment

2014 Act No. 121, Section 7.C, rewrote subsection (A).

SECTION 1-11-67. Rental charges for occupancy of state-controlled office buildings; apportionment among agency funding sources.

The Department of Administration shall assess and collect a rental charge from all state departments and agencies that occupy space in state-controlled office buildings under its jurisdiction. The amount charged each department or agency must be calculated on a square foot, or other equitable basis of measurement, and at rates that will yield sufficient total annual revenue to cover the annual principal and interest due or anticipated on the Capital Improvement Obligations for projects administered or planned by the department, and maintenance and operation costs of department-controlled office buildings. The amount collected must be deposited in a special account and must be expended only for payment on Capital Improvement Obligations and maintenance and operations costs of the buildings under the supervision of the department.

All departments and agencies against which rental charges are assessed and whose operations are financed in whole or in part by federal or other nonappropriated funds are both directed to apportion the payment of these charges equitably among all funds to ensure that each bears its proportionate share.

HISTORY: 2002 Act No. 356, Section 1, Pt XI.J; 2014 Act No. 121 (S.22), Pt V, Section 7.C, eff July 1, 2015.

Effect of Amendment

2014 Act No. 121, Section 7.C, rewrote the first undesignated paragraph, generally substituting "Department of Administration" for "State Budget and Control Board " and "Office of General Services".

SECTION 1-11-70. Lands subject to Department's control.

All vacant lands and lands purchased by the former land commissioners of the State are subject to the directions of the Department of Administration.

HISTORY: 1962 Code Section 1-357; 1952 Code Section 1-357; 1942 Code Section 2137; 1932 Code Section 2137; Civ. C. '22 Section 98; Civ. C. '12 Section 93; Civ. C. '02 Section 89; G. S. 61; R. S. 83; 1878 (16) 559; 1950 (46) 3605; 2014 Act No. 121 (S.22), Pt V, Section 7.C, eff July 1, 2015.

Effect of Amendment

2014 Act No. 121, Section 7.C, substituted "are subject to the directions of the Department of Administration" for "shall be subject to the directions of the State Budget and Control Board".

SECTION 1-11-80. Department authorized to grant easements for public utilities on vacant State lands.

The Department of Administration, upon approval of the State Fiscal Accountability Authority, is authorized to grant easements and rights of way to any person for construction and maintenance of power lines, pipe lines, water and sewer lines and railroad facilities over, on or under such vacant lands or marshland as are owned by the State, upon payment of the reasonable value thereof.

HISTORY: 1962 Code Section 1-357.1; 1963 (53) 177; 2014 Act No. 121 (S.22), Pt V, Section 7.C, eff July 1, 2015.

Effect of Amendment

2014 Act No. 121, Section 7.C, substituted " Department of Administration, upon approval of the State Fiscal Accountability Authority," for "State Budget and Control Board".

SECTION 1-11-90. Department authorized to grant rights of way over State marshlands for roads or power or pipe lines to State agencies or political subdivisions.

The Department of Administration, upon approval of the State Fiscal Accountability Authority, may grant to agencies or political subdivisions of the State, without compensation, rights of way through and over such marshlands as are owned by the State for the construction and maintenance of roads, streets and highways or power or pipe lines, if, in the judgment of the department, the interests of the State will not be adversely affected thereby.

HISTORY: 1962 Code Section 1-357.2; 1963 (53) 177; 2014 Act No. 121 (S.22), Pt V, Section 7.C, eff July 1, 2015.

Effect of Amendment

2014 Act No. 121, Section 7.C, substituted "Department of Administration, upon approval of the State Fiscal Accountability Authority," for "State Budget and Control Board" and substituted "judgment of the department" for "judgment of the Budget and Control Board".

SECTION 1-11-100. Execution of instruments conveying rights of way or easements over marshlands or vacant lands.

Deeds or other instruments conveying such rights of way or easements over such marshlands or vacant lands as are owned by the State shall be executed by the Governor in the name of the State, when authorized by the Department of Administration, upon approval of the State Fiscal Accountability Authority, and when duly approved by the office of the Attorney General; deeds or other instruments conveying such easements over property in the name of or under the control of State agencies, institutions, commissions or other bodies shall be executed by the majority of the governing body thereof, shall name both the State of South Carolina and the institution, agency, commission or governing body as grantors, and shall show the written approval of the Director of the Department of Administration and the State Fiscal Accountability Authority.

HISTORY: 1962 Code Section 1-357.3; 1963 (53) 177; 2014 Act No. 121 (S.22), Pt V, Section 7.C, eff July 1, 2015.

Effect of Amendment

2014 Act No. 121, Section 7.C, substituted "authorized by the Department of Administration, upon approval of the State Fiscal Accountability Authority," for "authorized by resolution of the Budget and Control Board, duly recorded in the minutes and records of such Board" and substituted "written approval of the Director of the Department of Administration and the State Fiscal Accountability Authority" for "written approval of the majority of the members of the State Budget and Control Board".

SECTION 1-11-110. Authorization of Department to acquire real property by gift, purchase, and condemnation.

(1) The Department of Administration, subject to the requirements of Section 1-11-65, is authorized to acquire real property, including any estate or interest therein, for, and in the name of, the State of South Carolina by gift, purchase, condemnation or otherwise.

(2) The Department of Administration shall make use of the provisions of the Eminent Domain Procedure Act (Chapter 2, Title 28) if it is necessary to acquire real property by condemnation. The actions must be maintained by and in the name of the department. The right of condemnation is limited to the right to acquire land necessary for the development of the Capitol Complex grounds in the City of Columbia.

HISTORY: 1962 Code Section 1-357.4; 1968 (55) 3067; 1987 Act No. 173, Section 2; 2014 Act No. 121 (S.22), Pt V, Section 7.C, eff July 1, 2015.

Effect of Amendment

2014 Act No. 121, Section 7.C, in subsection (1), substituted "Department of Administration, subject to the requirements of Section 1-11-65," for "State Budget and Control Board"; and in subsection (2), substituted "Department of Administration" for "State Budget and Control Board", substituted "Chapter 2, Title 28" for "Chapter 2 of Title 28", and substituted "Capitol Complex grounds" for "capitol complex mall".

SECTION 1-11-115. Use of proceeds of sale of State real property.

All proceeds from the sale of real property titled to or subject to the care and control of the Department of Administration must be deposited to the credit of the Sinking Fund and used by the department for the acquisition and maintenance of facilities owned by it for the use and occupancy of state departments and agencies.

HISTORY: 1999 Act No. 100, Part II, Section 39.

Code Commissioner's Note

At the direction of the Code Commissioner, references in this section to the offices of the former State Budget and Control Board, Office of the Governor, or other agencies, were changed to reflect the transfer of them to the Department of Administration or other entities, pursuant to the directive of the South Carolina Restructuring Act, 2014 Act No. 121, Section 5(D)(1), effective July 1, 2015.

SECTION 1-11-130. Authorization of Authority to cooperate in handling finances of State subdivisions.

The State Fiscal Accountability Authority may cooperate with and assist the authorities of the counties, municipalities, school districts and other subdivisions of the State in the handling, in whatever manner may be deemed by it desirable in each case, of the financial obligations of such counties, municipalities, school districts and other subdivisions. The Authority may, upon request of any such authorities, negotiate with the holders of such obligations and the authorities of the obligor to the end that such extensions and adjustments as may be desirable may be effected and may negotiate with any lending agency and perform any other act or service pursuant to the purpose hereof to the end that the credit of the subdivisions of the State and the rights of the holders of their obligations may be mutually protected.

HISTORY: 1962 Code Section 1-358; 1952 Code Section 1-358; 1942 Code Section 2146-1; 1933 (38) 291; 1950 (46) 3605.

Code Commissioner's Note

At the direction of the Code Commissioner, references in this section to the offices of the former State Budget and Control Board, Office of the Governor, or other agencies, were changed to reflect the transfer of them to the Department of Administration or other entities, pursuant to the directive of the South Carolina Restructuring Act, 2014 Act No. 121, Section 5(D)(1), effective July 1, 2015.

SECTION 1-11-135. Fees for processing revenue bonds.

To offset the costs incurred by the State in the review and processing of proposals by the governing bodies of counties and municipalities for the issuance or refunding of industrial, hospital, or pollution control revenue bonds or notes, the State Fiscal Accountability Authority may charge a single fee to cover initial processing including any amendments in accord with the following schedule:

Issue or Refunding Amount Fee

$1,000,000 or less $ 2,000 $1,000,001 through $25,000,000 3,000 $25,000,001 through $50,000,000 4,000 Over $50,000,000 5,000

The revenue received from these fees must be deposited in the General Fund.

HISTORY: 1984 Act No. 512, Part II, Section 3.

Code Commissioner's Note

At the direction of the Code Commissioner, references in this section to the offices of the former State Budget and Control Board, Office of the Governor, or other agencies, were changed to reflect the transfer of them to the Department of Administration or other entities, pursuant to the directive of the South Carolina Restructuring Act, 2014 Act No. 121, Section 5(D)(1), effective July 1, 2015.

SECTION 1-11-140. Authorization of Fiscal Accountability Authority, through the Office of Insurance Reserve Fund, to provide insurance.

(A) The State Fiscal Accountability Authority, through the Insurance Reserve Fund, is authorized to provide insurance for the State, its departments, agencies, institutions, commissions, boards, and the personnel employed by the State in its departments, agencies, institutions, commissions, and boards so as to protect the State against tort liability and to protect these personnel against tort liability arising in the course of their employment. The insurance also may be provided for physicians or dentists employed by the State, its departments, agencies, institutions, commissions, or boards against any tort liability arising out of the rendering of any professional services as a physician or dentist for which no fee is charged or professional services rendered of any type whatsoever so long as any fees received are directly payable to the employer of a covered physician or dentist, or to any practice plan authorized by the employer whether or not the practice plan is incorporated and registered with the Secretary of State; provided, any insurance coverage provided by the authority may be on the basis of claims made or upon occurrences. The insurance also may be provided for students of high schools, South Carolina Technical Schools, or state-supported colleges and universities while these students are engaged in work study, distributive education, or apprentice programs on the premises of private companies. Premiums for the insurance must be paid from appropriations to or funds collected by the various entities, except that in the case of the above-referenced students in which case the premiums must be paid from fees paid by students participating in these training programs. The authority has the exclusive control over the investigation, settlement, and defense of claims against the various entities and personnel for whom it provided insurance coverage and may promulgate regulations in connection therewith.

(B) Any political subdivision of the State including, without limitations, municipalities, counties, and school districts, may procure the insurance for itself and for its employees in the same manner provided for the procurement of this insurance for the State, its entities, and its employees, or in a manner provided by Section 15-78-140.

(C) The procurement of tort liability insurance in the manner provided is the exclusive means for the procurement of this insurance.

(D) The authority, through the Insurance Reserve Fund, also is authorized to offer insurance to governmental hospitals and any subsidiary of or other entity affiliated with the hospital currently existing or as may be established; and chartered, nonprofit, eleemosynary hospitals and any subsidiary of or other entity affiliated with the hospital currently existing or as may be established in this State so as to protect these hospitals against tort liability. Notwithstanding any other provision of this section, the procurement of tort liability insurance by a hospital and any subsidiary of or other entity affiliated with the hospital currently existing or as may be established supported wholly or partially by public funds contributed by the State or any of its political subdivisions in the manner herein provided is not the exclusive means by which the hospital may procure tort liability insurance.

(E) The authority, through the Insurance Reserve Fund, is authorized to provide insurance for duly appointed members of the boards and employees of health system agencies, and for members of the State Health Coordinating Council which are created pursuant to Public Law 93-641.

(F) The authority, through the Insurance Reserve Fund, is further authorized to provide insurance as prescribed in Sections 10-7-10 through 10-7-40, 59-67-710, and 59-67-790.

(G) Documentary or other material prepared by or for the Insurance Reserve Fund in providing any insurance coverage authorized by this section or any other provision of law which is contained in any claim file is subject to disclosure to the extent required by the Freedom of Information Act only after the claim is settled or finally concluded by a court of competent jurisdiction.

(H) The authority, through the Insurance Reserve Fund, is further authorized to provide insurance for state constables, including volunteer state constables, to protect these personnel against tort liability arising in the course of their employment, whether or not for compensation, while serving in a law enforcement capacity.

HISTORY: 1962 Code Section 1-359.1; 1973 (58) 646; 1974 (58) 2638; 1976 Act No. 744, Section 1; 1977 Act No. 182, Section 4; 1978 Act No. 418, Section 1; 1978 Act No. 502, Section 1; 1979 Act No. 77, Section 1; 1984 Act No. 424, Section 1; 1988 Act No. 389, Section 1; 1994 Act No. 380, Section 1; 2014 Act No. 121 (S.22), Pt VII, Section 19.B, eff July 1, 2015.

Editor's Note

2014 Act No. 121, Section 19.A, provides as follows:

"SECTION 19.A. (1) The Insurance Reserve Fund is transferred to the State Fiscal Accountability Authority on July 1, 2015, as a division of the authority.

"(2) The Insurance Reserve Fund, transferred to the authority, shall administer and perform all administrative and operational functions of the Office of Insurance Services, including the Insurance Reserve Fund, except that the Attorney General of this State must continue to approve the attorneys-at-law retained to represent the clients of the Insurance Reserve Fund in the manner provided by law."

Effect of Amendment

2014 Act No. 121, Section 19.B, substituted "authority" for "board" throughout; in subsection (A), substituted "The State Fiscal Accountability Authority, through the Insurance Reserve Fund" for "The State Budget and Control Board, through the Office of Insurance Services" in the first sentence, and substituted "authority" for "Budget and Control Board" in the second sentence; in subsection (B), added the reference to Section 15-78-140; in subsections (D), (E), (F), substituted "The authority, through the Insurance Reserve Fund" for "The State Budget and Control Board, through the Office of Insurance Services"; in subsection (G), substituted "Insurance Reserve Fund" for "Office of Insurance Services"; and in subsection (H), substituted "The authority, through the Insurance Reserve Fund" for "The board, through the Office of Insurance Services".

SECTION 1-11-141. Insurance on state-owned vehicles by agencies; liability of employees for cost of accident repairs.

(A) Agencies shall insure state-owned vehicles through the State Fiscal Accountability Authority or shall absorb the cost of accident repairs within the agency budget.

(B) State employees who, while driving state-owned vehicles on official business, are involved in accidents resulting in damages to the vehicles may not be held liable to the State for the cost of repairs, except in the following cases:

(1) If the operator was convicted of driving under the influence of alcohol or illegal drugs at the time of the accident and the Accident Review Board determines that the operator's impaired condition substantially was the cause of the accident, the operator may be assessed up to the full cost of repairs; and

(2) In all other cases, the employee operator may be assessed for an amount not to exceed two hundred dollars for each occurrence if he is found to be at

fault in the accident after a review of records conducted by a duly appointed Accident Review Board.

(C) Employees subjected to these assessments may appeal the assessment to the following bodies, in the following order:

(1) Agency Accident Review Board;

(2) Agency Executive Director or governing board or commission;

(3) State Motor Vehicle Management Council; and

(4) State Fiscal Accountability Authority.

HISTORY: 1995 Act No. 145, Part II, Section 17.

Code Commissioner's Note

At the direction of the Code Commissioner, references in this section to the offices of the former State Budget and Control Board, Office of the Governor, or other agencies, were changed to reflect the transfer of them to the Department of Administration or other entities, pursuant to the directive of the South Carolina Restructuring Act, 2014 Act No. 121, Section 5(D)(1), effective July 1, 2015.

SECTION 1-11-145. Employment of special agents to examine insurance risks carried by Authority.

The State Fiscal Accountability Authority may employ special agents to examine insurance risks carried by such authority and perform any other duties which may be required of them. The cost of necessary supplies, equipment and travel expenses of the special agents shall be paid from the revenues of the Insurance Reserve Fund.

HISTORY: 1979 Act No. 199, Part II, Section 10.

Code Commissioner's Note

At the direction of the Code Commissioner, references in this section to the offices of the former State Budget and Control Board, Office of the Governor, or other agencies, were changed to reflect the transfer of them to the Department

of Administration or other entities, pursuant to the directive of the South Carolina Restructuring Act, 2014 Act No. 121, Section 5(D)(1), effective July 1, 2015.

SECTION 1-11-147. Automobile liability reinsurance contract; letting for bid.

To underwrite automobile liability insurance provided by the board, the State Fiscal Accountability Authority is authorized to either self-insure, purchase reinsurance, or use a combination of self-insurance and reinsurance. Should the authority elect to purchase automobile liability reinsurance, the reinsurance shall be procured through a bid process in accordance with the South Carolina Consolidated Procurement Code with a contract term not to exceed three years.

HISTORY: 1999 Act No. 13, Section 1.

Code Commissioner's Note

At the direction of the Code Commissioner, references in this section to the offices of the former State Budget and Control Board, Office of the Governor, or other agencies, were changed to reflect the transfer of them to the Department of Administration or other entities, pursuant to the directive of the South Carolina Restructuring Act, 2014 Act No. 121, Section 5(D)(1), effective July 1, 2015.

SECTION 1-11-160. Execution by General Services Division of certificates of exemption from taxation on behalf of political subdivisions.

The General Services Division of the Department of Administration shall, when necessary, execute a certificate of exemption from taxation when a certificate is required for Federal tax purposes for or on behalf of political subdivisions that purchase property from or through the General Services Division and the certificate so executed shall then constitute the certificate of the political subdivision. The General Services Division shall accept the political subdivision's requisition or purchase order as conclusive proof that the property so requisitioned or purchased is for the exclusive use of the political subdivision.

HISTORY: 1962 Code Section 1-360; 1968 (55) 2697.

Code Commissioner's Note

At the direction of the Code Commissioner, references in this section to the offices of the former State Budget and Control Board, Office of the Governor, or other agencies, were changed to reflect the transfer of them to the Department

of Administration or other entities, pursuant to the directive of the South Carolina Restructuring Act, 2014 Act No. 121, Section 5(D)(1), effective July 1, 2015.

SECTION 1-11-170. Authorization to maintain revolving funds to finance certain inventories and accounts receivable.

The Department of Administration may maintain revolving funds adequate to finance inventories and accounts receivable for goods and services rendered by its Division of General Services on a reimbursement basis.

HISTORY: 1976 Act No. 602, Section 1.

Code Commissioner's Note

At the direction of the Code Commissioner, references in this section to the offices of the former State Budget and Control Board, Office of the Governor, or other agencies, were changed to reflect the transfer of them to the Department of Administration or other entities, pursuant to the directive of the South Carolina Restructuring Act, 2014 Act No. 121, Section 5(D)(1), effective July 1, 2015.

SECTION 1-11-175. Authorization of Authority to finance construction of correctional facilities.

The State Fiscal Accountability Authority is authorized to finance the construction of correctional facilities by issuance of capital improvement bonds or other methods of financing approved by the Board.

HISTORY: 1985 Act No. 201, Part II, Section 85.

Code Commissioner's Note

At the direction of the Code Commissioner, references in this section to the offices of the former State Budget and Control Board, Office of the Governor, or other agencies, were changed to reflect the transfer of them to the Department of Administration or other entities, pursuant to the directive of the South Carolina Restructuring Act, 2014 Act No. 121, Section 5(D)(1), effective July 1, 2015.

SECTION 1-11-180. Additional powers of the Department of Administration; condition of state property; blanket bonds; energy utilization management system; regulations.

(A) In addition to the powers granted the Department of Administration under this chapter or any other provision of law, the department may:

(1) survey, appraise, examine, and inspect the condition of state property to determine what is necessary to protect state property against fire or deterioration and to conserve the use of the property for state purposes;

(2) approve blanket bonds for a state department, agency, or institution including bonds for state officials or personnel. However, the form and execution of blanket bonds must be approved by the Attorney General; and

(3) contract to develop an energy utilization management system for state facilities under its control and to assist other agencies and departments in establishing similar programs. However, this does not authorize capital expenditures.

(B) The Department of Administration shall promulgate regulations necessary to carry out this section.

HISTORY: 1995 Act No. 145, Part II, Section 42; 2014 Act No. 121 (S.22), Pt V, Section 7.C, eff July 1, 2015.

Effect of Amendment

2014 Act No. 121, Section 7.C, in subsection (A), substituted "Department of Administration" for "Budget and Control Board" and substituted "department may" for "board may"; deleted former subsections (A)(2) and (A)(3) relating to destruction of agency records and submission of plans and specifications, and redesignated accordingly; and in subsection (B), substituted "Department of Administration shall" for "Budget and Control Board may".

SECTION 1-11-185. Additional powers of the Department of Administration; permanent improvement projects; regulations; goods and services to promote efficient and economical operations.

(A) In addition to the powers granted the Department of Administration pursuant to this chapter or another provision of law, the department may require submission and approval of plans and specifications for a permanent improvement project of a cost of one million dollars or less by a state department, agency, or institution of the executive branch before a contract is awarded for the permanent improvement project. If the cost of the permanent improvement project is more than one million dollars, approval of the State Fiscal Accountability Authority is required, in lieu of the department's approval, before the contract may be awarded and the authority may require submission of the plans and specifications for this purpose. The provisions of this subsection are in addition to any other requirements of law relating to permanent improvement projects, including the provisions of Chapter 47, Title 2.

(B) The Department of Administration may promulgate regulations necessary to carry out its duties.

(C) The respective divisions of the Department of Administration are authorized to provide to and receive from other governmental entities, including other divisions and state and local agencies and departments, goods and services as will in its opinion promote efficient and economical operations. The divisions may charge and pay the entities for the goods and services, the revenue from which must be deposited in the state treasury in a special account and expended only for the costs of providing the goods and services, and those funds may be retained and expended for the same purposes.

HISTORY: 2014 Act No. 121 (S.22), Pt V, Section 7.D, eff July 1, 2015.

SECTION 1-11-220. Division of General Services, Program of Fleet Management; Fleet Management Program.

There is hereby established within the Department of Administration, Division of General Services, Program of Fleet Management headed by the "State Fleet Manager", appointed by and reporting directly to the department. The department shall develop a comprehensive state Fleet Management Program. The program shall address acquisition, assignment, identification, replacement, disposal, maintenance, and operation of motor vehicles.

The department shall, through its policies and regulations, seek to:

(a) achieve maximum cost-effectiveness management of state-owned motor vehicles in support of the established missions and objectives of the agencies, boards, and commissions;

(b) eliminate unofficial and unauthorized use of state vehicles;

(c) minimize individual assignment of state vehicles;

(d) eliminate the reimbursable use of personal vehicles for accomplishment of official travel when this use is more costly than use of state vehicles;

(e) acquire motor vehicles offering optimum energy efficiency for the tasks to be performed;

(f) insure motor vehicles are operated in a safe manner in accordance with a statewide Fleet Safety Program; and

(g) improve environmental quality in this State by decreasing the discharge of pollutants.

HISTORY: 1978 Act No. 644 Part II Section 24(A); 1982 Act No. 429, Section 1; 2008 Act No. 203, Section 1, eff upon approval (became law without the Governor's signature on April 17, 2008); 2014 Act No. 121 (S.22), Pt V, Section 7.E.1, eff July 1, 2015.

Effect of Amendment

The 2008 amendment added item (g) relating to improving the environmental quality by decreasing discharge of pollutants.

2014 Act No. 121, Section 7.E.1, in the first undesignated paragraph, substituted " Department of Administration, Division of General Services, Program of Fleet Management headed by" for "Budget and Control Board the Division of Motor Vehicle Management headed by a Director, hereafter referred to as", substituted "department" for "Budget and Control Board, hereafter referred to as the Board", and substituted "The department shall" for "The Board shall"; in the second undesignated paragraph, substituted "department" for "Budget and Control Board"; and made other nonsubstantive changes.

SECTION 1-11-225. Cost allocation plan to recover cost of operating Fleet Management Program.

The Department of Administration shall establish a cost allocation plan to recover the cost of operating the comprehensive statewide Fleet Management Program. The division shall collect, retain, and carry forward funds to ensure continuous administration of the program.

HISTORY: 2002 Act No. 356, Section 1, Pt IX.A; 2014 Act No. 121 (S.22), Pt V, Section 7.E.2, eff July 1, 2015.

Effect of Amendment

2014 Act No. 121, Section 7.E.2, substituted "Department of Administration" for "Division of Operations".

SECTION 1-11-250. Division of General Services, Program of Fleet Management; definitions.

For purposes of Sections 1-11-220 to 1-11-330:

(a) "State agency" means all officers, departments, boards, commissions, institutions, universities, colleges, and all persons and administrative units of state government that operate motor vehicles purchased, leased, or otherwise held with the use of state funds, pursuant to an appropriation, grant or encumbrance of state funds, or operated pursuant to authority granted by the State.

(b) "Department" means the South Carolina Department of Administration.

HISTORY: 1978 Act No. 644, Part II, Section 24(D); 2002 Act No. 311, Section 2; 2014 Act No. 121 (S.22), Pt V, Section 7.E.3, eff July 1, 2015.

Effect of Amendment

2014 Act No. 121, Section 7.E.3, rewrote subsection (b), substituting "Department" for "Board, and substituted "Department of Administration" for "State Budget and Control Board".

SECTION 1-11-260. Division of General Services, Program of Fleet Management; annual reports; policies, procedures and regulations.

(A) The Fleet Manager shall report annually to the General Assembly concerning the performance of each state agency in achieving the objectives enumerated in Sections 1-11-220 through 1-11-330 and include in the report a summary of the program's efforts in aiding and assisting the various state agencies in developing and maintaining their management practices in accordance with the comprehensive statewide Fleet Management Program. This report also shall contain recommended changes in the law and regulations necessary to achieve these objectives.

(B) The department, after consultation with state agency heads, shall promulgate and enforce state policies, procedures, and regulations to achieve the goals of Sections 1-11-220 through 1-11-330 and shall recommend administrative penalties to be used by the agencies for violation of prescribed procedures and regulations relating to the Fleet Management Program.

HISTORY: 1978 Act No. 644 Part II Section 24(E); 1982 Act No. 429, Section 3; 2002 Act No. 311, Section 3; 2014 Act No. 121 (S.22), Pt V, Section 7.E.3, eff July 1, 2015.

Effect of Amendment

2014 Act No. 121, Section 7.E.3, in subsection (A), deleted "Budget and Control Board and the" after "report annually to the", substituted "summary of the program's efforts" for "summary of the division's efforts", and substituted "statewide Fleet Management Program" for "statewide Motor Vehicle Management Program"; and in subsection (B), substituted "department" for "board".

SECTION 1-11-270. Division of General Services, Program of Fleet Management; establishment of criteria for individual assignment of motor vehicles.

(A) The department shall establish criteria for individual assignment of motor vehicles based on the functional requirements of the job, which shall reduce the assignment to situations clearly beneficial to the State. Only the Governor, statewide elected officials, and agency heads are provided a state-owned vehicle based on their position.

(B) Law enforcement officers, as defined by the agency head, may be permanently assigned state-owned vehicles by their respective agency head. Agency heads may assign a state-owned vehicle to an employee when the vehicle carries or is equipped with special equipment needed to perform duties directly related to the employee's job, and the employee is either in an emergency response capacity after normal working hours or for logistical reasons it is determined to be in the agency's interest for the vehicle to remain with the employee. No other employee may be permanently assigned to a state-owned vehicle, unless the assignment is cost advantageous to the State under guidelines developed by the State Fleet Manager. Statewide elected officials, law enforcement officers, and those employees who have been assigned vehicles because they are in an emergency response capacity after normal working hours are exempt from reimbursing the State for commuting miles. Other employees operating a permanently assigned vehicle must reimburse the State for commuting between home and work.

(C) All persons, except the Governor and statewide elected officials, permanently assigned with automobiles shall log all trips on a log form approved by the board, specifying beginning and ending mileage and job function performed. However, trip logs must not be maintained for vehicles whose gross vehicle weight is greater than ten thousand pounds nor for vehicles assigned to full-time line law enforcement officers. Agency directors and commissioners permanently assigned state vehicles may utilize exceptions on a report denoting only official and commuting mileage in lieu of the aforementioned trip logs.

HISTORY: 1978 Act No. 644, Part II, Section 24(F); 1982 Act No. 429, Section 4; 1995 Act No. 145, Part II, Section 18; 2014 Act No. 121 (S.22), Pt V, Section 7.E.3, eff July 1, 2015.

Effect of Amendment

2014 Act No. 121, Section 7.E.3, in subsection (A), substituted "department" for "board".

SECTION 1-11-280. Division of General Services, Program of Fleet Management; interagency motor pools.

The department shall develop a system of agency-managed and interagency motor pools which are, to the maximum extent possible, cost beneficial to the State. All motor pools shall operate according to regulations promulgated by the department. Vehicles shall be placed in motor pools rather than being individually assigned except as specifically authorized by the department in accordance with criteria established by the department. Agencies utilizing motor pool vehicles shall utilize trip log forms approved by the department for each trip, specifying beginning and ending mileage and the job function performed.

The provisions of this section shall not apply to school buses and service vehicles.

HISTORY: 1978 Act No. 644, Part II, Section 24(G); 1982 Act No. 429, Section 5; 2014 Act No. 121 (S.22), Pt V, Section 7.E.3, eff July 1, 2015.

Effect of Amendment

2014 Act No. 121, Section 7.E.3, in the first undesignated paragraph, substituted "department" for board throughout, and deleted the former second to last sentence, relating to the transfer of the motor pool operated by the Division of General Services.

SECTION 1-11-290. Division of General Services, Program of Fleet Management; plan for maximally cost-effective vehicle maintenance.

The department in consultation with the agencies operating maintenance facilities shall study the cost-effectiveness of such facilities versus commercial alternatives and shall develop a plan for maximally cost-effective vehicle maintenance. The department shall promulgate rules and regulations governing vehicle maintenance to effectuate the plan.

The State Vehicle Maintenance program shall include:

(a) central purchasing of supplies and parts;

(b) an effective inventory control system;

(c) a uniform work order and record-keeping system assigning actual maintenance cost to each vehicle; and

(d) preventive maintenance programs for all types of vehicles.

All motor fuels shall be purchased from state facilities except in cases where such purchase is impossible or not cost beneficial to the State.

All fuels, lubricants, parts, and maintenance costs including those purchased from commercial vendors shall be charged to a state credit card bearing the license plate number of the vehicle serviced and the bill shall include the mileage on the odometer of the vehicle at the time of service.

HISTORY: 1978 Act No. 644, Part II, Section 24(H); 2014 Act No. 121 (S.22), Pt V, Section 7.E.3, eff July 1, 2015.

Effect of Amendment

2014 Act No. 121, Section 7.E.3, in the first undesignated paragraph, substituted "department" for "board" throughout, and added a comma after "parts" in the last undesignated paragraph.

SECTION 1-11-300. Agencies to develop and implement uniform cost accounting and reporting system; purchase of motor vehicle equipment and supplies; use of credit cards; determination of vehicle cost per mile.

In accordance with criteria established by the department, each agency shall develop and implement a uniform cost accounting and reporting system to ascertain the cost per mile of each motor vehicle used by the State under their control. Agencies presently operating under existing systems may continue to do so provided that departmental approval is required and that the existing systems are uniform with the criteria established by the department. All expenditures on a vehicle for gasoline and oil shall be purchased in one of the following ways:

(1) from state-owned facilities and paid for by the use of Universal State Credit Cards except where agencies purchase these products in bulk;

(2) from any fuel outlet where gasoline and oil are sold regardless of whether the outlet accepts a credit or charge card when the purchase is necessary or in the best interest of the State; and

(3) from a fuel outlet where gasoline and oil are sold when that outlet agrees to accept the Universal State Credit Card.

These provisions regarding purchase of gasoline and oil and usability of the state credit card also apply to alternative transportation fuels where available. The department shall adjust the budgetary appropriation for "Operating Expenses - Lease Fleet" to reflect the dollar savings realized by these provisions and transfer such amount to other areas of the State Fleet Management Program. The department shall promulgate regulations regarding the purchase of motor vehicle equipment and supplies to ensure that agencies within a reasonable distance are not duplicating maintenance services or purchasing equipment that is not in the best interest of the State. The department shall develop a uniform method to be used by the agencies to determine the cost per mile for each vehicle operated by the State.

HISTORY: 1978 Act No. 644, Part II Section 24(I); 1982 Act No. 429, Section 6; 1998 Act No. 419, Part II, Section 30; 2014 Act No. 121 (S.22), Pt V, Section 7.E.3, eff July 1, 2015.

Effect of Amendment

2014 Act No. 121, Section 7.E.3, substituted "department" for "board" throughout; in the last paragraph, substituted "adjust the budgetary appropriation" for "adjust the appropriation in Part IA, Section 63B"; and made other nonsubstantive changes.

SECTION 1-11-310. Division of General Services, Program of Fleet Management; acquisition and disposition of vehicles; titles.

(A) The Department of Administration shall purchase, acquire, transfer, replace, and dispose of all motor vehicles on the basis of maximum cost-effectiveness and lowest anticipated total life cycle costs.

(B) The standard state fleet sedan or station wagon must be no larger than a compact model and the special state fleet sedan or station wagon must be no larger than an intermediate model. The State Fleet Manager shall determine the types of vehicles which fit into these classes. Only these classes of sedans and station wagons may be purchased by the State for nonlaw enforcement use.

(C) The State shall purchase police sedans only for the use of law enforcement officers, as defined by the Internal Revenue Code. Purchase of a vehicle under this subsection must be concurred in by the State Fleet Manager and must be in accordance with regulations promulgated or procedures adopted under Sections 1-11-220 through 1-11-340 which must take into consideration the agency's mission, the intended use of the vehicle, and the officer's duties. Law enforcement agency vehicles used by employees whose job functions do not meet the Internal Revenue Service definition of "Law Enforcement Officer" must be standard or special state fleet sedans.

(D) All state motor vehicles must be titled to the State and must be received by and remain in the possession of the Program of Fleet Management pending sale or disposal of the vehicle.

(E) Titles to school buses and service vehicles operated by the State Department of Education and vehicles operated by the South Carolina Department of Transportation must be retained by those agencies.

(F) Exceptions to requirements in subsections (B) and (C) must be approved by the State Fleet Manager. Requirements in subsection (B) do not apply to the Department of Commerce.

(G) Preference in purchasing state motor vehicles must be given to vehicles assembled in the United States with at least seventy-five percent domestic content as determined by the appropriate federal agency.

(H) Preference in purchasing state motor vehicles must be given to hybrid, plug-in hybrid, biodiesel, hydrogen, fuel cell, or flex-fuel vehicles when the performance, quality, and anticipated life cycle costs are comparable to other available motor vehicles.

HISTORY: 1978 Act No. 644, Part II, Section 24(J); 1992 Act No. 449, Part V, Section 2, eff July 1, 1992; 1996 Act No. 459, Section 2; 2008 Act No. 203, Section 2, eff upon approval (became law without the Governor's signature on April 17, 2008); 2014 Act No. 121 (S.22), Pt V, Section 7.E.3, eff July 1, 2015.

Effect of Amendment

The 2008 amendment added item (H) relating to purchase of low emission motor vehicles by the State.

2014 Act No. 121, Section 7.E.3, in subsection (A), substituted "Department of Administration" for "State Budget and Control Board"; in subsections (B) and (C), substituted "State Fleet Manager" for "director of the Division of Motor Vehicle Management"; in subsection (D), substituted "Program of Fleet Management" for "Division of Motor Vehicle Management"; and in subsection (F), substituted "State Fleet Manager" for "director of the Division of Motor Vehicle Management" and substituted "Department of Commerce" for "State Development Board".

SECTION 1-11-315. Feasibility of using alternative transportation fuels for state fleet.

The Department of Administration, Division of General Services, Program of Fleet Management, shall determine the extent to which the state vehicle fleet can be configured to operate on alternative transportation fuels. This determination must be based on a thorough evaluation of each alternative fuel and the feasibility of using such fuels to power state vehicles. The state fleet must be configured in a manner that will serve as a model for other corporate and government fleets in the use of alternative transportation fuel. By March 1, 1993, the Program of Fleet Management must submit a plan to the General Assembly for the use of alternative transportation fuels for the state vehicle fleet that will enable the state vehicle fleet to serve as a model for corporate and other government fleets in the use of alternative transportation fuel. This plan must contain a cost/benefit analysis of the proposed changes.

HISTORY: 1992 Act No. 449, Pt. V, Section 17; 2014 Act No. 121 (S.22), Pt V, Section 7.E.3, eff July 1, 2015.

Effect of Amendment

2014 Act No. 121, Section 7.E.3, substituted "Department of Administration, Division of General Services, Program of Fleet Management," for "State Budget and Control Board Division of Motor Vehicle Management" and substituted "Program of Fleet Management" for "Division of Motor Vehicle Management".

SECTION 1-11-320. Division of General Services, Program of Fleet Management; plates and other identification requirements; exemptions.

The department shall ensure that all state-owned motor vehicles are identified as such through the use of permanent state government license plates and either state or agency seal decals. No vehicles shall be exempt from the requirements for identification except those exempted by the department.

This section shall not apply to vehicles supplied to law enforcement officers when, in the opinion of the department after consulting with the Chief of the State Law Enforcement Division, those officers are actually involved in undercover law enforcement work to the extent that the actual investigation of criminal cases or the investigators' physical well-being would be jeopardized if they were identified. The department is authorized to exempt vehicles carrying human service agency clients in those instances in which the privacy of the client would clearly and necessarily be impaired.

HISTORY: 1978 Act No. 644, Part II, Section 24(K); 1982 Act No. 429, Section 7; 2014 Act No. 121 (S.22), Pt V, Section 7.E.3, eff July 1, 2015.

Effect of Amendment

2014 Act No. 121, Section 7.E.3, substituted "department" for "board" throughout, and in the first paragraph, deleted the hyphen between "state" and "government".

SECTION 1-11-330. Division of Motor Vehicle Management; State Department of Education vehicles exempted.

The provisions of Sections 1-11-220 to 1-11-330 shall not apply to school buses and service vehicles operated by the State Department of Education.

HISTORY: 1978 Act No. 644, Part II, Section 24(N).

SECTION 1-11-335. Department of Administration may provide to and receive from other governmental entities goods and services.

The respective divisions of the Department of Administration are authorized to provide to and receive from other governmental entities, including other divisions and state and local agencies and departments, goods and services, as will in its opinion promote efficient and economical operations. The divisions may charge and pay the entities for the goods and services, the revenue from which shall be deposited in the state treasury in a special account and expended only for the costs of providing the goods and services, and such funds may be retained and expended for the same purposes.

HISTORY: 1995 Act No. 145, Part II, Section 6; 2014 Act No. 121 (S.22), Pt V, Section 7.E.3, eff July 1, 2015.

Effect of Amendment

2014 Act No. 121, Section 7.E.3, substituted "Department of Administration" for "Budget and Control Board".

SECTION 1-11-340. Department to develop and implement statewide Fleet Safety Program.

The department shall develop and implement a statewide Fleet Safety Program for operators of state-owned vehicles which shall serve to minimize the amount paid for rising insurance premiums and reduce the number of accidents involving state-owned vehicles. The department shall promulgate regulations requiring the establishment of an accident review board by each agency and mandatory driver training in those instances where remedial training for employees would serve the best interest of the State.

HISTORY: 1982 Act No. 429, Section 9; 2014 Act No. 121 (S.22), Pt V, Section 7.E.3, eff July 1, 2015.

Effect of Amendment

2014 Act No. 121, Section 7.E.3, twice substituted "department" for "board" and deleted "rules and" before "regulations".

SECTION 1-11-360. Office of Precinct Demographics; establishment and responsibilities.

There is created within the Revenue and Fiscal Affairs Office an Office of Precinct Demographics to be staffed by personnel as determined appropriate by the office and consistent with funds appropriated for the Office by the General Assembly in the annual general appropriation act. The Office of Precinct Demographics shall:

(1) Review existing precinct boundaries and maps for accuracy, develop and rewrite descriptions of precincts for submission to the legislative process.

(2) Consult with members of the General Assembly or their designees on matters related to precinct construction or discrepancies that may exist or occur in precinct boundary development in the counties they represent.

(3) Develop a system for originating and maintaining precinct maps and related data for the State.

(4) Represent the Division at public meetings, meetings with members of the General Assembly, and meetings with other state, county, or local governmental entities on matters related to precincts.

(5) Assist the appropriate county officials in the drawing of maps and writing of descriptions or precincts preliminary to these maps and descriptions being filed in this office for submission to the United States Department of Justice.

(6) Coordinate with the Census Bureau in the use of precinct boundaries in constructing census boundaries and the identification of effective uses of precinct and census information for planning purposes.

(7) Serve as a focal point for verifying official precinct information for the counties of South Carolina.

HISTORY: 1984 Act No. 512, Part II, Section 59.

Code Commissioner's Note

At the direction of the Code Commissioner, references in this section to the offices of the former State Budget and Control Board, Office of the Governor, or other agencies, were changed to reflect the transfer of them to the Department of Administration or other entities, pursuant to the directive of the South Carolina Restructuring Act, 2014 Act No. 121, Section 5(D)(1).

SECTION 1-11-370. Determination and designation of indebtedness to be included within any limits on "private activity bonds."

A. By the provisions of Title 4, Chapter 29, of Title 4 (the Industrial Revenue Bond Act), Chapter 3, of Title 48 (the Pollution Control Facilities Revenue Bond Act), Article 11 of Chapter 7 of Title 44 (the Hospital Revenue Bond Act), all of the 1976 Code, and certain other provisions of South Carolina law, various political subdivisions and agencies of the State of South Carolina are authorized or enabled to issue their debt for the benefit of certain private entities in order to encourage and promote certain undertakings and activities which promote the public health, welfare, and economy of the State. There is pending in the Congress of the United States legislation which, if enacted in its present form, would impose a maximum dollar limit on the amount of the debt, referred to as "private activity bonds", which could be issued by a state in a given year. The legislation purports to be effective, retroactively, to all the indebtedness issued subsequent to December 31, 1983. The legislation also provides that the inclusion of the indebtedness issued in any state within the limitation imposed must be determined in a manner as provided by the legislature of the state. The pendency of the legislation absent a mechanism for determining the inclusion of debt within the proposed limit has created uncertainty and difficulty in the issuance of debt to which the limitation, if imposed, might apply. In order to remove this uncertainty the General Assembly proposes to delegate to the State Fiscal Accountability Authority and the Joint Bond Review Committee, if a maximum limit upon the debt is imposed, the authority to designate which indebtedness is included within any limits on "private activity bonds", which may be imposed by federal law or regulations and to promulgate rules and regulations as the Board with the approval of the committee may consider necessary for the purposes.

B. The State Fiscal Accountability Authority and the Joint Bond Review Committee shall develop a plan pursuant to which the Authority shall determine which issue of indebtedness, or portions of indebtedness, issued by the State of South Carolina or any agency or political subdivision of the State must be included within any limitation on "private activity bonds" or any similar indebtedness, proposed or imposed by any federal legislation or regulations. The determination may be made without regard to the date of any agreements between the issuers and beneficiaries of any indebtedness, and no priority need be given any issue, issuer, or beneficiary based on any date.

C. The State Fiscal Accountability Authority, after review by the Joint Bond Review Committee, shall promulgate regulations as it considers necessary or useful in connection with the authority granted in this section.

HISTORY: 1984 Act No. 512, Part II, Section 39.

Code Commissioner's Note

At the direction of the Code Commissioner, references in this section to the offices of the former State Budget and Control Board, Office of the Governor, or other agencies, were changed to reflect the transfer of them to the Department of Administration or other entities, pursuant to the directive of the South Carolina Restructuring Act, 2014 Act No. 121, Section 5(D)(1), effective July 1, 2015.

SECTION 1-11-395. Use of vendors by state body providing health care or social services to recover reimbursement for providing services.

Any state governmental body which provides health care or social services and which has a legal right to be reimbursed from any private or governmental source for these services may contract with any vendor on a contingent basis to recover or to assist in the recovery of funds for reimbursement of the provided services. The governmental body may pay the vendor from funds actually collected from governmental or private sources as a result of the services provided by the vendor. The vendor must be selected pursuant to Section 11-35-1530, 11-35-1560, or 11-35-1570 and the contract must be approved by the State Fiscal Accountability Authority.

HISTORY: 1988 Act No. 658, Part II, Section 18C.

Code Commissioner's Note

At the direction of the Code Commissioner, references in this section to the offices of the former State Budget and Control Board, Office of the Governor, or other agencies, were changed to reflect the transfer of them to the Department of Administration or other entities, pursuant to the directive of the South Carolina Restructuring Act, 2014 Act No. 121, Section 5(D)(1), effective July 1, 2015.

SECTION 1-11-400. Authority of Budget and Control Board to enter lease purchase agreements to provide method of replacing Central Correctional Institution.

In furtherance of the State's interest in complying with the terms of Nelson v. Leeke, and in minimizing potential legal liability in the future, and in furtherance of achieving a cost effective and timely solution to this problem through innovative means available in the private sector, after consultation with the Joint Bond Review Committee and the State Reorganization Commission, the State Budget and Control Board is authorized to enter into lease purchase agreements consistent with the Consolidated Procurement Code of the State of South Carolina which would provide the State an economically feasible method of replacing the Central Correctional Institution (CCI), so long as these agreements (1) can be demonstrated to be comparably cost effective to traditional financing methods, (2) can result in long-term operational cost savings, (3) are in compliance with the standards enunciated in Nelson v. Leeke, (4) can result in the provision of a new facility of sufficient bed, program, and support space more expeditiously than traditional methods, (5) that will minimize the wasteful expenditure of funds for further capital improvements to CCI, and (6) will be subject to the year-to-year appropriation process of the General Assembly.

HISTORY: 1985 Act No. 201, Part II, Section 28.

SECTION 1-11-405. Aircraft purchase, lease, or lease-purchase by state agency.

No aircraft may be purchased, leased, or lease-purchased for more than a thirty-day period by any state agency without the prior authorization of the Department of Administration or the State Fiscal Accountability Authority, as appropriate, and the Joint Bond Review Committee.

HISTORY: 1995 Act No. 145, Part II, Section 44.

Code Commissioner's Note

At the direction of the Code Commissioner, references in this section to the offices of the former State Budget and Control Board, Office of the Governor, or other agencies, were changed to reflect the transfer of them to the Department of Administration or other entities, pursuant to the directive of the South Carolina Restructuring Act, 2014 Act No. 121, Section 5(D)(1), effective July 1, 2015.

SECTION 1-11-420. Reports to State Budget and Control Board.

All institutions, departments, and agencies shall file an annual report with the board at the time the board specifies. The board shall prescribe specifications and deadlines as are practicable for the reports, the objective being to limit the content and style of printing, and thus keep the cost of their publication within reasonable limits. The board shall have the reports printed and made available on or before January first to each member of the General Assembly at his request and to the State Library. The board shall report annually to the General Assembly on the expenditure of appropriations for the reports showing, by departments, the number of copies and cost of publication. State agency annual reports required under the provisions of this section and reports to the General Assembly may not be printed in a multicolor format unless that format can be purchased at the cost of black and white printing, nor may these reports contain pictures of board or commission members, agency officers, or employees.

HISTORY: 1988 Act No. 307, Section 1.

SECTION 1-11-425. Cost information to be included in publications; exceptions.

All agencies using appropriated funds shall print on the last page of all bound publications the following information:

(1) total printing cost;

(2) total number of documents printed; and

(3) cost per unit.

The President Pro Tempore of the Senate, the Speaker of the House, the Legislative Services Agency, the presidents of each institution of higher education, and the State Board for Technical and Comprehensive Education may exempt from this requirement documents published by their respective agencies. Agency publications which are produced for resale are also exempt from this requirement.

Publications of public relations nature produced by Parks, Recreation and Tourism and the Division of State Development are exempt from this requirement.

HISTORY: 2002 Act No. 356, Section 1, Pt XI.K; 2013 Act No. 31, Section 2, eff May 21, 2013.

Effect of Amendment

The 2013 amendment substituted "the Legislative Services Agency" for "Legislative Printing, Information and Technology Systems".

SECTION 1-11-430. Supply and use of telecommunication systems for state Government.

In post-divestiture circumstances, the State, its boards, committees, commissions, councils, and agencies, and other entities excluding counties, municipalities, and special service and school districts must be treated as a single enterprise for purposes of securing and utilizing local and long distance telecommunications equipment and services.

The Department of Administration shall secure all telecommunications equipment and services for the state government enterprise under terms it considers suitable and coordinate the supply of the equipment and services for state government use. No entity of state government may enter into an agreement or renew an existing agreement for telecommunications services unless approved by the board.

HISTORY: 1989 Act No. 189, Part II, Section 23.

Code Commissioner's Note

At the direction of the Code Commissioner, references in this section to the offices of the former State Budget and Control Board, Office of the Governor, or other agencies, were changed to reflect the transfer of them to the Department

of Administration or other entities, pursuant to the directive of the South Carolina Restructuring Act, 2014 Act No. 121, Section 5(D)(1), effective July 1, 2015.

SECTION 1-11-435. Protection of critical information technology infrastructure and data systems.

To protect the state's critical information technology infrastructure and associated data systems in the event of a major disaster, whether natural or otherwise, and to allow the services to the citizens of this State to continue in such an event, the Office of the State Chief Information Officer (CIO) should develop a Critical Information Technology Infrastructure Protection Plan devising policies and procedures to provide for the confidentiality, integrity, and availability of, and to allow for alternative and immediate on-line access to critical data and information systems including, but not limited to, health and human services, law enforcement, and related agency data necessary to provide critical information to citizens and ensure the protection of state employees as they carry out their disaster-related duties. All state agencies and political subdivisions of this State are directed to assist the Office of the State CIO in the collection of data required for this plan.

HISTORY: 2002 Act No. 339, Section 4.

SECTION 1-11-440. Defense of members of Fiscal Accountability Authority and the Director of the Department of Administration.

(A) The State must defend the members of the State Fiscal Accountability Authority and the Director of the Department of Administration against a claim or suit that arises out of or by virtue of their performance of official duties on behalf of the authority or the department, as applicable, and must indemnify them for a loss or judgment incurred by them as a result of the claim or suit, without regard to whether the claim or suit is brought against them in their individual or official capacities, or both. The State must defend officers and management employees of the authority, legislative employees performing duties for the authority's members or the department, and the department's officers and management employees against a claim or suit that arises out of or by virtue of the performance of official duties unless the officer, management employee, or legislative employee was acting in bad faith and must indemnify these officers, management employees, and legislative employees for a loss or judgment incurred by them as a result of such claim or suit, without regard to whether the claim or suit is brought against them in their individual or official capacities, or both. This commitment to defend and indemnify extends to members of the authority, the authority's officers and management employees, the department's director and officers and management employees, and legislative employees after they have left their employment with the authority, the General Assembly, or the department, as applicable, if the claim or suit arises out of or by virtue of their performance of official duties on behalf of their employer.

(B) The State must defend the members of the Retirement Systems Investment Panel established pursuant to Section 16, Article X of the Constitution of this State and Section 9-16-310 against a claim or suit that arises out of or by virtue of their performance of official duties on behalf of the panel and must indemnify these members for a loss or judgment incurred by them as a result of the claim or suit, without regard to whether the claim or suit is brought against them in their individual or official capacities, or both. This commitment to defend and indemnify extends to members of the panel after they have left their service with the panel if the claim or suit arises out of or by virtue of their performance of official duties on behalf of the panel.

HISTORY: 2003 Act No. 13, Section 1; 2014 Act No. 121 (S.22), Pt VII, Section 20.A, eff July 1, 2015.

Editor's Note

Section 9-16-310, referenced in subsection (B), was repealed by 2012 Act No. 278.

Effect of Amendment

2014 Act No. 121, Section 20.A, rewrote subsection (A).

SECTION 1-11-460. Payment of judgments against governmental employees and officials in excess of one million dollars; limitations; recovery of amount paid by assessment against entities purchasing tort liability insurance.

The State Fiscal Accountability Authority, through the Division of Insurance Services, is authorized to pay judgments against individual governmental employees and officials, in excess of one million dollars, subject to a maximum of four million dollars in excess of one million dollars for one employee and a maximum of twenty million dollars in excess of five million dollars in one fiscal year. These payments are limited to judgments rendered under 42 U.S.C. Section 1983 against governmental employees or officials who are covered by a tort liability policy issued by the Insurance Reserve Fund. These payments are also limited to judgments against governmental employees and officials for acts committed within the scope of employment. If a judgment is paid, the payment must be recovered by assessments against all governmental entities purchasing tort liability insurance from the Insurance Reserve Fund.

HISTORY: 1992 Act No. 509, Section 1.

Code Commissioner's Note

At the direction of the Code Commissioner, references in this section to the offices of the former State Budget and Control Board, Office of the Governor, or other agencies, were changed to reflect the transfer of them to the Department of Administration or other entities, pursuant to the directive of the South Carolina Restructuring Act, 2014 Act No. 121, Section 5(D)(1), effective July 1, 2015.

SECTION 1-11-470. Limitations on use of funds appropriated by General Assembly.

(A) No funds appropriated by the General Assembly may be used by a constitutional officer to purchase space including, but not limited to, notices or advertisements, in a print medium or time from a radio or television medium without unanimous prior written approval of the Budget and Control Board.

(B) No funds appropriated by the General Assembly may be used by a constitutional officer to print on, or distribute with, official documents extraneous promotional material or to purchase plaques, awards, citations, or other recognitions without unanimous prior written approval of the Budget and Control Board.

(C) If nonpublic funds are used for the purposes enumerated in subsection (A), the constitutional officer expending the funds must submit the source of the funds showing all contributors to the Budget and Control Board before the funds are expended.

(D) The provisions of this section do not apply to the Governor or to the General Assembly.

HISTORY: 1997 Act No. 155, Part II, Section 42A.

Code Commissioner's Note

At the direction of the Code Commissioner, reference in this section to the former Budget and Control Board has not been changed pursuant to the directive of the South Carolina Restructuring Act, 2014 Act No. 121, Section 5(D)(1), until further action by the General Assembly.

SECTION 1-11-475. Employee benefit appropriations; transfer of funds within agency to cover overruns.

It is the intent of the General Assembly that the amounts appropriated to each agency or institution in a fiscal year for employee benefits are sufficient to pay the employer contribution costs of that agency. The Department of Administration shall devise a plan for the expenditure of the funds appropriated for employer contributions and may require transfers of funds within an agency or institution if it becomes evident that the employer contribution costs exceed the funds available for that purpose.

HISTORY: 2002 Act No. 356, Section 1, Pt XI.F.

Code Commissioner's Note

At the direction of the Code Commissioner, references in this section to the offices of the former State Budget and Control Board, Office of the Governor, or other agencies, were changed to reflect the transfer of them to the Department of Administration or other entities, pursuant to the directive of the South Carolina Restructuring Act, 2014 Act No. 121, Section 5(D)(1), effective July 1, 2015.

SECTION 1-11-480. Hiring consultant or management firm to assist in administration of state employee unemployment compensation fund; annual reports to General Assembly.

The Department of Administration is authorized to hire consultants or a management firm to assist in the administration of the unemployment compensation program for state employees and, for that purpose, may use funds appropriated or otherwise made available for unemployment payments. The Department of Administration is authorized to make the transfers necessary to accomplish this purpose. The Department of Administration shall report in writing annually to the General Assembly the complete name, address, and amounts paid to the consultants or management firm.

HISTORY: 1999 Act No. 100, Part II, Section 86.

Code Commissioner's Note

At the direction of the Code Commissioner, references in this section to the offices of the former State Budget and Control Board, Office of the Governor, or other agencies, were changed to reflect the transfer of them to the Department of Administration or other entities, pursuant to the directive of the South Carolina Restructuring Act, 2014 Act No. 121, Section 5(D)(1), effective July 1, 2015.

SECTION 1-11-490. Breach of security of state agency data; notification; rights and remedies of injured parties; penalties; notification of Consumer Protection Division.

(A) An agency of this State owning or licensing computerized data or other data that includes personal identifying information shall disclose a breach of the security of the system following discovery or notification of the breach in the security of the data to a resident of this State whose unencrypted and unredacted personal identifying information was, or is reasonably believed to have been, acquired by an unauthorized person when the illegal use of the information has occurred or is reasonably likely to occur or use of the information creates a material risk of harm to the resident. The disclosure must be made in the most expedient time possible and without unreasonable delay, consistent with the legitimate needs of law enforcement, as provided in subsection (C), or with measures necessary to determine the scope of the breach and restore the reasonable integrity of the data system.

(B) An agency maintaining computerized data or other data that includes personal identifying information that the agency does not own shall notify the owner or licensee of the information of a breach of the security of the data immediately following discovery, if the personal identifying information was, or is reasonably believed to have been, acquired by an unauthorized person.

(C) The notification required by this section may be delayed if a law enforcement agency determines that the notification impedes a criminal investigation. The notification required by this section must be made after the law enforcement agency determines that it no longer compromises the investigation.

(D) For purposes of this section:

(1) "Agency" means any agency, department, board, commission, committee, or institution of higher learning of the State or a political subdivision of it.

(2) "Breach of the security of the system" means unauthorized access to and acquisition of computerized data that was not rendered unusable through encryption, redaction, or other methods that compromise the security, confidentiality, or integrity of personal identifying information maintained by the agency, when illegal use of the information has occurred or is reasonably likely to occur or use of the information creates a material risk of harm to the consumer. Good faith acquisition of personal identifying information by an employee or agent of the agency for the purposes of the agency is not a breach of the security of the system if the personal identifying information is not used or subject to further unauthorized disclosure.

(3) "Personal identifying information" has the same meaning as "personal identifying information" in Section 16-13-510(D).

(E) The notice required by this section may be provided by:

(1) written notice;

(2) electronic notice, if the person's primary method of communication with the individual is by electronic means or is consistent with the provisions regarding electronic records and signatures set forth in Section 7001 of Title 15 USC and Chapter 6, Title 26 of the 1976 Code;

(3) telephonic notice; or

(4) substitute notice, if the agency demonstrates that the cost of providing notice exceeds two hundred fifty thousand dollars or that the affected class of subject persons to be notified exceeds five hundred thousand or the agency has insufficient contact information. Substitute notice consists of:

(a) e-mail notice when the agency has an e-mail address for the subject persons;

(b) conspicuous posting of the notice on the agency's web site page, if the agency maintains one; or

(c) notification to major statewide media.

(F) Notwithstanding subsection (E), an agency that maintains its own notification procedures as part of an information security policy for the treatment of personal identifying information and is otherwise consistent with the timing requirements of this section is considered to be in compliance with the notification requirements of this section if it notifies subject persons in accordance with its policies in the event of a breach of security of the system.

(G) A resident of this State who is injured by a violation of this section, in addition to and cumulative of all other rights and remedies available at law, may:

(1) institute a civil action to recover damages;

(2) seek an injunction to enforce compliance; and

(3) recover attorney's fees and court costs, if successful.

(H) An agency that knowingly and wilfully violates this section is subject to an administrative fine up to one thousand dollars for each resident whose information was accessible by reason of the breach, the amount to be decided by the Department of Consumer Affairs.

(I) If the agency provides notice to more than one thousand persons at one time pursuant to this section, the business shall notify, without unreasonable delay, the Consumer Protection Division of the Department of Consumer Affairs and all consumer reporting agencies that compile and maintain files on a nationwide basis, as defined in 15 USC Section 1681a(p), of the timing, distribution, and content of the notice.

HISTORY: 2008 Act No. 190, Section 4.A, eff July 1, 2009.

SECTION 1-11-495. Repealed.

HISTORY: Former Section, titled Monitoring revenues and expenditures to determine year-end deficits; quarterly appropriations allocation; supplemental appropriations, had the following history: 2008 Act No. 353, Section 2, Pt 20A, eff July 1, 2009; 2010 Act No. 152, Section 4, eff May 6, 2010. Repealed by 2014 Act No. 121, Pt VI, Section 10.B, eff July 1, 2015.

SECTION 1-11-497. Across-the-board reduction in expenditures.

If the Executive Budget Office or the General Assembly mandates an across-the-board reduction, state agencies are encouraged to reduce general operating expenses including, but not limited to, travel, training, procurement, hiring of temporary and contractual employees before reductions are made to programs, special line items, or local provider services critical to an agency's mission.

HISTORY: 2008 Act No. 353, Section 2, Pt 20E, eff July 1, 2009.

Code Commissioner's Note

At the direction of the Code Commissioner, references in this section to the offices of the former State Budget and Control Board, Office of the Governor, or other agencies, were changed to reflect the transfer of them to the Department of Administration or other entities, pursuant to the directive of the South Carolina Restructuring Act, 2014 Act No. 121, Section 5(D)(1), effective July 1, 2015.

ARTICLE 3

Allocation of State Ceiling on Issuance of Private Activity Bonds

SECTION 1-11-500. Calculation and certification of state ceiling.

The state ceiling on the issuance of private activity bonds as defined in Section 146 of the Internal Revenue Code of 1986 (the Code) established in the act must be certified annually by the State Fiscal Accountability Authority secretary based upon the provisions of the act. The board secretary shall make this certification as soon as practicable after the estimates of the population of the State of South Carolina to be used in the calculation are published by the United States Bureau of the Census but in no event later than February first of each calendar year.

HISTORY: 1987 Act No. 117, Section 1.

Code Commissioner's Note

At the direction of the Code Commissioner, references in this section to the offices of the former State Budget and Control Board, Office of the Governor, or other agencies, were changed to reflect the transfer of them to the Department of Administration or other entities, pursuant to the directive of the South Carolina Restructuring Act, 2014 Act No. 121, Section 5(D)(1), effective July 1, 2015.

SECTION 1-11-510. Allocation of bond limit amounts.

(A) The private activity bond limit for all issuing authorities must be allocated by the board in response to authorized requests as described in Section 1-11-530 by the issuing authorities.

(B) The aggregate private activity bond limit amount for all South Carolina issuing authorities is allocated initially to the State for further allocation within the limits prescribed herein.

(C) Except as is provided in Section 1-11-540, all allocations must be made by the board on a first-come, first-served basis, to be determined by the date and time sequence in which complete authorized requests are received by the board secretary.

HISTORY: 1987 Act No. 117, Section 2.

SECTION 1-11-520. Private activity bond limits and pools.

(A) The private activity bond limit for all state government issuing authorities now or hereafter authorized to issue private activity bonds as defined in the act, to be known as the "state government pool", is forty percent of the state ceiling less any amount shifted to the local pool as described in subsection (B) of this section or plus any amount shifted from that pool.

(B) The private activity bond limit for all issuing authorities other than state government agencies, to be known as the "local pool", is sixty percent of the state ceiling plus any amount shifted from the state government pool or less any amount shifted to that pool.

(C) The board, with review and comment by the Joint Bond Review Committee, may shift unallocated amounts from one pool to the other at any time.

HISTORY: 1987 Act No. 117, Section 3.

SECTION 1-11-530. Authorized requests for allocation of bond limit amounts.

(A) For private activity bonds proposed for issue by other than state government issuing authorities, an authorized request is a request included in a petition to the board that a specific amount of the state ceiling be allocated to the bonds for which the petition is filed. The petition must be accompanied by a copy of the Inducement Contract, Inducement Resolution, or other comparable preliminary approval entered into or adopted by the issuing authority, if any, relating to the bonds. The board shall forward promptly to the committee a copy of each petition received.

(B) For private activity bonds proposed for issue by any state government issuing authority, an authorized request is a request included in a petition to the board that a specific amount of the state ceiling be allocated to the bonds for which the petition is filed. The petition must be accompanied by a bond resolution or comparable action by the issuing authority authorizing the issuance of the bonds. The board shall forward promptly to the committee a copy of each petition received.

(C) Each authorized request must demonstrate that the allocation amount requested constitutes all of the private activity bond financing contemplated at the time for the project and any other facilities located at or used as a part of an integrated operation with the project.

HISTORY: 1987 Act No. 117, Section 4.

SECTION 1-11-540. Limitations on allocations.

(A) The board, with review and comment by the committee, may disapprove, reduce, or defer any authorized request. If it becomes necessary to exercise this authority, the board and the committee shall take into account the public interest in promoting economic growth and job creation.

(B) Authorized requests for state ceiling allocations of more than ten million dollars for a single project are deferred until after July first unless the board, after review and comment by the committee, determines in any particular instance that the positive impact upon the State of approving an allocation of an amount greater than ten million dollars is of such significance that approval of the allocation is warranted.

HISTORY: 1987 Act No. 117, Section 5.

SECTION 1-11-550. Certificates by issuing authority and by board.

(A) An allocation of the state ceiling approved by the board is made formal initially by a certificate which allocates tentatively a specific amount of the state ceiling to the bonds for which the allocation is requested. This tentative allocation certificate must specify the state ceiling amount allocated, the issuing authority and the project involved, and the time period during which the tentative allocation is valid. This certificate must remind the issuing authority that the tentative allocation is made final after the issuing authority chairman or other duly authorized official or agent of the issuing authority, before the issue is made, certifies the issue amount and the projected date of issue, as is required by subsection (B) of this section. It also may include other information considered relevant by the board secretary.

(B) The chairman or other authorized official or agent of an issuing authority issuing any private activity bond for which a portion of the state ceiling has been allocated tentatively shall execute and deliver to the board secretary an issue amount certificate setting forth the exact amount of bonds to be issued and the projected bond issue date which date must not be more than ten business days after the date of the issue amount certificate and it must be before the state ceiling allocation involved expires. The issue amount certificate may be an executed copy of the appropriate completed Internal Revenue Service form to be submitted to the Internal Revenue Service on the issue or it may be in the form of a letter which certifies the exact amount of bonds to be issued and the projected date of the issue.

(C) In response to the issuing authority's issue amount certificate required by subsection (B) of this section, the board secretary is authorized to issue and, as may be necessary, to revise a certificate making final the ceiling allocation approved previously by the board on a tentative basis, if the secretary determines that:

(1) the issuing authority's issue amount certificate specifies an amount not in excess of the approved tentative ceiling allocation amount;

(2) the issue amount certificate was received prior to the issue date projected and that the certificate is dated not more than ten days prior to the issue date projected;

(3) the issue date projected is within the time period approved previously for the tentative ceiling allocation; and

(4) the bonds when issued and combined with the total amount of bonds requiring a ceiling allocation included in issue amount certificates submitted previously to the board by issuing authorities do not exceed the state ceiling for the calendar year. Except under extraordinary circumstances, the board secretary shall issue this certificate within two business days following the date the issue amount certificate is received.

(D) In accordance with Section 149(e)(2)(F) of the Code, the secretary of the State Fiscal Accountability Authority is designated as the state official responsible for certifying, if applicable, that certain bonds meet the requirements of Section 146 of the Code relating to the volume cap on private activity bonds.

(E) Any tentative or final state ceiling allocation granted by the board before the effective date of this act remains valid as an allocation of a portion of the volume cap for South Carolina provided under Section 146 of the Code. The allocations expire in accordance with the regulations under which they were granted or extended and their validity may be extended or reinstated in accordance with the provisions of Sections 1-11-500 through 1-11-570.

HISTORY: 1987 Act No. 117, Section 6.

Code Commissioner's Note

At the direction of the Code Commissioner, references in this section to the offices of the former State Budget and Control Board, Office of the Governor, or other agencies, were changed to reflect the transfer of them to the Department of Administration or other entities, pursuant to the directive of the South Carolina Restructuring Act, 2014 Act No. 121, Section 5(D)(1), effective July 1, 2015.

SECTION 1-11-560. Time limits on allocations.

(A) Any state ceiling allocation approved by the board is valid only for the calendar year in which it is approved, unless eligible and approved for carry-forward election or unless specified differently in the board certificates required by Section 1-11-550.

(B) Unless eligible and approved for carry- forward election or unless specified differently in board certificates required by Section 1-11-550, each state ceiling allocation expires automatically if the bonds for which the allocation is made are not issued within ninety consecutive calendar days from the date the allocation is approved by the board.

(C) In response to a written request by the chairman or other duly authorized official or agent of an issuing authority, the board, acting during the period an approved allocation is valid, may extend the period in which an allocation is valid in a single calendar year by thirty-one consecutive calendar days to a total of not more than one hundred twenty-one consecutive calendar days.

(D) In response to a written request by the chairman or other authorized official or agent of an issuing authority, the board may reinstate for a period of not more than thirty-one consecutive calendar days in any one calendar year part or all of an allocation approved but not extended previously in accordance with subsection (C) of this section in that same calendar year which has expired. The reinstatement request must certify that the authorized request submitted previously is still true and correct or a new authorized request must be submitted.

(E) A tentative ceiling allocation is canceled automatically if the chairman or other authorized official or agent of the issuing authority involved fails to deliver the issue amount certificate required by Section 1-11-550 to the board secretary before the bonds for which the allocation is made are issued.

(F) The chairman or other authorized official or agent of an issuing authority shall advise the board secretary in writing as soon as is practicable after a decision is made not to issue bonds for which a portion of the state ceiling has been allocated. All notices of relinquishment of ceiling allocations must be entered promptly in the board's records by the board secretary.

(G) Ceiling allocations which are eligible and approved for carry-forward election are not subject to the validity limits of this section. The board shall join with the issuing authorities involved in carry-forward election statements to meet the requirements of the Internal Revenue Service.

HISTORY: 1987 Act No. 117, Section 7.

SECTION 1-11-570. Fiscal Accountability Authority to adopt policies and procedures.

The State Fiscal Accountability Authority, after review and comment by the committee, may adopt the policies and procedures it considers necessary for the equitable and effective administration of Sections 1-11-500 through 1-11-570.

HISTORY: 1987 Act No. 117, Section 8.

Code Commissioner's Note

At the direction of the Code Commissioner, references in this section to the offices of the former State Budget and Control Board, Office of the Governor, or other agencies, were changed to reflect the transfer of them to the Department of Administration or other entities, pursuant to the directive of the South Carolina Restructuring Act, 2014 Act No. 121, Section 5(D)(1), effective July 1, 2015.

SECTION 1-11-580. Fiscal Accountability Authority to make quarterly payments on certain insurance contracts.

The State Fiscal Accountability Authority shall make quarterly payments on insurance contracts where the annual premium exceeds fifty thousand dollars. The board shall undertake necessary negotiations to implement this requirement. Where fees may be incurred for quarterly rather than annual payments, the State Fiscal Accountability Authority shall determine whether the investment income opportunity is greater or less than proposed fees and shall make the decision which best benefits South Carolina.

HISTORY: 1995 Act No. 145, Part II, Section 20.

Code Commissioner's Note

At the direction of the Code Commissioner, references in this section to the offices of the former State Budget and Control Board, Office of the Governor, or other agencies, were changed to reflect the transfer of them to the Department of Administration or other entities, pursuant to the directive of the South Carolina Restructuring Act, 2014 Act No. 121, Section 5(D)(1), effective July 1, 2015.

ARTICLE 5

Employees and Retirees Insurance-Accounting for Post-Employment Benefits

Editor's Note

2008 Act No. 195, Section 2, provides as follows:

"Article 5, Chapter 11, Title 1 of the 1976 Code is retitled 'Employees and Retirees Insurance-Accounting for Post-Employment Benefits'."

SECTION 1-11-703. Definitions.

As used in this article:

(1) "Actuarial accrued liability" means that portion, as determined by a particular actuarial cost method, of the actuarial present value of fund obligations and administrative expenses which is not provided for by future normal costs.

(2) "Actuarial assumptions" means assumptions regarding the occurrence of future events affecting costs of the SCRHI Trust Fund or LTDI Trust Fund such as mortality, withdrawal, disability, and retirement; changes in compensation; aging effects and cost trends for post-employment benefits; benefit election rates; rates of investment earnings and asset appreciation or depreciation; procedures used to determine the actuarial value of assets; and other such relevant items.

(3) "Actuarial cost method" means a method for determining the actuarial present value of the obligations and administrative expenses of the SCRHI Trust Fund or LTDI Trust Fund and for developing an actuarially equivalent allocation of such value to time periods, usually in the form of a normal cost and an actuarial-accrued liability. Acceptable actuarial methods are the aggregate, attained age, individual entry age, frozen attained age, frozen entry age, and projected unit credit methods.

(4) "Actuarial present value of total projected benefits" means the present value, at the valuation date, of the cost to finance benefits payable in the future, discounted to reflect the expected effects of the time value of money and the probability of payment.

(5) "Actuarial valuation" means the determination, as of a valuation date, of the normal cost, actuarial accrued liability, actuarial value of assets, and related actuarial present values for the SCRHI Trust Fund or LTDI Trust Fund.

(6) "Actuarially sound" means that calculated contributions to the SCRHI Trust Fund or LTDI Trust Fund are sufficient to pay the full actuarial cost of these trust funds. The full actuarial cost includes both the normal cost of providing for fund obligations as they accrue in the future and the cost of amortizing the unfunded actuarial accrued liability over a period of no more than thirty years.

(7) "Administrative expenses" means all expenses incurred in the operation of the SCRHI Trust Fund and LTDI Trust Fund, including all investment expenses.

(8) "LTDI Trust Fund" means the Long Term Disability Insurance Trust Fund established pursuant to Section 1-11-707 to fund benefits under the state's Basic Long Term Disability (BLTD) Income Benefit Plan.

(9) "Board" means the Board of Directors of the South Carolina Public Employee Benefit Authority.

(10) "Employee insurance program" or "EIP" means the office of the South Carolina Public Employee Benefit Authority designated by the board to operate insurance programs pursuant to this article.

(11) "IBNR" means unpaid health claims incurred but not reported. The liability for IBNR claims is actuarially estimated based on the most current historical claims experience of previous payments, inflation, award trends, and estimates of health care trend changes.

(12) "Operating account" means the health insurance program's business operating activities account maintained by the State Treasurer in which are deposited all premiums for enrollees in self-funded health plans authorized in this article, along with employer contributions for active employees covered by such self-funded health plans, and from which claims and administrative expenses of the self-funded health and dental plans administered by the employee insurance program are paid.

(13) "State-covered entity" means state agencies and institutions, however described, and school districts. It also includes political subdivisions of the State that participate in the state health and dental plans.

(14) "State health and dental plans" means any insurance program administered by the employee insurance program pursuant to this article.

(15) "SCRHI Trust Fund" means the South Carolina Retiree Health Insurance Trust Fund established pursuant to Section 1-11-705 to fund the employer cost for health benefits for retired state employees and retired public school district employees.

(16) "State Retirement System" or "State Retirement Systems" means all retirement systems established pursuant to Title 9 except for the National Guard Retirement System.

(17) "Unfunded actuarial accrued liability" means for any actuarial valuation the excess of the actuarial accrued liability over the actuarial value of the assets of the fund under an actuarial cost method utilized by the fund for funding purposes.

(18) "Trust fund paid premiums" means the employer premium for state health and dental plans coverage paid by the SCRHI Trust Fund on behalf of a retiree. When it is expressed as a percentage of trust fund paid premiums, it means that the SCRHI Trust Fund shall pay the stated percentage of the employer premiums, with the retiree paying the balance of the employer premiums and the entire employee premium.

HISTORY: 2008 Act No. 195, Section 3, eff May 1, 2008; 2012 Act No. 278, Pt IV, Subpt 2, Section 31, eff July 1, 2012.

Editor's Note

2008 Act No. 195, Section 8, provides as follows:

"This act takes effect on the first day of the month following the month during which this act is approved by the Governor [approved April 2, 2008]."

2012 Act No. 278, Pt IV, Subpt 3, Section 65(C), provides as follows:

"(C) The Code Commissioner is directed to change or correct all references to the Employee Insurance Program, the Retirement Division, and the Deferred Compensation Commission to reflect its transfer to the South Carolina Public Employee Benefit Authority. References to the name of the Employee Insurance Program, the Retirement Division, and the Deferred Compensation Commission in the 1976 Code or other provisions of law are considered to be and must be construed to mean appropriate references."

Effect of Amendment

The 2012 amendment substituted "Board of Directors of the South Carolina Public Employee Benefit Authority" for "State Budget and Control Board" in subsection (9); and substituted "South Carolina Public Employee Benefit Authority" for "board" in subsection (10).

SECTION 1-11-705. South Carolina Retiree Health Insurance Trust fund established; administration.

(A) There is established in the State Treasury separate and distinct from the general fund of the State and all other funds the South Carolina Retiree Health Insurance Trust Fund (SCRHI Trust Fund) to provide for the employer costs of retiree post-employment health insurance benefits for retired state employees and retired employees of public school districts. Earnings on the SCRHI Trust Fund must be credited to it and unexpended funds carried forward in it to succeeding fiscal years.

(B) The board is the trustee of the SCRHI Trust Fund and the State Treasurer is the custodian of the funds of the SCRHI Trust Fund.

(C) The employee insurance program shall administer the SCRHI Trust Fund.

(D) The employee insurance program shall engage actuarial and other services as required to transact the business of the SCRHI Trust Fund. The actuary engaged by the employee insurance program shall provide technical advice to the board regarding operation of the SCRHI Trust Fund.

(E) Upon recommendations of the actuary, the board shall adopt generally accepted and reasonable actuarial assumptions and methods for the operation and funding of the SCRHI Trust Fund as it considers necessary and prudent. The actuarial assumptions and methods adopted by the board must be appropriate for the purposes at hand and must be reasonable, individually and in the aggregate, taking into account the experience of the plan and reasonable expectations. Utilizing the actuarial assumptions most recently adopted by the board, the actuary engaged by the employee insurance program shall set the annual actuarial valuations of normal cost, actuarial liability, actuarial value of assets, and related actuarial present values for the SCRHI Trust Fund.

(F) The board may adopt policies and procedures and promulgate regulations as necessary for the proper administration of the SCRHI Trust Fund.

(G)(1) The funds of the SCRHI Trust Fund must be invested and reinvested by the State Treasurer in the manner allowed by law. The State Treasurer shall consult with the employee insurance program and the employee insurance program's actuary to develop an annual investment plan for the SCRHI Trust Fund taking into account the cash flow needs of the employee insurance program with regard to payment of the employer share of premiums and claims for covered retirees.

(2) Effective beginning with the first fiscal year after the ratification of an amendment to Section 16, Article X of the Constitution of this State allowing funds in post-employment benefits trust funds to be invested in equity securities, the Retirement System Investment Commission (RSIC) established pursuant to Chapter 16 of Title 9, shall invest and reinvest the funds of the SCRHI Trust Fund as assets of a retirement system are invested. The chief investment officer shall consult with the employee insurance program and the employee insurance program's actuary to develop an annual investment plan for the SCRHI Trust Fund taking into account the cash flow needs of the employee insurance program with regard to payment of the employer share of premiums and claims for covered retirees. After the initial fiscal year the RSIC assumes this investing function, the annual investment plan for the SCRHI Trust Fund must be approved by the commission no later than June first of each year for the fiscal year beginning July first of the same calendar year.

(H) The board annually shall determine the minimum annual required contributions to the SCRHI Trust Fund on an actuarially sound basis in accordance with Governmental Accounting Standards Board Statement No. 45, or any other Governmental Accounting Standards Board statements that may be applicable to the SCRHI Trust Fund.

(I) The board shall fund the SCRHI Trust Fund:

(1) through the employer contributions for the South Carolina Retirement Systems as provided in Section 1-11-710(A)(2). The total employer contributions collected from the State and school districts for post-employment benefits must be transferred immediately to the SCRHI Trust Fund for investment, reinvestment, and the payment of post-employment benefits;

(2) by transfer of the Employee Insurance Program as of January thirty-first of each calendar year to the trust fund from the employee insurance program's operating account, the cash balance in the operating account in excess of one hundred forty percent of the actuarially-determined IBNR reserves of the state's health plans as of December thirty-first of the preceding year. On May 1, 2008, an initial transfer must take place applicable to the cash balance as of December 31, 2007; and

(3) with funding as authorized by the General Assembly pursuant to Section 1-11-710(D).

(J) Each month, the employee insurance program shall determine the monthly amount of the state-funded employer premium with respect to retired state employees and retired public school district employees who are eligible for state-paid employer premiums pursuant to Section 1-11-730, and shall transfer this amount to the operating account from the SCRHI Trust Fund. In addition, the employee insurance program shall transfer the total cost of post-employment benefits for retirees and their dependents, net of premium contributions made on behalf of retirees and other sources of revenue attributable to retirees, in accordance with Governmental Accounting Standards Board Statements Nos. 43 and 45 and the Implementation Guide.

(K) The funds of the SCRHI Trust Fund may only be used for the payment of employer-provided other post-employment benefits under the terms of the state health and dental plans. The administrative costs related to the administration of the SCRHI Trust Fund, and the investment and reinvestment of its funds, may be funded from the earnings of the SCRHI Trust Fund.

(L) As a trust, the funds of the SCRHI Trust Fund are not assets of the State or the school districts or their respective agencies. The contributions to the SCRHI Trust Fund are irrevocable and may not revert to the employer except upon complete satisfaction of all liabilities and administrative expenses of the state health and dental plans of other post-employment benefits provided pursuant to the state health and dental plans.

HISTORY: 2008 Act No. 195, Section 3, eff May 1, 2008.

Editor's Note

2008 Act No. 195, Section 7, provides as follows:

"The Code Commissioner shall insert the effective date of this act [May 1, 2008] for the phrase 'reference date' where it appears in Section 1-11-705 of the 1976 Code as added by this act and in Section 1-11-730 of the 1976 Code as amended by this act."

2008 Act No. 195, Section 8, provides as follows:

"This act takes effect on the first day of the month following the month during which this act is approved by the Governor [approved April 2, 2008]."

2012 Act No. 278, Pt IV, Subpt 3, Section 65(C), provides as follows:

"(C) The Code Commissioner is directed to change or correct all references to the Employee Insurance Program, the Retirement Division, and the Deferred Compensation Commission to reflect its transfer to the South Carolina Public Employee Benefit Authority. References to the name of the Employee Insurance Program, the Retirement Division, and the Deferred Compensation Commission in the 1976 Code or other provisions of law are considered to be and must be construed to mean appropriate references."

SECTION 1-11-707. South Carolina Long Term Disability Insurance Trust Fund established; administration.

(A) There is established in the State Treasury separate and distinct from the general fund of the State and all other funds the South Carolina Long Term Disability Insurance Trust Fund (LTDI Trust Fund) to provide for the payment of benefits under the state's Basic Long Term Disability Income Benefit Plan. Earnings on the LTDI Trust Fund must be credited to it and unexpended funds carry forward in it to succeeding fiscal years.

(B) The board is the trustee of the LTDI Trust Fund and the State Treasurer is the custodian of the funds of the LTDI Trust Fund.

(C) The employee insurance program shall administer the LTDI Trust Fund.

(D) The employee insurance program shall engage actuarial and other services as required to transact the business of the LTDI Trust Fund. The actuary engaged by the employee insurance program shall provide technical advice to the board regarding operation of the LTDI Trust Fund.

(E) Upon recommendations of the actuary, the board shall adopt generally accepted and reasonable actuarial assumptions and methods for the operation and funding of the LTDI Trust Fund as it considers necessary and prudent. The actuarial assumptions and methods adopted by the board must be appropriate for the purposes at hand and must be reasonable, individually and in the aggregate, taking into account the experience of the plan and reasonable expectations. Utilizing the actuarial assumptions most recently adopted by the board, the actuary engaged by the employee insurance program shall set the annual actuarial valuations of normal cost, actuarial liability, actuarial value of assets, and related actuarial present values for the LTDI Trust Fund.

(F) The board may adopt policies and procedures and promulgate regulations as necessary for the proper administration of the LTDI Trust Fund.

(G)(1) The funds of the LTDI Trust Fund must be invested and reinvested by the State Treasurer in the manner allowed by law. The State Treasurer shall consult with the employee insurance program and the employee insurance program's actuary to develop an annual investment plan for the LTDI Trust Fund taking into account the cash flow needs of the employee insurance program with regard to payment of the employer share of premiums and claims for covered retirees.

(2) Effective beginning with the first fiscal year after the ratification of an amendment to Section 16, Article X of the Constitution of this State allowing funds in post-employment benefits trust funds to be invested in equity securities, the Retirement System Investment Commission (RSIC) established pursuant to Chapter 16 of Title 9, shall invest and reinvest the funds of the LTDI Trust Fund as assets of a retirement system are invested. The chief investment officer shall consult with the employee insurance program and the employee insurance program's actuary to develop an annual investment plan for the LTDI Trust Fund taking into account the cash flow needs of the employee insurance program with regard to payment of the employer share of premiums and claims for covered retirees. After the initial fiscal year the RSIC assumes this investing function, the annual investment plan for the LTDI Trust Fund must be approved by the commission no later than June first of each year for the fiscal year beginning July first of the same calendar year.

(H) The board annually shall determine the minimum annual required contributions to the LTDI Trust Fund on an actuarially sound basis in accordance with Governmental Accounting Standards Board Statement No. 45, or any other Governmental Accounting Standards Board statements that may be applicable to the LTDI Trust Fund.

(I) The board shall increase the employer contributions used to fund the BLTD Plan by an amount equal to or greater than the minimum annual required contribution for the LTDI Trust Fund as determined in subsection (H) of this section. The increased employer contributions remitted to the employee insurance program under this subsection must be deposited in the LTDI Trust Fund.

(J) Each month, the employee insurance program shall transfer to the operating account from the LTDI Trust Fund the amount invoiced by the third-party administrator for the BLTD Plan for payment of LTDI claims, including reasonable expenses associated with claims administration of the BLTD Plan.

(K) The assets of the LTDI Trust Fund may only be used for the payment of the state's claims under the BLTD Plan along with reasonable expenses associated with the operation of the BLTD Plan, and the assets of the LTDI Trust Fund may not be used for any other purpose. The administrative costs related to the administration of the LTDI Trust Fund, and the investment and reinvestment of its funds, must be funded from the earnings of the LTDI Trust Fund.

(L) As a trust, the funds of the LTDI Trust Fund are not assets of the State or the school districts or their respective agencies. The contributions to the LTDI Trust Fund are irrevocable and may not revert to the employer except upon complete satisfaction of all liabilities and administrative expenses of the State Basic Long Term Disability Income Benefit Plan of other post-employment benefits provided pursuant to the State Basic Long Term Disability Income Benefit Plan.

HISTORY: 2008 Act No. 195, Section 3, eff May 1, 2008.

Editor's Note

2008 Act No. 195, Section 8, provides as follows:

"This act takes effect on the first day of the month following the month during which this act is approved by the Governor [approved April 2, 2008]."

2012 Act No. 278, Pt IV, Subpt 3, Section 65(C), provides as follows:

"(C) The Code Commissioner is directed to change or correct all references to the Employee Insurance Program, the Retirement Division, and the Deferred Compensation Commission to reflect its transfer to the South Carolina Public Employee Benefit Authority. References to the name of the Employee Insurance Program, the Retirement Division, and the Deferred Compensation Commission in the 1976 Code or other provisions of law are considered to be and must be construed to mean appropriate references."

SECTION 1-11-710. Board to make insurance available to active and retired employees; Insurance Reserve Fund to provide reinsurance; cost to be paid out of appropriated and other funds.

(A) The board shall:

(1) make available to active and retired employees of this State and its public school districts and their eligible dependents group health, dental, life, accidental death and dismemberment, and disability insurance plans and benefits in an equitable manner and of maximum benefit to those covered within the available resources;

(2) approve by August fifteenth of each year a plan of benefits, eligibility, and employer, employee, retiree, and dependent contributions for the next calendar year. The board shall devise a plan for the method and schedule of payment for the employer and employee share of contributions and by July first of the current fiscal year, develop and implement a plan increasing the employer contribution rates of the State Retirement Systems to a level adequate to cover the employer's share for the current fiscal year's cost of providing health and dental insurance to retired state and school district employees. The state health and dental plans must include a method for the distribution of the funds appropriated as provided by law which are designated for retiree insurance and also must include a method for allocating to school districts, excluding EIA funding, sufficient general fund monies to offset the additional cost incurred by these entities in their federal and other fund activities as a result of this employer contribution charge. The funds collected through increasing the employer contribution rates for the State Retirement Systems under this section must be deposited in the SCRHI Trust Fund established pursuant to Section 1-11-705. The amounts appropriated in this section shall constitute the State's pro rata contributions to these programs except the State shall pay its pro rata share of health and dental insurance premiums for retired state and public school employees for the current fiscal year;

(3) adjust the plan, benefits, or contributions, at any time to insure the fiscal stability of the system;

(4) set aside in separate continuing accounts in the State Treasury, appropriately identified, all funds, state-appropriated and other, received for actual health and dental insurance premiums due. Funds credited to these accounts may be used to pay the costs of administering the state health and dental plans and may not be used for purposes of other than providing insurance benefits for employees and retirees. A reserve equal to not less than one and one-half months' claims must be maintained in the accounts.

(B) The board may authorize the Insurance Reserve Fund to provide reinsurance, in an approved format with actuarially developed rates, for the operation of the group health insurance or cafeteria plan program, as authorized by Section 9-1-60, for active and retired employees of the State, and its public school districts and their eligible dependents. Premiums for reinsurance provided pursuant to this subsection must be paid out of state appropriated and other funds received for actual health insurance or cafeteria plan premiums due.

(C) Notwithstanding Sections 1-23-310 and 1-23-320 or any other provision of law, claims for benefits under any self-insured plan of insurance offered by the State to state and public school district employees and other eligible individuals must be resolved by procedures established by the board, which shall constitute the exclusive remedy for these claims, subject only to appellate judicial review consistent with the standards provided in Section 1-23-380.

(D) The General Assembly intends to authorize funding for the SCRHI Trust Fund in order to make progress toward reaching or maintaining the minimum annual required contribution under Governmental Accounting Standards Board Statement No. 45. The board shall determine the minimum annual required contribution pursuant to Section 1-11-705(H).

HISTORY: 1992 Act No. 364, Section 1; 1995 Act No. 145, Part II, Section 19; 1996 Act No. 312, Section 1; 2001 Act No. 62, Sections 1, 2; 2008 Act No. 195, Section 4, eff May 1, 2008; 2012 Act No. 278, Pt IV, Subpt 2, Section 32, eff July 1, 2012.

Editor's Note

2008 Act No. 195, Section 8, provides as follows:

"This act takes effect on the first day of the month following the month during which this act is approved by the Governor [approved April 2, 2008]."

Effect of Amendment

The 2008 amendment, in subparagraph (A)(2), combined the second and third sentences by substituting "and" for "Provided that the Budget and Control Board," preceding "by July first", in the third sentence substituted "state health and dental plans" for "plan", and added the fourth sentence referring to the SCRHI Trust Fund; in subparagraph (A)(4), in the second sentence substituted "plans" for "insurance programs" and in the third sentence deleted "an average of" preceding "one and one-half months" and at the end "and all funds in excess of the reserve must be used to reduce premium rates or improve or expand benefits as funding permits"; and added subsection (D) relating to maintaining the minimum annual required contribution.

The 2012 amendment substituted "board" for "State Budget and Control Board" in subsection (A).

SECTION 1-11-715. Incentive program to encourage participation in health promotion and disease prevention programs

The Employee Insurance Program of the Public Employee Benefit Authority is directed to develop and implement, for employees and their spouses who participate in the health plans offered by the Employee Insurance Program, an incentive plan to encourage participation in programs offered by the Employee Insurance Program that promote health and the prevention of disease. The Employee Insurance Program is further directed to implement a premium reduction or other financial incentive, beginning on January 1, 2012, for those employees and their spouses who participate in these programs.

HISTORY: 2011 Act No. 31, Section 1, eff May 26, 2011.

Code Commissioner's Note

At the direction of the Code Commissioner, references in this section to the offices of the former State Budget and Control Board, Office of the Governor, or other agencies, were changed to reflect the transfer of them to the Department of Administration or other entities, pursuant to the directive of the South Carolina Restructuring Act, 2014 Act No. 121, Section 5(D)(1).

Editor's Note

2012 Act No. 278, Pt IV, Subpt 3, Section 65(C), provides as follows:

"(C) The Code Commissioner is directed to change or correct all references to the Employee Insurance Program, the Retirement Division, and the Deferred Compensation Commission to reflect its transfer to the South Carolina Public Employee Benefit Authority. References to the name of the Employee Insurance Program, the Retirement Division, and the Deferred Compensation Commission in the 1976 Code or other provisions of law are considered to be and must be construed to mean appropriate references."

SECTION 1-11-720. Entities whose employees and retirees are eligible for state health and dental insurance plans; requirements for eligibility.

(A) In addition to the employees and retirees and their eligible dependents covered under the state health and dental insurance plans pursuant to Section 1-11-710, employees and retirees and their eligible dependents of the following entities are eligible for coverage under the state health and dental insurance plans pursuant to the requirements of subsection (B):

(1) counties;

(2) regional tourism promotion commissions funded by the Department of Parks, Recreation and Tourism;

(3) county intellectual disability boards funded by the State Mental Retardation Department;

(4) regional councils of government established pursuant to Article 1, Chapter 7 of Title 6;

(5) regional transportation authorities established pursuant to Chapter 25 of Title 58;

(6) alcohol and drug abuse planning agencies designated pursuant to Section 61-12-20;

(7) special purpose districts created by act of the General Assembly that provide gas, water, fire, sewer, recreation, hospital, or sanitation service, or any combination of these services;

(8) municipalities;

(9) local councils on aging or other governmental agencies providing aging services funded by the Office on Aging, Office of the Lieutenant Governor;

(10) community action agencies that receive funding from the Community Services Block Grant Program administered by the Governor's Office, Division of Economic Opportunity;

(11) a residential group care facility providing on-site teaching for residents if the facility's staff are currently members of the South Carolina Retirement System

established pursuant to Chapter 1, Title 9 and if it provides at no cost educational facilities on its grounds to the school district in which it is located.

(12) the South Carolina State Employees' Association;

(13) the Palmetto State Teachers' Association;

(14) the South Carolina Education Association;

(15) the South Carolina Association of School Administrators;

(16) the South Carolina School Boards Association;

(17) the South Carolina Student Loan Corporation.

(18) legislative caucus committees as defined in Section 8-13-1300(21).

(19) soil and water conservation districts established pursuant to Title 48, Chapter 9.

(20) housing authorities as provided for in Chapter 3, Title 31;

(21) the Greenville-Spartanburg Airport District;

(22) cooperative educational service center employees.

(23) the South Carolina Sheriff's Association.

(24) the Pee Dee Regional Airport District.

(25) the Children's Trust Fund as established pursuant to Section 63-11-910.

(26) a residential group facility which provides on-site teaching for residents if the facility's employees are currently members of the South Carolina Retirement System or if it provides, at no cost, educational facilities on its grounds to the school district in which it is located.

(27) a federally qualified health center.

(28) County First Steps Partnership established pursuant to Section 59-152-60.

(29) Palmetto Pride as established pursuant to paragraph 26.7, Part 1B, Act 115 of 2005.

(30) joint agencies established pursuant to Chapter 23, Title 6.

(B) To be eligible to participate in the state health and dental insurance plans, the entities listed in subsection (A) shall comply with the requirements established by the board, and the benefits provided must be the same benefits provided to state and school district employees. These entities must agree to participate for a minimum of four years and the board may adjust the premiums during the coverage period based on experience. An entity which withdraws from participation may not subsequently rejoin during the first four years after the withdrawal date.

(C) If an entity participating in the plans pursuant to subsection (A) is delinquent in remitting proper payments to cover its obligations, the board's Office of Insurance Services shall certify the delinquency to the department or agency of the State holding funds payable to the delinquent entity, and that department or agency shall withhold from those funds an amount sufficient to satisfy the unpaid obligation and shall remit that amount to the Office of Insurance Services in satisfaction of the delinquency.

HISTORY: 1992 Act No. 364, Section 1; 1994 Act No. 310, Section 1; 1994 Act No. 342, Section 2; 1994 Act No. 497, Part II, Sections 42A, 42B; 1996 Act No. 458, Part II, Section 81; 1997 Act No. 62, Section 1; 1998 Act No. 317, Section 1; 1999 Act No. 100, Part II, Sections 40, 89; 2000 Act No. 377, Sections 1 to 5; 2006 Act No. 316, Section 1, eff May 31, 2006; 2008 Act No. 353, Section 2, Pt 25D.3, eff July 1, 2008; 2011 Act No. 31, Sections 2, 3, eff May 26, 2011; 2012 Act No. 278, Pt IV, Subpt 2, Section 33, eff July 1, 2012.

Code Commissioner's Note

At the direction of the Code Commissioner, the reference to Section 20-7-5010 in paragraph (A)(25) was changed to Section 63-11-910 in accordance with 2008 Act No. 361 (Children's Code).

Pursuant to 2011 Act No. 47, Section 14(B), the Code Commissioner substituted "intellectual disability" for "mentally retarded" and "person with intellectual disability" or "persons with intellectual disability" for "mentally retarded".

Effect of Amendment

The 2006 amendment, in subsection (A), added items (25) to (29).

The 2008 amendment, in paragraph (A)(9), substituted "Office of the Lieutenant Governor" for "Department of Health and Human Services".

The 2011 amendment, in subsection (A), in paragraph (7), inserted ", or sanitation", and added paragraph (30).

The 2012 amendment substituted "board" for "Statute Budget and Control Board" in subsection (B).

SECTION 1-11-725. Rating of local disabilities and special needs providers as single group.

The board's experience rating of all local disabilities and special needs providers pursuant to Section 1-11-720(A)(3) must be rated as a single group when rating all optional groups participating in the state employee health insurance program.

HISTORY: 2008 Act No. 353, Section 2, Pt 20I, eff July 1, 2009; 2012 Act No. 278, Pt IV, Subpt 2, Section 34, eff July 1, 2012.

Effect of Amendment

The 2012 amendment substituted "board's" for "State Budget and Control Board's".

SECTION 1-11-730. Persons eligible for state health and dental plan coverage.

(A) If a person began employment eligible for coverage under the state health and dental plans on or before May 1, 2008, the following eligibility provisions govern that person's participation in state health and dental plans as a retiree:

(1) A person covered by the state health and dental plans who terminates employment with at least twenty years' retirement service credit by a state-covered entity before eligibility for retirement under a state retirement system is eligible for state health and dental plans coverage, effective on the date of retirement under a state retirement system, if the last five years are consecutive and in a full-time permanent position with a state-covered entity. With respect to a retiree eligible for coverage pursuant to this subsection, the retiree is eligible

for trust fund paid premiums and the retiree is responsible for the entire employee premium.

(2) A member of the General Assembly who leaves office or retires with at least eight years' credited service in the General Assembly Retirement System is eligible to participate in the state health and dental plans by paying the full premium as determined by the board.

(3) With respect to an active employee: (a) employed by the State or a public school district, (b) retiring with ten or more years of state-covered entity service credited under a state retirement system, and (c) with the last five years of earned service credit consecutive and in a full-time permanent position with the State or a public school district, the retiree is eligible for trust fund paid premiums and the retiree is responsible for the entire employee premium.

(4) A person covered by the state health and dental plans who retires with at least five years' state-covered entity service credited under a state retirement system is eligible to participate in the state health and dental plans by paying the full premium as determined by the board, if the last five years are consecutive and in a full-time permanent position with a state-covered entity.

(5) A spouse or dependent of a person covered by the plans who is killed in the line of duty after December 31, 2001, shall receive equivalent coverage under the state health and dental plans for a period of twelve months and the State is responsible for paying the full premium. After the twelve-month period, a spouse or dependent is eligible for trust fund paid premiums. A spouse is eligible for trust fund paid premiums under this subsection until the spouse remarries. A dependent is eligible for trust fund paid premiums under this subsection until the dependent's eligibility for coverage under the plans would ordinarily terminate.

(6) A former municipal or county council member of a county or municipality which participates in the state health and dental plans who served on the council for at least twelve years and who was covered under the plans at the time of termination is eligible to maintain coverage under the plans if the former member pays the full employer and employee contributions and if the county or municipal council elects to allow this coverage for former members.

(7) A person covered by the state health and dental plans who terminated employment with at least eighteen years' retirement service credit by a state-covered entity before eligibility for retirement under a state retirement system before 1990 is eligible for the plans effective on the date of retirement, if this

person returns to a state-covered entity and is covered by the state health and dental plans and completes at least two consecutive years in a full-time permanent position before the date of retirement.

(B) If a person began employment eligible for coverage under the state health and dental plans after May 1, 2008, the following eligibility provisions govern that person's participation in state health and dental plans as a retiree:

(1) An active employee covered by the state health and dental plans who retires with at least five years of earned retirement service credit under a state retirement system with a state-covered entity is eligible to participate as a retiree in the state health and dental plans if the last five years of the person's covered employment were consecutive and in a full-time permanent position.

(2) A person covered by the state health and dental plans who terminates employment before the person's date of retirement with at least twenty years of earned retirement service credit under a state retirement system with a state-covered entity is eligible to participate as a retiree in the state health and dental plans on the person's date of retirement under a state retirement system, if the last five years of the person's covered employment before termination were consecutive and in a full-time permanent position.

(3) A retired state employee or a retired employee of a public school district who retires under a state retirement system and who is eligible for state health and dental plan coverage under the provisions of item (1) or (2) of this subsection, is eligible for trust fund paid premiums as follows:

(a) If the retiree's earned service credit in a state retirement system is five or more years but fewer than fifteen years with a state-covered entity, then the retiree shall pay the full premium for health and dental plans.

(b) If the retiree's earned service credit in a state retirement system is more than fifteen years, but fewer than twenty-five years with a state-covered entity, then the retiree is eligible for fifty percent trust fund paid premiums and the retiree shall pay the remainder of the premium cost.

(c) If the retiree's earned service credit in a state retirement system is twenty-five or more years with a state-covered entity, then the retiree is eligible for trust fund paid premiums and the retiree is responsible for the entire employee premium.

(4) If a retiree under a state retirement system was employed by an entity that participates in the state health and dental plans pursuant to the provisions of Section 1-11-720 and is eligible to participate in state health and dental plans as a retiree pursuant to the provisions of item (1) or (2) of this subsection, then the retiree's employer, at its discretion, may elect to pay all or a portion of the premium for the retiree's state health and dental plans.

(5) A spouse or dependent of a person covered by the plans who is killed in the line of duty on or after May 1, 2008, shall continue to maintain coverage under state health and dental plans for a period of twelve months after the covered person's death and the State is responsible for paying the full premium. After the twelve-month period, a spouse or dependent is eligible for trust fund paid premiums and the spouse or dependent is responsible for the entire employee premium. A spouse is eligible for trust fund paid premiums under this subsection until the spouse remarries. A dependent is eligible for trust fund paid premiums pursuant to this subsection until the dependent's eligibility for coverage under the plans would ordinarily terminate.

(C) For employees who participate in the state health and dental plans pursuant to the provisions of Section 1-11-720 but who are not members of the State Retirement Systems, one year of full-time employment or its equivalent under their employment relation equates to one year of earned retirement service credit under a state retirement system for purposes of the requirements of subsection (B)(1) and (2) of this section. The EIP shall implement the provisions of this subsection and make determinations pursuant to it. A person aggrieved by a determination of the EIP pursuant to this subsection may appeal that determination as a contested case as provided in Chapter 23 of Title 1, the Administrative Procedures Act.

(D)(1) A person who retires from employment with a solicitor's office under a state retirement system is eligible to participate in the state health and dental plans by paying the full premium as determined by the board if at least one county in the judicial circuit covered by that solicitor's office participates in the state health and dental plans and the person's last five years of employment prior to retirement are consecutive and in a full-time permanent position with that solicitor's office or another entity that participates in the state health and dental plans.

(2) The provisions of this subsection must be interpreted to provide eligibility to the employee, retiree, and their eligible dependents.

HISTORY: 1992 Act No. 364, Section 1; 1994 Act No. 342, Section 1; 1996 Act No. 230, Section 1; 2000 Act No. 387, Part II, Section 67W.1; 2003 Act No. 80, Section 1; 2008 Act No. 195, Section 5, eff May 1, 2008; 2012 Act No. 278, Pt IV, Subpt 2, Section 35, eff July 1, 2012; 2014 Act No. 248 (S.897), Section 1, eff June 6, 2014.

Editor's Note

2008 Act No. 195, Section 7, provides as follows:

"The Code Commissioner shall insert the effective date of this act [May 1, 2008] for the phrase 'reference date' where it appears in Section 1-11-705 of the 1976 Code as added by this act and in Section 1-11-730 of the 1976 Code as amended by this act."

2008 Act No. 195, Section 8, provides as follows:

"This act takes effect on the first day of the month following the month during which this act is approved by the Governor [approved April 2, 2008]."

2014 Act No. 248, Section 2, provides as follows:

"SECTION 2. This act takes effect upon approval by the Governor and is retroactive to January 1, 2012.

Effect of Amendment

The 2008 amendment rewrote this section.

The 2012 amendment substituted "board" for "State Budget and Control Board".

2014 Act No. 248, Section 1, added subsection (D).

SECTION 1-11-740. Division of Insurance Services authorized to develop optional long-term care insurance program.

The Division of Insurance Services of the board may develop an optional long-term care insurance program for active and retired members of the various state retirement systems depending on the availability of a qualified vendor. A program must require members to pay the full insurance premium.

HISTORY: 1992 Act No. 364, Section 1; 2012 Act No. 278, Pt IV, Subpt 2, Section 36, eff July 1, 2012.

Effect of Amendment

The 2012 amendment substituted "board" for "State Budget and Control Board".

SECTION 1-11-750. Withholding long-term care insurance premiums for State retirees.

The board shall devise a method of withholding long-term care insurance premiums offered under Section 1-11-740 for retirees if sufficient enrollment is obtained to make the deductions feasible.

HISTORY: 1995 Act No. 145, Part II, Section 21; 2012 Act No. 278, Pt IV, Subpt 2, Section 36, eff July 1, 2012.

Effect of Amendment

The 2012 amendment substituted "board" for "Budget and Control Board".

SECTION 1-11-770. South Carolina 211 Network.

(A) Subject to appropriations, the General Assembly authorizes the board to plan, develop, and implement a statewide South Carolina 211 Network, which must serve as the single point of coordination for information and referral for health and human services. The objectives for establishing the South Carolina 211 Network are to:

(1) provide comprehensive and cost-effective access to health and human services information;

(2) improve access to accurate information by simplifying and enhancing state and local health and human services information and referral systems and by fostering collaboration among information and referral systems;

(3) electronically connect local information and referral systems to each other, to service providers, and to consumers of information and referral services;

(4) establish and promote standards for data collection and for distributing information among state and local organizations;

(5) promote the use of a common dialing access code and the visibility and public awareness of the availability of information and referral services;

(6) provide a management and administrative structure to support the South Carolina 211 Network and establish technical assistance, training, and support programs for information and referral-service programs;

(7) test methods for integrating information and referral services with local and state health and human services programs and for consolidating and streamlining eligibility and case-management processes;

(8) provide access to standardized, comprehensive data to assist in identifying gaps and needs in health and human services programs; and

(9) provide a unified systems plan with a developed platform, taxonomy, and standards for data management and access.

(B) In order to participate in the South Carolina 211 Network, a 211 provider must be certified by the board. The board must develop criteria for certification and must adopt the criteria as regulations.

(1) If any provider of information and referral services or other entity leases a 211 number from a local exchange company and is not certified by the agency, the agency shall, after consultation with the local exchange company and the Public Service Commission, request that the Federal Communications Commission direct the local exchange company to revoke the use of the 211 number.

(2) The agency shall seek the assistance and guidance of the Public Service Commission and the Federal Communications Commission in resolving any disputes arising over jurisdiction related to 211 numbers.

HISTORY: 2002 Act No. 339, Section 5; 2012 Act No. 278, Pt IV, Subpt 2, Section 37, eff July 1, 2012.

Effect of Amendment

The 2012 amendment substituted "board" for "State Budget and Control Board".

SECTION 1-11-780. Mental health insurance.

The State Employee Insurance Program shall continue to provide mental health parity in the same manner and with the same management practices as included in the plan beginning in 2002, and is not under the jurisdiction of the Department of Insurance. The continuation by the State Employee Insurance Program of providing mental health parity in accordance with the plan set forth in 2002 constitutes compliance with this act.

HISTORY: 2005 Act No. 76, Section 3, eff June 30, 2006.

Code Commissioner's Note

This section was codified at the direction of the Code Commissioner.

Editor's Note

2012 Act No. 278, Pt IV, Subpt 3, Section 65(C), provides as follows:

"(C) The Code Commissioner is directed to change or correct all references to the Employee Insurance Program, the Retirement Division, and the Deferred Compensation Commission to reflect its transfer to the South Carolina Public Employee Benefit Authority. References to the name of the Employee Insurance Program, the Retirement Division, and the Deferred Compensation Commission in the 1976 Code or other provisions of law are considered to be and must be construed to mean appropriate references."

ARTICLE 7

South Carolina Confederate Relic Room and Military Museum [Repealed]

Editor's Note

This article is repealed effective July 1, 2015, by 2014 Act No. 121, Section 17.B. See Chapter 17, Title 60 for new provisions effective July 1, 2015.

SECTIONS 1-11-1110 to 1-11-1140. Repealed.

HISTORY: Former Section, titled Director of South Carolina Confederate Relic Room and Military Museum; appointment, had the following history: 2002 Act No. 356, Section 1, Pt IX.C. Repealed by 2014 Act No. 121, Pt VI, Section 17.B, eff July 1, 2015.

HISTORY: Former Section, titled Authority to receive donations of funds and artifacts and admission fees, had the following history: 2002 Act No. 356, Section 1, Pt IX.C. Repealed by 2014 Act No. 121, Pt VI, Section 17.B, eff July 1, 2015.

HISTORY: Former Section, titled Removal or disposition of artifacts in permanent collection, had the following history: 2002 Act No. 356, Section 1, Pt IX.C. Repealed by 2014 Act No. 121, Pt VI, Section 17.B, eff July 1, 2015.

HISTORY: Former Section, titled Legislative intent, had the following history: 2002 Act No. 356, Section 1, Pt IX.C. Repealed by 2014 Act No. 121, Pt VI, Section 17.B, eff July 1, 2015.

CHAPTER 13

State Human Affairs Commission

SECTION 1-13-10. Short title.

This chapter shall be known as the "South Carolina Human Affairs Law."

HISTORY: 1962 Code Section 1-360.21; 1972 (57) 2651.

SECTION 1-13-20. Declaration of policy.

This chapter is an expression of the concern of the State for the promotion of harmony and the betterment of human affairs. The General Assembly declares the practice of discrimination against an individual because of race, religion, color, sex, age, national origin, or disability as a matter of state concern and declares that this discrimination is unlawful and in conflict with the ideals of South Carolina and the nation, as this discrimination interferes with opportunities of the individual to receive employment and to develop according to the individual's own ability and is degrading to human dignity. The General Assembly further declares that to alleviate these problems a state agency is created which shall seek to eliminate and prevent discrimination because of race, religion, color, sex, age, national origin, or disability.

HISTORY: 1962 Code Section 1-360.22; 1972 (57) 2651; 1979 Act No. 24, Section 1; 1996 Act No. 426, Section 2.

SECTION 1-13-30. Definitions.

The following words and phrases used herein shall be construed as follows:

(a) "Commission" means the State Human Affairs Commission.

(b) "National origin" includes ancestry.

(c) "Age" means at least forty years.

(d) "Person" means individuals, labor unions and organizations, joint apprenticeship committees, partnerships, associations, corporations, legal representatives, mutual companies, joint-stock companies, trusts, unincorporated organizations, trustees, trustees in bankruptcy, receivers, other legal or commercial entities located in part or in whole in the State or doing business in the State, the State and any of its agencies and departments or local subdivisions of state agencies and departments; and municipalities, counties, special purpose districts, school districts and other local governments.

(e) "Employer" means any person who has fifteen or more employees for each working day in each of twenty or more calendar weeks in the current or preceding calendar year, and any agent of such a person, but such term does not include an Indian tribe or a bona fide private membership club other than a labor organization.

(f) "Employment agency" means any person regularly undertaking to procure employees for an employer or to procure for employees opportunities to work for an employer and includes an agent of such a person.

(g) "Labor organization" means any agent of a labor organization, and includes any organization of any kind, any agency, or employee representation committee, group, association, or plan in which employees participate and which exists for the purpose, in whole or in part, of dealing with employers concerning grievances, labor disputes, wages, rates of pay, hours or other terms or conditions of employment, and any conference, general committee, joint or system board, or joint council which is subordinate to a national or international labor organization.

(h) "Employee" means an individual employed by an employer, except that the term "employee" shall not include any person elected to public office in this State, or any person chosen by such officer to be on such officer's personal staff, or an appointee on the policy-making level or an immediate adviser with respect to the exercise of the constitutional or legal powers of the office. The exemption set forth in the preceding sentence shall not include employees subject to the civil service laws of the State or any of its agencies, departments, local subdivisions, or political subdivisions of the State, local government, or local governmental agencies.

(i) "Complainant" means an individual alleging to have been aggrieved by an employment practice which is unlawful under this chapter.

(j) "Respondent" means a person against whom a charge of violation has been filed.

(k) The term "religion" means all aspects of religious observance and practice, as well as belief, unless an employer demonstrates that he is unable to reasonably accommodate to an employee's or prospective employee's religious observance or practice without undue hardship on the conduct of the employer's business.

(l) The terms "because of sex" or "on the basis of sex" include, but are not limited to, because of or on the basis of pregnancy, childbirth, or related medical conditions; and women affected by pregnancy, childbirth, or related medical conditions shall be treated the same for all employment-related purposes, including receipt of benefits under fringe benefit programs, as other persons not so affected but similar in their ability or inability to work, and nothing in item (3) of subsection (h) of Section 1-13-80 shall be interpreted to permit otherwise. This subsection shall not require an employer to pay for health insurance benefits for abortion, except where the life of the mother would be endangered if the fetus were carried to term, or except where medical complications have arisen from an abortion. Provided, that nothing herein shall preclude an employer from providing abortion benefits or otherwise affect bargaining agreements in regard to abortion. This subsection shall not apply to any fringe benefit fund or insurance program which was in effect on October 31, 1978, until April 30, 1979. Until after October 31, 1979 or, if there was an applicable collective bargaining agreement in effect on October 31, 1978, until the termination of that agreement, no person who, on October 31, 1978, was providing either by direct payment or by making contributions to a fringe benefit fund or insurance program, benefits in violation of the provisions of this chapter relating to sex discrimination in employment shall, in order to come into compliance with such provisions, reduce the benefits or the compensation provided any employee on October 31, 1978, either directly or by failing to provide sufficient contributions to a fringe benefit fund or insurance program: Provided, That where the costs of such benefits on October 31, 1978 are apportioned between employers and employees, the payments or contributions required to comply with the provisions of this chapter relating to sex discrimination in employment may be made by employers and employees in the same proportion: And provided, further, That nothing in this section shall prevent the readjustment of benefits or compensation for reasons unrelated to compliance with the provisions of this chapter relating to sex discrimination in employment.

(M) "Covered entity" means an employer, employment agency, labor organization, or joint labor-management committee.

(N) "Disability" means with respect to an individual:

(1) a physical or mental impairment that substantially limits one or more of the major life activities of the individual;

(2) a record of an impairment; or

(3) being regarded as having an impairment.

The definition of "disability" must be interpreted in a manner consistent with federal regulations promulgated pursuant to the Americans with Disabilities Act of 1990, as amended, Public Law 101-336.

(O) "Auxiliary aids and services" means:

(1) qualified interpreters or other effective methods of making aurally delivered materials available to individuals with hearing impairments;

(2) qualified readers, taped texts, or other effective methods of making visually delivered materials available to individuals with visual impairments;

(3) acquisition or modification of equipment or devices; and

(4) other similar services and actions.

(P) "Direct threat" means a significant risk to the health or safety of the employee or of others that cannot be eliminated by reasonable accommodation.

(Q) "Illegal use of drugs" means the use of drugs, the possession and distribution of which is unlawful under Chapter 53, Title 44. This term does not include the use of a drug taken under supervision by a licensed health care professional or other lawful uses. Nothing in this chapter prohibits a covered entity from requiring employees to conform to drug-free workplace laws and regulations or from establishing and enforcing rules, policies, or guidelines concerning use of alcohol or illegal drugs in the workplace.

(R) "Drug" means a controlled substance as defined in Section 44-53-10.

(S) "Qualified individual with a disability" means an individual with a disability who, with or without reasonable accommodation, can perform the essential functions of the employment position that the individual holds or desires. For the purposes of this chapter, consideration must be given to the employer's judgment as to what functions of a job are essential, and if an employer has prepared a written job description before advertising or interviewing applicants for the job, this description must be considered evidence of the essential functions of the job. "Qualified individual with a disability" does not include an employee or applicant who is currently engaging in the illegal use of drugs when the covered entity acts on the basis of the use.

(T) "Reasonable accommodation" may include:

(1) making existing facilities used by employees readily accessible to and usable by individuals with disabilities; and

(2) job restructuring, part-time or modified work schedules, reassignment to a vacant position, acquisition or modification of equipment or devices, appropriate adjustment or modifications of examinations, training materials or policies, the provision of qualified readers or interpreters, and other similar accommodations for individuals with disabilities.

(U) "Undue hardship" means an action requiring significant difficulty or expense, when considered in light of the following factors:

(1) the nature and cost of the accommodation needed under this chapter;

(2) the overall financial resources of the facility involved in the provision of the reasonable accommodation, the number of persons employed at the facility, the effect on expenses and resources, or the impact otherwise of the accommodation upon the operation of the facility;

(3) the overall financial resources of the covered entity, the overall size of the business of a covered entity with respect to the number of its employees, the number, type, and location of its facilities; and

(4) the type of operation of the covered entity, including the composition, structure, and functions of the workforce of the entity, the geographic separateness and the administrative or fiscal relationship of the facility in question to the covered entity.

HISTORY: 1962 Code Section 1-360.23; 1972 (57) 2651; 1973 (58) 698; 1979 Act No. 24, Section 2; 1988 Act No. 663, Section 1; 1996 Act No. 426, Section 3.

SECTION 1-13-40. Creation of South Carolina Commission on Human Affairs.

(a) There is hereby created in the executive department the South Carolina Human Affairs Commission, to encourage fair treatment for, and to eliminate and prevent discrimination against, any member of a group protected by this chapter, and to foster mutual understanding and respect among all people in this State.

(b) The commission shall consist of a member from each congressional district appointed by the Governor, with the advice and consent of the Senate, and two members at large appointed by the Governor. Each member shall serve for a term of three years and until their successors are appointed and qualify. Vacancies must be filled in the manner of the original appointment for the unexpired term.

(c) No member of the Commission shall serve more than two consecutive terms. A member having served two consecutive terms shall be eligible for reappointment one year after the expiration of his second term.

(d) The Governor shall appoint one of the at large members to serve as chairman and may appoint any member to serve as vice-chairman, each to serve a term of one year. In the absence of appointment of a vice-chairman, the members may elect one of their number to fill that office. The Commission may elect other officers from among its members as necessary, except that the Commissioner may be elected to serve as secretary.

(e) The Commission shall meet at such times and in such places as it may determine.

(f) A quorum for transacting business shall consist of a majority of the membership as constituted at the time of a meeting.

(g) Each member shall be entitled to one vote on each issue presented, a majority of the votes cast determining the issue. Votes may be cast only in person. Voting may be by secret ballot or by voice vote.

(h) A vacancy in the Commission shall not impair the right of the remaining members to exercise all the powers of the Commission.

(i) Members of the Commission shall be entitled to such per diem, mileage and subsistence as is provided for by law for boards, committees and commissions.

(j) The Commission shall render each year to the Governor and to the General Assembly a written report of its activities and of its recommendations.

HISTORY: 1962 Code Section 1-360.24; 1972 (57) 2651; 1979 Act No. 24, Section 3; 1983 Act No. 80, Sections 1-3; 1991 Act No. 248, Section 6; 2012 Act No. 279, Section 1, eff June 26, 2012.

Editor's Note

2012 Act No. 279, Section 33, provides as follows:

"Due to the congressional redistricting, any person elected or appointed to serve, or serving, as a member of any board, commission, or committee to represent a congressional district, whose residency is transferred to another district by a change in the composition of the district, may serve, or continue to serve, the term of office for which he was elected or appointed; however, the appointing or electing authority shall appoint or elect an additional member on that board, commission, or committee from the district which loses a resident member as a result of the transfer to serve until the term of the transferred member expires. When a vacancy occurs in the district to which a member has been transferred, the vacancy must not be filled until the full term of the transferred member expires. Further, the inability to hold an election or to make an appointment due to judicial review of the congressional districts does not constitute a vacancy."

Effect of Amendment

The 2012 amendment rewrote subsection (b).

SECTION 1-13-50. Commissioner and personnel.

(a) The Commission shall recommend to the Governor a person who shall be employed as Commissioner and shall, with the approval of the Governor, employ such person who shall be subject to dismissal by the Commission with the approval of the Governor. The Commissioner shall be the chief administrative officer of the Commission, and shall perform such duties as are incident to such office or are required of him by the Commission.

(b) The Commissioner shall receive such compensation as may be provided by law.

(c) The Commissioner shall recommend to the Commission, and with its approval, employ attorneys, secretaries, clerks, investigators and conciliators for the expeditious discharge of the Commission's duties.

HISTORY: 1962 Code Section 1-360.25; 1972 (57) 2651; 1973 (58) 698.

SECTION 1-13-60. Duties of chairman and vice-chairman.

The chairman shall be the presiding officer at meetings of the Commission and shall promote the orderly transaction of its business. In the chairman's absence, or his inability to act, the vice-chairman or if no vice-chairman has been appointed or elected a commissioner designated by the chairman shall act in his stead.

HISTORY: 1962 Code Section 1-360.26; 1972 (57) 2651.

SECTION 1-13-70. Powers of Commission.

The Commission shall have the power:

(a) To establish and maintain its principal office in the city of Columbia and such other offices within the State as it may deem necessary.

(b) To adopt bylaws.

(c) To promulgate, in accordance with the provisions of this chapter, regulations including, but not limited to, regulations requiring the posting of notices prepared or approved by the Commission and the submission of equal employment opportunity plans and reports by any state agency or department or local subdivisions of a state agency or department, according to a format and schedule approved by the Commission.

(d) To formulate policies to effectuate the purposes of this chapter and to make recommendations to appropriate parties in furtherance of such policies.

(e) To obtain and utilize upon request the services of all governmental departments and agencies.

(f) To create or recognize advisory agencies and conciliation councils, local, regional, or statewide, as will aid in effectuating the purposes of this chapter and of Section 3 of Article I of the Constitution of this State. The commission may empower these agencies and councils to study problems of discrimination in all or specific fields of human affairs or in specific instances of discrimination because of race, religion, color, sex, age, national origin, or disability and to foster through community effort, or otherwise, goodwill, cooperation, and conciliation among the groups and elements of the population of the State. These agencies and councils also may make recommendations to the commission for the development of policies and procedures in general and in specific instances and for programs of formal or informal education which the commission may in turn recommend to the appropriate state agency. These advisory agencies and conciliation councils, as far as practicable, must be composed of representative citizens.

(g) To seek the understanding and cooperation of or to enter into agreement with any existing or later-created councils, agencies, commissions, task forces, institutions or organizations, public or private, which are, in the judgment of the Commission, dedicated to the promotion of human rights and affairs.

(h) To issue publications and results of investigations and research as in its judgment will tend to promote goodwill and the betterment of human affairs.

(i) To require from any state agency or department or local subdivisions of a state agency or department such reports and information at such times as it may deem reasonably necessary to effectuate the purposes of this chapter.

(j) To prepare and distribute copies of this chapter, of any regulations promulgated pursuant to subsection (c) of this section, of policies formulated pursuant to subsection (d) of this section or of any other materials effectuating the purposes of this chapter; to make the chapter available to the public and to require the chapter to be posted in places conspicuous to employees of state agencies or departments or local subdivisions of a state agency or department and to applicants for employment therewith.

(k) To cooperate with the United States Equal Employment Opportunity Commission created by the Civil Rights Act of 1964 (78 Stat. 241) in order to achieve the purposes of that act and with other Federal, State and local agencies and departments.

(l) To accept reimbursement pursuant to section 709(b) of the Civil Rights Act of 1964 (78 Stat. 241) for services rendered to the United States Equal Employment Opportunity Commission.

(m) To accept gifts or bequests, grants or other donations, public or private.

(n) To investigate problems in human affairs in the State and in connection therewith, to hold hearings, to request the attendance of persons who shall give testimony, to receive for the record of any such hearing written statements, documents, exhibits and other items pertinent to the subject matter of any such hearing, and following any such investigation or hearing to issue such report and recommendations as in its opinion will assist in effectuating the purposes of this chapter.

(o) To receive and resolve complaints in accordance with the provisions of Section 1-13-90.

(p) Pursuant to subsections (e) and (i), if a person fails to permit access, or otherwise refuses to cooperate, the Commission may request an order of a court of competent jurisdiction requiring access and other related good faith compliance.

(q) To furnish technical assistance requested by persons subject to this chapter to assist them in their compliance with this chapter, the regulations promulgated hereunder, a conciliation agreement or an order issued thereunder.

(r) To petition for an order of a court of competent jurisdiction requiring compliance with an order issued by the Commission pursuant to the procedure set forth in item (16) of subsection (c) of Section 1-13-90; provided, that a complainant, respondent or intervenor aggrieved by an order of the Commission is entitled to judicial review. The procedure for compliance, enforcement or review shall be as set forth in item (19) of subsection (c) of Section 1-13-90.

(s) To institute proceedings in a court of competent jurisdiction, for cause shown, to prevent or restrain any person from violating any provision of this chapter.

(t) To contract with persons and organizations to perform services as it may deem reasonably necessary to effectuate the purposes of this chapter and to accept reimbursement for services rendered pursuant to the contract.

(u) To make contractual agreements, within the scope and authority of this chapter, with any agency of the federal government, which agreements may include provisions under which the Federal Equal Employment Opportunity Commission shall refrain from processing a charge in South Carolina in any class specified in such agreements.

(v) To perform the functions specified in this chapter.

HISTORY: 1962 Code Section 1-360.27; 1972 (57) 2651; 1973 (58) 698; 1979 Act No. 24 Sections 4-7; 1996 Act No. 426, Section 4.

SECTION 1-13-80. Unlawful employment practices; exceptions.

(A) It is an unlawful employment practice for an employer:

(1) to fail or refuse to hire, bar, discharge from employment or otherwise discriminate against an individual with respect to the individual's compensation or terms, conditions, or privileges of employment because of the individual's race, religion, color, sex, age, national origin, or disability;

(2) to limit, segregate, or classify employees or applicants for employment in a way which would deprive or tend to deprive an individual of employment opportunities, or otherwise adversely affect the individual's status as an employee, because of the individual's race, color, religion, sex, age, national origin, or disability;

(3) to reduce the wage rate of an employee in order to comply with the provisions of this chapter relating to age.

(B) It is an unlawful employment practice for an employment agency to fail or refuse to refer for employment or otherwise to discriminate against an individual because of the individual's race, color, religion, sex, age, national origin, or disability, or to classify or refer for employment an individual on the basis of the individual's race, color, religion, sex, age, national origin, or disability.

(C) It is an unlawful employment practice for a labor organization:

(1) to exclude or to expel from its membership or otherwise to discriminate against an individual because of the individual's race, color, religion, sex, age, national origin, or disability;

(2) to limit, segregate, or classify its membership or applicants for membership or to classify or fail or refuse to refer for employment an individual in a way which would deprive or tend to deprive an individual of employment opportunities or would limit employment opportunities or otherwise adversely affect the individual's status as an employee or as an applicant for employment because of the individual's race, color, religion, sex, age, national origin, or disability;

(3) to cause or attempt to cause an employer to discriminate against an individual in violation of this section.

(D) It is an unlawful employment practice for a covered entity:

(1) to exclude or otherwise deny equal jobs or benefits to a qualified individual because of a known disability of an individual with whom the qualified individual is known to have a relationship or association;

(2) to fail or make reasonable accommodations to the known physical or mental limitations of an otherwise qualified individual with a disability who is an applicant or employee, unless the covered entity can demonstrate that the accommodation would impose an undue hardship on the operations of the business of the covered entity; or to deny employment opportunities to a job applicant or employee who is an otherwise qualified individual with a disability, if the denial is based on the need of the covered entity to make reasonable accommodation to the physical or mental impairments of the employee or applicant;

(3) to use qualification standards, employment tests, or other selection criteria that screen out or tend to screen out an individual with a disability or a class of individuals with disabilities unless the standard, test, or other selection criteria, as used by the covered entity, is shown to be job related for the position in question and is consistent with business necessity;

(4) to fail to select and administer tests concerning employment in the most effective manner to ensure that, when the test is administered to a job applicant or employee who has a disability that impairs sensory, manual, or speaking skills, the test results accurately reflect the skills, aptitude, or whatever other factor of the applicant or employee that the test purports to measure, rather than reflecting the impaired sensory, manual, or speaking skills of the employee or applicant, except where the skills are the factors that the test purports to measure.

(E) It is an unlawful employment practice for an employer, labor organization, or joint labor-management committee controlling apprenticeship or other training or retraining, including on-the-job training programs, to discriminate against an individual because of the individual's race, color, religion, sex, national origin, or disability in admission to or employment in a program established to provide apprenticeship or other training.

(F) It is an unlawful employment practice for an employer to discriminate against an employee or applicant for employment, for an employment agency, or joint labor-management committee controlling apprenticeship or other training or retraining, including on-the-job training programs, to discriminate against an individual or for a labor organization to discriminate against a member or applicant for membership because the individual has opposed a practice made an unlawful employment practice by this chapter or because the individual has made a charge, testified, assisted, or participated in an investigation, proceeding, or hearing under this chapter.

(G) It is an unlawful employment practice for an employer, labor organization, employment agency, or joint labor-management committee controlling apprenticeship or other training or retraining, including on-the-job training programs, to print or publish or cause to be printed or published a notice or advertisement relating to employment by the employer or membership in or a classification or referral for employment by the labor organization or relating to a classification or referral for employment by the employment agency or relating to admission to or employment in a program established to provide apprenticeship or other training by the joint labor-management committee indicating a preference, limitation, specification, or discrimination based on race, color, religion, sex, national origin, or disability, except that the notice or advertisement may indicate a preference, limitation, specification, or discrimination based on religion, sex, or national origin when religion, sex, or national origin is a bona fide occupational qualification for employment.

(H) It is unlawful for an employer, labor organization, or employment agency to print or publish or cause to be printed or published a notice or advertisement relating to employment by the employer or membership in or a classification or referral for employment by the labor organization or relating to a classification or referral for employment by the employment agency indicating a preference, limitation, specification, or discrimination based on age.

(I) Notwithstanding any other provision of this chapter:

(1) It is not an unlawful employment practice for an employer to employ employees, for an employment agency to classify or refer for employment an individual, for a labor organization to classify its membership or to classify or refer for employment an individual, or for an employer, labor organization, or joint labor-management committee controlling apprenticeship or other training or retraining programs to admit or employ an individual in a program on the basis of the individual's religion, sex, or national origin in those certain instances where religion, sex, or national origin is a bona fide occupational qualification reasonably necessary to the normal operation of that particular business or enterprise.

(2) It is not an unlawful employment practice for a party subject to the provisions of this section to compile or assemble information as may be required pursuant to Section 1-13-70(i) or Federal Equal Employment Opportunity Commission or federal contract compliance requirements or pursuant to another law not inconsistent with this chapter.

(3) It is not an unlawful employment practice for an employer to apply different standards of compensation or different terms, conditions, or privileges of employment pursuant to a bona fide seniority or merit system or a system which measures earnings by quantity or quality of production or to employees who work in different locations if the differences are not the result of an intention to discriminate because of race, religion, color, sex, national origin, or disability; nor is it an unlawful employment practice for an employer to give and to act upon the results of a professionally developed ability test if the test, its administration, or action upon the results is not designed, intended, or used to

discriminate because of race, color, religion, sex, national origin, or disability. It is not an unlawful employment practice under this chapter for an employer to differentiate upon the basis of sex in determining the amount of wages or compensation paid or to be paid to employees of the employer if the differentiation is authorized by Section 6(d) of the Fair Labor Standards Act of 1938, as amended (29 U.S.C. 206(d)).

(4) Nothing contained in this chapter applies to a business or enterprise on or near an Indian reservation with respect to a publicly announced employment practice of the business or enterprise under which a preferential treatment is given to an individual because the individual is an Indian living on or near a reservation.

(5) This chapter does not apply to a religious corporation, association, educational institution, or society with respect to the employment of individuals of a particular religion to perform work connected with the carrying on by the corporation, association, educational institution, or society of its activities. It is not an unlawful employment practice for a school, college, university, or other educational institution or institution of learning to hire and employ employees of a particular religion if the school, college, university, or other educational institution or institution of learning is, in whole or in substantial part, owned, supported, controlled, or managed by a particular religion or by a particular religious corporation, association, or society, or if the curriculum of the school, college, university, or other educational institution or institution of learning is directed toward the propagation of a particular religion.

(6) Nothing contained in this chapter may be interpreted to require an employer, employment agency, labor organization, or joint labor-management committee subject to this chapter to grant preferential treatment to an individual or to a group because of race, color, religion, sex, national origin, or disability of the individual or group on account of an imbalance which may exist with respect to the total number or percentage of persons of a race, color, religion, sex, national origin, or disability employed by an employer, referred or classified for employment by an employment agency or labor organization admitted to membership or classified by a labor organization, or admitted to, or employed in, an apprenticeship or other training program in comparison with the total number or percentage of persons of the race, color, religion, sex, national origin, or disability in a community, state, section, or other area or in the available work force in a community, state, section, or other area.

(7) It is not unlawful for an employer, employment agency, or labor organization:

(i) to take an action otherwise prohibited under this chapter where age is a bona fide occupational qualification reasonably necessary to the normal operation of the particular business or where the differentiation is based on reasonable factors other than age;

(ii) to observe the terms of a bona fide seniority system or a bona fide employee benefit plan such as retirement, pension, or insurance plan which is not a subterfuge to evade the purposes of this chapter except that no employee benefit plan may excuse the failure to hire an individual.

Notwithstanding the provisions of subitem (ii), no seniority system or employee benefit plan may require or permit the involuntary retirement of an individual covered by the provisions of this chapter relating to age because of the age of the individual; however, employees covered by a collective bargaining agreement which was in effect on June 30, 1986, and which would otherwise be prohibited by the provisions of this subitem, this subitem takes effect upon the termination of the agreement or on January 1, 1990, whichever occurs first.

(8) Nothing in this chapter may be construed to prohibit compulsory retirement of an employee who has attained sixty-five years of age and who, for the two-year period immediately before retirement, is employed in a bona fide executive or high policymaking position, if the employee is entitled to an immediate nonforfeitable annual retirement benefit from a pension, profit sharing, savings, or deferred compensation plan or a combination of these plans of the employer of the employee which equals in aggregate at least forty-four thousand dollars.

(9) In applying subsection (I)(8), the retirement benefit test, if a retirement benefit is in a form other than a straight life annuity with no ancillary benefits or if employees contribute to a plan or make rollover contributions, the benefit must be adjusted in accordance with regulations prescribed by the commissioner so that the benefit is the equivalent of a straight life annuity with no ancillary benefits under a plan to which employees do not contribute and under which no rollover contributions are made.

(10) Nothing in this chapter relating to age discrimination in employment may be construed to prohibit compulsory retirement of an employee who has attained seventy years of age and who is serving under a contract of unlimited tenure or similar arrangement providing for unlimited tenure at an institution of higher education. This item is effective until December 31, 1993.

(11) It is an unlawful employment practice for a person to forcibly resist, prevent, impede, or interfere with the commission or any of its members or representatives in the lawful performance of duty under this chapter.

(12) It is not unlawful for an employer which is the State, a political subdivision of the State, an agency or instrumentality of the State or of a political subdivision of the State, or an interstate agency to fail or refuse to hire or to discharge an individual because of the individual's age if the action is taken:

(i) with respect to the employment of an individual as a firefighter or as a law enforcement officer and the individual has attained the age of hiring or retirement in effect under applicable law on March 3, 1983;

(ii) pursuant to a bona fide hiring or retirement plan that is not a subterfuge to evade the purposes of this chapter.

This item is effective until December 31, 1993.

The term "firefighter" means an employee the duties of whose position are primarily to perform work directly connected with the control and extinguishment of fires or the maintenance and use of firefighting apparatus and equipment, including an employee engaged in this activity who is transferred to a supervisory or administrative position.

The term "law enforcement officer" means an employee the duties of whose position are primarily the investigation, apprehension, or detention of individuals suspected or convicted of offenses against the criminal laws of the State, including an employee engaged in this activity who is transferred to a supervisory or administrative position. For the purpose of this item, "detention" includes the duties of employees assigned to guard individuals incarcerated in a penal institution.

Nothing contained in items (8), (10), and (12) may override Sections 9-1-1530 and 9-1-1537.

(13) It is not an unlawful employment practice for a private employer to give preference in employment to a veteran. This preference is also extended to the veteran's spouse if the veteran has a service-connected permanent and total disability. A private employer who gives a preference in employment provided by this item does not violate any other provision of this chapter by virtue of

giving the preference. For purposes of this item, "veteran" has the same meaning as provided in Section 25-11-40.

HISTORY: 1962 Code Section 1-360.28; 1972 (57) 2651; 1979 Act No. 24, Section 8; 1988 Act No. 663, Section 2; 1996 Act No. 426, Section 5; 2014 Act No. 210 (H.4922), Section 1, eff June 2, 2014.

Effect of Amendment

2014 Act No. 210, Section 1, added subsection (I)(13), relating to veteran employment preference.

SECTION 1-13-85. Medical examinations and inquiries.

(A) The prohibition against unlawful employment practices set forth in Section 1-13-80 (a) through (d) includes the prohibition against conducting medical examinations and inquiries except as provided for in this section.

(B) Except as provided in subsection (C), a covered entity must not conduct a medical examination or make inquiries of a job applicant as to whether the applicant is an individual with a disability or as to the nature or severity of the disability. A covered entity may make preemployment inquiries into the ability of an applicant to perform job-related functions.

(C) A covered entity may require a medical examination after an offer of employment has been made to a job applicant and before the commencement of the employment duties of the applicant, and may condition an offer of employment on the results of the examination, if:

(1) all entering employees are subjected to the examination regardless of disability;

(2) information obtained regarding the medical condition or history of the applicant is collected and maintained on separate forms and in separate medical files and is treated as a confidential medical record, except that:

(a) supervisors and managers may be informed regarding necessary restrictions on the work or duties of the employee and necessary accommodations;

(b) first aid and safety personnel may be informed, when appropriate, if the disability might require emergency treatment;

(c) government officials investigating compliance with this chapter must be provided relevant information on request; and

(3) the results of the examination are used only in accordance with this chapter.

(D) For purposes of this chapter, drug and alcohol exams, tests, or screens may not be considered a medical examination.

(E)(1) A covered entity may not require a medical examination and may not make inquiries of an employee as to whether the employee is an individual with a disability or as to the nature or severity of the disability, unless the examination or inquiry is shown to be job-related and consistent with business necessity.

(2) A covered entity may conduct voluntary medical examinations including voluntary medical histories which are part of an employee health program available to employees at that work site. A covered entity may make inquiries into the ability of an employee to perform job-related functions.

(3) Information obtained under subsection (E)(2) regarding the medical condition or history of an employee is subject to the requirements of subsection (C)(2) and (3).

(F)(1) It may be a defense to a charge of discrimination under this chapter that an alleged application of qualification standards, tests, or selection criteria that screens out or tends to screen out or otherwise denies a job or benefit to an individual with a disability has been shown to be job related and consistent with business necessity, and the performance cannot be accomplished by reasonable accommodation, as required under this title.

(2) The term "qualification standards" may include a requirement that an individual may not pose a direct threat to the safety of that individual or of other individuals in the workplace.

(3) This chapter may not prohibit a religious corporation, association, educational institution, or society from giving preference in employment to individuals of a particular religion to perform work connected with the carrying on of its activities by the corporation, association, educational institution, or society. Under this chapter, a religious organization may require that all applicants and employees conform to the religious tenets of the organization.

(4) If an individual has an infectious or communicable disease that is transmitted to others through the handling of food, that is included on the list developed by the Secretary of Health and Human Services pursuant to the requirements of the Americans with Disabilities Act of 1990, Public Law 101-336, and which cannot be eliminated by reasonable accommodation, a covered entity may refuse to assign or continue to assign the individual to a job involving food handling.

Nothing in this chapter may be construed to preempt, modify, or amend a state, county, or local law, ordinance, or regulation applicable to food handling which is designed to protect the public health from individuals who pose a significant risk to the health or safety of others and which cannot be eliminated by reasonable accommodation, pursuant to the list of infectious or communicable diseases and the modes of transmissibility published by the Secretary of Health and Human Services.

HISTORY: 1996 Act No. 426, Section 1.

SECTION 1-13-90. Complaints, investigations, hearings and orders.

(a) Any person shall complain in writing under oath or affirmation to the Commission within one hundred eighty days after the alleged discriminatory practice occurred. The Commissioner, his employees or agents, shall assist complainants in reducing verbal complaints to writing and shall assist in setting forth such information as may be required by the Commission. The Commission shall serve a copy of the complaint upon the respondent within ten days after the complaint is received by the Commission, except that if the Commission determines for good cause that such service will impede its investigation of the complaint, it shall serve notice of the complaint, including the date, place, and circumstances of the alleged unlawful employment practice upon the respondent within ten days after the complaint is received by the Commission.

(b) Any complainant who is a member of the Commission shall be disqualified from participation except as the complainant in the processing and resolution of the complaint.

(c) For complaints asserting expressly or in substance a violation by a state agency or department or local subdivisions of a state agency or department of Section 1-13-80 the procedure shall be as follows:

(1) The Commissioner shall assign one or more of his employees or agents to investigate the complaint, in which case one shall be designated the investigator in charge of the complaint. Information gathered during an investigation under this subsection shall not be made public by the Commission, its officers or employees, except for information made public as a result of being offered or received into evidence in an action brought under this subsection.

(2) The Chairman of the Commission or, upon the request of the Chairman, the Commissioner shall designate a member of the Commission to supervise the processing of the complaint.

(3) The complaint may be resolved at any time before a hearing by conference, conciliation and persuasion with the complainant and the respondent, such resolution to be embodied in a conciliation agreement, which shall include an agreement by the respondent to refrain from committing unlawful discriminatory practices in the future, and which may contain such further provisions as are agreed upon by the complainant and the respondent. No conciliation agreement shall be deemed an effective resolution by the Commission unless the supervisory commission member shall have reviewed and approved the terms thereof. Positions taken by a witness in connection with such efforts toward conciliation shall not be made public or used against the interest of the witness in a subsequent proceeding.

(4) In undertaking its investigation of a complaint the Commission shall have the authority:

(i) To issue a subpoena or subpoena duces tecum and thereby compel attendance of witnesses or production for examination of books, papers, and records, whenever it is deemed necessary to compel the attendance of witnesses, or the production for examination of any books, payrolls, personnel records, correspondence, documents, papers or any other evidence relating to any matter under investigation or in question before the Commission. The power may be exercised only by the joint action by the Chairman of the Commission and the Commissioner.

(ii) To require any party or witness to answer interrogatories at any time after the complaint is filed.

(iii) To take depositions of witnesses including any party pursuant to a complaint or investigation made by the Commission.

(iv) Pursuant to subitems (i), (ii), (iii), above, if a person fails to permit access, fails to comply with a subpoena, refuses to have his or her deposition taken, refuses to answer interrogatories, or otherwise refuses to allow discovery, the Commission may request an order of a court of competent jurisdiction requiring discovery and other related good faith compliance.

(5) If not sooner resolved, the investigator shall upon completion of his investigation submit to the supervisory commission member a statement of the facts disclosed by his investigation and recommend either that the complaint be dismissed or that a panel of commission members be designated to hear the complaint. The supervisory commission member, after review of the case file and the statement and recommendation of the investigator shall issue an order either of dismissal or for a hearing, which order shall not be subject to judicial or other further review.

(6) If the order be of dismissal, the supervisory commission member shall mail a copy of the order to the complainant and the respondent at their last known addresses.

(7) If the order be for a hearing, the supervisory commission member shall annex thereto a notice and a copy of the complaint and require the respondent to answer the complaint at a hearing at a time and place specified in the notice and shall serve upon the respondent a copy of the order, the complaint, and the notice.

(8) At any time before a hearing a complaint may be amended by the supervisory commission member upon the request of the investigator or of the complainant or of the respondent. Complaints may be amended during a hearing only upon a majority vote of the panel of commission members for such hearing.

(9) Upon request by any party, the Commissioner shall issue appropriate subpoenaes or subpoenaes duces tecum to any witnesses or other custodians of documents desired to be present at the hearing, or at prehearing depositions, unless the Commissioner determines that issuance of the subpoenaes or subpoenaes duces tecum would be unreasonable or unduly burdensome.

(10) Upon notification by any party that any party or witness has failed to permit access, failed to comply with a subpoena or subpoena duces tecum, refused to have his or her deposition taken, refused to answer interrogatories, or otherwise refused to allow discovery, the Commission, shall, upon notice to the party or

witness, apply to a court of competent jurisdiction for an order requiring discovery and other good faith compliance unless the Commission determines that the discovery would be unreasonably or unduly burdensome.

(11) Upon request by the supervisory commission member, the Chairman of the Commission shall designate a panel of three members of the Commission to sit as the Commission to hear the complaint; provided, that no member of the Commission shall be a member of a panel to hear a complaint for which he has been a supervisory commission member.

(12) At any hearing held pursuant to this subsection, the case in support of the complaint shall be presented before the panel by one or more of the commission's employees or agents, and, with consent of the panel, by legal representatives of the complaining party; provided, that endeavors at conciliation by the investigator shall not be received into evidence nor otherwise made known to the members of the panel.

(13) The respondent shall submit a written answer to the complaint and appear at such hearing in person or by counsel and may submit evidence. The respondent shall have the power reasonably and fairly to amend his answer.

(14) The complainant shall be permitted to be present and submit evidence.

(15) Proceedings under this section shall be subject to the Administrative Procedures Act, Sections 1-23-310 through 1-23-400 of the Code of Laws of South Carolina, 1976, as amended, and in case of conflict between the provisions of this chapter and the Administrative Procedures Act, the Administrative Procedures Act shall govern. A recording of the proceedings shall be made, which may be subsequently transcribed upon request and payment of a reasonable fee by the complainant or the respondent. The fee shall be set by the Commission or upon motion of the panel, in which case copies of such transcription shall be made available to the complainant or the respondent upon request and payment of a reasonable fee to be set by the Commission.

(16) If upon all the evidence at the hearing the panel shall find that the respondent has engaged in any unlawful discriminatory practice, it shall state its findings of fact and serve upon the respondent in the name of the Commission an opinion and order requiring that such unlawful discriminatory practice be discontinued and requiring such other action including, but not limited to, hiring, reinstatement or upgrading of employees, with or without back pay to the

persons aggrieved by such practice as, in the judgment of the panel, will effectuate the purposes of this chapter. Back pay liability shall not accrue from a date more than two years prior to the filing of a charge with the Commission. The Commission may retain jurisdiction of any such case until it is satisfied of compliance by the respondent with its order.

(17) If upon all the evidence at the hearing the panel shall find that the respondent has not engaged in any such unlawful discriminatory practice, the panel shall state its findings of fact and serve upon the complainant and the respondent an opinion and order dismissing the complaint as to the respondent.

(18) A copy of the opinion and order of the Commission shall be delivered in all cases to the Attorney General and to such other public officers as the Commission deems proper. Copies of the opinion and order shall be available to the public for inspection upon request, and copies shall be made available to any person upon payment of a reasonable fee set by the Commission.

(19)(i) If an application for review is made to the commission within fourteen days from the date the order of the commission is given, the commission, for good cause shown, shall review the order and evidence, receive further evidence, rehear the parties or their representatives, and, if proper, amend the order.

(ii) The order of the commission, as provided in item (16) of subsection (c) of this section, if not reviewed in due time, or an order of the commission upon review, as provided for in subitem (i) of item (19) of this subsection, is conclusive and binding as to all questions of fact unless clearly erroneous in view of the reliable, probative, and substantive evidence in the whole record. Either party to the dispute, within thirty days after receipt of notice to be sent by registered mail of the order may appeal the decision of the commission to the Administrative Law Court as provided in Sections 1-23-380(B) and 1-23-600(D). In case of an appeal from the decision of the commission, the appeal operates as a supersedeas for thirty days only, unless otherwise ordered by the administrative law judge, and the respondent is required to comply with the order involved in the appeal or certification until the questions at issue are fully determined in accordance with the provisions of this chapter.

(iii) The commission may institute a proceeding for enforcement of its order of item (16) of subsection (c) of this section, or its amended order of subitem (i) of item (19) of this subsection after thirty days from the date of the order, by filing a notice of appeal in the court of common pleas of the county in which the hearing occurred, or where a person required in the order to cease and desist from a practice which is the subject of the commission's order, or to take other affirmative action, resides, or transacts business.

If no appeal pursuant to subitem (ii) of item (19) of this subsection is initiated, the commission may obtain a decree of the court for enforcement of its order upon a showing that a copy of the petition for enforcement was served upon the party subject to the dictates of the commission's order.

(d) For complaints asserting expressly or in substance a violation of Section 1-13-80 by employers, employment agencies or labor organizations, including municipalities, counties, special purpose districts, school districts, and local governments, but not including employers, employment agencies or labor organizations covered by Section 1-13-90(c), the procedure shall be as follows:

(1) The Commissioner shall assign one or more of his employees or agents to investigate the complaint, in which case one shall be designated the investigator in charge of the complaint.

(2) The Commission shall institute an investigation by its employees to ascertain the facts relating to such alleged unlawful employment practice. In its investigation of a charge filed under this chapter, the Commission or its designated employees shall at all reasonable times have access to, for the purposes of examination, and the right to copy any evidence of any person being investigated that relates to unlawful employment practices covered by this chapter and is relevant to the charge under investigation. If any persons fail to permit access to such evidence, the Commission may issue a subpoena duces tecum and thereby compel the production for examination and copying of such evidence. If any person fails to comply with a subpoena issued under this chapter, the Commission may request an order of a court of competent jurisdiction requiring compliance with the subpoena. The person against whom an order of court is sought shall be given at least four days' notice of the time and place of the court hearing and may appear and oppose the granting of any order. Any person may, after giving the Commission at least four days' notice, move before a court of competent jurisdiction for an order quashing any subpoena issued under this subsection. Information gathered during an investigation under this subsection shall not be made public by the Commission, its officers or employees, except for information made public as a result of being offered or received into evidence in an action brought under this subsection.

(3) The complaint may be resolved at any time by conference, conciliation and persuasion with the complainant and the party complained of, such resolution to be embodied in a conciliation agreement, which may include an agreement by the respondent to refrain from committing unlawful discriminatory practices in the future, and which may contain such further provisions as are agreed upon by the complainant and the party complained of. Nothing said or done during and as part of such informal endeavors may be made public by the Commission or used as evidence in a subsequent proceeding.

(4) If not sooner resolved, the investigator shall upon completion of his investigation submit to the Commissioner a statement of the facts disclosed by his investigation and recommend either that the complaint be dismissed or that the Commission bring an action in equity in circuit court against the respondent. The Commissioner, after a review of the case file and the statement and recommendation of the investigator, may issue an order either to dismiss the charge or to bring an action in equity in circuit court against the respondent, which order shall not be subject to judicial or other further review.

(5) If the order be of dismissal, the Commissioner shall mail a copy of the order to the complainant and to the respondent at their last known addresses.

(6) If a charge filed with the commission by a complainant pursuant to this chapter is dismissed by the commission, or if within one hundred eighty days from the filing of the charge the commission has not filed an action under this chapter or entered into a conciliation agreement to which the complainant is a party, the complainant may bring an action in equity against the respondent in circuit court. The action must be brought within one year from the date of the violation alleged, or within one hundred twenty days from the date the complainant's charge is dismissed, whichever occurs earlier, except that this period may be extended by written consent of the respondent.

(7) If within thirty days after issuance of its determination the Commission is unable to secure from the respondent a conciliation agreement acceptable to the Commission, or if the Commission determines after investigation that the respondent has violated the terms of a conciliation agreement, the Commission may bring an action in equity against the respondent in circuit court. Such action shall be brought within one year from the date of the violation alleged, except that this period may be extended by written consent of the respondent.

(8) No action may be brought under this chapter by a complainant if an action based on the same charge has been brought by the Commission, and no action

may be brought under this chapter by the Commission if an action based on the same charge has been brought by the complainant. No action may be brought under this chapter if an action alleging essentially the same facts and seeking relief for the same complainant has been brought in any federal court. Any action brought under this chapter shall be promptly dismissed if an action alleging essentially the same facts and seeking relief for the same complainant is brought in any federal court.

(9) If the court finds that the respondent has intentionally engaged in or is intentionally engaging in an unlawful employment practice charged in the complaint, the court may enjoin the respondent from engaging in such unlawful employment practice, and order such affirmative action as may be appropriate, which may include, but is not limited to, reinstatement of hiring of employees, with or without back pay payable by the employer, employment agency, or labor organization, as the case may be, responsible for the unlawful employment practice or any other equitable relief as the court deems appropriate. Back pay liability shall not accrue from a date more than two years prior to the filing of a charge with the Commission. Unemployment compensation, interim earnings, or amount earnable with reasonable diligence, by the person or persons discriminated against shall operate to reduce the back pay otherwise allowable. No order of the court shall require the admission or reinstatement of an individual as a member of a union, of the hiring, reinstatement, or promotion of an individual as an employee, or the payment to him of any back pay if such individual was refused admission, suspended or expelled, or was refused employment or advancement or was suspended or discharged for any reason other than discrimination on account of race, color, religion, sex, age or national origin in violation of this chapter, or discrimination in violation of subsection (e) of Section 1-13-80.

(e) For complaints of the existence or occurrence of a practice asserted to be discriminatory on the basis of race, religion, color, age, sex, national origin, or disability, other than those discriminatory practices declared unlawful by Section 1-13-80, or of any other dispute regarding human affairs, the procedure of the commission is as follows:

The commissioner shall assign one or more of the commission's employees or agents who may resolve the complaint by conference, conciliation, and persuasion with the complainant and the respondent, the resolution to be embodied in a conciliation agreement which shall include such provisions as are agreed upon by the complainant and the respondent. If the employee or agent is unable after reasonable efforts to resolve the complaint, the employee or agent shall withdraw from the matter and not participate further and the commission file of the complaint must be closed. If the complainant and the respondent thereafter resolve the complaint and submit a record of the resolution to the commission, the record must be entered into the commission file of the complaint.

(f) If in the course of processing any complaint under the procedure set forth in (e) above sufficient facts shall appear warranting the processing of the complaint under the procedure provided by subsection (c) or (d) of this section upon notice to the complainant and to the respondent, such other procedure shall thereafter be followed for the processing of the complaint.

(g) The Commission shall establish such rules as may be necessary to govern, expedite and effectuate the procedures prescribed in this section.

HISTORY: 1962 Code Section 1-360.29; 1972 (57) 2651; 1973 (58) 698; 1979 Act No. 24 Section 9; 1990 Act No. 333, Section 1; 1996 Act No. 426, Section 6; 2006 Act No. 387, Section 1, eff July 1, 2006.

Editor's Note

2006 Act No. 387, Section 53, provides as follows:

"This act is intended to provide a uniform procedure for contested cases and appeals from administrative agencies and to the extent that a provision of this act conflicts with an existing statute or regulation, the provisions of this act are controlling."

2006 Act No. 387, Section 57, provides as follows:

"This act takes effect on July 1, 2006, and applies to any actions pending on or after the effective date of the act. No pending or vested right, civil action, special proceeding, or appeal of a final administrative decision exists under the former law as of the effective date of this act, except for appeals of Department of Health and Environmental Control Ocean and Coastal Resource Management and Environmental Quality Control permits that are before the Administrative Law Court on the effective date of this act and petitions for judicial review that are pending before the circuit court. For those actions only, the department shall hear appeals from the administrative law judges and the circuit court shall hear pending petitions for judicial review in accordance with the former law. Thereafter, any appeal of those actions shall proceed as provided in this act for review. For all other actions pending on the effective date of this act, the action proceeds as provided in this act for review."

Effect of Amendment

The 2006 amendment, subparagraph (c)(19)(ii), in the second sentence substituted "Administrative Law Court as provided in Sections 1-23-380(B) and 1-23-600(D)" for "court of common pleas of the county in which the hearing occurred, or in which the respondent resides or has his principal office", and in the third sentence substituted "administrative law judge" for "court"; in subparagraph (c)(19)(iii), substituted "date" for "day" and"notice of appeal" for "petition"; and made nonsubstantive changes throughout.

SECTION 1-13-100. Construction and application of chapter.

Nothing in this chapter may be construed to create a cause of action other than those specifically described in Section 1-13-90 of this chapter. Nothing in this chapter may be construed to create a cause of action against a person not covered by Title VII of the Civil Rights Act of 1964, as amended, 42 U. S. C. Section 2000e et seq., if the cause of action arises from discrimination on the basis of race, color, religion, sex, or national origin. Nothing in this chapter may be construed to create a cause of action against a person not covered by the Age Discrimination in Employment Act of 1967, as amended, 29 U. S. C. Section 621 et seq., if the cause of action arises from discrimination on the basis of age. Nothing in this chapter may be construed to create a cause of action against a person not covered by the Americans with Disabilities Act of 1990, as amended, Public Law 101-336.

HISTORY: 1962 Code Section 1-360.30; 1972 (57) 2651; 1979 Act No. 24, Section 10; 1996 Act No. 426, Section 7.

SECTION 1-13-110. Affirmative action plans by State agencies; approval by Commission; action by General Assembly.

Each State agency shall develop an Affirmative Action Plan to assure equitable employment for members of minorities (race and sex) and shall present such Plans to the Human Affairs Commission. On or before February 1 of each year, the Human Affairs Commission shall submit a report to the General Assembly concerning the status of the Affirmative Action Plans of all State agencies. If any Affirmative Action Plans have been disapproved, the report shall contain the reasons for such disapproval. If the General Assembly takes no action within sixty (60) days on those Plans which have been disapproved, the action of the Human Affairs Commission shall be final.

HISTORY: 1978 Act No. 644, Part II, Section 3A.

CHAPTER 15

Commission on the Status of Women

SECTION 1-15-10. Commission created; appointment, qualifications and terms of members; vacancies.

There is created a Commission on Women to be composed of sixteen members appointed by the Governor with the advice and consent of the Senate from among persons with a competency in the area of public affairs and women's activities. One member must be appointed from each congressional district and the remaining members from the State at large. The commission must be under and a part of the Department of Administration. Members of the commission shall serve for terms of four years and until their successors are appointed and qualify, except of those members first appointed after the expansion of the commission to fifteen members, two members shall serve a term of one year, two members shall serve a term of two years, two members shall serve a term of three years, and two members shall serve a term of four years. Members appointed prior to and after the expansion of the commission to fifteen members must be designated by the Governor as being appointed to serve either from a particular congressional district or at large. The member first appointed from the Seventh Congressional District after the expansion of the commission to sixteen members shall serve a four-year term. Vacancies must be filled in the manner of the original appointment for the unexpired portion of the term only. No member must be eligible to serve more than two consecutive terms.

HISTORY: 1962 Code Section 9-451; 1970 (56) 2321; 1978 Act No. 591, Section 1; 1993 Act No. 181, Section 8; 2008 Act No. 249, Section 1, eff upon approval (became law without the Governor's signature on June 5, 2008); 2012 Act No. 279, Section 2, eff June 26, 2012; 2014 Act No. 121 (S.22), Pt V, Section 7.F, eff July 1, 2015.

Editor's Note

2012 Act No. 279, Section 33, provides as follows:

"Due to the congressional redistricting, any person elected or appointed to serve, or serving, as a member of any board, commission, or committee to represent a congressional district, whose residency is transferred to another district by a change in the composition of the district, may serve, or continue to serve, the term of office for which he was elected or appointed; however, the appointing or electing authority shall appoint or elect an additional member on that board, commission, or committee from the district which loses a resident member as a result of the transfer to serve until the term of the transferred member expires. When a vacancy occurs in the district to which a member has been transferred, the vacancy must not be filled until the full term of the transferred member expires. Further, the inability to hold an election or to make an appointment due to judicial review of the congressional districts does not constitute a vacancy."

Effect of Amendment

The 2008 amendment rewrote this section.

The 2012 amendment substituted "sixteen" for "fifteen"; inserted "The member first appointed from the Seventh Congressional District after the expansion of the commission to sixteen members shall serve a four-year term."; and, made other, nonsubstantive, changes.

2014 Act No. 121, Section 7.F, in the third sentence, substituted "Department of Administration" for "Office of the Governor".

SECTION 1-15-20. Per diem, mileage and subsistence.

The members of the Commission shall be paid the usual per diem, mileage and subsistence as provided by law for members of boards, commissions and committees to be paid from the general fund of the State.

HISTORY: 1962 Code Section 9-452; 1970 (56) 2321.

SECTION 1-15-30. Organization; officers; quorum.

The commission shall meet as soon after appointment as practicable and shall organize itself by electing one of its members as chairman, one of its members as vice-chairman, and one of its members as secretary. A quorum for transacting business at all meetings of the commission shall consist of a majority of the membership of the commission.

HISTORY: 1962 Code Section 9-453; 1970 (56) 2321; 1978 Act No. 591, Section 2.

SECTION 1-15-40. Duties.

(1) The commission shall study the status of women and make periodic reports to the Governor with its recommendations concerning the following areas:

(a) Education needs and education opportunities pertaining to women.

(b) Social insurance and tax laws as they affect the net earnings and other income of women.

(c) Federal and state labor laws dealing with such matters as hours, night work and wages to determine whether they are accomplishing the purposes for which they were established and whether they should be adapted to changing technological, economic and social conditions.

(d) Differences in legal treatment of men and women in regard to political and civil rights, property rights, and family relations.

(e) New and expanded services that may be required for women as wives and mothers, and workers, including education, counseling, training, home services, and arrangements for care of children during the working day.

(f) The employment policies and practices of the State of South Carolina with reference to additional affirmative steps which should be taken through legislation, executive or administrative action to assure nondiscrimination on the basis of sex and to enhance constructive employment opportunities for women.

(g) At appropriate intervals of five or more years, an updated report shall be issued by the commission.

(2) The commission shall also be empowered to:

(a) Receive and disburse state and federal grants for furtherance of the commission's objectives.

(b) Disseminate pertinent material relating to the rights, responsibilities and status of women.

HISTORY: 1962 Code Section 9-454; 1970 (56) 2321; 1978 Act No. 591, Section 3.

SECTION 1-15-50. Cooperation.

All executive departments and agencies of the State government shall cooperate with the Commission in the performance of its duties.

HISTORY: 1962 Code Section 9-455; 1970 (56) 2321.

CHAPTER 17

Interstate Cooperation

SECTION 1-17-10. Commission on Interstate Cooperation.

The Commission on Interstate Cooperation shall be composed of fifteen members, namely: The five members of the Committee on Interstate Cooperation of the Senate, the five members of the Committee on Interstate Cooperation of the House of Representatives and five officials of the State government named by the Governor, one of whom shall be designated by him as the chairman of the Commission. The State officials, when so named, shall serve ex officio. The Governor shall be an honorary member of the Commission.

HISTORY: 1962 Code Section 9-101; 1952 Code Section 9-101; 1942 Code Section 3442-14; 1936 (39) 1322.

SECTION 1-17-20. Committee on Interstate Cooperation of Senate.

The standing Committee on Interstate Cooperation of the Senate shall consist of five Senators. The members and chairman of this Committee shall be designated in the same manner as is customary in the case of the members and chairmen of other standing committees of the Senate. The Lieutenant Governor may serve ex officio as one of the five members of this Committee.

HISTORY: 1962 Code Section 9-102; 1952 Code Section 9-102; 1942 Code Section 3442-12; 1936 (39) 1322.

SECTION 1-17-30. Committee on Interstate Cooperation of House of Representatives.

The standing Committee on Interstate Cooperation of the House of Representatives shall consist of five members. The members and chairman of this Committee shall be designated in the same manner as is customary in the case of the members and chairmen of other standing committees of the House of Representatives.

HISTORY: 1962 Code Section 9-103; 1952 Code Section 9-103; 1942 Code Section 3442-13; 1936 (39) 1322.

SECTION 1-17-40. Terms of members of Commission and Committees.

The standing Committee of the Senate and the standing Committee of the House of Representatives shall function during the regular sessions of the legislature and also during the interim periods between such sessions. Their members shall serve until their successors are designated and they shall respectively constitute the Senate and House councils of the American Legislators' Association for this State. The terms of each administration member of the Commission appointed by the Governor shall extend until the next gubernatorial inauguration and thereafter until his successor is appointed.

HISTORY: 1962 Code Section 9-104; 1952 Code Section 9-104; 1942 Code Section 3442-17; 1936 (39) 1322.

SECTION 1-17-50. Duties of Commission.

The South Carolina Commission on Interstate Cooperation shall encourage and arrange conferences with officials of other states and of other units of government, carry forward the participation of this State as a member of the council of state governments, both regionally and nationally, and formulate proposals for cooperation between this State and other states.

HISTORY: 1962 Code Section 9-105; 1952 Code Section 9-105; 1942 Code Section 3442-11; 1936 (39) 1322.

SECTION 1-17-60. Committees established by Commission to conduct conferences and formulate proposals concerning cooperation; advisory boards.

The Commission shall establish such committees as it deems advisable to conduct conferences and to formulate proposals concerning subjects of intergovernmental cooperation. Subject to the approval of the Commission the members of every such committee shall be appointed by the chairman of the Commission. State officials who are not members of the Commission may be appointed as members of any such committee but at least one member of the Commission shall be a member of every such committee. The Commission may provide such rules as it considers appropriate concerning the membership and functioning of any committee which it establishes. The Commission may provide for advisory boards for itself and for its various committees and for the service of private citizens on such boards.

HISTORY: 1962 Code Section 9-106; 1952 Code Section 9-106; 1942 Code Section 3442-15; 1936 (39) 1322.

SECTION 1-17-70. Reports; compensation and powers of Commission.

The Commission shall report to the Governor and to the legislature within fifteen days after the convening of each regular legislative session and at such other times as it deems appropriate. Its members and the members of all committees which it establishes shall serve without compensation but they shall be paid their necessary expenses in carrying out their obligations under this chapter. The Commission may employ a secretary and a stenographer. It may incur such other expenses as may be necessary for the proper performance of its duties and it may, by contributions to the council of state governments, participate with other states in maintaining said council's regional and central secretariats and its other governmental services.

HISTORY: 1962 Code Section 9-107; 1952 Code Section 9-107; 1942 Code Section 3442-16; 1936 (39) 1322.

CHAPTER 18

Review of Occupational Registration & Licensing

SECTION 1-18-10. Definitions.

(A) "Licensure" means the process by which an agency, board, or commission of the State grants permission to persons meeting predetermined qualifications to have the exclusive use of an occupational title and to engage in an occupation to the exclusion of unlicensed persons.

(B) "Registration" means the process by which an agency, board, or commission identifies and lists those persons who meet predetermined qualifications and who are the only persons permitted to use an occupational title.

(C) "Commission" means the State Reorganization Commission.

HISTORY: 1988 Act No. 572, Section 1.

SECTION 1-18-20. Public hearings on whether occupation should be regulated.

Upon the filing of any bill proposing to regulate an occupation not regulated by the State, the subcommittee of the standing committee of the House of Representatives or the Senate to which the bill has been referred may request that the commission conduct the public hearing or that the commission assist the subcommittee in conducting the public hearing. Upon the request of the subcommittee, the commission may hold hearings for the purpose of determining whether or not occupations not regulated by the State should be regulated.

HISTORY: 1988 Act No. 572, Section 1.

SECTION 1-18-30. Notice of hearings; review panel; report of commission.

When requested by the subcommittee, the commission shall provide notice of the hearings to the public and to any organizations or state agencies or boards whose members could reasonably be expected to be affected by any proposed regulation or changes in regulation. In addition, the commission may solicit the participation, as part of the review panel, of representatives of state agencies currently authorized to regulate a profession related to that under review. The subcommittee, as referred to in Section 1-18-70, shall sit in conjunction with the commission at the hearings. Upon receipt of testimony at the hearing, and pursuant to any other research or inquiries it considers appropriate, the commission shall report its findings and conclusions to the subcommittee of the Senate and the House, as referred to in Section 1-18-70.

HISTORY: 1988 Act No. 572, Section 1.

SECTION 1-18-40. Factors to be considered in evaluating whether occupation should be regulated; limits on recommendation to regulate.

In evaluating whether an occupation should be regulated, the commission shall consider whether:

(1) the unregulated practice of an occupation presents a clear and recognizable danger to the health, safety, or welfare of the public;

(2) the practice of the occupation requires such a specialized skill that the public is not qualified to select a competent practitioner without assurances that he has met minimum qualifications;

(3) the public is or may be effectively protected by other means, such as academic credentials, certification by a nongovernmental entity, or membership in occupational associations;

(4) current laws are ineffective or inadequate to protect the public health, safety, and welfare and whether strengthening the laws would not provide adequate protection to the public;

(5) the practitioner performs a service for others which would qualify for payment of part or all of those services by a third party if the practitioners were to be regulated by the State;

(6) regulation will increase the cost of goods;

(7) regulation will increase or decrease the availability of services to the public;

(8) regulation will assure the competency of practitioners of the occupation;

(9) regulation can be provided through an existing agency or under supervision of presently licensed practitioners.

In determining any recommendation for regulation of an occupation, the commission shall recommend the least extensive and restrictive form of regulation consistent with the public interest. The commission may not recommend any regulation unless necessary to protect the health, safety, or welfare of the public.

HISTORY: 1988 Act No. 572, Section 1.

SECTION 1-18-50. Degrees of regulation of occupation; limits on recommendation of regulation by licensure.

(A) If the commission determines that existing remedies do not adequately protect the public health, safety, or welfare, it shall consider the following degrees of regulation of the practice of that occupation in the following order:

(1) statutory change to provide for civil causes of action or criminal penalties;

(2) inspection of a practitioner's premises and activities and authorization of an appropriate state board, agency, or commission to enjoin an activity which is detrimental to the public health, safety, or welfare;

(3) listing of a practitioner's location, nature, and operation of practice;

(4) registration as defined in this chapter;

(5) licensure as defined in this chapter.

(B) Licensure must be recommended only where the commission determines that registration or other means of regulation is not adequate to protect the health, safety, or welfare of the public. The commission may recommend one or more means of regulation or statutory change, whether or not it is included in subsection (A) of this section.

HISTORY: 1988 Act No. 572, Section 1.

SECTION 1-18-60. Recommendations to General Assembly.

In making its recommendations to the General Assembly, the commission may recommend that no regulation be created, that regulations be assigned to an existing board, agency, or commission, or that a new board be established. If registration or licensure is recommended, the commission shall recommend what qualifications are specified for the registration or licensure and describe the activities that may be engaged in by persons pursuing the occupation.

HISTORY: 1988 Act No. 572, Section 1.

SECTION 1-18-70. Recommendations to be based on evidence; recommendations to be in writing; persons who are to receive copy of recommendations.

All recommendations formulated by the commission must be based upon evidence gathered by the commission in public hearings from testimony submitted orally or in writing by interested parties including the commission and upon evidence compiled by the commission in studies conducted by the commission. The recommendations of the commission must be made in writing and delivered to the chairman of the subcommittee of the standing committee of the House or the Senate to which a bill proposing to regulate an occupation has been referred. Copies of the commission's recommendations must also be delivered to the President Pro Tempore of the Senate, the Speaker of the House of Representatives, and the Governor. Copies of the commission's recommendations must be mailed to any person who has made a request concerning occupational regulation that was considered by the commission. If the commission recommends no changes with respect to the regulation of an occupation, the commission shall notify by mail any person who has requested that regulations or changes be recommended.

HISTORY: 1988 Act No. 572, Section 1.

CHAPTER 21

Uniformity of Legislation

SECTION 1-21-10. Board of Commissioners for Promotion of Uniformity of Legislation in the United States.

The Governor shall appoint three suitable persons who, with their successors, shall constitute a "Board of Commissioners for the Promotion of Uniformity of Legislation in the United States." Any vacancy in the Board shall be filled by the appointment by the Governor of a suitable person.

HISTORY: 1962 Code Section 9-401; 1952 Code Section 9-401; 1942 Code Section 3440; 1932 Code Section 3440; Civ. C. '22 Section 1049; Civ. C. '12 Section 926; 1909 (26) 127.

SECTION 1-21-20. Duty of Board.

The Board shall:

(1) Examine the subjects of insolvency, the descent and distribution of property, the execution and probate of wills and other subjects upon which uniformity of legislation in the various states and territories of the union is desirable but which are outside the jurisdiction of the Congress of the United States;

(2) Confer upon these matters with the commissioners appointed by other states and territories for the same purpose;

(3) Consider and draft uniform laws to be submitted for approval and adoption of the several states; and

(4) Generally devise and recommend such other or further course of action as shall accomplish the purposes of this chapter.

HISTORY: 1962 Code Section 9-402; 1952 Code Section 9-402; 1942 Code Section 3441; 1932 Code Section 3441; Civ. C. '22 Section 1050; Civ. C. '12 Section 927; 1909 (26) 127.

SECTION 1-21-30. Record; annual report.

The Board shall keep a record of all its transactions and shall at each regular session of the legislature in each year, and may at any other time, make a report of its doings and of its recommendations to the General Assembly.

HISTORY: 1962 Code Section 9-403; 1952 Code Section 9-403; 1942 Code Section 3442; 1932 Code Section 3442; Civ. C. '22 Section 1051; Civ. C. '12 Section 928; 1909 (26) 127.

CHAPTER 23

State Agency Rule Making and Adjudication of Contested Cases

ARTICLE 1

State Register and Code of Regulations

SECTION 1-23-10. Definitions.

As used in this article:

(1) "Agency" or "State agency" means each state board, commission, department, executive department or officer, other than the legislature, the courts, the South Carolina Tobacco Community Development Board, or the Tobacco Settlement Revenue Management Authority, authorized by law to make regulations or to determine contested cases;

(2) "Document" means a regulation, notice or similar instrument issued or promulgated pursuant to law by a state agency;

(3) "Person" means any individual, partnership, corporation, association, governmental subdivision or public or private organization of any character other than an agency;

(4) "Regulation" means each agency statement of general public applicability that implements or prescribes law or policy or practice requirements of any agency. Policy or guidance issued by an agency other than in a regulation does not have the force or effect of law. The term "regulation" includes general licensing criteria and conditions and the amendment or repeal of a prior regulation, but does not include descriptions of agency procedures applicable only to agency personnel; opinions of the Attorney General; decisions or orders in rate making, price fixing, or licensing matters; awards of money to individuals; policy statements or rules of local school boards; regulations of the National Guard; decisions, orders, or rules of the Board of Probation, Parole, and Pardon Services; orders of the supervisory or administrative agency of a penal, mental, or medical institution, in respect to the institutional supervision, custody, control, care, or treatment of inmates, prisoners, or patients; decisions of the governing board of a university, college, technical college, school, or other educational institution with regard to curriculum, qualifications for admission, dismissal and readmission, fees and charges for students, conferring degrees and diplomas, employment tenure and promotion of faculty and disciplinary proceedings; decisions of the Human Affairs Commission relating to firms or individuals; advisory opinions of agencies; and other agency actions relating only to specified individuals.

(5) "Promulgation" means final agency action to enact a regulation after compliance with procedures prescribed in this article.

(6) "Office" means the Office of Research and Statistics of the Revenue and Fiscal Affairs Office.

(7) "Substantial economic impact" means a financial impact upon:

(a) commercial enterprises;

(b) retail businesses;

(c) service businesses;

(d) industry;

(e) consumers of a product or service;

(f) taxpayers; or

(g) small businesses as defined in Section 1-23-270.

HISTORY: 1977 Act No. 176, Art. I, Section 1; 1992 Act No. 507, Section 2; 1996 Act No. 411, Section 1; 1999 Act No. 77, Section 2; 2000 Act No. 387, Part II, Section 69A.3; 2004 Act No. 231, Section 3, eff January 1, 2005.

Code Commissioner's Note

At the direction of the Code Commissioner, references in this section to the offices of the former State Budget and Control Board, Office of the Governor, or other agencies, were changed to reflect the transfer of them to the Department of Administration or other entities, pursuant to the directive of the South Carolina Restructuring Act, 2014 Act No. 121, Section 5(D)(1).

Effect of Amendment

The 2004 amendment added subparagraph (7)(g).

SECTION 1-23-20. Custody, printing and distribution of documents charged to Legislative Council; establishment of State Register.

The Legislative Council is charged with the custody, printing and distribution of the documents required or authorized to be published in this article and with the responsibility for incorporating them into a State Register. Such Register shall include proposed as well as finally adopted documents required to be filed with the Council; provided, however, that publication of a synopsis of the contents of proposed regulations meets the requirements of this section. Additions to the State Register shall be published by the Legislative Council at least once every thirty days.

HISTORY: 1977 Act No. 176, Art. I, Section 2.

SECTION 1-23-30. Filing of documents with Legislative Council; public inspection; distribution.

The original and either two additional originals or two certified copies of each document authorized or required to be published in the State Register by this article shall be filed with the Legislative Council by the agency by which it is promulgated. Filing may be accomplished at all times when the Council office is open for official business.

The Council shall note upon each document filed the date and hour of filing and shall as soon as practicable publish such document in the State Register. Copies of all documents filed shall be available at the Council office for public inspection during office hours.

The Council shall transmit to the Clerk of Court of each county a copy of the State Register and all additions thereto when published. Clerks of Court shall maintain their copies of the Register in current form and provide for public inspection thereof. The Council shall transmit one original or certified copy of each document filed with the Council to the Department of Archives and History which shall be made available for public inspection in the office of the department.

HISTORY: 1977 Act No. 176, Art. I, Section 3.

SECTION 1-23-40. Documents required to be filed and published in State Register.

There shall be filed with the Legislative Council and published in the State Register:

(1) All regulations promulgated or proposed to be promulgated by state agencies which have general public applicability and legal effect, including all of those which include penalty provisions. Provided, however, that the text of regulations as finally promulgated by an agency shall not be published in the State Register until such regulations have been approved by the General Assembly in accordance with Section 1-23-120.

(2) Any other documents, upon agency request in writing. Comments and news items of any nature shall not be published in the Register.

HISTORY: 1977 Act No. 176, Art. I, Section 4.

SECTION 1-23-50. Legislative Council to establish procedures.

The Legislative Council shall establish procedures for carrying out the provisions of this article relating to the State Register and the form and filing of regulations. These procedures may provide among other things:

(1) The manner of certification of copies required to be filed under Section 1-23-40;

(2) The manner and form in which the documents or regulations shall be printed, reprinted, compiled, indexed, bound and distributed, including the compilation of the State Register ;

(3) The number of copies of the documents, regulations or compilations thereof, which shall be printed and compiled, the number which shall be distributed without charge to members of the General Assembly, officers and employees of the State or state agencies for official use and the number which shall be available for distribution to the public;

(4) The prices to be charged for individual copies of documents or regulations and subscriptions to the compilations and reprints and bound volumes of them.

HISTORY: 1977 Act No. 176, Art. I, Section 5; 1979 Act No. 188, Section 2.

SECTION 1-23-60. Effect of filing and of publication of documents and regulations; rebuttable presumption of compliance; judicial notice of contents.

A document or regulation required by this article to be filed with the Legislative Council shall not be valid against a person who has not had actual knowledge of it until the document or regulation has been filed with the office of the Legislative Council, printed in the State Register and made available for public inspection as provided by this article. Unless otherwise specifically provided by statute, filing and publication of a document or regulation in the State Register as required or authorized by this article is sufficient to give notice of the contents of the document or regulation to a person subject to or affected by it. The publication of a document filed in the office of the Legislative Council creates a rebuttable presumption:

(1) That it was duly issued, prescribed or promulgated subject to further action required under this article;

(2) That it was filed and made available for public inspection at the day and hour stated in the printed notation thereon required under Section 1-23-30;

(3) That the copy on file in the Legislative Council is a true copy of the original;

The contents of filed documents shall be judicially noticed and, without prejudice to any other mode of citation, may be cited by volume and page number or the numerical designation assigned to it by the Legislative Council.

HISTORY: 1977 Act No. 176, Art. I, Section 6.

SECTION 1-23-70. Duty of Attorney General.

The Attorney General shall be responsible for the interpretation of this article and for the compliance by agencies required to file documents with the Legislative Council under the provisions of this article and shall upon request advise such agencies of necessary procedures to insure compliance therewith.

HISTORY: 1977 Act No. 176, Art. I, Section 7.

SECTION 1-23-80. Costs incurred and revenues collected by Legislative Council.

The cost of printing, reprinting, wrapping, binding and distributing the documents, regulations or compilations thereof, including the State Register, and other expenses incurred by the Legislative Council in carrying out the duties placed upon it by this article shall be funded by the appropriations to the council in the annual state general appropriations act. All revenue derived from the sale of the documents and regulations shall be deposited in the general fund of the State.

HISTORY: 1977 Act No. 176, Art. I, Section 8.

SECTION 1-23-90. Complete codifications of documents; Code of State Regulations designated.

(a) The Legislative Council may provide for, from time to time as it considers necessary, the preparation and publication of complete codifications of the documents of each agency having general applicability and legal effect, issued or promulgated by the agency which are relied upon by the agency as authority for, or are invoked or used by it in the discharge of, its activities or functions.

(b) A codification published under item (a) of this section shall be designated as the "Code of State Regulations". The Legislative Council may regulate the binding of the printed codifications into separate books with a view to practical usefulness and economical manufacture. Each book shall contain an explanation of its coverage and other aids to users that the Legislative Council may require. A general index to the entire Code of State Regulations may be separately printed and bound.

(c) The Legislative Council shall regulate the supplementation and republication of the printed codifications with a view to keeping the Code of State Regulations as current as practicable.

(d) The authority granted in this section is supplemental to and not in conflict with the establishment of the State Register as provided for in other provisions of this article.

HISTORY: 1977 Act No. 176, Art. I, Section 9.

SECTION 1-23-100. Exemptions for Executive Orders, proclamations or documents issued by Governor's Office; treatment of some Executive Orders for information purposes.

This article shall not apply to Executive Orders, proclamations or documents issued by the Governor's Office. However, Governor's Executive Orders, having general applicability and legal effect shall be transmitted by the Secretary of State to the Legislative Council to be published in a separate section of the State Register for information purposes only. Such orders shall not be subject to General Assembly approval.

HISTORY: 1977 Act No. 176, Art. I, Section 10.

SECTION 1-23-110. Procedures for publication of notice of proposed promulgation of regulations; public participation; contest of regulation for procedural defects.

(A) Before the promulgation, amendment, or repeal of a regulation, an agency shall:

(1) give notice of a drafting period by publication of a notice in the State Register. The notice must include:

(a) the address to which interested persons may submit written comments during the initial drafting period before the regulations are submitted as proposed;

(b) a synopsis of what the agency plans to draft;

(c) the agency's statutory authority for promulgating the regulation;

(2) submit to the office, no later than the date the notice required in item (3) is published in the State Register, a preliminary assessment report prepared in accordance with Section 1-23-115 on regulations having a substantial economic impact;

(3) give notice of a public hearing at which the agency will receive data, views, or arguments, orally and in writing, from interested persons on proposed regulations by publication of a notice in the State Register if requested by twenty-five persons, by a governmental subdivision or agency, or by an association having not less than twenty-five members. The notice must include:

(a) the address to which written comments must be sent and the time period of not less than thirty days for submitting these comments;

(b) the date, time, and place of the public hearing which must not be held sooner than thirty days from the date the notice is published in the State Register;

(c) a narrative preamble and the text of the proposed regulation. The preamble shall include a section-by-section discussion of the proposed regulation and a justification for any provision not required to maintain compliance with federal law including, but not limited to, grant programs;

(d) the statutory authority for its promulgation;

(e) a preliminary fiscal impact statement prepared by the agency reflecting estimates of costs to be incurred by the State and its political subdivisions in complying with the proposed regulation. A preliminary fiscal impact statement is not required for those regulations which are not subject to General Assembly review under Section 1-23-120;

(f) a summary of the preliminary assessment report submitted by the agency to the office and notice that copies of the preliminary report are available from the agency. The agency may charge a reasonable fee to cover the costs associated with this distribution requirement. A regulation that does not require an assessment report because it does not have a substantial economic impact, must include a statement to that effect. A regulation exempt from filing an assessment report pursuant to Section 1-23-115(E) must include an explanation of the exemption;

(g) statement of the need and reasonableness of the regulation as determined by the agency based on an analysis of the factors listed in Section 1-23-115(C)(1) through (11). At no time is an agency required to include items (4) through (8) in the reasonableness and need determination. However, comments related to items (4) through (8) received by the agency during the public comment periods must be made part of the official record of the proposed regulations.

(h) the location where a person may obtain from the agency a copy of the detailed statement of rationale as required by this item. For new regulations and significant amendments to existing regulations, an agency shall prepare and make available to the public upon request a detailed statement of rationale which shall state the basis for the regulation, including the scientific or technical basis, if any, and shall identify any studies, reports, policies, or statements of professional judgment or administrative need relied upon in developing the regulation. This subitem does not apply to regulations which are not subject to General Assembly review under Section 1-23-120.

(B) Notices required by this section must be mailed by the promulgating agency to all persons who have made timely requests of the agency for advance notice of proposed promulgation of regulations.

(C)(1) The agency shall consider fully all written and oral submissions respecting the proposed regulation.

(2) Following the public hearing and consideration of all submissions, an agency must not submit a regulation to the General Assembly for review if the regulation contains a substantive change in the content of regulation as proposed pursuant to subsection (A)(3) and the substantive change was not raised, considered, or discussed by public comment received pursuant to this section. The agency shall refile such a regulation for publication in the State Register as a proposed regulation pursuant to subsection (A)(3).

(D) A proceeding to contest a regulation on the ground of noncompliance with the procedural requirements of this section must be commenced within one year from the effective date of the regulation.

HISTORY: 1977 Act No. 176, Art. I, Section 11; 1980 Act No. 442, Section 1; 1985 Act No. 190, Section 2; 1988 Act No. 605, Section 1; 1989 Act No. 91, Section 1; 1992 Act No. 507, Section 3; 1993 Act No. 181, Section 11; 1996 Act No. 411, Sections 2, 3; 2002 Act No. 231, Section 1; 2007 Act. No. 104, Section 1, eff July 1, 2008.

Code Commissioner's Note

At the direction of the Code Commissioner, references in this section to the offices of the former State Budget and Control Board, Office of the Governor, or other agencies, were changed to reflect the transfer of them to the Department of Administration or other entities, pursuant to the directive of the South Carolina Restructuring Act, 2014 Act No. 121, Section 5(D)(1).

Editor's Note

2007 Act No. 104, Section 5, provides as follows:

"This act takes effect July 1, 2008, and applies to regulations for which a notice of a public hearing has been published in the State Register, in accordance with Section 1-23-110(A)(3) of the 1976 Code, after June 30, 2008; all other regulations under General Assembly review on this act's effective date must be processed and reviewed in accordance with the law in effect on June 30, 2008."

Effect of Amendment

The 2007 amendment designated paragraph (C)(1) and added paragraph (C)(2) relating to regulations containing substantive changes.

SECTION 1-23-111. Regulation process; public hearings; report of presiding official; options upon unfavorable determination.

(A) When a public hearing is held pursuant to this article involving the promulgation of regulations by a department for which the governing authority is a single director, it must be conducted by an administrative law judge assigned by the chief judge. When a public hearing is held pursuant to this article involving the promulgation of regulations by a department for which the governing authority is a board or commission, it must be conducted by the board or commission, with the chairman presiding. The administrative law judge or chairman, as the presiding official, shall ensure that all persons involved in the public hearing on the regulation are treated fairly and impartially. The agency shall submit into the record the jurisdictional documents, including the statement of need and reasonableness as determined by the agency based on an analysis of the factors listed in Section 1-23-115(C)(1) through (11), except items (4) through (8), and any written exhibits in support of the proposed regulation. The agency may also submit oral evidences. Interested persons may present written or oral evidence. The presiding official shall allow questioning of agency representatives or witnesses, or of interested persons making oral statements, in order to explain the purpose or intended operation of the proposed regulation, or a suggested modification, or for other purposes if material to the evaluation or formulation of the proposed regulation. The presiding official may limit repetitive or immaterial statements or questions. At the request of the presiding official or the agency, a transcript of the hearing must be prepared.

(B) After allowing all written material to be submitted and recorded in the record of the public hearing no later than five working days after the hearing ends, unless the presiding official orders an extension for not more than twenty days, the presiding official shall issue a written report which shall include findings as to the need and reasonableness of the proposed regulation based on an analysis of the factors listed in Section 1-23-115(C)(1) through (11), except items (4) through (8), and other factors as the presiding official identifies and may include suggested modifications to the proposed regulations in the case of a finding of lack of need or reasonableness.

(C) If the presiding official determines that the need for or reasonableness of the proposed regulation has not been established, the agency shall elect to:

(a) modify the proposed regulation by including the suggested modifications of the presiding official;

(b) not modify the proposed regulation in accordance with the presiding official's suggested modifications in which case the agency shall submit to the General Assembly, along with the promulgated regulation submitted for legislative review, a copy of the presiding official's written report; or

(c) terminate the promulgation process for the proposed regulation by publication of a notice in the State Register and the termination is effective upon publication of the notice.

HISTORY: 1993 Act No. 181, Section 11A; 1996 Act No. 411, Section 4.

SECTION 1-23-115. Regulations requiring assessment reports; report contents; exceptions; preliminary assessment reports.

(A) Upon written request by two members of the General Assembly, made before submission of a promulgated regulation to the General Assembly for legislative review, a regulation that has a substantial economic impact must have an assessment report prepared pursuant to this section and in accordance with the procedures contained in this article. In addition to any other method as may be provided by the General Assembly, the legislative committee to which the promulgated regulation has been referred, by majority vote, may send a written notification to the promulgating agency informing the agency that the committee cannot approve the promulgated regulation unless an assessment report is prepared and provided to the committee. The written notification tolls the running of the one hundred-twenty-day legislative review period, and the period does not begin to run again until an assessment report prepared in accordance with this article is submitted to the committee. Upon receipt of the assessment report, additional days must be added to the days remaining in the one hundred-twenty-day review period, if less than twenty days, to equal twenty days. A copy of the assessment report must be provided to each member of the committee.

(B) A state agency must submit to the Office of Research and Statistics of Revenue and Fiscal Affairs Office, a preliminary assessment report on regulations which have a substantial economic impact. Upon receiving this report the office may require additional information from the promulgating agency, other state agencies, or other sources. A state agency shall cooperate and provide information to the office on requests made pursuant to this section. The office shall prepare and publish a final assessment report within sixty days after the public hearing held pursuant to Section 1-23-110. The office shall forward the final assessment report and a summary of the final report to the promulgating agency.

(C) The preliminary and final assessment reports required by this section must disclose the effects of the proposed regulation on the public health and environmental welfare of the community and State and the effects of the economic activities arising out of the proposed regulation. Both the preliminary and final reports required by this section may include:

(1) a description of the regulation, the purpose of the regulation, the legal authority for the regulation, and the plan for implementing the regulation;

(2) a determination of the need for and reasonableness of the regulation as determined by the agency based on an analysis of the factors listed in this subsection and the expected benefit of the regulation;

(3) a determination of the costs and benefits associated with the regulation and an explanation of why the regulation is considered to be the most cost-effective, efficient, and feasible means for allocating public and private resources and for achieving the stated purpose;

(4) the effect of the regulation on competition;

(5) the effect of the regulation on the cost of living and doing business in the geographical area in which the regulation would be implemented;

(6) the effect of the regulation on employment in the geographical area in which the regulation would be implemented;

(7) the source of revenue to be used for implementing and enforcing the regulation;

(8) a conclusion on the short-term and long-term economic impact upon all persons substantially affected by the regulation, including an analysis containing a description of which persons will bear the costs of the regulation and which persons will benefit directly and indirectly from the regulation;

(9) the uncertainties associated with the estimation of particular benefits and burdens and the difficulties involved in the comparison of qualitatively and quantitatively dissimilar benefits and burdens. A determination of the need for the regulation shall consider qualitative and quantitative benefits and burdens;

(10) the effect of the regulation on the environment and public health;

(11) the detrimental effect on the environment and public health if the regulation is not implemented. An assessment report must not consider benefits or burdens on out-of-state political bodies or businesses. The assessment of

benefits and burdens which cannot be precisely quantified may be expressed in qualitative terms. This subsection must not be interpreted to require numerically precise cost-benefit analysis. At no time is an agency required to include items (4) through (8) in a preliminary assessment report or statement of the need and reasonableness; however, these items may be included in the final assessment report prepared by the office.

(D) If information required to be included in the assessment report materially changes at any time before the regulation is approved or disapproved by the General Assembly, the agency must submit the corrected information to the office which must forward a revised assessment report to the Legislative Council for submission to the committees to which the regulation was referred during General Assembly review.

(E) An assessment report is not required on:

(1) regulations specifically exempt from General Assembly review by Section 1-23-120; however, if any portion of a regulation promulgated to maintain compliance with federal law is more stringent than federal law, then that portion is not exempt from this section;

(2) emergency regulations filed in accordance with Section 1-23-130; however, before an emergency regulation may be refiled pursuant to Section 1-23-130, an assessment report must be prepared in accordance with this section;

(3) regulations which control the hunting or taking of wildlife including fish or setting times, methods, or conditions under which wildlife may be taken, hunted, or caught by the public, or opening public lands for hunting and fishing.

HISTORY: 1992 Act No. 507, Section 1; 1993 Act No. 181, Section 12; 1996 Act No. 411, Sections 5, 6.

Code Commissioner's Note

At the direction of the Code Commissioner, references in this section to the offices of the former State Budget and Control Board, Office of the Governor, or other agencies, were changed to reflect the transfer of them to the Department of Administration or other entities, pursuant to the directive of the South Carolina Restructuring Act, 2014 Act No. 121, Section 5(D)(1).

SECTION 1-23-120. Approval of regulations; submission to Legislative Council for submission to General Assembly; contents, requirements and procedures; compliance with federal law.

(A) All regulations except those specifically exempted pursuant to subsection (H) must be filed with Legislative Council for submission to the General Assembly for review in accordance with this article; however, a regulation must not be filed with Legislative Council for submission to the General Assembly more than one year after publication of the drafting notice initiating the regulation pursuant to Section 1-23-110, except those regulations requiring a final assessment report as provided in Sections 1-23-270 and 1-23-280.

(B) To initiate the process of review, the agency shall file with the Legislative Council for submission to the President of the Senate and the Speaker of the House of Representatives a document containing:

(1) a copy of the regulations promulgated;

(2) in the case of regulations proposing to amend an existing regulation or any clearly identifiable subdivision or portion of a regulation, the full text of the existing regulation or the text of the identifiable portion of the regulation; text that is proposed to be deleted must be stricken through, and text that is proposed to be added must be underlined;

(3) a request for review;

(4) a brief synopsis of the regulations submitted which explains the content and any changes in existing regulations resulting from the submitted regulations;

(5) a copy of the final assessment report and the summary of the final report prepared by the office pursuant to Section 1-23-115. A regulation that does not require an assessment report because the regulation does not have a substantial economic impact must include a statement to that effect. A regulation exempt from filing an assessment report pursuant to Section 1-23-115(E) must include an explanation of the exemption;

(6) a copy of the fiscal impact statement prepared by the agency as required by Section 1-23-110;

(7) a detailed statement of rationale which states the basis for the regulation, including the scientific or technical basis, if any, and identifies any studies,

reports, policies, or statements of professional judgment or administrative need relied upon in developing the regulation;

(8) a copy of the economic impact statement, as provided in Section 1-23-270(C)(1)(a); and

(9) a copy of the regulatory flexibility analysis, as provided in Section 1-23-270(C)(1)(b).

(C) Upon receipt of the regulation, the President and Speaker shall refer the regulation for review to the standing committees of the Senate and House which are most concerned with the function of the promulgating agency. A copy of the regulation or a synopsis of the regulation must be given to each member of the committee, and Legislative Council shall notify all members of the General Assembly when regulations are submitted for review either through electronic means or by addition of this information to the website maintained by the Legislative Services Agency, or both. The committees to which regulations are referred have one hundred twenty days from the date regulations are submitted to the General Assembly to consider and take action on these regulations. However, if a regulation is referred to a committee and no action occurs in that committee on the regulation within sixty calendar days of receipt of the regulation, the regulation must be placed on the agenda of the full committee beginning with the next scheduled full committee meeting.

(D) If a joint resolution to approve a regulation is not enacted within one hundred twenty days after the regulation is submitted to the General Assembly or if a joint resolution to disapprove a regulation has not been introduced by a standing committee to which the regulation was referred for review, the regulation is effective upon publication in the State Register. Upon introduction of the first joint resolution disapproving a regulation by a standing committee to which the regulation was referred for review, the one-hundred-twenty-day period for automatic approval is tolled. A regulation may not be filed under the emergency provisions of Section 1-23-130 if a joint resolution to disapprove the regulation has been introduced by a standing committee to which the regulation was referred. Upon a negative vote by either the Senate or House of Representatives on the resolution disapproving the regulation and the notification in writing of the negative vote to the Speaker of the House of Representatives and the President of the Senate by the Clerk of the House in which the negative vote occurred, the remainder of the period begins to run. If the remainder of the period is less than ninety days, additional days must be added to the remainder to equal ninety days. The introduction of a joint resolution by the committee of either house does not prevent the introduction of a joint resolution by the committee of the other house to either approve or disapprove the regulations concerned. A joint resolution approving or disapproving a regulation must include:

(1) the synopsis of the regulation as required by subsection (B)(4);

(2) the summary of the final assessment report prepared by the office pursuant to Section 1-23-115 or, as required by subsection (B)(5), the statement or explanation that an assessment report is not required or is exempt.

(E) The one-hundred-twenty-day period of review begins on the date the regulation is filed with the President and Speaker. Sine die adjournment of the General Assembly tolls the running of the period of review, and the remainder of the period begins to run upon the next convening of the General Assembly excluding special sessions called by the Governor.

(F) Any member of the General Assembly may introduce a joint resolution approving or disapproving a regulation thirty days following the date the regulations concerned are referred to a standing committee for review and no committee joint resolution approving or disapproving the regulations has been introduced and the regulations concerned have not been withdrawn by the promulgating agency pursuant to Section 1-23-125, but the introduction does not toll the one-hundred-twenty-day period of automatic approval.

(G) A regulation is deemed withdrawn if it has not become effective, as provided in this article, by the date of publication of the next State Register published after the end of the two-year session in which the regulation was submitted to the President and Speaker for review. Other provisions of this article notwithstanding, a regulation deemed withdrawn pursuant to this subsection may be resubmitted by the agency for legislative review during the next legislative session without repeating the requirements of Section 1-23-110, 1-23-111, or 1-23-115 if the resubmitted regulation contains no substantive changes for the previously submitted version.

(H) General Assembly review is not required for regulations promulgated:

(1) to maintain compliance with federal law including, but not limited to, grant programs; however, the synopsis of the regulation required to be submitted by subsection (B)(4) must include citations to federal law, if any, mandating the promulgation of or changes in the regulation justifying this exemption. If the

underlying federal law which constituted the basis for the exemption of a regulation from General Assembly review pursuant to this item is vacated, repealed, or otherwise does not have the force and effect of law, the state regulation is deemed repealed and without legal force and effect as of the date the promulgating state agency publishes notice in the State Register that the regulation is deemed repealed. The agency must publish the notice in the State Register no later than sixty days from the effective date the underlying federal law was rendered without legal force and effect. Upon publication of the notice, the prior version of the state regulation, if any, is reinstated and effective as a matter of law. The notice published in the State Register shall identify the specific provisions of the state regulation that are repealed as a result of the invalidity of the underlying federal law and shall provide the text of the prior regulation, if any, which is reinstated. The agency may promulgate additional amendments to the regulation by complying with the applicable requirements of this chapter;

(2) by the state Board of Financial Institutions in order to authorize state-chartered banks, state-chartered savings and loan associations, and state-chartered credit unions to engage in activities that are authorized pursuant to Section 34-1-110;

(3) by the South Carolina Department of Revenue to adopt regulations, revenue rulings, revenue procedures, and technical advice memoranda of the Internal Revenue Service so as to maintain conformity with the Internal Revenue Code as defined in Section 12-6-40;

(4) as emergency regulations under Section 1-23-130.

(I) For purposes of this section, only those calendar days occurring during a session of the General Assembly, excluding special sessions, are included in computing the days elapsed.

(J) Each state agency, which promulgates regulations or to which the responsibility for administering regulations has been transferred, shall by July 1, 1997, and every five years thereafter, conduct a formal review of all regulations which it has promulgated or for which it has been transferred the responsibility of administering, except that those regulations described in subsection (H) are not subject to this review. Upon completion of the review, the agency shall submit to the Code Commissioner a report which identifies those regulations:

(1) for which the agency intends to begin the process of repeal in accordance with this article;

(2) for which the agency intends to begin the process of amendment in accordance with this article; and

(3) which do not require repeal or amendment.

Nothing in this subsection may be construed to prevent an agency from repealing or amending a regulation in accordance with this article before or after it is identified in the report to the Code Commissioner.

HISTORY: 1977 Act No. 176, Art. I, Section 12; 1979 Act No. 188, Section 3; 1980 Act No. 442, Section 2; 1981 Act No. 21, Section 1; 1982 Act No. 414, Section 1; 1986 Act No. 414, Section 14; 1988 Act No. 605, Section 2; 1989 Act No. 91, Section 2; 1992 Act No. 507, Section 4; 1993 Act No. 181, Section 13; 1996 Act No. 411, Section 7; 1996 Act No. 411, Section 8; 1997 Act No. 114, Section 1; 2002 Act No. 231, Section 2; 2004 Act No. 231, Sections 4, 5, eff January 1, 2005; 2007 Act No. 104, Section 2, eff July 1, 2008; 2011 Act No. 33, Section 1, eff June 7, 2011; 2013 Act No. 31, Section 3, eff May 21, 2013.

Code Commissioner's Note

At the direction of the Code Commissioner, references in this section to the offices of the former State Budget and Control Board, Office of the Governor, or other agencies, were changed to reflect the transfer of them to the Department of Administration or other entities, pursuant to the directive of the South Carolina Restructuring Act, 2014 Act No. 121, Section 5(D)(1).

Editor's Note

2007 Act No. 104, Section 5, provides as follows:

"This act takes effect July 1, 2008, and applies to regulations for which a notice of a public hearing has been published in the State Register, in accordance with Section 1-23-110(A)(3) of the 1976 Code, after June 30, 2008; all other regulations under General Assembly review on this act's effective date must be processed and reviewed in accordance with the law in effect on June 30, 2008."

Effect of Amendment

The 2004 amendment, in subsection (A), added the exception at the end of the first sentence relating to Sections 1-23-270 and 1-23-280 and, in subsection (B), added paragraphs (B)(7) and (B)(8).

The 2007 amendment rewrote this section to provide for submission of regulations to the Legislative Council for submission to the General Assembly; added paragraph (B)(2) requiring amendments to be clearly indicated; and added subsection (G) relating to when regulations are deemed withdrawn.

The 2011 amendment, in subsection (H)(1), added the last five sentences.

The 2013 amendment, in subsection (C), substituted "the Legislative Services Agency" for "Legislative Printing Information and Technology Services".

SECTION 1-23-125. Approval, disapproval and modification of regulations.

(A) The legislative committee to which a regulation is submitted is not authorized to amend a particular regulation and then introduce a joint resolution approving the regulation as amended; however, this provision does not prevent the introduction of a resolution disapproving one or more of a group of regulations submitted to the committee and approving others submitted at the same time or deleting a clearly separable portion of a single regulation and approving the balance of the regulation in the committee resolution.

(B) If a majority of a committee determines that it cannot approve a regulation in the form submitted, it shall notify the promulgating agency in writing along with its recommendations as to changes that would be necessary to obtain committee approval. The agency may:

(1) withdraw the regulation from the General Assembly and resubmit it with the recommended changes to the Speaker and the Lieutenant Governor, but any regulation not resubmitted within thirty days is considered permanently withdrawn;

(2) withdraw the regulation permanently;

(3) take no action and abide by whatever action is taken or not taken by the General Assembly on the regulation concerned.

(C) The notification tolls the one-hundred-twenty-day period for automatic approval, and when an agency withdraws regulations from the General

Assembly prior to the time a committee resolution to approve or disapprove the regulation has been introduced, the remainder of the period begins to run only on the date the regulations are resubmitted to the General Assembly. Upon resubmission of the regulations, additional days must be added to the days remaining in the review period for automatic approval, if less than twenty days, to equal twenty days, and a copy of the amended regulation must be given to each member of the committee. If an agency decides to take no action pursuant to subsection (B)(3), it shall notify the committee in writing and the remainder of the period begins to run only upon this notification.

(D) This section, as it applies to approval, disapproval, or modification of regulations, does not apply to joint resolutions introduced by other than the committees to which regulations are initially referred by the Lieutenant Governor or the Speaker of the House of Representatives.

(E) A regulation submitted to the General Assembly for review may be withdrawn by the agency for any reason. The regulation may be resubmitted by the agency for legislative review during the legislative session without repeating the requirements of Section 1-23-110, 1-23-111, or 1-23-115 if the resubmitted regulation contains no substantive changes from the previously submitted version.

HISTORY: 1979 Act No. 188, Section 1; 1980 Act No. 442, Section 3; 1982 Act No. 414, Section 1; 1979 Act No. 188, Section 1; 1980 Act No. 442, Section 3; 1982 Act No. 414, Section 1; 1988 Act No. 605, Section 3; 1996 Act No. 411, Section 9; 2007 Act No. 104, Section 3, eff July 1, 2008.

Editor's Note

2007 Act No. 104, Section 5, provides as follows:

"This act takes effect July 1, 2008, and applies to regulations for which a notice of a public hearing has been published in the State Register, in accordance with Section 1-23-110(A)(3) of the 1976 Code, after June 30, 2008; all other regulations under General Assembly review on this act's effective date must be processed and reviewed in accordance with the law in effect on June 30, 2008."

Effect of Amendment

The 2007 amendment, in subsection (A), deleted the last sentence relating to withdrawal or modification of a regulation under legislative review and rewrote subsection (E) which required public comment on regulations containing a substantive change.

SECTION 1-23-126. Petition requesting promulgation, amendment or repeal of regulation.

An interested person may petition an agency in writing requesting the promulgation, amendment or repeal of a regulation. Within thirty days after submission of such petition, the agency shall either deny the petition in writing (stating its reasons for the denial) or shall initiate the action in such petition.

HISTORY: 1980 Act No. 442, Section 6.

SECTION 1-23-130. Emergency regulations.

(A) If an agency finds that an imminent peril to public health, safety, or welfare requires immediate promulgation of an emergency regulation before compliance with the procedures prescribed in this article or if a natural resources related agency finds that abnormal or unusual conditions, immediate need, or the state's best interest requires immediate promulgation of emergency regulations to protect or manage natural resources, the agency may file the regulation with the Legislative Council and a statement of the situation requiring immediate promulgation. The regulation becomes effective as of the time of filing.

(B) An emergency regulation filed under this section which has a substantial economic impact may not be refiled unless accompanied by the summary of the final assessment report prepared by the office pursuant to Section 1-23-115 and a statement of need and reasonableness is prepared by the agency pursuant to Section 1-23-111.

(C) If emergency regulations are either filed or expire while the General Assembly is in session, the emergency regulations remain in effect for ninety days only and may not be refiled; but if emergency regulations are both filed and expire during a time when the General Assembly is not in session they may be refiled for an additional ninety days.

(D) Emergency regulations and the agency statement as to the need for and reasonableness of immediate promulgation must be published in the next issue of the State Register following the date of filing. The summary of the final assessment report required for refiling emergency regulations pursuant to subsection (B) must also be published in the next issue of the State Register.

(E) An emergency regulation promulgated pursuant to this section may be permanently promulgated by complying with the requirements of this article.

HISTORY: 1977 Act No. 176, Art. I, Section 13; 1980 Act No. 442, Section 4; 1986 Act No. 478, Section 1; 1992 Act No. 507, Section 5; 1993 Act No. 181, Section 14.

Code Commissioner's Note

At the direction of the Code Commissioner, references in this section to the offices of the former State Budget and Control Board, Office of the Governor, or other agencies, were changed to reflect the transfer of them to the Department of Administration or other entities, pursuant to the directive of the South Carolina Restructuring Act, 2014 Act No. 121, Section 5(D)(1).

SECTION 1-23-140. Duties of state agencies; necessity for public inspection.

(a) In addition to other requirements imposed by law, each agency shall:

(1) Adopt and make available for public inspection a description of its organization, stating the general course and method of its operations and the methods whereby the public may obtain information or make submissions or requests;

(2) Adopt and make available for public inspection a written policy statement setting forth the nature and requirements of all formal and informal procedures available, including a description of all forms and instructions used by the agency;

(3) Make available for public inspection all final orders, decisions and opinions except as otherwise provided by law.

(b) No agency rule, order or decision is valid or effective against any person or party, nor may it be invoked by the agency for any purpose until it has been made available for public inspection as required by this article and Article 2. This provision is not applicable in favor of any person or party who has actual knowledge thereof.

HISTORY: 1977 Act No. 176, Art. I, Section 14.

SECTION 1-23-150. Appeals contesting authority of agency to promulgate regulation.

(a) Any person may petition an agency in writing for a declaratory ruling as to the applicability of any regulation of the agency or the authority of the agency to promulgate a particular regulation. The agency shall, within thirty days after receipt of such petition, issue a declaratory ruling thereon.

(b) After compliance with the provisions of paragraph (a) of this section, any person affected by the provisions of any regulation of an agency may petition the Circuit Court for a declaratory judgment and/or injunctive relief if it is alleged that the regulation or its threatened application interferes with or impairs, or threatens to interfere with or impair, the legal rights or privileges of the plaintiff or that the regulation exceeds the regulatory authority of the agency. The agency shall be made a party to the action.

HISTORY: 1977 Act No. 176, Art. I, Section 15; 1980 Act No. 442, Section 5.

SECTION 1-23-160. Prior filed regulations unaffected.

All regulations of state agencies promulgated according to law and filed with the Secretary of State as of January 1, 1977, shall have the full force and effect of law. All regulations of state agencies promulgated under this article and effective as of June 30, 1994 shall have the full force and effect of law.

HISTORY: 1977 Act No. 176, Art. I, Section 16; 1993 Act No. 181, Section 15.

ARTICLE 2

Small Business Regulatory Flexibility

SECTION 1-23-270. Small business defined; economic impact statements; impact reduction options; judicial review of agency compliance; periodic review of regulations.

(A) This article may be cited as the "South Carolina Small Business Regulatory Flexibility Act of 2004".

(B) As used in this article "small business" means a commercial retail service, industry entity, or nonprofit corporation, including its affiliates, that:

(1) is, if a commercial retail service or industry service, independently owned and operated; and

(2) employs fewer than one hundred full-time employees or has gross annual sales or program service revenues of less than five million dollars.

(C) Before an agency submits to the General Assembly for review a regulation that may have a significant adverse impact on small businesses, the agency, if directed by the Small Business Regulatory Review Committee, shall prepare:

(1) an economic impact statement that includes the following:

(a) an identification and estimate of the number of small businesses subject to the proposed regulation;

(b) the projected reporting, recordkeeping, and other administrative costs required for compliance with the proposed regulation, including the type of professional skills necessary for preparation of the report or record;

(c) a statement of the economic impact on small businesses; and

(d) a description of less intrusive or less costly alternative methods of achieving the purpose of the proposed regulation;

(2) a regulatory flexibility analysis in which the agency, where consistent with health, safety, and environmental and economic welfare, shall consider utilizing regulatory methods that accomplish the objectives of applicable statutes while minimizing a significant adverse impact on small businesses.

(D) The agency shall consider, without limitation, each of the following methods of reducing the impact of the proposed regulation on small businesses:

(1) establishment of less stringent compliance or reporting requirements for small businesses;

(2) establishment of less stringent schedules or deadlines for compliance or reporting requirements for small businesses;

(3) consolidation or simplification of compliance or reporting requirements for small businesses;

(4) establishment of performance standards for small businesses to replace design or operational standards required in the proposed regulation; and

(5) exemption of small businesses from all or a part of the requirements contained in the proposed regulation.

(E) A small business that is adversely impacted or aggrieved in connection with the promulgation of a regulation is entitled to judicial review of agency compliance with the requirements of this article. A small business may seek that review during the period beginning on the date of final agency action.

(F)(1) Each state agency, which promulgates regulations or to which the responsibility for administering regulations has been transferred, shall by July 1, 1997, and every five years thereafter, conduct a formal review of all regulations which it has promulgated or for which it has been transferred the responsibility of administering, except that those regulations described in Section 1-23-120(H) are not subject to this review. Upon completion of the review, the agency shall submit to the Code Commissioner a report which identifies those regulations:

(a) for which the agency intends to begin the process of repeal in accordance with this article;

(b) for which the agency intends to begin the process of amendment in accordance with this article; and

(c) which do not require repeal or amendment.

Nothing in this subsection may be construed to prevent an agency from repealing or amending a regulation in accordance with Article 1 before or after it is identified in the report to the Code Commissioner.

(2) Regulations that take effect on or after the effective date of this article must be reviewed within five years of the publication of the final regulation in the State Register and every five years after that to ensure that they minimize economic impact on small businesses in a manner consistent with the stated objectives of applicable statutes.

(3) In reviewing regulations to minimize their economic impact on small businesses, the agency shall consider the:

(a) continued need for the regulation;

(b) nature of complaints or comments received concerning the regulation from the public;

(c) complexity of the regulation;

(d) extent to which the regulation overlaps, duplicates, or conflicts with other federal, state, and local governmental regulations; and

(e) length of time since the regulation has been evaluated or the degree to which technology, economic conditions, or other factors have changed in the area affected by the regulation.

HISTORY: 2004 Act No. 231, Section 2, eff January 1, 2005; 2007 Act No. 104, Section 4, eff July 1, 2008.

Code Commissioner's Note

Paragraphs (D)(a) to (D)(e) were redesignated as paragraphs (D)(1) to (D)(5) at the direction of the Code Commissioner.

Editor's Note

2007 Act No. 104, Section 5, provides as follows:

"This act takes effect July 1, 2008, and applies to regulations for which a notice of a public hearing has been published in the State Register, in accordance with Section 1-23-110(A)(3) of the 1976 Code, after June 30, 2008; all other regulations under General Assembly review on this act's effective date must be processed and reviewed in accordance with the law in effect on June 30, 2008."

Effect of Amendment

The 2007 amendment rewrote paragraph (F)(1).

SECTION 1-23-280. Small Business Regulatory Review Committee; membership; terms.

(A)(1) There is established a Small Business Regulatory Review Committee within the South Carolina Department of Commerce. For purposes of this article, "committee" is the Small Business Regulatory Review Committee and "department" is the South Carolina Department of Commerce.

(2) The duties of the committee, in determining if a proposed permanent regulation has a significant adverse impact on small businesses, are to:

(a) direct the promulgating agency to prepare the regulatory flexibility analysis described in Section 1-23-270(C)(2) no later than the end of the public comment period that follows the notice of proposed regulation, as provided in Section 1-23-110(A)(3); and

(b) request, at the committee's discretion, the Revenue and Fiscal Affairs Office to prepare a final assessment report, as provided in Section 1-23-115(B), of the proposed permanent regulation no later than the end of the public comment period that follows the notice of proposed regulation, as provided in Section 1-23-110(A)(3). The committee may request a final assessment report from the Revenue and Fiscal Affairs Office only in cases where the committee determines that information in addition to the agency's economic impact as provided in Section 1-23-270(C)(1) is critical in the committee's determination that a proposed permanent regulation has a significant adverse impact on small business. The Revenue and Fiscal Affairs Office:

(i) within the review and comment period, shall perform a final assessment report of the regulation on small businesses within sixty days of a request for assessment by the committee, and the promulgating agency has sixty days to complete a regulatory flexibility analysis; and

(ii) may request additional information from the agency. The sixty-day final assessment report deadline must be tolled until the time that the Office of Research and Statistics receives the requested additional information. The one-year deadline for submission of regulations to the General Assembly as provided in Section 1-23-120(A) also must be tolled until the time that both analyses are prepared and presented to the committee; and

(c) submit to the promulgating agency, no later than thirty days after receipt of the regulatory flexibility analysis prepared by the promulgating agency and, if requested by the committee, after receipt of the final assessment report prepared by the Office of Research and Statistics, a written statement advising the agency that a proposed permanent regulation has a significant adverse impact on small business.

(3) This subsection does not limit the committee's ability to petition a state agency to amend, revise, or revoke an existing regulation.

(4) Staff support for the committee must be provided by the department. The department shall act only as a coordinator for the committee, and may not provide legal counsel for the committee.

(B) The committee shall consist of eleven members, appointed as follows:

(1) five members to be appointed by the Governor;

(2) three members to be appointed by the President Pro Tempore of the Senate; and

(3) three members to be appointed by the Speaker of the House of Representatives.

(C) In addition, the Chairman of the Labor, Commerce and Industry Committee of the South Carolina Senate and the Chairman of the Labor, Commerce and Industry Committee of the South Carolina House of Representatives, or their designees, shall serve as nonvoting, ex officio members of the committee. During the committee review process, the director or his designee, of the promulgating agency shall be available at the request of the committee for comment on the proposed regulation.

(D) Appointments to the committee must be representative of a variety of small businesses in this State. All appointed members shall be either current or former owners or officers of a small business.

(E) The initial appointments to the committee must be made within sixty days from the effective date of this act. The department shall provide the name and address of each appointee to the Governor, the President Pro Tempore of the Senate, the Speaker of the House of Representatives, and the Chairmen of the House and Senate Labor, Commerce and Industry Committees.

(F)(1) Members initially appointed to the committee shall serve for terms ending December 31, 2005. Thereafter, appointed members shall serve two-year terms that expire on December thirty-first of the second year.

(2) The Governor shall appoint the initial chairman of the committee from the appointed members for a term ending December 31, 2006, and shall appoint

subsequent chairs of the committee from the appointed members for two-year terms that expire on December thirty-first of the second year.

(3) The committee shall meet as determined by its chairman.

(4) A majority of the voting members of the committee constitutes a quorum to do business. The concurrence of a majority of the members of the committee present and voting is necessary for an action of the committee to be valid.

(5) An appointed committee member may not serve more than three consecutive terms.

HISTORY: 2004 Act No. 231, Section 2, eff January 1, 2005.

Code Commissioner's Note

At the direction of the Code Commissioner, the reference in subparagraph (A)(2)(a) was changed from "1-23-270(C)(1)" to "1-23-270(C)(2)".

At the direction of the Code Commissioner, references in this section to the offices of the former State Budget and Control Board, Office of the Governor, or other agencies, were changed to reflect the transfer of them to the Department of Administration or other entities, pursuant to the directive of the South Carolina Restructuring Act, 2014 Act No. 121, Section 5(D)(1).

SECTION 1-23-290. Petition opposing regulation having significant adverse impact; determination of whether impact statement or public hearing addressed economic impact; waiver or reduction of administrative penalties.

(A) For promulgated regulations, the committee may file a written petition with the agency that has promulgated the regulations opposing all or part of a regulation that has a significant adverse impact on small business.

(B) Within sixty days after the receipt of the petition, the agency shall determine whether the impact statement or the public hearing addressed the actual and significant impact on small business or if conditions justifying the regulation have changed. The agency shall submit a written response of its determination to the committee within sixty days after receipt of the petition. If the agency determines that the petition merits the amendment, revision, or revocation of a regulation, the agency may initiate proceedings in accordance with the applicable requirements of the Administrative Procedures Act.

(C) If the agency determines that the petition does not merit the amendment or repeal of a regulation, the committee promptly shall convene a meeting for the purpose of determining whether to recommend that the agency initiate proceedings to amend or repeal the regulation in accordance with the Administrative Procedures Act. The review must be based upon the actual record presented to the agency. The committee shall base its recommendation on any of the following reasons:

(1) the actual impact on small business was not reflected in, or significantly exceeded, the economic impact statement formulated by the Revenue and Fiscal Affairs Office, pursuant to Section 1-23-280(A)(2);

(2) the actual impact was not previously considered by the agency in its economic impact statement formulated pursuant to Section 1-23-270(C) or its regulatory flexibility analysis formulated pursuant to Section 1-23-280(A)(2); or

(3) the technology, economic conditions, or other relevant factors justifying the purpose for the regulations have changed or no longer exist.

(D) If the committee recommends that an agency initiate regulation proceedings for a reason provided in subsection (C), the committee shall submit to the Speaker of the House of Representatives and the President Pro Tempore of the Senate an evaluation report and the agency's response as provided in Section 1-23-290(B). The General Assembly may take later action in response to the evaluation report and the agency's response as the General Assembly finds appropriate.

(E)(1) Notwithstanding another provision of law, an agency authorized to assess administrative penalties or administrative fines upon a business may waive or reduce an administrative penalty or administrative fine for a violation of a regulation by a small business if the:

(a) small business corrects the violation within thirty days or less after receipt of a notice of violation or citation; or

(b) violation was the result of an excusable misunderstanding of the agency's interpretation of a regulation.

(2) Item (1) does not apply if:

(a) a small business has been notified previously of the violation of a regulation by the agency pursuant to Section 1-23-290(E)(1) and has been given an opportunity to correct the violation on a previous occasion;

(b) a small business fails to exercise good faith in complying with the regulation;

(c) a violation involves wilful or criminal conduct;

(d) a violation results in imminent or adverse health, safety, or environmental impact; or

(e) the penalty or fine is assessed pursuant to a federal law or regulation, for which a waiver or reduction is not authorized by the federal law or regulation.

HISTORY: 2004 Act No. 231, Section 2, eff January 1, 2005.

Code Commissioner's Note

At the direction of the Code Commissioner, references in this section to the offices of the former State Budget and Control Board, Office of the Governor, or other agencies, were changed to reflect the transfer of them to the Department of Administration or other entities, pursuant to the directive of the South Carolina Restructuring Act, 2014 Act No. 121, Section 5(D)(1).

SECTION 1-23-300. Applicability.

This article does not apply to emergency regulations promulgated pursuant to Section 1-23-130 or regulations promulgated pursuant to Chapter 9 of Title 46 or Chapter 4 of Title 47 or to proposed regulations by an agency to implement a statute or ordinance that does not require an agency to interpret or describe the requirements of the statute or ordinance, such as state legislative or federally mandated provisions that do not allow discretion to consider less restrictive alternatives or to a federal regulation that has gone through the federal regulatory flexibility act, if the federal review process is the same as or is stricter than the requirements of these sections.

HISTORY: 2004 Act No. 231, Section 2, eff January 1, 2005.

ARTICLE 3

Administrative Procedures

SECTION 1-23-310. Definitions.

As used in this article:

(1) "Administrative law judge" means a judge of the South Carolina Administrative Law Court created pursuant to Section 1-23-500;

(2) "Agency" means each state board, commission, department, or officer, other than the legislature, the courts, or the Administrative Law Court, authorized by law to determine contested cases;

(3) "Contested case" means a proceeding including, but not restricted to, ratemaking, price fixing, and licensing, in which the legal rights, duties, or privileges of a party are required by law to be determined by an agency after an opportunity for hearing;

(4) "License" includes the whole or part of any agency permit, franchise, certificate, approval, registration, charter, or similar form of permission required by law, but it does not include a license required solely for revenue purposes;

(5) "Party" means each person or agency named or admitted as a party, or properly seeking and entitled as of right to be admitted as a party;

(6) "Person" means any individual, partnership, corporation, association, governmental subdivision, or public or private organization of any character other than an agency.

HISTORY: 1977 Act No. 176, Art. II, Section 1; 1980 Act No. 442, Section 7; 1993 Act No. 181, Section 16; 1998 Act No. 359, Section 1; 2008 Act No. 334, Section 3, eff June 16, 2008.

Effect of Amendment

The 2008 amendment, in item (1), substituted "Administrative Law Court" for "administrative law judge division"; and, in item (2), substituted ", the courts, or the Administrative Law Court," for "or the courts, but to include the administrative law judge division".

SECTION 1-23-320. Notice and hearing in contested case; depositions; subpoenas; informal disposition; content of record.

(A) In a contested case, all parties must be afforded an opportunity for hearing after notice of not less than thirty days, except in proceedings before the Department of Employment and Workforce, which are governed by the provisions of Section 41-35-680.

(B) The notice must include a:

(1) statement of the time, place, and nature of the hearing;

(2) statement of the legal authority and jurisdiction under which the hearing is to be held;

(3) reference to the particular sections of the statutes and rules involved;

(4) short and plain statement of the matters asserted. If the agency or other party is unable to state the matters in detail at the time the notice is served, the initial notice may be limited to a statement of the issues involved. Thereafter, upon application, a more definite and detailed statement must be furnished.

(C) A party to these proceedings may cause to be taken the depositions of witnesses within or without the State and either by commission or de bene esse. Depositions must be taken in accordance with and subject to the same provisions, conditions, and restrictions as apply to the taking of like depositions in civil actions at law in the court of common pleas; and the same rules with respect to the giving of notice to the opposite party, the taking and transcribing of testimony, the transmission and certification of it, and matters of practice relating to it apply.

(D) The agency hearing a contested case may issue subpoenas in the name of the agency for the attendance and testimony of witnesses and the production and examination of books, papers, and records on its own behalf or, upon request, on behalf of another party to the case.

A party to the proceeding may seek enforcement of or relief from an agency subpoena before the Administrative Law Court pursuant to Section 1-23-600(F).

(E) Opportunity must be afforded all parties to respond and present evidence and argument on all issues involved.

(F) Unless precluded by law, informal disposition may be made of a contested case by stipulation, agreed settlement, consent order, or default.

(G) The record in a contested case must include:

(1) all pleadings, motions, intermediate rulings, and depositions;

(2) evidence received or considered;

(3) a statement of matters officially noticed;

(4) questions and offers of proof, objections, and rulings on the contested case;

(5) proposed findings and exceptions;

(6) any decision, opinion, or report by the officer presiding at the hearing.

(H) Oral proceedings or any part of the oral proceedings must be transcribed on request of a party.

(I) Findings of fact must be based exclusively on the evidence and on matters officially noticed.

HISTORY: 1977 Act No. 176, Art. II, Section 2; 1983 Act No. 56, Section 1; 1993 Act No. 181, Section 17; 1998 Act No. 359, Section 2; 2008 Act No. 334, Section 4, eff June 16, 2008.

Code Commissioner's Note

Pursuant to the directive to the Code Commissioner in 2010 Act No. 146, Section 122, "Department of Employment and Workforce" was substituted for all references to "Employment Security Commission", and "Executive Director of the Department of Employment and Workforce" or "executive director" was substituted for all references to the "Chairman of the Employment Security Commission" or "chairman" that refer to the Chairman of the Employment Security Commission, as appropriate.

Effect of Amendment

The 2008 amendment substituted (A) to (I) for (a) to (i) as the subsection designations; in subsection (D), rewrote the second undesignated paragraph relating to enforcement of or relief from an agency subpoena; and made nonsubstantive language changes throughout.

SECTION 1-23-330. Evidentiary matters in contested cases.

In contested cases:

(1) Irrelevant, immaterial or unduly repetitious evidence shall be excluded. Except in proceedings before the Industrial Commission the rules of evidence as applied in civil cases in the court of common pleas shall be followed. Agencies shall give effect to the rules of privilege recognized by law. Objections to evidentiary offers may be made and shall be noted in the record. Subject to these requirements, when a hearing will be expedited and the interests of the parties will not be prejudiced substantially, any part of the evidence may be received in written form;

(2) Documentary evidence may be received in the form of copies or excerpts, if the original is not readily available. Upon request, parties shall be given an opportunity to compare the copy with the original;

(3) Any party may conduct cross-examination;

(4) Notice may be taken of judicially cognizable facts. In addition, notice may be taken of generally recognized technical or scientific facts within the agency's specialized knowledge. Parties shall be notified either before or during the hearing or by reference in preliminary reports or otherwise of the material noticed including any staff memoranda or data, and they shall be afforded an opportunity to contest the material so noticed. The agency's experience, technical competence and specialized knowledge may be utilized in the evaluation of the evidence.

HISTORY: 1977 Act No. 176, Art. II, Section 3; 1979 Act No. 188, Section 6.

SECTION 1-23-340. Procedure in contested cases where majority of those who are to render final decision are unfamiliar with case.

When in a contested case a majority of the officials of the agency who are to render the final decision have not heard the case or reviewed the record, the decision, if adverse to a party to the proceeding other than the agency itself, shall not be made until a proposal for decision is served upon the parties, and an opportunity is afforded to each party adversely affected to file exceptions and present briefs and oral argument to the officials who are to render the decision. The proposal for decision shall contain a statement of the reasons therefor and of each issue of fact or law necessary to the proposed decision, prepared by the person who conducted the hearing or one who has read the record. The parties by written stipulation may waive compliance with this section.

HISTORY: 1977 Act No. 176, Art. II, Section 4.

SECTION 1-23-350. Final decision or order in contested case.

A final decision or order adverse to a party in a contested case shall be in writing or stated in the record. A final decision shall include findings of fact and conclusions of law, separately stated. Findings of fact, if set forth in statutory language, shall be accompanied by a concise and explicit statement of the underlying facts supporting the findings. If, in accordance with agency rules, a party submitted proposed findings of fact, the decision shall include a ruling upon each proposed finding. Parties shall be notified either personally or by mail of any decision or order. Upon request a copy of the decision or order shall be delivered or mailed forthwith to each party and to his attorney of record.

HISTORY: 1977 Act No. 176, Art. II, Section 5.

SECTION 1-23-360. Communication by members or employees of agency assigned to decide contested case.

Unless required for the disposition of ex parte matters authorized by law, members or employees of an agency assigned to render a decision or to make findings of fact and conclusions of law in a contested case shall not communicate, directly or indirectly, in connection with any issue of fact, with any person or party, nor, in connection with any issue of law, with any party or his representative, except upon notice and opportunity for all parties to participate. An agency member:

(1) May communicate with other members of the agency; and

(2) May have the aid and advice of one or more personal assistants.

Any person who violates the provisions of this section shall be deemed guilty of a misdemeanor and upon conviction shall be fined not more than two hundred fifty dollars or imprisoned for not more than six months.

HISTORY: 1977 Act No. 176, Art. II, Section 6.

SECTION 1-23-370. Procedures regarding issuance, denial or renewal of licenses.

(a) When the grant, denial or renewal of a license is required to be preceded by notice and opportunity for hearing, the provisions of this article and Article 1 concerning contested cases apply.

(b) When a licensee has made timely and sufficient application for the renewal of a license or a new license with reference to any activity of a continuing nature, the existing license does not expire until the application has been finally determined by the agency, and, in case the application is denied or the terms of the new license limited, until the last day for seeking review of the agency order or a later date fixed by order of the reviewing court.

(c) No revocation, suspension, annulment, or withdrawal of any license is lawful unless, prior to the institution of agency proceedings, the agency gave notice by mail to the licensee of facts or conduct which warrant the intended action, and the licensee was given an opportunity to show compliance with all lawful requirements for the retention of the license. If the agency finds that public health, safety or welfare imperatively requires emergency action, and incorporates a finding to that effect in its order, summary suspension of a license may be ordered pending proceedings for revocation or other action. These proceedings shall be promptly instituted and determined.

HISTORY: 1977 Act No. 176, Art. II, Section 7.

SECTION 1-23-380. Judicial review upon exhaustion of administrative remedies.

A party who has exhausted all administrative remedies available within the agency and who is aggrieved by a final decision in a contested case is entitled to judicial review pursuant to this article and Article 1. This section does not limit utilization of or the scope of judicial review available under other means of review, redress, relief, or trial de novo provided by law. A preliminary, procedural, or intermediate agency action or ruling is immediately reviewable if review of the final agency decision would not provide an adequate remedy. Except as otherwise provided by law, an appeal is to the court of appeals.

(1) Proceedings for review are instituted by serving and filing notice of appeal as provided in the South Carolina Appellate Court Rules within thirty days after the final decision of the agency or, if a rehearing is requested, within thirty days after the decision is rendered. Copies of the notice of appeal must be served upon the agency and all parties of record.

(2) Except as otherwise provided in this chapter, the serving and filing of the notice of appeal does not itself stay enforcement of the agency decision. The serving and filing of a notice of appeal by a licensee for review of a fine or penalty or of its license stays only those provisions for which review is sought and matters not affected by the notice of appeal are not stayed. The serving or filing of a notice of appeal does not automatically stay the suspension or revocation of a permit or license authorizing the sale of beer, wine, or alcoholic liquor. The agency may grant, or the reviewing court may order, a stay upon appropriate terms, upon the filing of a petition under Rule 65 of the South Carolina Rules of Civil Procedure.

(3) If a timely application is made to the court for leave to present additional evidence, and it is shown to the satisfaction of the court that the additional evidence is material and that there were good reasons for failure to present it in the proceeding before the agency, the court may order that the additional evidence be taken before the agency upon conditions determined by the court. The agency may modify its findings and decision by reason of the additional evidence and shall file the evidence and modifications, new findings, or decisions with the reviewing court.

(4) The review must be conducted by the court and must be confined to the record. In cases of alleged irregularities in procedure before the agency, not shown in the record, and established by proof satisfactory to the court, the case may be remanded to the agency for action as the court considers appropriate.

(5) The court may not substitute its judgment for the judgment of the agency as to the weight of the evidence on questions of fact. The court may affirm the decision of the agency or remand the case for further proceedings. The court may reverse or modify the decision if substantial rights of the appellant have been prejudiced because the administrative findings, inferences, conclusions, or decisions are:

(a) in violation of constitutional or statutory provisions;

(b) in excess of the statutory authority of the agency;

(c) made upon unlawful procedure;

(d) affected by other error of law;

(e) clearly erroneous in view of the reliable, probative, and substantial evidence on the whole record; or

(f) arbitrary or capricious or characterized by abuse of discretion or clearly unwarranted exercise of discretion.

HISTORY: 1977 Act No. 176, Art. II, Section 8; 1993 Act No. 181, Section 18; 2006 Act No. 387, Section 2, eff July 1, 2006; 2008 Act No. 334, Section 5, eff June 16, 2008.

Editor's Note

2006 Act No. 387, Section 53, provides as follows:

"This act is intended to provide a uniform procedure for contested cases and appeals from administrative agencies and to the extent that a provision of this act conflicts with an existing statute or regulation, the provisions of this act are controlling."

2006 Act No. 387, Section 57, provides as follows:

"This act takes effect on July 1, 2006, and applies to any actions pending on or after the effective date of the act. No pending or vested right, civil action, special proceeding, or appeal of a final administrative decision exists under the former law as of the effective date of this act, except for appeals of Department of Health and Environmental Control Ocean and Coastal Resource Management and Environmental Quality Control permits that are before the Administrative Law Court on the effective date of this act and petitions for judicial review that are pending before the circuit court. For those actions only, the department shall hear appeals from the administrative law judges and the circuit court shall hear pending petitions for judicial review in accordance with the former law. Thereafter, any appeal of those actions shall proceed as provided in this act for review. For all other actions pending on the effective date of this act, the action proceeds as provided in this act for review."

Effect of Amendment

The 2006 amendment rewrote this section to provide for review by an administrative law judge and appeal to the South Carolina Court of Appeals.

The 2008 amendment deleted subsection (B) relating to review by an administrative law judge of a final decision in a contested case; deleted the designation of the first paragraph as subsection (A) and at the end of the first sentence substituted "pursuant to this article and Article 1" for "under this article, Article 1, and Article 5"; in paragraph (1) deleted ", the Administrative Law Court," following "agency"; in the fourth sentence of paragraph (2) deleted "or administrative law judge" following "agency"; and in the second sentence of paragraph (4) deleted "or the Administrative Law Court" following "agency" in two places.

SECTION 1-23-390. Supreme Court review.

An aggrieved party may obtain a review of a final judgment of the circuit court or the court of appeals pursuant to this article by taking an appeal in the manner provided by the South Carolina Appellate Court Rules as in other civil cases.

HISTORY: 1977 Act No. 176, Art. II, Section 9; 1999 Act No. 55, Section 4; 2006 Act No. 387, Section 3, eff July 1, 2006.

Editor's Note

2006 Act No. 387, Section 53, provides as follows:

"This act is intended to provide a uniform procedure for contested cases and appeals from administrative agencies and to the extent that a provision of this act conflicts with an existing statute or regulation, the provisions of this act are controlling."

2006 Act No. 387, Section 57, provides as follows:

"This act takes effect on July 1, 2006, and applies to any actions pending on or after the effective date of the act. No pending or vested right, civil action, special proceeding, or appeal of a final administrative decision exists under the former law as of the effective date of this act, except for appeals of Department of Health and Environmental Control Ocean and Coastal Resource Management and Environmental Quality Control permits that are before the Administrative Law Court on the effective date of this act and petitions for judicial review that are pending before the circuit court. For those actions only, the department shall hear appeals from the administrative law judges and the circuit court shall hear pending petitions for judicial review in accordance with the former law. Thereafter, any appeal of those actions shall proceed as provided in this act for review. For all other actions pending on the effective date of this act, the action proceeds as provided in this act for review."

Effect of Amendment

The 2006 amendment added "or the court of appeals" and made nonsubstantive changes.

SECTION 1-23-400. Application of article.

The provisions of this article shall not apply to any matters pending on June 13, 1977. The provisions of Sections 1-23-360 and 1-23-370 shall not apply to any agency which under existing statutes have established and follow notice and hearing procedures which are in compliance with such sections.

HISTORY: 1977 Act No. 176, Art. II, Section 10.

ARTICLE 5

South Carolina Administrative Law Court

Editor's Note

2004 Act No. 202, Section 3, provides as follows:

"Wherever the term 'Administrative Law Judge Division' appears in any provision of law, regulation, or other document, it must be construed to mean the Administrative Law Court established by this act."

SECTION 1-23-500. South Carolina Administrative Law Court created; number of judges.

There is created the South Carolina Administrative Law Court, which is an agency and a court of record within the executive branch of the government of this State. The court shall consist of a total of six administrative law judges. The administrative law judges shall be part of the state employees retirement system.

HISTORY: 1993 Act No. 181, Section 19; 1994 Act No. 452, Section 9; 2004 Act No. 202, Section 1, eff April 26, 2004.

Effect of Amendment

The 2004 amendment deleted the designation preceding former subsection (A) and rewrote the paragraph, substituting "Administrative Law Court" for "Administrative Law Judge Division", and deleted subsection (B) relating to a feasibility study by the Judicial Council.

SECTION 1-23-505. Definitions.

As used in this article:

(1) "Administrative law judge" means a judge of the South Carolina Administrative Law Court created pursuant to Section 1-23-500.

(2) "Agency" means a state agency, department, board, or commission whose action is the subject of a contested case hearing or an appellate proceeding heard by an administrative law judge, or a public hearing on a proposed regulation presided over by an administrative law judge.

(3) "Contested case" means a proceeding including, but not restricted to, ratemaking, price fixing, and licensing, in which the legal rights, duties, or privileges of a party are required by law or by Article I, Section 22, Constitution of the State of South Carolina, 1895, to be determined by an agency or the Administrative Law Court after an opportunity for hearing.

(4) "License" includes the whole or part of any agency permit, franchise, certificate, approval, registration, charter, or similar form of permission required by law, but does not include a license required solely for revenue purposes.

(5) "Party" means each person or agency named or admitted as a party, or properly seeking and entitled as of right to be admitted as a party.

(6) "Person" means any individual, partnership, corporation, association, governmental subdivision, or public or private organization of any character other than an agency.

HISTORY: 2008 Act No. 334, Section 1, eff June 16, 2008.

SECTION 1-23-510. Election of judges; terms.

(A) The judges of the division must be elected by the General Assembly in joint session, for a term of five years and until their successors are elected and qualify; provided, that of those judges initially elected, the chief judge, elected to Seat 1 must be elected for a term of five years, the judge elected to Seat 2 must be elected for a term of three years, the judge elected to Seat 3 must be elected for a term of one year. The remaining judges of the division must be elected for terms of office to begin February 1, 1995, for terms of five years and until their successors are elected and qualify; provided, that those judges elected to seats whose terms of office are to begin on February 1, 1995, to Seat 4 must be initially elected for a term of five years, the judge elected to Seat 5 must be initially elected for a term of three years, and the judge elected to Seat 6 must be initially elected for a term of one year. The terms of office of the judges of the division for Seats 1, 2, and 3 shall begin on March 1, 1994. The terms of office of the judges of the division for Seats 4, 5, and 6 shall begin on February 1, 1995. The terms of office of each of the seats shall terminate on the thirtieth day of June in the final year of the term for the respective seats.

(B) In electing administrative law judges, race, gender, and other demographic factors including age, residence, type of practice, and law firm size should be considered to assure nondiscrimination, inclusion, and representation to the greatest extent possible of all segments of the population of this State.

(C) Before election as an administrative law judge, a candidate must undergo screening pursuant to the provisions of Section 2-19-10, et seq.

(D) Each seat on the division must be numbered. Elections are required to be for a specific seat. The office of chief administrative law judge is a separate and distinct office for the purpose of an election.

(E) In the event that there is a vacancy in the position of the chief administrative law judge or for any reason the chief administrative law judge is unable to act, his powers and functions must be exercised by the most senior administrative law judge as determined by the date of their election to the division.

HISTORY: 1993 Act No. 181, Section 19; 1999 Act No. 39, Section 1.

SECTION 1-23-520. Eligibility for office.

No person is eligible for the office of law judge of the division who does not at the time of his election meet the qualification for justices and judges as set forth in Article V of the Constitution of this State.

HISTORY: 1993 Act No. 181, Section 19.

SECTION 1-23-525. Members of General Assembly disqualified for office of law judge.

No member of any General Assembly who is not otherwise prohibited from being elected to an administrative law judge position may be elected to such position while he is a member of the General Assembly and for a period of four years after he ceases to be a member of the General Assembly.

HISTORY: 1993 Act No. 181, Section 19.

SECTION 1-23-530. Oath of office.

The judges of the division shall qualify after the date of their election by taking the constitutional oath of office.

HISTORY: 1993 Act No. 181, Section 19.

SECTION 1-23-535. Official seal.

The Administrative Law Court shall have a seal with a suitable inscription, an impression of which must be filed with the Secretary of State.

HISTORY: 2008 Act No. 334, Section 2, eff June 16, 2008.

SECTION 1-23-540. Compensation; full-time position.

The chief judge (Seat 1) shall receive as annual salary equal to ninety percent of that paid to the circuit court judges of this State. The remaining judges shall receive as annual salary equal to eighty percent of that paid to the circuit court judges of this State. They are not allowed any fees or perquisites of office, nor may they hold any other office of honor, trust, or profit. Administrative law judges in the performance of their duties are also entitled to that per diem, mileage, expenses, and subsistence as is authorized by law for circuit court judges.

Each administrative law judge shall devote full time to his duties as an administrative law judge, and may not practice law during his term of office, nor may he during this term be a partner or associate with anyone engaged in the practice of law in this State.

HISTORY: 1993 Act No. 181, Section 19.

SECTION 1-23-550. Vacancies.

All vacancies in the office of administrative law judge must be filled in the manner of original appointment. When a vacancy is filled, the judge elected shall hold office only for the unexpired term of his predecessor.

HISTORY: 1993 Act No. 181, Section 19.

SECTION 1-23-560. Application of Code of Judicial Conduct; complaints against administrative law judges; attending judicial-related functions.

Administrative law judges are bound by the Code of Judicial Conduct, as contained in Rule 501 of the South Carolina Appellate Court Rules. The sole grounds for discipline and sanctions for administrative law judges are those contained in the Code of Judicial Conduct in Rule 502, Rule 7 of the South Carolina Appellate Court Rules. The Commission on Judicial Conduct, under the authority of the Supreme Court, shall handle complaints against administrative law judges for possible violations of the Code of Judicial Conduct in the same manner as complaints against other judges. Notwithstanding another provision of law, an administrative law judge and the judge's spouse or guest may accept an invitation to attend a judicial-related or bar-related function, or an activity devoted to the improvement of the law, legal system, or the administration of justice.

HISTORY: 1993 Act No. 181, Section 19; 2008 Act No. 334, Section 6, eff June 16, 2008; 2014 Act No. 146 (S.405), Section 1, eff April 7, 2014.

Effect of Amendment

The 2008 amendment added the second sentence referring to Code of Judicial Conduct, Rule 502, Rule 7, and the fourth sentence relating to invitations to judicial-related functions; and, in the third sentence, added ", which" following "Commission" and substituted "shall use the procedure contained in" for "pursuant to".

2014 Act No. 146, Section 1, rewrote the third sentence, removing reference to the State Ethics Commission.

SECTION 1-23-570. Chief Judge responsible for administration of division.

The Chief Judge of the Administrative Law Judge Division is responsible for the administration of the division, including budgetary matters, assignment of cases, and the administrative duties and responsibilities of the support staff. The chief judge shall assign judges of the division to hear all cases of the various state departments and commissions for which it is responsible on a general rotation and interchange basis by scheduling and assigning administrative law judges based upon subject matter no less frequently than every six months.

HISTORY: 1993 Act No. 181, Section 19; 1998 Act No. 359, Section 3.

SECTION 1-23-580. Clerk of division; assistants to administrative law judges; other staff.

(A) A clerk of the division, to be appointed by the chief judge, must be appointed and is responsible for the custody and keeping of the records of the division. The clerk of the division shall perform those other duties as the chief judge may prescribe.

(B) Each administrative law judge may appoint, hire, contract, and supervise an administrative assistant as individually allotted and authorized in the annual general appropriations act.

(C) The other support staff of the division is as authorized by the General Assembly in the annual general appropriations act and shall be hired, contracted, and supervised by the chief judge. The division may engage stenographers for the transcribing of the proceedings in which an administrative law judge presides. It may contract for these stenographic functions, or it may use stenographers provided by the agency or commission.

HISTORY: 1993 Act No. 181, Section 19; 1998 Act No. 359, Section 4.

SECTION 1-23-590. Appropriation of funds.

The General Assembly in the annual general appropriations act shall appropriate those funds necessary for the operation of the Administrative Law Judge Division.

HISTORY: 1993 Act No. 181, Section 19.

SECTION 1-23-600. Hearings and proceedings.

(A) An administrative law judge shall preside over all hearings of contested cases as defined in Section 1-23-505 or Article I, Section 22, Constitution of the State of South Carolina, 1895, involving the departments of the executive branch of government as defined in Section 1-30-10 in which a single hearing officer, or an administrative law judge, is authorized or permitted by law or regulation to hear and decide these cases, except those arising under the:

(1) Consolidated Procurement Code;

(2) Public Service Commission;

(3) Department of Employment and Workforce;

(4) Workers' Compensation Commission, except as provided in Section 42-15-90; or

(5) other cases or hearings which are prescribed for or mandated by federal law or regulation, unless otherwise by statute or regulation specifically assigned to the jurisdiction of the Administrative Law Court. Unless otherwise provided by statute, the standard of proof in a contested case is by a preponderance of the evidence. The South Carolina Rules of Evidence apply in all contested case proceedings before the Administrative Law Court.

(B) All requests for a hearing before the Administrative Law Court must be filed in accordance with the court's rules of procedure. A party that files a request for a hearing with the Administrative Law Court must simultaneously serve a copy of the request on the affected agency. Upon the filing of the request, the chief judge shall assign an administrative law judge to the case. Notice of the contested case hearing must be issued in accordance with the rules of procedure of the Administrative Law Court.

(C) A full and complete record must be kept of all contested cases and regulation hearings before an administrative law judge. All testimony must be reported, but need not be transcribed unless a transcript is requested by a party. The party requesting a transcript is responsible for the costs involved. Proceedings before administrative law judges are open to the public unless confidentiality is allowed or required by law. The presiding administrative law judge shall render the decision in a written order. The decisions or orders of administrative law judges are not required to be published but are available for public inspection unless confidentiality is allowed or required by law.

(D) An administrative law judge also shall preside over all appeals from final decisions of contested cases pursuant to the Administrative Procedures Act, Article I, Section 22, Constitution of the State of South Carolina, 1895, or another law, except that an appeal from a final order of the Public Service Commission and the State Ethics Commission is to the Supreme Court or the court of appeals as provided in the South Carolina Appellate Court Rules, an appeal from the Procurement Review Panel is to the circuit court as provided in Section 11-35-4410, and an appeal from the Workers' Compensation Commission is to the court of appeals as provided in Section 42-17-60. An administrative law judge shall not hear an appeal from an inmate in the custody of the Department of Corrections involving the loss of the opportunity to earn sentence-related credits pursuant to Section 24-13-210(A) or Section 24-13-230(A) or an appeal involving the denial of parole to a potentially eligible inmate by the Department of Probation, Parole and Pardon Services.

(E) Review by an administrative law judge of a final decision in a contested case, heard in the appellate jurisdiction of the Administrative Law Court, must be in the same manner as prescribed in Section 1-23-380 for judicial review of final agency decisions with the presiding administrative law judge exercising the same authority as the court of appeals, provided that a party aggrieved by a final decision of an administrative law judge is entitled to judicial review of the decision by the court of appeals pursuant to the provisions of Section 1-23-610.

(F) Notwithstanding another provision of law, a state agency authorized by law to seek injunctive relief may apply to the Administrative Law Court for injunctive or equitable relief pursuant to Section 1-23-630. The provisions of this section do not affect the authority of an agency to apply for injunctive relief as part of a civil action filed in the court of common pleas.

(G) Notwithstanding another provision of law, the Administrative Law Court has jurisdiction to review and enforce an administrative process issued by an agency or by a department of the executive branch of government, as defined in Section 1-30-10, such as a subpoena, administrative search warrant, cease and desist order, or other similar administrative order or process. A department or agency of the executive branch of government authorized by law to seek an administrative process may apply to the Administrative Law Court to issue or enforce an administrative process. A party aggrieved by an administrative process issued by a department or agency of the executive branch of government may apply to the Administrative Law Court for relief from the process as provided in the Rules of the Administrative Law Court.

(H)(1) This subsection applies to timely requests for a contested case hearing pursuant to this section of decisions by departments governed by a board or commission authorized to exercise the sovereignty of the State.

(2) A request for a contested case hearing for an agency order stays the order. A request for a contested case hearing for an order to revoke or suspend a license stays the revocation or suspension. A request for a contested case hearing for a decision to renew a license for an ongoing activity stays the renewed license, the previous license remaining in effect pending completion of administrative review. A request for a contested case hearing for a decision to issue a new license stays all actions for which the license is a prerequisite; however, matters not affected by the request may not be stayed by the filing of the request. If the request is filed for a subsequent license related to issues substantially similar to those considered in a previously licensed matter, the license may not be automatically stayed by the filing of the request. If the requesting party asserts in the request that the issues are not substantially similar to those considered in a previously licensed matter, then the license must be stayed until further order of the Administrative Law Court. Requests for contested case hearings challenging only the amount of fines or penalties must be deemed not to affect those portions of orders imposing substantive requirements.

(3) The general rule of subsection (H)(2) does not stay emergency actions taken by an agency pursuant to an applicable statute or regulation.

(4) After a contested case is initiated before the Administrative Law Court, a party may move before the presiding administrative law judge to lift the stay imposed pursuant to this subsection. Upon motion by any party, the court shall lift the stay for good cause shown or if no irreparable harm will occur, then the stay shall be lifted. A hearing must be held within thirty days after the motion is filed with the court and served upon the parties to lift the automatic stay or for a determination of the applicability of the automatic stay. The judge must issue an order no later than fifteen business days after the hearing is concluded.

(5) A final decision issued by the Administrative Law Court in a contested case may not be stayed except by order of the Administrative Law Court or the court of appeals.

(6) Nothing contained in this subsection constitutes a limitation on the authority of the Administrative Law Court to impose a stay as otherwise provided by statute or by rule of court.

(I) If a final order of the Administrative Law Court is not appealed in accordance with the provisions of Section 1-23-610, upon request of a party to the proceedings, the clerk of the Administrative Law Court shall file a certified copy of the final order with a clerk of the circuit court, as requested, or court of competent jurisdiction, as requested. After filing, the certified order has the same effect as a judgment of the court where filed and may be recorded, enforced, or satisfied in the same manner as a judgment of that court.

(J) If an attorney of record is called to appear in actions pending in other tribunals in this State, the action in the Administrative Law Court has priority as is appropriate. Courts and counsel have the obligation to adjust schedules to accord with the spirit of comity between the Administrative Law Court and other state courts.

HISTORY: 1993 Act No. 181, Section 19; 1994 Act No. 452, Sections 1, 5; 1995 Act No. 92, Section 1; 2004 Act No. 202, Section 2, eff April 26, 2004; 2006 Act No. 381, Section 1, eff June 13, 2006; 2006 Act No. 387, Section 4, eff July 1, 2006; 2007 Act No. 111, Pt I, Section 1, eff July 1, 2007, applicable to injuries that occur on or after that date; 2008 Act No. 188, Section 1, eff January 1, 2009; 2008 Act No. 201, Section 13, eff February 10, 2009; 2008 Act No. 334, Section 7, eff June 16, 2008; 2010 Act No. 278, Section 23, eff July 1, 2010; 2012 Act No. 183, Section 2, eff June 7, 2012; 2012 Act No. 212, Section 1, eff June 7, 2012.

Code Commissioner's Note

At the direction of the Code Commissioner, the 2006 amendments were read together. The text of the section as amended by Act 387 is set forth above, except that in subsection (B), "those matters which are otherwise provided for in title 56" was deleted following "Occupational Health and Safety Act", in subparagraph (G)(3), "(G)" was substituted for "(F)", and subsection (E) from Act 381 was added as subsection (H).

At the direction of the Code Commissioner, the amendment of this section by 2008 Act No. 334, Section 1, effective June 16, 2008, was deemed to prevail over the amendment by 2008 Act No. 201, Section 13, effective February 10, 2009, because it was enacted later. The section was also amended by 2008 Act No. 188, Section 1, effective January 1, 2009, to delete the reference to cases arising under the Occupational Safety and Health Act in subsection (B). Among other changes, the amendment by Act 334 redesignated subsection (B) as subsection (A) and included cases arising under the Occupational Safety and Health Act as item (1). At the direction of the Code Commissioner, the deletion of the reference to the Occupational Safety and Health Act by Act 188 effective January 1, 2009 was applied to subsection (A) as amended by Act 334 on the basis that the reference to OSHA was inadvertently included in the later act and its inclusion was not consistent with the intent of the General Assembly in passing Act 188. Accordingly, in subsection (A) as amended by Act 334, item (1) was deleted effective January 1, 2009, and items (2) to (6) redesignated as items (1) to (5).

At the direction of the Code Commissioner, the reference in subsection (E) to Section 1-23-380(A) was changed to Section 1-23-380 to conform to the amendment of that section by 2008 Act No. 334, Section 5.

Pursuant to the directive to the Code Commissioner in 2010 Act No. 146, Section 122, "Department of Employment and Workforce" was substituted for all references to "Employment Security Commission", and "Executive Director of the Department of Employment and Workforce" or "executive director" was substituted for all references to the "Chairman of the Employment Security Commission" or "chairman" that refer to the Chairman of the Employment Security Commission, as appropriate.

Editor's Note

2006 Act No. 387, Section 53, provides as follows:

"This act is intended to provide a uniform procedure for contested cases and appeals from administrative agencies and to the extent that a provision of this act conflicts with an existing statute or regulation, the provisions of this act are controlling."

2006 Act No. 387, Section 57, provides as follows:

"This act takes effect on July 1, 2006, and applies to any actions pending on or after the effective date of the act. No pending or vested right, civil action, special proceeding, or appeal of a final administrative decision exists under the former law as of the effective date of this act, except for appeals of Department of Health and Environmental Control Ocean and Coastal Resource Management and Environmental Quality Control permits that are before the Administrative Law Court on the effective date of this act and petitions for judicial review that are pending before the circuit court. For those actions only, the department shall hear appeals from the administrative law judges and the circuit court shall hear pending petitions for judicial review in accordance with the former law. Thereafter, any appeal of those actions shall proceed as provided in this act for review. For all other actions pending on the effective date of this act, the action proceeds as provided in this act for review."

2010 Act 278, Section 26, provides as follows:

"This act takes effect July 1, 2010; provided, the provisions of this act do not apply to any matter pending before a court of this State prior to June 1, 2010."

Effect of Amendment

The 2004 amendment in subsection (A) substituted "must" for "shall" and "is responsible" for "shall be responsible"; in subsections (B) and (D) deleted "of the division" following "administrative law judge"; in subsection (B) substituted "Court" for "Judge Division"; in subsection (D), inserted ", or as otherwise provided by law," following "Licensing and Regulation"; rewrote subsection (C); deleted subsection (E) relating to cases initiated before and after May 1, 1994; and made nonsubstantive changes.

The first 2006 amendment, in subsection (B), deleted "those matters which are otherwise provided for in Title 56," following "Occupational Health and Safety Act"; and added subsection (E) [redesignated as (H)] relating to the filing of final orders.

The second 2006 amendment rewrote subsections (B) and (D) and added subsection (E), (F) and (G) relating to appeal of orders of the State Human Affairs Commission to the Administrative Law Court.

The 2007 amendment, in subsection (D), substituted "Court of Appeals" for "circuit court" relating to appeals from the Workers' Compensation Commission.

The first 2008 amendment, in subsection (B), deleted "arising under the Occupational Safety and Health Act,".

The second 2008 amendment, in subsection (B), added the second sentence relating to the standard of proof in a contested case' and, in subsection (H), in the first sentence deleted "petition for judicial review of a" preceding "final order" and substituted "appealed" for "filed".

The third 2008 amendment, deleted subsection (A) relating to the keeping and availability of records and reenacted it as subsection (C); redesignated subsections (B) and (C) as subsections (A) and (B); in subsection (A) substituted "1-23-505" for "1-23-310", designated paragraphs (1) to (6) [redesignated as (1) to (5) effective January 1, 2009 at the direction of the Code Commissioner] from existing text, and added the second and third sentences of (6) [redesignated as (5)] relating to standard of proof and applicability of the South Carolina Rules of Evidence; in subsection (B), added the fourth sentence relating to notice of the contested case hearing; in subsection (D), added the second sentence relating to certain appeals from inmates; added subsection (E); redesignated subsections (E) to (H) as (F) to (I); in subsection (G), substituted "Administrative Law Court" for "chief administrative law judge" and added references to agencies of the executive branch in two places; in paragraph (H)(2), in the fourth sentence added "however," and the fifth and sixth sentences; in paragraph (H)(3), substituted "(H)(2)" for "(G)(2)"; in paragraph (H)(4), added the second through fourth sentences; in paragraph (H)(5), deleted from the end ", or cases when Section 1-23-610(A) applies, the appropriate board or commission"; and, in subsection (I), in the first sentence deleted "petition for judicial review of a" preceding "final order" and substituted "filed" for "appealed", "1-23-610" for "1-23-600" and 'shall" for "must".

The 2010 amendment added subsection (J) relating to priority of actions in different courts.

The first 2012 amendment in subsection (A)(4), inserted ", except as provided in Section 42-15-90".

The second 2012 amendment in subsection (D), deleted ", and an appeal from the Department of Employment and Workforce is to the circuit court as provided in Section 41-35-750", and made other changes.

SECTION 1-23-610. Judicial review of final decision of administrative law judge; stay of enforcement of decision.

(A)(1) For judicial review of a final decision of an administrative law judge, a notice of appeal by an aggrieved party must be served and filed with the court of appeals as provided in the South Carolina Appellate Court Rules in civil cases and served on the opposing party and the Administrative Law Court not more than thirty days after the party receives the final decision and order of the administrative law judge. Appeal in these matters is by right.

(2) Except as otherwise provided in this chapter, the serving and filing of the notice of appeal does not itself stay enforcement of the administrative law judge's decision. The serving and filing of a notice of appeal by a licensee for review of a fine or penalty or of its license stays only those provisions for which review is sought and matters not affected by the notice of appeal are not stayed. The serving or filing of a notice of appeal does not automatically stay the suspension or revocation of a permit or license authorizing the sale of beer, wine, or alcoholic liquor. Upon motion, the administrative law judge may grant, or the court of appeals may order, a stay upon appropriate terms.

(B) The review of the administrative law judge's order must be confined to the record. The court may not substitute its judgment for the judgment of the administrative law judge as to the weight of the evidence on questions of fact. The court of appeals may affirm the decision or remand the case for further proceedings; or, it may reverse or modify the decision if the substantive rights of the petitioner have been prejudiced because the finding, conclusion, or decision is:

(a) in violation of constitutional or statutory provisions;

(b) in excess of the statutory authority of the agency;

(c) made upon unlawful procedure;

(d) affected by other error of law;

(e) clearly erroneous in view of the reliable, probative, and substantial evidence on the whole record; or

(f) arbitrary or capricious or characterized by abuse of discretion or clearly unwarranted exercise of discretion.

HISTORY: 1993 Act No. 181, Section 19; 2006 Act No. 387, Section 5, eff July 1, 2006; 2008 Act No. 334, Section 8, eff June 16, 2008.

Editor's Note

2006 Act No. 387, Section 53, provides as follows:

"This act is intended to provide a uniform procedure for contested cases and appeals from administrative agencies and to the extent that a provision of this act conflicts with an existing statute or regulation, the provisions of this act are controlling."

2006 Act No. 387, Section 57, provides as follows:

"This act takes effect on July 1, 2006, and applies to any actions pending on or after the effective date of the act. No pending or vested right, civil action, special proceeding, or appeal of a final administrative decision exists under the former law as of the effective date of this act, except for appeals of Department of Health and Environmental Control Ocean and Coastal Resource Management and Environmental Quality Control permits that are before the Administrative Law Court on the effective date of this act and petitions for judicial review that are pending before the circuit court. For those actions only, the department shall hear appeals from the administrative law judges and the circuit court shall hear pending petitions for judicial review in accordance with the former law. Thereafter, any appeal of those actions shall proceed as provided in this act for review. For all other actions pending on the effective date of this act, the action proceeds as provided in this act for review."

Effect of Amendment

The 2006 amendment rewrote this section.

The 2008 amendment rewrote this section.

SECTION 1-23-630. Powers of law judges.

(A) Each administrative law judge of the division has the same power at chambers or in open hearing as do circuit court judges and to issue those remedial writs as are necessary to give effect to its jurisdiction.

(B) An administrative law judge may authorize the use of mediation in a manner that does not conflict with other provisions of law and is consistent with the division's rules of procedure.

HISTORY: 1993 Act No. 181, Section 19; 2003 Act No. 39, Section 1.

SECTION 1-23-640. Principal offices of court; where cases heard.

The court shall maintain its principal offices in the City of Columbia. However, judges of the court shall hear contested cases at the court's offices or at a suitable location outside the City of Columbia when determined by the chief judge.

HISTORY: 1993 Act No. 181, Section 19; 1994 Act No. 452, Section 6; 2008 Act No. 334, Section 9, eff June 16, 2008.

Effect of Amendment

The 2008 amendment substituted "court" for "division" throughout and in the second sentence deleted "offices or location of the involved department or commission as prescribed by the agency or commission, at the division's" following "hear contested cases at the" and made minor language changes.

SECTION 1-23-650. Promulgation of rules.

(A) Rules governing the internal administration and operations of the Administrative Law Court must be:

(1) proposed by the chief judge of the court and adopted by a majority of the judges of the court; or

(2) proposed by any judge of the court and adopted by seventy-five percent of the judges of the court.

(B) Rules governing practice and procedure before the court which are:

(1) consistent with the rules of procedure governing civil actions in courts of common pleas; and

(2) not otherwise expressed in Chapter 23, Title 1; upon approval by a majority of the judges of the court must be promulgated by the court and are subject to

review as are rules of procedure promulgated by the Supreme Court under Article V of the Constitution.

(C) All hearings before an administrative law judge must be conducted exclusively in accordance with the rules of procedure promulgated by the court pursuant to this section. All other rules of procedure for the hearing of contested cases or appeals by individual agencies, whether promulgated by statute or regulation, are of no force and effect in proceedings before an administrative law judge.

HISTORY: 1993 Act No. 181, Section 19; 1994 Act No. 452, Section 2; 1998 Act No. 359, Section 5; 2006 Act No. 387, Section 6, eff July 1, 2006.

Editor's Note

2006 Act No. 387, Section 53, provides as follows:

"This act is intended to provide a uniform procedure for contested cases and appeals from administrative agencies and to the extent that a provision of this act conflicts with an existing statute or regulation, the provisions of this act are controlling."

2006 Act No. 387, Section 57, provides as follows:

"This act takes effect on July 1, 2006, and applies to any actions pending on or after the effective date of the act. No pending or vested right, civil action, special proceeding, or appeal of a final administrative decision exists under the former law as of the effective date of this act, except for appeals of Department of Health and Environmental Control Ocean and Coastal Resource Management and Environmental Quality Control permits that are before the Administrative Law Court on the effective date of this act and petitions for judicial review that are pending before the circuit court. For those actions only, the department shall hear appeals from the administrative law judges and the circuit court shall hear pending petitions for judicial review in accordance with the former law. Thereafter, any appeal of those actions shall proceed as provided in this act for review. For all other actions pending on the effective date of this act, the action proceeds as provided in this act for review."

Effect of Amendment

The 2006 amendment designated subsections (A) and (B); in subsection (A), in the introductory statement substituted "Administrative Law Court must" for "administrative law judge division shall"; added subsection (C); and substituted "court" for "division" and made nonsubstantive changes throughout.

SECTION 1-23-660. Office of Motor Vehicle Hearings; conduct of hearings; applicability of Code of Judicial Conduct; appeals.

(A) There is created within the Administrative Law Court the Office of Motor Vehicle Hearings. The chief judge of the Administrative Law Court shall serve as the director of the Office of Motor Vehicle Hearings. The duties, functions, and responsibilities of all hearing officers and associated staff of the Department of Motor Vehicles are devolved upon the Administrative Law Court effective January 1, 2006. The hearing officers and staff positions, together with the appropriations relating to these positions, are transferred to the Office of Motor Vehicle Hearings of the Administrative Law Court on January 1, 2006. The hearing officers and staff shall be appointed, hired, contracted, and supervised by the chief judge of the court and shall continue to exercise their adjudicatory functions, duties, and responsibilities under the auspices of the Administrative Law Court as directed by the chief judge and shall perform such other functions and duties as the chief judge of the court prescribes. All employees of the office shall serve at the will of the chief judge. The chief judge is solely responsible for the administration of the office, the assignment of cases, and the administrative duties and responsibilities of the hearing officers and staff. Notwithstanding another provision of law, the chief judge also has the authority to promulgate rules governing practice and procedures before the Office of Motor Vehicle Hearings. These rules are subject to review as are the rules of procedure promulgated by the Supreme Court pursuant to Article V of the South Carolina Constitution.

(B) Notwithstanding another provision of law, the hearing officers shall conduct hearings in accordance with Chapter 23 of Title 1, the Administrative Procedures Act, and the rules of procedure for the Office of Motor Vehicle Hearings, at suitable locations as determined by the chief judge. For purposes of this section, any law enforcement agency that employs an officer who requested a breath test and any law enforcement agency that employs a person who acted as a breath test operator resulting in a suspension pursuant to Section 56-1-286 or 56-5-2951 is a party to the hearing and shall be served with appropriate notice, afforded the opportunity to request continuances and participate in the hearing, and provided a copy of all orders issued in the action. Representatives of the Department of Motor Vehicles are not required to appear at implied consent, habitual offender, financial responsibility, or point suspension hearings. However, if the Department of Motor Vehicles elects not to appear through a representative at any implied consent hearing, or through the submission of documentary evidence at any habitual offender, financial responsibility, or point suspension hearing, and it wishes to appeal the decision, it must first file a motion for reconsideration with the Office of Motor Vehicle Hearings within ten days after receipt of the hearing officer's decision. The hearing officer must issue a written order upon the motion for reconsideration within thirty days. The Department of Motor Vehicles may file a notice of appeal with the Administrative Law Court within thirty days after receipt of the hearing officer's order on the motion for reconsideration. The Administrative Law Court must dismiss any appeal which does not meet the requirements of this subsection.

(C) The hearing officers are bound by the Code of Judicial Conduct, as contained in Rule 501 of the South Carolina Appellate Court Rules. The State Ethics Commission is responsible for the enforcement and administration of those rules and for the issuance of advisory opinions on the requirements of those rules for administrative law judges and hearing officers pursuant to the procedures contained in Section 8-13-320. Notwithstanding another provision of law, an administrative law judge or hearing officer, and the judge's or hearing officer's spouse or guest, may accept an invitation to and attend a judicial-related or bar-related function, or an activity devoted to the improvement of the law, the legal system, or the administration of justice.

(D) Appeals from decisions of the hearing officers must be taken to the Administrative Law Court pursuant to the court's appellate rules of procedure. Recordings of all hearings will be made part of the record on appeal, along with all evidence introduced at hearings, and copies will be provided to parties to those appeals at no charge. The chief judge shall not hear any appeals from these decisions.

HISTORY: 1993 Act No. 181, Section 19; 2005 Act No. 128, Section 22, eff July 1, 2005; 2006 Act No. 381, Section 2, eff June 13, 2006; 2006 Act No. 387, Section 7, eff July 1, 2006; 2008 Act No. 201, Section 14, eff February 10, 2009; 2008 Act No. 279, Section 1, eff October 1, 2008.

Code Commissioner's Note

At the direction of the Code Commissioner, both 2006 amendments were read together. The text of the section from the second amendment by Act 387 is set forth above, except that the eighth and ninth sentences in the first undesignated paragraph and the second and sixth sentences of the third undesignated paragraph were added from first amendment by Act 381.

This section was amended by 2008 Act Nos. 201 and 279. At the direction of the Code Commissioner, the text of Act 279 appears above because it was enacted later.

Editor's Note

2006 Act No. 387, Section 53, provides as follows:

"This act is intended to provide a uniform procedure for contested cases and appeals from administrative agencies and to the extent that a provision of this act conflicts with an existing statute or regulation, the provisions of this act are controlling."

2006 Act No. 387, Section 57, provides as follows:

"This act takes effect on July 1, 2006, and applies to any actions pending on or after the effective date of the act. No pending or vested right, civil action, special proceeding, or appeal of a final administrative decision exists under the former law as of the effective date of this act, except for appeals of Department of Health and Environmental Control Ocean and Coastal Resource Management and Environmental Quality Control permits that are before the Administrative Law Court on the effective date of this act and petitions for judicial review that are pending before the circuit court. For those actions only, the department shall hear appeals from the administrative law judges and the circuit court shall hear pending petitions for judicial review in accordance with the former law. Thereafter, any appeal of those actions shall proceed as provided in this act for review. For all other actions pending on the effective date of this act, the action proceeds as provided in this act for review."

Effect of Amendment

The 2005 amendment rewrote this section.

The first 2006 amendment, in the first undesignated paragraph, added the eighth and ninth sentences relating to promulgation of rules; and in the third undesignated paragraph, added the second sentence relating to breath tests, the third sentence relating to appearance by representatives of the Department of Motor Vehicles, and the seventh sentence relating to tape recordings of hearings.

The second 2006 amendment rewrote this section.

The first 2008 amendment deleted the last four sentences of the first undesignated paragraph relating to hiring a law clerk to assist the judges who hear Department of Motor Vehicle Hearing appeals; deleted the second undesignated paragraph relating to the role of the Budget and Control Board in the transition; and rewrote the third undesignated paragraph.

The second 2008 amendment rewrote this section, designating the subsections and substituting "Office of Motor Vehicle Hearings" for "Division of Motor Vehicle Hearings" throughout.

SECTION 1-23-670. Filing fees.

Each request for a contested case hearing, notice of appeal, or request for injunctive relief before the Administrative Law Court must be accompanied by a filing fee equal to that charged in circuit court for filing a summons and complaint, unless another filing fee schedule is established by rules promulgated by the Administrative Law Court, subject to review as in the manner of rules of procedure promulgated by the Supreme Court pursuant to Article V of the Constitution of this State. This fee must be retained by the Administrative Law Court in order to help defray the costs of the proceedings. No filing fee is required in administrative appeals by inmates from final decisions of the Department of Corrections or the Department of Probation, Parole and Pardon Services. However, if an inmate files three administrative appeals during a calendar year, then each subsequent filing during that year must be accompanied by a twenty-five dollar filing fee. If the presiding administrative law judge determines at the conclusion of the proceeding that the case was frivolous or taken solely for the purpose of delay, the judge may impose such sanctions as the circumstances of the case and discouragement of like conduct in the future may require.

HISTORY: 2008 Act No. 353, Section 2, Pt 18A, eff July 1, 2009.

SECTION 1-23-680. Cost of South Carolina Code, supplements, and replacement volumes.

The South Carolina Administrative Law Court is not required to reimburse the South Carolina Legislative Council for the cost of the Code of Laws, code supplements, or code replacement volumes distributed to the court.

HISTORY: 2008 Act No. 353, Section 2, Pt 18B, eff July 1, 2009.

South Carolina General Assembly
General Statues Order Form

Fax Orders:	1-980-299-5965
Phone Orders:	1-980-729-3505
E-mail Orders:	www.visionbooks.org
Mail Orders:	Vision Books P.O. Box 42406, Charlotte, NC 28215-1985

Shipp To:
Name_____
Address_____
City_____State_____Zip_____
Phone_____Fax_____
Email_____@_____

Bill To: We can bill a third party on your behalf.
Name_____
Address_____
City_____State_____Zip_____
Phone____(_____)_____Fax_____
Email_____@_____

Pamphlet Number ($15.00 Each)	Qty	Total Cost
_____	_____	_____
_____	_____	_____
_____	_____	_____
_____	_____	_____
_____	_____	_____
_____	_____	_____
_____	_____	_____
_____	_____	_____
Full Volume Set 1-92	92 Pamphlets	1,380.00

Free Shipping & Handling on Full Volume Orders
Add $1.00 Shipping & Handling per pamphlet $_____

Total Cost $_____

Thank You for Your Support. Management!

Order General Assembly General Reference Guides for other States

Fax Orders:	1-980-299-5965
Phone Orders:	1-980-729-3505
E-mail Orders:	www.visionbooks.org
Mail Orders:	Vision Books P.O. Box 42406, Charlotte, NC 28215-1985

Shipp To:
Name_____
Address_____
City_____State_____Zip_____
Phone_____Fax_____
Email_____@_____

Bill To: We can bill a third party on your behalf.
Name_____
Address_____
City_____State_____Zip_____
Phone____(_____)_____Fax_____
Email_____@_____

This order form is for a General Reference Guide Only. It will contain your pamphlet numbers and information on how to order your state's individual pamphlets.

Item   Qty   Total Cost

General Reference Guide for the state of:

_____   _____ $_____

Write your state name on this line.
($7.00 each General Reference Guide)

Add $1.00 Shipping & Handling per pamphlet $_____

Total Cost $_____

Thank You for Your Support. Management!

Did you enjoy this book?

Something you want to tell us? Please do, we'd like to hear your thoughts.

Send all written correspondence to:

Vision Books
P.O. Box 42406
Charlotte, NC 28215-1985
Email: staff@visionbooks.org

Phone Orders:	1-980-729-3505
E-mail Orders:	www.visionbooks.org
Mail Orders:	Vision Books P.O. Box 42406 Charlotte, NC 28215-1985

www.ingramcontent.com/pod-product-compliance
Lightning Source LLC
Chambersburg PA
CBHW021349210526
45463CB00001B/37